D1607466

MODERN AMERICAN HISTORY

New Studies and Outstanding Dissertations

Edited by
Robert E. Burke
and
Frank Freidel

A Garland Series

Library of Congress Cataloging-in-Publication Data

Woods, Gerald, 1930–
    The police in Los Angeles : reform and professionali-
zation / Gerald Woods.
        p.   cm. — (Modern American history)
    ISBN 0-8153-1096-X (alk. paper)
    1. Police—California—Los Angeles—History. I. Title.
II. Series.
HV8148.L55W66   1993
363.2'09794'94—dc20   92-34899
                                                             CIP

Design by Marisel Tavárez

Printed on acid-free, 250-year-life paper.
Manufactured in the United States of America

DEDICATION

For Elizabeth, Stephen and Allan, and for all police reformers who believe with August Vollmer that policing could be and should be "the highest form of social work."

Acknowledgment

I cannot list all of the individuals who helped in some way to make this book possible but I must thank Stanley Coben, Stephan Thernstrom, Gary Nash, Mae Churchill, Robert Burke, Robert M. Fogelson, Lawrence Sherman, George Kelling, Sidney Harring, Gene E. Carte, Steven P. Erie, Harold Brackman and Gregory H. Singleton. I owe a great debt also to the management of the *Los Angeles Times,* who granted access to their "morgue" files, and to the staffs of the Graduate Research Library of the University of California at Los Angeles and the Bancroft Library of the University of California at Berkeley.

CONTENTS

The Police in Los Angeles

INTRODUCTION

This book is a study of police reform. In conjunction, the words "police and "reform" reveal the paradox of American law enforcement. The modern police service is a response to the nineteenth century industrial metropolis, where propertyless masses, crime and disorder appeared to threaten the foundations of civilized society. In the United States, unfortunately, the police often seemed more a cause of urban crisis than a solution to it. Police malpractice has been a staple of newspaper commentary since the 1840's, when the first American police departments were established. Police reform, then, is an intrinsic part of the story of urban reform in America.[1]

Progressivism and Professionalization, the two significant police reform movements, provide the major themes of this work. Progressivism is the better known. Among other goals, the progressives hoped to enlist honorable police officers, eliminate spoils politics from government and suppress protected commercial vice operations. Their enduring monument is the municipal civil service.

Professionalization has roots in the 1870's but its influence has been greatest since World War II. The movement is led by career police officers who direct their efforts mainly to operational and technological efficiency. In this context, "professional law enforcement" refers to the centralized, paramilitary bureaucracy that is the current norm for American cities.[2]

The study deals with police history in Los Angeles since 1850, with emphasis upon the period since World War I. Although a large and comprehensive police literature has been published since the 1960's, most of it has been produced by social scientists and does not have a historical focus. Only a few systematic, longitudinal studies of twentieth century American police forces are available. Nevertheless, the existing scholarly historical literature reveals striking similarities between police problems and the nature of reform in American cities of the east, the midwest and the Pacific coast.[3]

Impressionistic history and certain work in other disciplines is less helpful. It is clear that until sufficient data for southern and western cities are available, urban theories based only on evidence from immigrant-swollen northeastern and midwestern cities must be approached with caution. The "ethos" theory, for example, identifies the urban political machine as an unAmerican product of immigrant cultures. It is an unworkable explanation for Los Angeles, where machine politicians, venal policemen, civic reformers and the electorate were mainly native-born, white, middle class Protestant Republicans. The criminal class also was predominantly white and native born, notwithstanding implied links between urban criminality and foreign birth. For similar reasons, the view of Progressivism as a status revolution, though it may be valid, is not verified by this research.[4]

The alleged peculiarities of Los Angeles politics have generated other questionable theories. One scholar asserts that a political vacuum has existed in Los Angeles since the decline of the good government movement in 1913. Others see decentralized municipal institutions as the source of political reform. The absence of a political elite is suggested and the validity of the terms "boss" and "machine" is questioned. These deficient theses perhaps reflect an acceptance of progressive institutions and reform rhetoric at face value.[5]

In fact, the boss and the machine immediately filled any vacuum that might have followed the collapse of the old reform coalition. The most visible sign of his presence was the persistence of open commercial vice in the center of the downtown business district, despite an unflagging reform campaign that continued through the successive administrations of six different mayors. The reformers, a fairly self-conscious and cohesive political elite drawn largely from the six most prestigious Protestant denominations, controlled the city between 1909 and 1915. After many setbacks, they finally destroyed the machine in 1938.

The influential Chandler and Hearst newspapers usually ignored civic corruption on the grounds that bad publicity hurt business. A misleading lack of information in the major journals may have encouraged the idea that decentralized decisionmaking and fragmentary political associations produced reformed government. In truth, the administrative structure and the informal political system have not changed much since the glory days of the machine. Until the 1950's, reform administrations used machine methods to purge their enemies from the city government. The same progressive city charter under which corrupt government flourished is in force today.

Fortunately for the historian, several smaller Los Angeles newspapers engaged in periodic reform crusades. Whether in the cause of honest government or higher circulation, many civic scandals came to light. The

Record, a feisty link in the Scripps Canfield chain, fought the good fight from 1905 until mid-1932. After the *Record* failed, two independent dailies, the *Illustrated Daily News* and the *Hollywood Citizen-News,* carried on the struggle. On occasion, and for reasons not always identifiable, the massive resources of Harry Chandler's *Times* or W.R. Hearst's *Examiner* might also be employed in the service of reform. Together, the newspaper reports, the recollections of participants, the private papers of principal figures and pertinent documentary materials from city, county and state archives provide a fascinating picture of Los Angeles in the days of the boss, the machine and the good government crusade.

This analysis, though not divided into sections, falls into three parts. The first section deals briefly with events leading to the formation of the Los Angeles Police Department in 1876, but its main theme is the continuing effort by progressive citizens to suppress commercial, protected vice through blue laws and police action. The significant period begins in 1889 and ends in 1924. Chapter One deals with the progressive movement from 1889, when police reform was first written into the city charter, until 1915, when, after three charter revisions, the abolition of wards and the winning of every elective office, the Los Angeles reform coalition disintegrated. Chapter Two describes the reorganization of a new progressive movement, led by Protestant clergymen. It ends in 1923, with the appointment of August Vollmer as chief of the LAPD. The arrival of Vollmer, America's foremost police administrator, was thought to presage a new era of honest, efficient law enforcement. Chapter Three describes Vollmer's year in Los Angeles and the reasons for his defeat.

The second section covers the period 1924-1938, when the machine reached its zenith and the police plumbed new depths of infamy. At the same time, the department won important benefits in return for cooperation with anti-labor business interests on one hand and corrupt politicians on the other. Chapter Four deals with "Boss" Parrot's Los Angeles, when the police became known as "the Cossacks" for their unlawful treatment of vagrants, labor organizers and political radicals. Chapter Five describes the strange period from 1929 to 1933, when the Church Brotherhood ruled city hall and rampant bigotry was the rule. Chapter Six is an analysis of the last great reform campaign, leading to the recall of Mayor Frank Shaw and the overthrow of the machine, which was impelled by the attempted murder of a civic investigator by members of the police intelligence squad.

The reformed era since 1939 is the subject of Section Three. It is concerned mainly with the sixteen year tenure of Chief William Parker.

Parker, a leading spokesman and architect of professionalization, was one of the most important figures in the postwar history of American Law enforcement. Between 1950 and 1966, Parker gained an international reputation as a police administrator. He made the LAPD America's model police force, studied and copied by executives from other jurisdictions. His theories and methods became the conventional wisdom of police professionalization.

Finally, this book questions the place of professional police in democratic society. To a considerable degree, William Parker's decisions in Los Angeles ordained the course of events in distant metropolitan areas. The general significance of Parker and the LAPD stems from that fact, because Parker explicitly rejected August Vollmer's view of the policeman as "the highest kind of social worker." Parker took a a garrison outlook. He argued that the police formed a "thin blue line" of heroes, arrayed against the forces of evil. In limiting police professionalism to this narrow and paranoid view, Parker did a lasting disservice to residents of American cities, to the ideal of a police profession and to police officers, who have been denied the larger vision of August Vollmer.

Chief Parker's legacy has not been glorious. His successors, Thomas Reddin, Edward Davis and Daryl Gates, allowed or did not prevent a decline to the Cossack style of policing for which the department was infamous during the 1920's and 1930's. The current LAPD may be judged a failure by almost all pertinent criteria. The allegedly "nonpartisan" police department takes an aggressive role in politics, lobbying at every level of government and denouncing elected officials. This blights the theory and threatens the practice of municipal government. High wages, generous pensions and modern equipment have not reduced the crime rate. Rigorous civil service standards of selection, training and promotion, and security of employment, have not produced an impartial public agency that can be trusted to perform its duties in a lawful manner.

This may be illustrated by a single recent example of many that could be cited. Early in March, 1991, television viewers across the United States and around the world observed a shocking spectacle, filmed by an unobserved amateur photographer. More than twenty white police officers, including a supervising sergeant, looked on while three other officers beat, kicked and shocked Rodney Glen King, a lone black man who lay on the ground handcuffed. The helpless victim was struck as many as fifty-six times and kicked as many as seven times. His injuries included a fractured eye socket, a broken cheek bone, a broken leg, facial nerve damage, a severe concussion and burns from a police stun gun.

To add insult to injury, the police wanted to charge the victim with battery on an officer and resisting arrest. After two days in hospital, he was transferred to the Los Angeles County Jail and held there pending investigation of charges of evading police officers and evading parole. He also was accused of driving at high speed. No charges were filed and the victim was released. He would undoubtedly have been charged and probably convicted if the episode had not been filmed, putting the lie to police testimony.

Unfortunately, although the number of police officers present was unusual, the violent assault on Rodney King was not a rare event. It was only a highly publicised example of something that is a common occurrence in Los Angeles. Predictably, the chief of police asserted that the assault was an aberration and that the department should not be judged on one event.

The daily victims of unprofessional police conduct know that the chief was wrong. The organizations that work daily with the victims—the American Civil Liberties Union, the Police Misconduct Lawyers Referral Service, the black and hispanic advocacy groups and similar organizations—know that the chief was wrong. As long as the chief did not know that he was wrong, however, there could be no change from within. External authorities such as police commissions, city councils, district attorneys, civil rights lawyers and judges would have to compel the necessary reform.

The major conclusion of this study is that contemporary police professionalization negates the fundamental American precept of honest, impartial, efficient and humane public service. Moreover, urban police departments are becoming potent political machines. Given the reactionary nature of police politics, the consequences for pluralistic, libertarian society could be momentous. Eternal vigilance may well be the price of freedom.

NOTES

[1] For origins and rationale of British models of American institutions see Charles Reith, *The Police Idea: Its History and Evolution in England in the Eighteenth Century and After* (Oxford University Press, 1938); T.A. Critchley, *A History of Police in England and Wales,1900-1966* (Constable & Co., Ltd. 1967); and Allen Silver, "The Demand for Order in Civil Society; A Review of Some Themes in the History of Urban Crime, Police and Riot," in David Bordua, ed., *The Police: Six Sociological Essays* (John Wiley & Sons; Inc., 1967), 1-24 and notes.

[2]. The first known national convention of American police administrators, in 1871, is a convenient starting point for the professionalization movement; see *Official Proceedings of the National Police Convention. Held at the City of St. Louis, Missouri, on the 20th, 21th, and 23rd days of October, 1871.*(St. Louis, 1871; reprinted by the Arno Press, New York, 1973).

[3] Raymond B. Fosdick, *American Police Systems* (New York, 1920); Roger Lane, *Policing the City: Boston, 1822-1885* (Harvard University Press, 1967); James F. Richardson, *The New York Police: Colonial Times to 1901* (Oxford University Press, 1970); Lyle W. Dorsett, *The Pendergast Machine* (Oxford University Press, 1968). For a perceptive review of the police literature see Robert Reiner, *The Politics of the Police* (Brighton: Wheatsheaf Books, 1985).

[4] Edward C. Banfield and James Q. Wilson, *City Politics* (N.Y.: Vintage Books, 1963), esp.46; the authors offer no evidence to substantiate their theory. For an especially good critique, see Raymond E. Wolfinger and John O. Field, "Political Ethos and the Structure of Urban Government," *American Political Science Review* 60:2 (June 1966), 306-326; Michael Banton, *The Policeman in the Community* (N.Y.: Basic Books, 1964); Richard Hofstadter, *The Age of Reform* (New York: Vintage Books, 1955).

[5] James Q. Wilson, *The Amateur Democrat* (University of Chicago Press, 1962), 96-98; Wilson's faulty analysis is compounded by J. David Greenstone, *Labor in American Politics* (N.Y.: Alfred A. Knopf, 1969), 144; Beatrice Dinerman & Winston Crouch, *Southern California Metropolis* (University of California Press, 1963); Francis M. Carney, "The Decentralized Politics of Los Angeles," *The Annals of the American Academy of Social and Political Science* 253 (May 1964), 107-121; it should be noted that other studies find decentralization and fragmenta-

tion the norm for large American cities, even "machine-ridden" Chicago. See John C. Bollens and Henry J. Schmardt, *The Metropolis* (N.Y.: Harper & Row, 1965); also Edward E. Banfield, *Political Influence* (Free Press of Glencoe, 1962), esp. 286-303.

CHAPTER ONE

VICE, VIRTUE, AND POLITICS:
The Illusion of Police Reform, 1850-1915.

The City of the Angels is as yet far away from the ideal city.
The dollar still rules. Material things are more sought for
than spiritual. Low political ideals still hold sway. Nevertheless, a brighter day is dawning.

Dana W. Bartlett
The Better City

Los Angeles, founded in 1781 by a small garrison sent from Mexico to bar British expansion in the Pacific, existed in relative solitude and
tranquillity until the American conquest and the subsequent goldrush of
1849. Hordes of rapacious fortune seekers then destroyed the old way of
life and established classic frontier conditions. Almost overnight, the
once somnolent hide and tallow depot became "the toughest town in the
West," a reputation maintained through two boisterous and bloody
decades.

Gambling halls, saloons, brothels and opium dens flourished.
"Hard Cases" of every breed and color jostled in the streets. Bandit
gangs and marauding Indians waylaid travellers, sometimes in daylight
within sight of the pueblo. Deadly violence became commonplace. Several lawmen were killed in gun battles. Fresh candidates for the sheriff's
and marshal's jobs were scarce.

"Law-abiding" residents, determined to maintain order, reacted
with equal savagery. Troops of citizen guards and rangers conducted
ruthless campaigns against highway bandits. Lynch mobs, led on at least
one occasion by a mayor of Los Angeles, dealt "popular justice" to suspected criminals, often seizing their victims from the custody of a county
sheriff or town marshal. These actions dismayed even the vigilantes who
rode in the ranger battalions. Popular justice defeated its own ends, however. Meeting violence with violence eliminated numerous malefactors
but did nothing for the concept of rule by law. [1]

11

Urban growth eventually forced the Common Council to establish a more comprehensive police service. Between incorporation in 1850, and 1869, the town grew from 1100 to about 5700 residents. The council then doubled, to six, the number of permanent deputies under City Marshal William Warren's command. The deputies wore uniforms, displayed six-pointed, star-shaped badges and carried rifles. The night shift toted lanterns.

The Common Council wanted fulltime police protection without cost to the taxpayer, which proved to be a long-term characteristic of Los Angeles politicians. The council provided no salaries. Remuneration depended upon the collection of fees for services, such as returning lost or stolen property or serving legal writs. Presumably, this system encouraged efficient policework by rewarding the most proficient deputies.

The experiment failed. The fee system encouraged corrupt practices. A deputy ordered to deliver several warrants to a single location usually made a separate trip with each document and collected multiple fees. Payment of rewards promoted connivance between thief and deputy at worst, quarrels over spoils at best. In 1870, Marshal Warren was slain by Deputy Joe Dye in a fight over division of rewards. [2]

Moreover, the marshal's department still seemed unable or unwilling to protect prisoners from lynch mobs. In 1871, when a white mob murdered a score of innocent Chinese, some officers evidently participated in the massacre. The Council later enlarged and reorganized the department and paid standard wages but the controversial force finally was disbanded in 1876. Former First Ward councilman J.T. Gerkens became the first chief of the new, thirteen-man, Los Angles Police Department. [3]

The passing of the marshal's department marked an important stage in the transformation from frontier village to commercial metropolis. Growth, the entrepreneurial ethnic, required a constantly increasing population but middleclass American migrants desired safe streets and a good moral climate. The deputy marshals, who arrested only the worst drunks and rowdies, kept commercial vice indoors and maintained uncertain control over street traffic, no longer sufficed. The new political majority demanded a formal law enforcement agency similar to those of large eastern cities.

Traditionally, policemen pursued burglars, bandits and other threats to life and property, hunted for stolen goods, arrested vagrants, searched and questioned suspicious persons, found runaways and performed casual acts of valor; preventing drownings, forestalling accidents, guarding or removing fallen wires and aiding the fire department. When necessary they engaged in gunbattles with desperados. In such circumstances, policework appeared to be an important and respectable public service.

Most patrolmen, however, spent their days at mundane tasks that required no special expertise, virtue or courage and could not be reconciled with dynamic interpretations of the police vocation. Indeed, these duties scarcely qualified as law enforcement, and tended to degrade the status of the police service. Officers enforced foot-and-mouth disease regulations, removed dead animals and loose paper from the streets, guarded "saleable" trash and removed weeds.

They admonished citizens who burned rubbish at other than prescribed hours or who wasted a valuable resource through excessive watering of lawns. They abated nuisances, from hurdy-gurdy men to merchants who stacked crates on sidewalks. They notified businessmen of police auctions and inspected commercial premises to ensure that the owners held valid business permits.

The normal workweek expanded enormously when fire, flood, earthquake or other disaster struck. Furthermore, each man purchased and maintained his own equipment: uniforms, hats, boots, revolver, belt and cartridges, handcuffs and nightstick. The remuneration was not overgenerous. The marshal's deputies in the early 1870's received $90 per month. The first LAPD officers earned similar sums but salaries declined when hard times depressed prices and produced a surplus of unemployed candidates for the department.

Above all, the policeman had no job security. Tenure of office during good behavior, a Federalist notion then being debated by reformers, made no headway in Los Angeles. The Jacksonian spoils system flourished. Policemen served at the councilmen's pleasure. Politicians awarded municipal jobs to loyal partisans and retention depended upon continued service to the donor rather than to the public. Appointments, promotions, demotions and dismissals at the direction of politicians were routine. [4]

Chiefs came and went in bewildering succession. Between 1877 and 1889, at least sixteen men held the position, for periods ranging from seventy-five days to nineteen months. A change of chief often toppled the captains and sergeants as well. Ambitious officers openly solicited support for promotion to higher ranks. The unstable command structure negated efficiency, discipline and morale. [5]

Political loyalty, a rude tongue and a ready fist seemed the only necessary qualifications for police work. Citizens as well as politicians apparently considered the LAPD a lowly patronage bureau rather than a respected public service. Very few capable, honest men accepted the small salary, unrewarding chores and low social status of the police department. Some completed honorable careers but most soon resigned.

Others, less ethical, seized the opportunities that police work offered the enterprising man. These officers used the statute book as a license to gather profits. Much wrongdoing could be overlooked, for a price. A small minority perceived the true nature of local conditions. They applied themselves diligently to municipal politics, the surest path to higher rank and privilege.

Los Angeles therefore adopted a system already found wanting in other American cities. Predictably, the police force became a center of political controversy, especially in connection with the enforcement (or non-enforcement) of local blue laws. The new middleclass Protestant migrants—or at least their vociferous religious leaders—abhorred the brothel, the casino and the saloon. Their determination to regulate and eventually suppress "sin" brought vice entrepreneurs into politics in support of "permissive" councilmen and encouraged the outright bribery of politicians and police officials.

Old-timers remembered "about 400" gambling halls during the 1850's and 1860's. Many casinos also provided liquor and women. As the central business and residential district expanded, a series of ordinances forbade vice within prescribed boundaries but ignored it elsewhere. In 1876, the city council established a legal vice district but later rescinded the law. The state supreme court overturned a subsequent statute which forbade unattached women to reside on the ground floor of any dwelling.

The council forbade gambling but illicit casinos continued to operate. So did saloons. Beginning with early closing and Sunday closing laws, church organizations pressed successfully for a steady reduction in the number of licensed saloons, despite a rapid increase in population. This invited collusion between tavern-keeper and policeman and almost ensured the operation of unlicensed "blind tiger" premises. [6]

Thus the small western city suffered the same kinds of police problems, involving vice, extortion, brutality, rudeness and inefficiency, that beset older and larger eastern centers. Public dissatisfaction with police operations mounted over the years, as did the moral reformers' determination to reorganize the department. Their chance came in 1889, when they rewrote the city charter and established a municipal corporation befitting a city of 50,000 residents.

The new charter marked the first Los Angeles victory of an emerging national phenomenon known afterwards as Progressivism. A self-conscious portion of the native American middleclass rose to contend with other interests for control of the city. The progressives evinced great faith in charter reform as a solution to civic problems; the revision of 1889 was only the first of many attempts to deal with ethical and social issues through constitutional amendments. Ironically, as the progressive numbers increased, making charter reform easier to accomplish, the progressives' puritanical moralism and parsimonious attitude toward municipal expenditures perpetuated old problems and perhaps created more new ones than the reformed statutes eliminated. [7]

The charter established a formal police commission to oversee the department. The commission controlled appointments, promotions, dismissals and general policy. The progressives hoped to neutralize politics within the LAPD by dividing and balancing the police commission membership and powers. The commission included four private citizens—two Democrats and two Republicans—appointed by the city council. The mayor sat on the board but could not serve as chairman. [8]

Because the mayor and the commissioners were themselves political partisans, they failed to depoliticize the police department. The first commission, however, accomplished some worthy deeds, most notably the appointment of Chief John M. Glass. Glass held office from 1889 to 1900. Longevity permitted the chief to gradually and systematically upgrade the department.

Chief Glass and his secretary, Charles R. Moffat, were the department's first professionals. The two presided over a significant change in the departmental ethos. What had been essentially a group of watchmen became a formal agent of the dominant social group, "impartially" enforcing laws designed to create a particular kind of urban social environment. The politically vulnerable policeman's impartiality when dealing with a socially prominent offender may be doubted; nevertheless, the department conformed generally to the legalistic style of contemporary "professional" police forces.

During Glass' term, a significant cooperation between progressive reformers and career police administrators began. The progressives admired "scientific" business management and modern technology. They tinkered with the city charter, seeking the most efficient system, and adopted technical improvements in transportation and communications. By and large, however, they emphasized such personal qualities as honesty, intelligence and responsibility. Their greatest efforts were on behalf of proposals endorsing individual merit: higher entrance standards, promotional examinations and secure job tenure during good behavior.

"Professional" police administrators, though mindful of the importance of personal qualities, concerned themselves more with material gains. In seeking professional status, the police attempted to participate in the important post-Civil War movement that laid the foundations of modern professions. Whereas academic training constituted the fundamental base of the medical, legal and educational professions, however, the police scarcely recognized the need for formal recruit training. The police exhibited the outward show of professionalism—a national association, a journal, an annual convention—but their main goals were those of the bureaucrat and the labor leader: efficient management and modern technology on one hand, better wages, pensions and working conditions on the other. This proved to be an enduring characteristic of non-academic police professionals.

Glass and Moffat introduced as much as possible of the program advocated by the national police chiefs' association. Between 1889 and 1891 they divided the growing city into four administrative districts, devised a way to locate any policeman at any given time and organized a detective bureau under Moffat's command. They appointed the first matron, to deal with female prisoners, opened the first branch police station and established minimum physical and mental entrance standards. [9]

The two men also initiated a rudimentary records bureau, which consisted of several clothespins hung on strings outside the chief's office. One held Glass' orders to his men, others the policemen's reports to their superior. The significance lay in the requirement that records be kept and daily reports submitted. Previously, police activity could not be measured. Officers wrote citizens' complaints on odd slips of paper that they carried in their pockets until the crime was solved or forgotten, or the paper disintegrated. [10]

The city charter required that the police chief report annually to the mayor and council. Glass' official report of 1897, the first to be separately published, maintained a tradition yet to be broken by a Los Angeles chief. Although the department had just been presented with a large new central station on First Street, the chief requested further increases in men, plant and equipment. He called for twenty per cent more personnel, two additional substations and a Gamewell communications system (a central switchboard with local telephones in boxes on the beats). He achieved partial success. In 1899, technicians installed the initial fifty-box system at a cost of $50,000. That year the LAPD also adopted the Bertillon method of criminal identification by physical measurements. [11]

In purchasing labor-saving devices, the council responded to the enduring reality of police budgets: personnel costs exceeded ninety per cent of the annual appropriation. One patrolman, from appointment to retirement, represented a salary outlay in excess of $20,000. Telephones, call-boxes, substations, bicycles, motorcycles and automobiles substituted for costly increases in manpower. A commitment to low taxation characterized Los Angeles mayors and councilmen. Indeed, the official attitude toward property taxes, as opposed to jobs, may be the most significant difference between "reform" and "traditional" machine politics.

Although relatively successful in modernizing operations, Glass found upgrading personnel and providing a proper level of protection more difficult. The police commission could and did transfer officers, decrease salaries, restrict recruitment and add to the department's responsibilities. Despite attempts to enforce minimum entrance requirements, personnel standards were low. Glass forbade drinking, smoking and card-playing while in uniform but the problems remained. His dress regulations were straightforward: "You will keep your coats buttoned, stars pinned over the left breast...and hold your clubs firmly." [12]

The city doubled in size during the decade of the 1890's, to 100,000 inhabitants. The proportion of police to citizens exceeded the recommended minimum (1:1000) in 1890 but fell to 1:0.93 by 1897 and continued to decline. Newcomers, spreading into the corners of the city, increased the protection problem. A spate of new ordinances placed further strain on the undermanned police force.

Excellent record notwithstanding, Glass survived for eleven years because he avoided vice scandals. Purveyors of "the social evils" continued to operate during his administration but they did so with caution. Visitors from the East frequently remarked on the climate of virtue maintained by Chief Glass and the LAPD. Apparently this created enemies for the chief. Late in 1899 he was forced from office in a dispute involving moral turpitude on the part of one of his captains. Glass' attempt to discipline his subordinate resulted in his own dismissal.

A Committee of Fifteen, appointed by the Chamber of Commerce, investigated the affair and exonerated Glass but could not force his reinstatement. A dispute between mayor and council paralyzed the police commission. So ended one of the most notable careers in LAPD annals.

Various officers appealed to their friends for aid in securing the positions of displaced sergeants and captains. [13]

Although Glass was out of office, the repercussions were far from over. The progressives, led by Charles Dwight Willard and John R. Haynes, proposed to amend the 1889 charter and reorganize the police force. The affront to the progressive ideal of nonpolitical police service led to charter reform that enhanced the chief's powers at the expense of the police commissioners and other outside influences.

The Glass fiasco added an important local dimension to a campaign constructed around the issues of direct legislation and the merit system. In the resounding victory of 1902, progressive voters ratified the initiative, referendum and recall, established a municipal civil service and changed the rules governing the police commission and police force.

The civil service amendment classified every police rank except the chief and his secretary. The charter certified the minimum physical and mental entrance requirements already in force, instituted competitive promotional examinations and mandated police salaries. It required that all requests or orders involving the police be forwarded directly to the chief for action. Finally, the mayor became chairman of the police commission and could remove other commissioners with consent of the council. By these measures the progressives hoped to establish the independence of the individual officer and place control of day-to-day administration in the chief's hands. The mayor, as chief executive officer, was given greater responsibility for the overall management of the department. [14]

The 1902 amendments included the first formal advances toward departmental independence. Civil service tenure commenced a trend toward insulation of policemen from public control. Regulations requiring that all police matters be channelled through the chief started a process that eventually gave the chief legal authority to centralize or decentralize the force, create or abolish divisions, deploy personnel and make or remake policy at will. Increased mayoral power vis-a-vis the police commission led to complete control over the chief. (This in turn led, much later, to a radical curtailment of the chief's power to punish or dismiss his subordinates, regardless of their conduct). [15]

The charter revisions, no matter how important in the long run, failed to achieve the reformers' immediate goals. The reformed department consisted of the previous force given civil service tenure. Of 139 incumbents, 112 passed the examination. Twenty-seven failed but received tutoring while on probation. The entrance qualifications allotted more importance to physical condition than to intelligence and character, reducing the screening procedure to an absurd level. Even these standards produced criticism. *The Los Angeles Times* noted that the civil service examiner discriminated against recruits by requiring them to have brains, although the incumbent police were "innocent of that." [16]

The charter battle of 1902 had two unexpected results. First, the reformers wrote their aversion to vice into the fundamental law, forbidding prostitution and gambling within the city limits, only to find themselves in an era of corruption without previous example in local history. Second, the anti-vice crusade became the standard campaign tactic in municipal elections for half a century afterward. That vice should be the most volatile political issue over a period of five decades spoke volumes about the voters. [17]

The demi-monde began to blossom after Mayor Clement Eaton and Chief John Glass left office. Commercial vice prospered in the "segregated zone" during the administration of Mayor Meredith Snyder and Chief John Elton (1900-1904). In mid-1902, two ministers discovered the "Ballarino," a building of many narrow cells, or "cribs," designed specifically for prostitution. They and their followers soon closed the Balarino, while casting many aspersions on the police. [18]

Perhaps the progressives arranged to have the churchmen find the brothel to ensure their support in the charter campaign. In any case, the fervid moral crusade of 1902 was repeated endlessly in subsequent election years. This was not entirely political cynicism. Despite the will of the political majority, the city suffered scandal after scandal as the twentieth century advanced. Again and again the progressives elected "reform" candidates, only to lose the victory when their standard-bearers unaccountably turned coats.

Between 1904 and 1909 the voters rejected three mayors accused of misconduct. Five police chiefs departed in disgrace. Chief John Elton and Mayor M.P. Snyder, Democrats, survived the Balarino scandal of 1902 because the progressives put their entire effort into charter reform but Elton resigned prior to the 1904 election to avoid questioning by members of the city council. Snyder lost to the Republican, Owen McAleer. McAleer, known as "the whisky mayor" because he refused to support proposed saloon regulations, lasted one two-year term and did not run again. The progressives lost the 1906 mayoralty election to Arthur Harper but that campaign and its aftermath foreshadowed the final triumph of reform.

The progressives, especially those who eventually formed the Progressive Party, were most often young Republicans as much opposed to

Republican machine government as to Democratic machine government. The "regular" Republicans understood clearly that the new movement would uproot their organization and deny them the spoils of office
if it could. The schism between progressive and regular Republicans
continued through the reform era. During the 1906 mayoralty campaign,
therefore, after progressive Republicans exposed the regular Republican
candidate as a tool of the Southern Pacific Railroad, the S.P. and the
machine Republicans switched to the machine Democrat, Arthur Harper,
and helped to elect him. This stymied the progressives'plan to reform the
police department through the mayor's office. [19]

Harper intended to seek a further term. Well before the election,
however, the progressives mounted a fullscale "oust Harper" campaign.
As always, vice provided the major issue. Operations in the segregated
zone, described in lurid terms by Sydney Kendall, in *Queen of the Red
Lights* and *The Soundings of Hell,* had become more overt. Underworld
bosses such as "Chowderhouse Jim" Dunne, Tom Savage and Nick
Oswald provided one dimension. Pearl Morton and other famous
madams provided another, riding about on Sundays in fancy carriages,
showing off their most comely employees.

No stranger need be lonely. A directory of the demimonde guided
travellers to such as Madam Weir, who held forth at 312 North Alameda
Street: to the sportively inclined people of Los Angeles,...she is the most
popular landlady of the coast. To strangers we would advise, if they are
looking for a nice, quiet time not to miss this cosy little place. Madame
Weir has four charming young ladies to assist her in entertaining guests,
who go away with words of praise for her and the young ladies.[20]

Victorianism, Comstockery, puritanism or whatever the reform
ethos might be called, had not yet triumphed over the frontier spirit. Attitudes toward "fallen women" were marked by a liberality and *joie de
vivre* that was unimaginable by 1920. As one participant fondly recalled:
"Figueroa from Jefferson Street to Washington Street was during the
race meet, left to the ladies of the night. As soon as the carriages reached
Figueroa, they all turned to and broke into a run...the girls standing up in
the boxes of the hacks whooping and yelling, calling each other names
and making bets on which team would beat. In addition to their rigs,
there would be as many as fifty buggies and carts filled with young men
of the town racing along right with them...me on my saddlehorse right in
the middle of it." [21]

The moral temper began to change following the partial reform victory of 1906. In 1908, the city attorney closed Pearl Morton's establishment.

The same year, Thomas L. Woolwine, an assistant district attorney, alleged in the *Los Angeles Examiner* that Mayor Arthur Harper protected vice operations in the segregated zone. District Attorney John D. Fredericks immediately dismissed Woolwine but the *Los Angeles Express* developed the young prosecutor's charges in a series entitled "Is Vice Protected"? [22]

Mayor Harper responded that he did not protect vice, he condoned it, regardless of state and local laws forbidding prostitution and gambling. He then filed a $600,000 lawsuit against the *Express*. The county grand jury investigated and found brothels in operation. Further testimony revealed that Harper's frequent "inspections" occasionally resembled orgies.

The mayor and police commissioners owned hotels and other rental properties in the vice district. Saloonkeepers had purchased $250,000 worth of stock in Harper's nondescript oil and sugar companies. Police Chief Edward Kern, a former teamster and Seventh Ward Democratic councilman, directed a firm which sold fire insurance to local businesses, both licensed and unlicensed. Nevertheless, the grand jury found no evidence that city officials protected illegal enterprises. [23]

The *Express* continued to investigate. Chief Kern resigned, to be replaced by his vice squad commander, Captain Thomas Broadhead. The Municipal League, formed in 1901 by Charles Dwight Willard, then initiated a drive to recall Mayor Harper. Other reform clubs quickly joined the campaign. These included John R. Haynes' Direct Legislation League, Edward A. Dickson's City Club and Meyer Lissner's Good Government Organization.

These groups formed the vanguard of the Lincoln-Roosevelt League, which soon became a powerful, state-wide reform organization. The progressives could also rely on the support of the Anti-Saloon League, the Anti-Racetrack Gambling League, the Sunday Rest League and the League of Justice, a civil rights organization. [24]

Meyer Lissner emerged as a leading progressive. His Good Government Organization became, in the short run, the most important political club. Lissner, a lawyer, arrived in Los Angeles during the 1890's and made a fortune in real estate speculation. In 1906, recommended to Edward Dickson as "too young to retire and too rich to practise law," he turned to local politics. By devoting almost all of his time to reform politics he became extremely influential. Lissner, a true progressive, cared only for the construction of an ideal civic constitution that would preserve public control of government. Then the "best" men—disinterested, public-spirited progressives—could be elected. Corrupt political machines would be destroyed. [25]

Lissner envisioned a reform political party that would cut across all strata of society. He appealed to the black community to vote for middleclass progressives instead of saloon and vice candidates. He expected strong working class support for honest, frugal government. Yet Lissner and his progressive associates had scant interest in social or economic reform. They made no attempt to nominate minority political candidates and actively resented "the tyranny of organized labor." Nevertheless, Lissner achieved remarkable early success. [26]

Local newspapers also played an important role. E.T. Earl owned and published the morning *Tribune* and the evening *Express,* edited by Edward A. Dickson. From 1906 until about 1916 the two newspapers provided the strongest and most consistent support for civic reform and progressivism. Earl's positions generally gained the support of the *Herald,* an independent Democratic journal. Thomas Gibbon, the *Herald* editor, was among the first "Progressive Democrats," a term that became more common with each reform victory. [27]

The *Record* proclaimed no party affiliation but its sympathies lay with the common man. The *Record* favored municipal socialism and direct legislation but opposed the reform movement between 1906 and 1909. The editors implied that reform was a Republican trick, designed to rob the working man of his saloons, boxing matches and horse races. [28]

William Randolph Hearst's *Examiner* remained firmly behind the traditional Democratic party organization. Hearst founded the *Examiner* in 1903 at the request of striking newspapermen who wanted an alternative to the *Times.* By remaining loyal to his original constituents, Hearst placed the *Examiner* in opposition to both civic and moral reform. Governmental reform meant defeating Democratic incumbents, while the saloons, brothels and gaming houses to be suppressed were in the working class, ethnic, Democratic wards.

At the conservative end of the spectrum stood Harrison Gray Otis' *Times,* the city's most reactionary bastion against organized labor and other "socialistic" developments. Invariably, Otis aligned his paper with the traditional or machine Republicans, tied closely to the Southern Pacific Railway political organization. Otis would not openly support a nonRepublican against the progressive candidates, however. For about a decade, the *Times* howled in the political wilderness, unable to direct the course of city politics.

The progressives gathered enough signatures on recall petitions to request an election to recall Arthur Harper. The recall vote was scheduled for March 27, 1909, but on March 11 the campaign took a stunning turn. The *Record,* in a banner headline, demanded Harper's immediate resignation. The mayor complied at once but neither he nor the editors would discuss the mysterious event. The Earl newspapers, chagrined at losing the story after conducting a long investigation, accused the *Record* of blackmailing Harper by threatening to expose his sordid personal life.

The grand jury summoned E.T. Earl to justify his continued allegations of official malfeasance. Earl's testimony resulted in the indictment of ex-mayor Harper, ex-chief Kern, ex-police commissioner Samuel Schenk and Chief of Police Thomas Broadhead. Earl got his information by paying $10,000 to Nick Oswald, a long-time entrepreneur in the segregated zone. Oswald, forced out of business in the post-1902 reform campaign, regained his place after Harper's election in 1906. Police Commissioner Schenk put him in charge of a new district, bounded by Alameda, Ducommun, Garcia and Aliso streets, while Chief Kern and Captain Broadhead closed the old district controlled by Tom Savage. [29]

At the new syndicate's office in the Hellman Building, Oswald paid $500 per month each to Harper, Kern, Broadhead and Schenk. These sums may have been less than the proceeds from the sale of worthless stock and fire insurance but still were double the monthly salaries of the chief and mayor. (After Schenk had to resign due to involvement in another scandal, his share went to Tom Savage, the deposed vice boss.) Oswald further testified that he only turned informer because he needed the money. District Attorney Frederick, determined not to be caught in the Harper-Kern scandal, had completely closed the segregated zone. [30]

Harper's resignation created a brief political dilemma. The *Times* and the Democrats argued that no further basis for recall existed; the five machine politicians among the nine city councilmen could therefore appoint someone to complete Harper's unexpired term. City Attorney Leslie Hewitt, a progressive elected in 1906, ruled that the unexpired portion consisted only of the period between Harper's resignation and the scheduled recall election. The council then appointed W.D. Stephens, a solid progressive and future governor, to serve the remaining sixteen days. [31]

The progressives nominated George Alexander, a seventy year-old immigrant Scottish grain merchant, to replace Harper. Fred Wheeler, a socialist, provided the only opposition. Wheeler, however, received support from the Southern Pacific, some regular Republicans and many Democrats. The *Times* remained neutral, fortunately perhaps for Alexander, who won by 1508 votes of 26,350 cast in a rather light turnout. [32]

The progressives proceeded to consolidate their victory. During the decade 1900-1909, the city had tripled in size, to 300,000 residents. It appeared that most newcomers were American-born Protestants of reformist sentiments. The electorate approved a charter amendment that abolished the ward system and established non-partisan election laws. Future candidates would run "at large" and would be forbidden to reveal their party affiliation.

In effect, the progressives abolished the municipal Democratic party. In the regular election of December, 1909, the reformers won all twenty-three elective offices: mayor, nine councilmen, city attorney, prosecutor, clerk, assessor, tax collector, auditor and seven schoolboard members. To the dismay of some progressives, George Alexander still occupied the mayor's office. "Uncle Alex" changed his mind about being an interim mayor and the good government organizations acquiesced rather than provoke a party quarrel.

Police reorganization presented complex problems. The progressives' first chief, Edward Dishman, was strictly a political appointment. Dishman, a reporter for the *Times,* had no experience but the progressives hoped to neutralize the *Times* in the regular 1909 election. This they accomplished, although Otis could not have supported a socialist in any case.

Otherwise, Dishman was the worst possible progressive choice. He upheld "personal liberty" with regard to vice and denounced the reformers' "fanatical" determination to suppress the segregated zone. Moreover, when the Harper-Kern syndicate escaped conviction for suborning bribery, Dishman reappointed ex-chief Thomas Broadhead to a captaincy. [33]

The angry reformers rejected Broadhead. The police commission overruled the appointment and shortly afterward dismissed Dishman. In his place they appointed Alexander Galloway, another outsider with no law enforcement experience. This continued a long but not unbroken tradition. In theory, an experienced "civilian" executive could effectively administer a government bureaucracy. Undoubtedly, an outside chief would be more attuned to the wishes of the mayor and less committed to the internal goals of the agency. This system paid no heed to the legitimate ambitions of career policemen. The use of managerial and technical experts from outside the service later became a tenet of professionalization but in 1910 the only virtue of the outside chief was his ignorance of the department's internecine conflicts. [34]

Two major parties struggled for dominance. Prior to the reform victory the Kern-Broadhead group held the best and most lucrative positions. A second faction, led by Captain Charles Dixon, rallied to the good government cause. Whether this reflected ideological affinity or was only a tactic of the "out" party is not clear. Rumor held that Captain Dixon gave the *Record* the information that forced Mayor Harper's mysterious resignation. Dixon evidently expected the chief's job and the chance to place his cronies in key positions. [35]

In addition to the contest for job preferment and graft, other internal conflicts (or "tong wars", as the *Times* put it) including competition over arrests, newspaper publicity and rewards, and rivalries between uniformed and plain-clothes divisions and between squads within divisions, kept the department in turmoil. Civil libertarians excoriated the police for unconstitutional, brutal and inhumane practises. The League of Justice specifically denounced arrests made "on suspicion," "third degree" interrogations, unlawful imprisonment, rudeness and profanity directed toward citizens, and filthy, vermin-ridden jails. [36]

No chief could immediately resolve such long standing problems but an impartial outsider, by refusing to place one faction at the mercy of the other, might gradually restore the merit system while disciplining the unruly minority among patrolmen. Unfortunately, Edward Dishman had openly supported the discredited Kern-Broadhead group. This denied Dixon's faction any reward for supporting the progressives and further exacerbated the internal strife. Alexander Galloway accepted Dixon's guidance but was too inept and too ignorant of police procedures to restore order within the department. After ten months, the police commission accepted his resignation. Dixon served briefly as interim chief until the Council appointed Charles Sebastian, another veteran police officer.

At the same time, the progressives decided to reorganize the command structure. The charter revision of 1911 established a three member, nonpartisan board—the mayor and two appointees acceptable to the council—in place of the five-member, politically balanced commission. So passed the last office where the Democrats retained a voice. The charter amendment also granted the mayor full powers to appoint, direct and dismiss the chief of police. Thus, between 1888 and 1911, command of the department passed from the city council, through the hands of an appointed board, into the control of a single elected official. [37]

Charter reform did nothing to improve working conditions and wages, important indices of efficiency and morale. Although modest "professional" technological advances were made, salaries remained low and personnel numbers at the minimum. In 1910, 250 officers protected 310,000 people. Chief Dishman requested 100 additional men in lieu of two proposed substations. After considerable prodding he got his way but salaries remained at the 1902 level, seventy-five dollars per month. This sum did not attract the best candidates. [38]

Circumstances changed dramatically, late in 1910. Members of the International Iron Workers' Union dynamited the *Los Angeles Times* building, killing a score of workmen. In the anti-radical hysteria that followed, the police force was raised to 500 men. Subsequent experience indicated that a large increase in police strength was a predictable response to social crisis in Los Angeles.

Police later discovered bombs at the homes of *Times* publisher Harrison Gray Otis and Felix Zeehandelaar, secretary of the anti-labor Merchants and Manufacturers Association. On December 24, another explosion damaged the Llewellyn Iron Works. During the subsequent trial of the brothers J.B. and J.J. McNamara for the murders of *Times* employees, their accomplice revealed sixty-nine other bomb plots planned by the radicals.

Members of the Burns Detective Agency found the McNamaras in other states, kidnapped them and returned them to Los Angeles for trial. These and other illegal acts outraged civil libertarians, who took the brothers' innocence for granted. Many labor leaders, union members and assorted radicals and liberals saw the McNamaras as victims of a classic frame-up by vengeful anti-labor reactionaries. [39]

The McNamaras' trial proceeded concurrently with the 1911 municipal election campaign. Job Harriman, a socialist lawyer defending the brothers, entered the mayoralty race and collected a large vote in the primary election. Harriman's candidacy frightened traditional politicians. Regular Republicans and Democrats joined the good government movement—and incidentally destroyed it. The *Times* suddenly found much that was praiseworthy in George Alexander's administration. A few days before the election, the corrupt dealings revealed later by Lincoln Steffens extracted the McNamaras' confession to the heinous crime. The anti-socialist coalition of fear then won an overwhelming victory. [40]

It became a popular fiction that the confession swung the election from Harriman to Alexander. Although two Socialist councilmen won seats, little in previous or subsequent Los Angeles history suggests that a majority of voters supported Harriman or socialism. The electorate actually turned more conservative. In 1913, Fred Rose, an old-line Republican police magistrate, edged out the Socialist candidate in the primary and then defeated the progressive candidate for mayor in the regular election.

By that time the reform political coalition had begun to disintegrate. Both the E.T. Earl and Meyer Lissner progressive factions opposed labor unions and social welfare legislation. They deserted Mayor Alexander when he accepted a few mild social reform measures. The suicidal progressives then supported an anti-reform petition to recall the city administration in June, 1913. Afterward, they failed to regain power. [41]

By 1915 the destruction of the original, politically-oriented municipal progressive movement was complete. True, Hiram Johnson, the progressive warhorse, could still flagellate the ultraconservative publisher of the *Times:*

> there is nothing so low, nothing so debased, nothing so infamous as Harrison Gray Otis. He sits there in senile dementia, with gangrened heart and rotting brain, grimacing at every reform, chattering impotently at all things that are decent, frothing, fuming, violently gibbering, going down to his grave in snarling infamy...anything that is disgraceful, corrupt, crooked and putrescent—that is Harrison Gray Otis.

Otis, however, could anticipate with pleasure an editorial description of "The Rise and Fall of the Goo-Goo." Already the Earl newspapers refused to print Lissner's name in their columns. Factional rivalry destroyed the once all-powerful good government movement. [42]

So ended the first quarter-century of progressive reform. It was directed mainly to political reorganization, with a major emphasis on proper police administration. By and large, the early political goals were accomplished, beginning with the charter of 1889 and continuing through the revisions of 1902, 1909 and 1911. Professionalization of the police was underway, although the specific term was seldom heard outside police conventions. "Direct democracy" existed. Theoretically, citizens could remove unsatisfactory officeholders and amend the laws to suit themselves. Whatever the other effects of "non-partisanship," it had placed the city government entirely in the hands of native, white, Protestant Republicans.

For six years, the police suppressed organized commercial vice. In this they had been aided by a platoon of ministers sworn in as special constables, and the Morals Efficiency League, also staffed by clergymen. Racetrack gambling and prizefighting had been abolished. To suppress prostitution, the reformers had passed an ordinance forbidding sexual intercourse between persons not married to one another, thus making conviction sure under one law or the other. The technicalities of this law led to an unsuccessful attempt to frame a puritanical city prosecutor on a phoney morals charge. It also meant that every year a few unfortunate lovers were convicted of adultery or fornication. As Willard Huntington Wright bitterly observed, the once exciting city became "Los Angeles, the Chemically Pure". [43]

NOTES

[1] This account of nineteenth century Los Angeles history is derived from a combination of pioneer accounts, early histories, recent general history, twentieth century scholarship and official documents. See two books by Horace Bell, *Reminiscences of A Ranger* (Los Angeles, 1881), and *On The Old West Coast: Being Further Reminiscences of A Ranger* (New York, 1902); Harris Newmark, *Sixty Years in Southern California, 1853-1913* (New York, 1916); J. Albert Wilson, *History of Los Angeles* (Oakland, 1880); Dwight Willard, *A History of Los Angeles City* (Los Angeles, 1901); J.M. Guinn, *Historical and Biographical Record of Southern California* (Chicago, 1902); Remi A. Nadeau, *City Makers* (Garden City, 1948), and *Los Angeles: From Mission to Modern City* (New York, 1960); descriptions of social violence are found in E. Caroline Gabard, "The Development of Law Enforcement in Early California," (M.A. thesis, University of Southern California, 1960); Patricia A. Poos, "The Era of Do-It-Yourself Justice: The First Twenty-One Years of the Los Angeles County Sheriff's Department (senior project, California State Polytechnic College at Pomona, 1972); Arthur W. Sjoquist, "From Posses to Professionals: A History of the Los Angeles Police Department," (M.A. thesis, California State University at Los Angeles, 1971); and Leonard Pitt, *The Decline of the Californios* (Berkeley, 1966). For a scholarly overview of the early period see Robert M. Fogelson, *The Fragmented Metropolis: Los Angeles, 1850-1930* (Cambridge, Mass., 1967). Population statistics are drawn from U.S. census returns. Also Norton Stern and William Kramer, "Emil Harris: Los Angeles Jewish Police Chief," *Southern California Quarterly* LV 2 (July 1973).

[2] Homer B. Cross, "Out of the Past," *The Guardian*, 27; Sjoquist, 42; Newmark, 418. Lyndley Bynum and Idwal Jones, *Biscailuz: Sheriff of the New West* (New York, 1950), *passim*.

[3] See photograph of lynching at Fort Moore Hill, c. 1870, in *The Guardian*, 23; an eyewitness said that members of the L.A.P.D. led the mob; Bell, *On the Old West Coast*, 169-173; see Common Council *Minutes*, vols. 11-13, for deliberations involving establishment of the police force.

[4] *Ibid.*, 310; v.13, 666-691; v.10, 381; Cross, *passim*.

[5] "Chiefs of Police, LAPD, 1876-1973," n.d.

[6] Cross, 17. Hubert Howe Bancroft, quoted by W.W. Robinson in *Tarnished Angels: Paradisaical Turpitude in Los Angeles* (L.A., 1969),

13, 15, 16, 21; W.W. Robinson, *Los Angeles From the Days of the Pueblo* (L.A.,1959), *passim*; Dana W. Bartlett, *The Better City* (L.A., 1907), 131-134; Gregory H. Singleton, "American Protestant Culture and Urbanization," (unpublished ms.), ch. 3 and 4, *passim*.

[7] L.A. City Charter, 1889; Lorin Peterson, *The Day of the Mugwump* (New York, 1961), 234-246.

[8] Marvin Abrahams, "The Functioning of Boards and Commissions in the Los Angeles City Government" (doctoral dissertation, U.C.L.A., 1967), 12 and *passim*.

[9] The first national convention of police chiefs took place in St. Louis in 1871. The discussion topics were intended to "advance the science and art of Police Services." The report of the 1871 convention and the annual meetings since 1893 are collected in *Police in America,* 5 vols. (New York: Arno Press, 1971). The first professional police journals were *The Police Chief* and the International Association of Chiefs of Police *Yearbook.;* See International Association ofChiefs of Police *Yearbook* (1959), 163-166; for California see John P. Kenney, *The California Police* (Springfield, Ill., 1969), esp. 5-7, 21-29, 73-75.

[10] Cross, 41-42; see Glass' impressive criminal identification ledgers in the LAPD archives.

[11] LAPD *Annual Report,* 1897; Glass' reports were quite short— even the 1897 pamphlet was only 11 pages—and were reprinted in the newspapers; see *Express,* 12-19-1891, in Moffat Scrapbook, LAPD Archives.

[12] George Wilson, "History of the Los Angeles Police Department," typescript, n.d.

[13] *Times,* 1-20-1891, 2-10-1891; *Ibid.,* 12-31-1899, 1-3-1900, 1-4-1900.

[14] Los Angeles City Charter, 1903; Peterson, *loc. cit.*

[15] cf. the charters of 1889 and 1903, esp. Sec. 53, 91-96, and Article 13.

[16] Civil Service Commission *Annual Report* (1904), 17-23; Cross, 41-45. *Times,* 11-19-06.

[17] Charter of 1903, S. 13 and 95a.

[18] For a fictional treatment of these events, see Sydney C. Kendall, *The Soundings of Hell* (Los Angeles, 1903), and *Queen of the Red Lights* (Los Angeles, 1906). The factual account is in the *Times,* June through December, 1902.

[19] Albert H. Clodius, "The Quest for Good Government in Los Angeles, 1900-1910" (doctoral dissertation, Claremont Graduate

School, 1953), 150-160; Janice Jaques, "The Political Reform Movement in Los Angeles, 1900-1910" (master's thesis, Claremont Graduate School, 1948), 44-65; Bartlett, 146-185, 248.

[20] Robinson, 15,16,21.

[21] P.L. Bonebrake, *The Westerner's Brand Book* (1947), quoted in Robinson, *Tarnished Angels,* 20.

[22] *Herald,* 9-27-08, 9-28-08; *Express,* 10-1-08, 10-13-08.

[23] Clodius, 187-188; Jaques, 90.

[24] Clodius, 170-230; Jaques, 65-85; Alice Rose, "The Rise of California Insurgency" (doctoral dissertation, Stanford University, 1942), *passim*; Kern later committed suicide.

[25] Clodius, 478; Russ Avery to E.A. Dickson, 3-15-06, E.A. Dickson Papers, Box 1, Folder 2; Avery, an attorney, was president of the Los Angeles Voters' League; George Mowry, *The California Progressives* (Chicago: Quadrangle Books, 1963), 43-44.

[26] Clodius, 409-411, 483-490; E.T. Earl to E.A. Dickson, 7-8-07, Dickson, Box 1, Folder 4; A.S. Petterson, "The Los Angeles Non-Partisan Movement of 1906," typescript in Dickson, Box 17, Folder 3. Mowry, 43, 93, 144-147.

[27] Clodius, 559-560.

[28] *Ibid.*

[29] *Record,* 3-11-09; *Herald,* 4-13-09; *Times,* 3-7-09 through 3-12-09.

[30] *Herald,* 4-12-09 through 4-15-09.

[31] *Ibid.,* 3-16-09; 3-24-09.

[32] Mowry, 42-43; Clodius, 150-159.

[33] *Ibid.,* 218-225; *Times,* 4-22-09, 2-14-10.

[34] *Ibid.*; Between 1900 and 1911, only 2 of 7 chiefs, Auble and Broadhead, came from the LAPD ranks.

[35] Clodius, 223. See *Times,* 4-5-09, 4-11-09 for discussion of factions which the newspaper likened to "Chinatown tongs."

[36] *Times,* 4-3-09, 4-5-09, 4-11-09; *Examiner,* 1-4-10, 2-17-10.

[37] Los Angeles City Charter, 1911; Abrahams, 12-16.

[38] See the chief's comments in the LAPD *Annual Reports,* 1909, 1910; Times, 4-18-09, 4-27-09.

[39] Louis Adamic, *Dynamite: The Story of Class Violence in America* (London, 1931), 200-253; daily reports of the trial are in defense attorney Joseph Le Compte Davis' Scrapbooks; see especially the McNamaras' handwritten confession in the Davis Papers Box 5. Mowry, 500-51; Nadeau, 121-141, esp. photo of demolished building at pp. 110-

111; the newspaper did not miss an issue; other presses printed the *Times* until new equipment was obtained.

[40] Lincoln Steffens, *The Autobiography of Lincoln Steffens* (New York, 1931), 680-682.

[41] Clodius, 531-535.

[42] Moro Mayo, *Los Angeles* (New York, 1933), 153; *Times,* 10-12-17; Mowry, 201-206; Clodius, 522-528; E.T. Earl to E.A. Dickson, forbidding the mention of Lissner in the *Tribune* or *Express,* Dickson, Box 3, Folder 17.

[43] Adela Rogers St. John, *Final Verdict* (Garden City, N.Y., 1962), 461-468; Willard H. Wright, "Los Angeles, the Chemically Pure," in Burton Rascoe and Graff Conklin, eds., *The Smart Set Anthology* (New York, 1934), 90-102.

CHAPTER TWO

THE SECOND PROGRESSIVE
MOVEMENT, 1915-1923

Los Angeles, California is an excellent illustration of the
hold that vice has upon the government. Through the efforts
of a small group led by preachers, an effort was made to
eliminate gambling and prostitution from that city, with the
result that the underworld people, in order to protect their
business interests, were obliged to form a defense organization, and to pay large sums of money to a political group,
ostensibly for campaign purposes. Any chief of police who
attempted to do his duty and eliminate those iniquitous dens
would soon have suffered a shortening of his career. The
business of vice therefore continued to flourish, the protests
of the people were wantonly flouted, the morale of the law-
enforcing officers was inevitably threatened, and the result
of the whole matter was to strengthen the hands of the politicians who daily corrupt the government of our cities.

August Vollmer,
*The Police and
Modern Society*

The moral reformers who provided the voting strength of the earlier political movement formed the vanguard of a new progressive crusade. The reform constituency survived—every politician styled himself
or herself a progressive—but a different leadership emerged. The Protestant clergy, traditionally important but not preeminent in local politics,
superseded Earl, Lissner and other theorists of government. Ministerial
organizations and federations of denominational laity replaced the political clubs of the past but lacked the cohesion and efficiency of the good
government associations.

Without rich philanthropists such as Earl and Lissner, reform fell
on hard times. Political campaigns required money, "the mother's milk

of politics," but civil service regulations curtailed patronage; nonpartisan laws vitiated precinct organizations; and abolition of the crib district eliminated the most willing and generous contributors. Since the reformers could not or would not finance their own slate of municipal candidates, they had to support the most promising individuals from among those who stood for office. This played into the hands of would-be grafters and vice entrepreneurs.

The experience of 1906-1915 proved that the numerous and potentially all-powerful reformers could not be ignored. Nevertheless, they could be circumvented. The machine regained power by financing ostensible reformers who in practise cooperated with the corrupt interests, especially through manipulation of the police department. As a result, the department again functioned as a sort of licensing and inspection bureau for organized vice operations.

Moreover, the protection of illegal enterprises encouraged other illegal activities. The indictment of police officers became commonplace, providing a continuing cause for sharp newspaper commentary and aggressive reform oratory. On the other hand, the department received broad progressive support for its vigilant and violent effort to make Los Angeles an unhealthy place for "radicals," labor organizers and vagrants. The American Legion provided enthusiastic aid. While the suppression of civil rights appalled certain liberals, the department's actions probably mitigated the effects of other forms of malfeasance.

Los Angeles at the time was in one sense a cosmopolitan city, supporting a polyglot population of Sikhs, Filipinos, Chinese, Japanese, Mexicans, negroes and whites from southern and eastern Europe. In a more significant sense it was a large provincial town: "the capitol of Iowa" on the west coast. Three orthodoxies shaped the society. The political dogma was a nativist progressivism. The economic standard was the "American system," or open shop. The religious creed was Protestant, especially as professed by Methodists and Presbyterians.

In general, the native middle class Protestants who controlled business and government considered the colored races to be superstitious and congenitally vicious. Whites also, from "backward" countries, were often immoral and sometimes dangerous. They habitually used beer or wine. They were Catholics or Jews or atheists. They proclaimed "alien" doctrines of class conflict and social reform inconsistent with the American system. Muckraking journalists had shown that agglomerations of such people in cities opened the door to municipal corruption, the very evil that made the progressive movement necessary.

Against such a development stood the Protestant churches. Many ministers involved themselves deeply in politics as unpaid speakers for "the right sort" of candidates but few considered significant economic or social change as necessary or even desirable. For them, reform meant the enforcement of municipal ordinances which forbade gambling, prostitution and alcoholic beverages. The churchmen knew that commercial vice required protection. This led to repeated clashes between reformers and police administrators.

A significant change soon occurred in the church-centered progressive movement. The reticent leadership provided by Dr. C.C. Selectman and Dr. R.C. Barton of the Morals Efficiency League gave way to an enterprising new breed exemplified by the Reverend Gustav A. Briegleb, of Westlake Presbyterian, and Robert P. "Fighting Bob" Shuler, of Trinity Methodist Church. Many differences separated Briegleb and Shuler but they were alike in two important characteristics: the will to power and the love of publicity.

Gustav Briegleb, born in Jersey City in 1881, attended Moody Bible Institute and the Biblical Seminary of New York. Ordained in 1905 and immediately successful, he left a good position in Philadelphia during World War I and enrolled in Whitman College of Walla Walla, Washington. After receiving the doctor of divinity degree in 1917, he became pastor at Westlake. Briegleb rose quickly, becoming president of the Los Angeles Ministerial Union by 1921. From that office he exerted pressure upon the police commission in the matter of public morals. Small but gratifying early successes—the closing of a roadhouse and dancehall—gave him the confidence to exploit larger opportunities when they occurred.

Briegleb persuaded the police commission that women should be forbidden to smoke "in any room or place adjacent to or connected with any ballroom or dancing academy" and achieved a ban on dancing with the cheek or head touching one's partner. The male could place his hand only on his partner's back, between shoulder and waist; the female could place her hand only in the left hand of the male. Music "suggestive of bodily contortions" was forbidden. Briegleb's insinuations regarding the way "immoral" dance halls received licenses frequently angered the police commissioners. At least one official threatened to strike him.

Gustav Briegleb became known in high places and was invited to meet President Coolidge when their paths crossed at a summer resort. The Lord's Day Alliance, an organization devoted to blue laws and Sunday closing, offered Briegleb the national leadership but he refused it in

order to remain in Los Angeles. A perceptive reporter, having visited
Briegleb's busy "plant," warned the public to beware "this preaching
Babbitt," who meant to convince businessmen that Sunday closing
would be "money in their pockets." [1]

Robert Shuler resembled William Jennings Bryan. He came from
the Blue Ridge by way of Texas. He upheld the Bible as literal revealed
truth and liked to chide Briegleb publicly for holding "modern" religious
ideas. Shuler's speech, ideas and congregation lacked the smooth sophistication of Briegleb's but his brain was as quick and his ultimate success
was greater.

Shuler exercised formidable political influence. On one occasion
he withdrew his endorsement of a conservative female schoolboard candidate because the woman smoked cigarets. Although she promised
never to smoke again, if elected, Fighting Bob remained adamant. In his
view, the possibility of a liberal on the schoolboard was less pressing
than the immediate evil of tobacco.

Shuler like to write, and his private magazine grew quickly to a
circulation of 11,000 by 1923. Even more, he liked to talk, and opportunities abounded because he was fearless on the podium. He made few
direct statements, always having "heard" or "been told" the juicy gossip
that he freely dispensed. The police were corrupt. Vice was protected.
The chief or the mayor or perhaps the district attorney, must go. Roman
Catholic District Attorney T.L. Woolwine's counter-attack on "pussy-
footing, publicity-seeking, religious despots" did no harm to Shuler, who
praised the Ku Klux Klan "for the enemies it had made." [2]

After succeeding Briegleb as president of the Ministerial Union,
Shuler instituted a devastating practise. Delegations of clergymen and
faithful would arrive unheralded at the office of the mayor or police chief
and there hold public inquests into vice conditions. Invariably, Shuler
and Briegleb were the star performers, although the two preachers
accomplished little of lasting importance. Briegleb eventually found it
more profitable to support the administration than to attack it.

Shuler also flirted with the machine but soon returned to his place
on the outside. In later years he was remembered with distaste by moder-
ates of all faiths, whereas Briegleb was largely forgotten. But Shuler had
enormous short-term significance. Observers credited him with unseating at least one mayor and one police chief. [3]

Notwithstanding the dismay which their antics aroused, Shuler and
Briegleb infused a fire into reform. The public willingly responded.
Reform took on the attributes of revival and stole many a headline from

competitors such as Amy Semple McPherson. Despite an apparent unity of purpose, however, the struggle for supremacy between Shuler and Briegleb was for twenty years an important political fact. The two ministers became constants in the Los Angeles political equation. Mayors, chiefs and bosses rose and fell. Shuler and Briegleb endured.

Organized commercial vice reappeared at the beginning of the second progressive era and seemed impossible to eradicate. Political expediency, war, urban growth and sumptuary laws spurred the demand for gambling, prostitution and illegal liquor. The number of transient males, the "consumers" of vice, increased with the opening of the Panama Canal in conjunction with construction of the Los Angeles harbor and the onset of World War I. The city became at once a seaport, a naval station and an army camp. New industries attracted more mechanics. "Factories in the fields" employed many laborers. The continuing migration required thousands of workmen to provide shelter and facilities.

The population rose to 576,000 by 1920 and reached about 770,000 by 1923. Concurrently, wartime liquor prohibition under the municipal Gandier Act in 1916, followed later by the Eighteenth Amendment and the Volstead Act, produced a law enforcement crisis of unprecedented dimensions. Opportunities for graft exceeded anything previously known. The proportion of policemen and other officials eager to share in the bonanza increased as the profits grew. With the vice lords ascendant, the progressives found themselves concerned almost entirely with moral issues. The old cycle of scandal and reform and scandal began again.

The career of Charles E. Sebastian, reform chief and mayor, foreshadowed the coming civic chaos. The tall, handsome Missourian epitomized the ethnic, religious and political traditions of the LAPD. He arrived in the city after service in the Spanish-American War and joined the force in 1900. A sergeant by 1908, Sebastian gained a reputation as a vice-raider in Chinatown. In 1909, however, he was named as a courier for the Harper-Kern syndicate. Perhaps the reformers considered him the hapless tool of corrupt superiors. At any rate, he escaped dismissal and went on to become chief in January, 1911. [4]

Chief Sebastian survived the good government defeat of 1913 and served through Fred Rose's term by maintaining a closed city. Purveyors of illicit entertainment were difficult to find. Willard H. Wright described the general atmosphere as "a frenzy of virtue." Pleasureseekers found themselves "thwarted by some ordinance, the primary object of which is to force Middle West moralities on every inhabitant. Puritanism is the inflexible doctrine of Los Angeles." The complaint had merit when published in 1913 but relief was at hand. The puritanical era scarcely outlasted the good government movement. [5]

Sebastian decided to forsake police work for politics, choosing to begin at the top, in the mayor's office. Scandal touched the chief early in the 1915 campaign when he was accused of illicit relationships with young women. After the girls admitted to perjury a wave of public joy floated the popular policeman into the mayor's chair. Disaster struck in 1916. By obtaining Sebastian's correspondence, the *Record* proved him guilty of adultery. In Los Angeles, this alone meant ruin, but extortion, suborning perjury and a staged pre-election attempt on his life contributed to the former hero's downfall. Sebastian resigned and faded away. [6]

The city council elected Frederick T. Woodman, an ascetic, child-less widower of forty-seven years, to complete Sebastian's term. Wood-man appointed a career officer, Captain John L. Butler, to replace Chief C.E. Snively, an ex-newsman and Sebastian's former secretary. Horace Karr, the *Times'* city hall reporter, became Woodman's closest advisor. To finance the 1919 mayoralty campaign, Woodman and Karr decided to open a section of Central Avenue to gambling, girls and liquor. Karr arranged the deal with George Henderson and George Brown, two Negro veterans of the lively old days. The vice dealers offered $25,000 in instalments for permission to operate. Someone, perhaps Chief Butler, "lined up" the vice squad. The *Record* editors then published the details, toppling their third mayor within a decade.

The grand jury indicted Woodman, Karr, Brown, Henderson, vice squad sergeant William "Wild Bill" Hackett and three patrolmen. In typ-ical local fashion, no convictions resulted. Karr and Brown received immunity and testified against the mayor. Woodman denied all knowl-edge of Karr's misdeeds. A crucial witness, last seen at the train station accompanied by a police officer, "disappeared." Someone "stole" an important notebook from Woodman's home. The confused jurors acquit-ted the mayor, who then campaigned for re-election.

Juries also acquitted the police officers but by no means exonerat-ed them. Trial testimony clearly established the existence of protected vice. For a time George Henderson seemed bound for prison. He refused to speak and was convicted. The court reversed this judgement on the basis of "new evidence" and the second jury failed to reach a verdict. District Attorney T.L. Woolwine then withdrew the charges, claiming that juries would not convict the little men if the mayor and others went free. This trial established the close-mouthed, retiring Henderson as the most powerful black boss. Although the flashy and boastful Brown described himself as "the King of Central Avenue," the white underworld leaders who ran the city refused to trust anyone who had turned state's witness to save himself. [7]

The electorate chose Woodman's opponent, Meredith Pinxton "Pinky" Snyder, giving him 61 percent of the ballots cast. Snyder ran as a progressive reformer, referring constantly to his record of clean government during three previous terms as mayor. The record, compiled between 1896 and 1904, apparently meant that none of his appointees went to jail. Oldtimers might recall that Snyder's police chief resigned in 1904 during a vice investigation and that the reformers then defeated Snyder's re-election bid. Relatively few could remember, of course. The population had increased 400 percent during the interval. [8]

Snyder nominated Detective Captain George K. Home to replace Chief Butler. Home, a saturnine man of forty, had fifteen years of service. He had risen fast, due in part to his predilection for vigorous law enforcement. As a rookie patrolman, he broke his club on the first head he struck with it but soon rid Chinatown of the youthful muggers who operated there. By 1916 he was a deputy chief under Clarence Sniveley. As head of the "Strong-arm Squad," his exploits against vagrants and wobblies pleased the business community, but the departmental politics that facilitated his rise ordained his fall when John L. Butler replaced Chief Sniveley. [9]

George Home's administration introduced the Roaring Twenties. A combination of phenomena produced what Home called "a breakdown of moral restraint." Anarchists, Communists and I.W.W. organizers denounced the American system. Striking A.F.L. unionists disrupted transportation and distribution services. Violent liquor wars and widespread public lawbreaking marked the commencement of prohibition. A vast increase in automobiles allowed "flaming youth" to escape neighborhood sanctions. The city's pell-mell growth continued, as did the influx of unwanted, jobless persons. According to Home's indices, the crime rate reached new peaks. [10]

The LAPD too, from chief to patrolmen, suffered an apparent breakdown of restraint. Home rehired a number of ex-policemen who had been dismissed for such crimes as assault, theft, and bribery and put some of them in positions of authority over the incumbent officers. Home also kept two irregular advisers of such malodorous reputation that they could not be hired through civil service procedures. One, Herbert "Brute" Kittle, had been dismissed in 1916 after a *Record* expose of his sadistic treatment of prisoners. By 1920 he was back, on Home's "secret service" payroll.

The *Record* again forced him out, however, by reporting (unlike other newspapers) a wild scene during which the drunken Kittle fired several shots through the floor of the detective bureau, threatened numerous witnesses and boasted that his friends were so powerful that he could not be fired. After Kittle resigned, evidence found in his desk pointed to his involvement in certain robberies. As the police closed in on his home, Kittle committed suicide to avoid arrest. [11]

The other irregular, Harry J. Raymond, might have been the model for the corrupt policemen often found in the novels of Dashiel Hammett and Raymond Chandler. Raymond's most recent official job had been that of police chief in Venice, California. After several suits for false arrest, fisticuffs with his subordinates and other personnel problems, Raymond found himself indicted for extortion. The prosecution fell through when the plaintiff fled from the state, claiming that his life was in danger. Venice, though not unaccustomed to garish characters, found Raymond a little too much so and ousted him. Like Kittle, Raymond resigned following the *Record* attack on Chief Home, but his career with the LAPD was by no means finished. [12]

The employment of Kittle, Raymond, and the other men rehired after dismissal for cause had a direct relationship to the protection of organized crime. A few trustworthy rogues could control the vice squad, act as collectors or "bag men" and ensure that no criminal enterprise succeeded except as part of the combination which ruled the underworld. When necessary, they could arrange "sweeping police raids" that invariably failed to net the significant criminal leaders. During Home's term the city reverted almost to frontier conditions, with open gambling, bootlegging and prostitution. Pick-pockets and "bunco" artists operated under the direct supervision of the LAPD detective bureau.

The *Record,* along with Robert Shuler, Gustav Briegleb and the Morals Efficiency League, led the progressive attack on open vice conditions. The critics pointed out that despite the presence of detectives from the LAPD and the district attorney's office, gamblers operated at bootlegged race meets that violated state and local laws. Gambling halls, bordellos and Chinese lotteries ran wide open, with each enterprise accepting an arrest ("taking a pinch") each month to satisfy public opinion. [13]

"Chief Home MUST know," the *Record* charged, to which Mayor Snyder replied that Los Angeles was the cleanest city in the world. This contradicted Snyder's earlier remark that the Mexican racing season had drawn "more bunko men and bad women here than in any city of like size in the country." (Bunco encompassed a wide range of tricks, including the sale of everything from nonexistent or fraudulent stocks and bonds to "gold" bricks and castles in Spain.) The mayor's allusion to bunco quickly returned to haunt him. The *Record* learned of several very large swindles in which the police appeared to be implicated. [14]

Eventually, five LAPD detective sergeants were dismissed although neither the police nor the district attorney sought indictments. The evidence showed that swindlers bilked visitors and residents of millions of dollars but the police made no arrests. Victims were told that nothing could be done and that they should go quietly home. Rumor held that the thieves paid about seventeen percent of their gross "take" to members of the detective bureau.

Police Commissioner R.T. Burge, a progressive favorite, alleged that a number of policemen had banked $50,000 to $100,000 although their salaries were only about $225 per month. Burge asked Chief Home to step aside and allow District Attorney Woolwine to investigate the department. Commissioner Burge, having conducted a secret investigation of the department, made further allegations. The LAPD had made no arrests of pickpockets for several months until a local private detective agency responded to complaints from its clients. Then fourteen arrests occurred within a few days. If Chief Home did not know these facts, Burge charged, then he was inefficient; if he did know his position was even worse.

These comments led to a heated dispute between Burge and Meredith Snyder, after which the mayor dismissed the commissioner. Snyder accused Burge of playing politics with a view to becoming mayor. An enterprising newsman soon published a dramatic *roman a clef* based on Snyder's comment, in which Burge, thinly disguised, played the villain. [15]

Burge's dismissal did not prevent an outside investigation. District Attorney Thomas Woolwine, also looking ahead to an election, sent his detectives into action. One of the arrested swindlers received immunity and freedom in return for his testimony. He revealed that bunco men and pickpockets, on arriving in Los Angeles, reported to the police and received their "licenses" to operate. Corrupt officers kept track of the "take" through the complaints made by victims. During the investigation, two police informers were murdered, which perhaps reduced the flow of information, but not before several banks and brokerage houses were implicated in the bunco scandals.

Woolwine's investigation drew the attention of every local newspaper except the *Times,* but only the *Record* continued to report the depredations of rank-and-file police criminals. Extortion from minor bootleggers, small time gamblers and erring motorists was the most common offense. Robbery, burglary, bootlegging and assaults against females were not unusual. Nor was public drunkenness. [16]

Aside from sexual assaults, police crimes may have represented the determination of individual officers to maintain an acceptable standard of living. The postwar inflation struck hard at the low paid policeman. Chief Home nevertheless forbade his officers to work as motion-picture extras or as special policemen in hotels and dancehalls, or to accept free board and room at hotels in return for unspecified protective services. He turned down a request that other sorts of "moon-lighting" be allowed.

The patrolmen knew that others received special treatment. Captain R. Lee Heath conducted his law practise between the hours of 10:00 A.M. and 4:00 P.M. Ranking officers operated two different funeral parlors and engaged in unseemly competition for cadavers that came under police jurisdiction by offering bonuses for bodies directed to the their mortuaries. The departmental printing office was conducted in a most irregular manner. Inevitably, lower ranking policemen also took advantage of illegal opportunities that the job presented. [17]

The cumulative effect on the public of repeated unorganized criminal acts by policemen is open to speculation. For some, it may have represented merely the little man seeking a share of the loot. If he got it from bootleggers and gamblers, who suffered? The person who bribed an officer to avoid a traffic ticket might have difficulty damning the recipient. Others may have found further evidence of a general moral decline in American society. Perhaps repetition dulled the senses to the point that further disclosures provoked neither outrage nor dismay. Whatever the case, continued malfeasance reinforced the negative opinion of the "cop."

The progressives, however, maintained their fervor. Chief Home threatened to resign if the attacks did not stop. Mayor Snyder, attempting a political manoeuvre, requested a grand jury investigation of the LAPD. Snyder, having noted the difficulty of getting a good police chief for $300 a month and the problems of cleaning up the city "alone," had not inspired public confidence in his administration or the department. The request to the grand jury permitted him to take action without admitting anything or blaming anyone, to place the matter in the hands of a responsible public body and to forestall to some degree an election year campaign by the district attorney.

The grand jury report upheld the progressive allegations in almost every respect. The *Record* therefore increased its coverage of vice conditions, reporting the number of illicit enterprises, the hours of operation and the fact that patrolmen on duty in Chinatown admitted seeing and hearing the barkers calling people in to gamble. Having already said that Chief Home must go, the editors added Mayor Snyder to the list. Only a new administration could reform the city and its corrupt police force. [18]

Meredith Snyder faced a serious dilemma. He was halfway through his term. To win in 1921, he needed the progressives but the price of their support included a "clean" city as well as an independent labor system and business-like government. The first priority was a reform police chief acceptable to the progressive voter organizations. Whether such a man could be found within the LAPD remained doubtful; few believed that anyone from the higher ranks could satisfy the reform leadership. An outside chief seemed the wisest choice.

On September 15, 1920, the *Record* could finally rejoice that "Chief Home is Out." Home reverted to his civil service rank of captain, took a year's leave of absence and departed to work in the oil business. An official announcement of 8190 arrests during September, the highest total for that month in LAPD history, seemed to add a statistical superlative to Home's record. It also appeared to justify his warning of a crime wave and his boast of increased efficiency.

In fact, neither case could be made, although a slight increase in the per capita crime rate did occur. The department achieved only a vast increase in traffic arrests. Arrests for crimes against persons and property fell below the figure for previous years, notwithstanding population growth. Indeed, a decline in arrests had characterized Home's earlier direction of the detective bureau. There was no crime wave, only a reduction in efficiency. Home's misuse of arrest statistics was a tested tactic of departmental politics. [19]

Lyle Pendegast, a deputy city prosecutor, replaced Home. He had a unblemished personal record and he came from outside the department. Having been executive secretary to four chiefs during the old days between 1905 and 1910, he undoubtedly understood the political realities. Pendegast hoped to decentralize the force, double the number of policemen and install a merit system by which to judge their efficiency. He also asked the council to pay the cost of uniforms. None of his ideas was accepted. The council refused to supply uniforms because that would be "in the nature of a pay raise" that the city could not afford. For the same reason, the force could not be enlarged. [20]

Wittingly or not, the council foreclosed police reform as a campaign issue for Snyder. Anti-radicalism usually provided a good platform but vigorous police action had made radicals a scarce commodity. Anti-vagrancy, a companion issue, also had community support and might have been successfully exploited. Police officials asserted that the petty crime rate rose twenty per cent every winter, when hordes of drifters arrived from the north and east. Unfortunately for Snyder, a botched raid on "Brother Tom" Liddecott's Midnight Mission had serious repercussions. A police raid at 4:30 A.M. netted seventy-nine homeless men, who were taken before a police judge and sentenced to 100 days each for vagrancy. Chief Pendegast claimed to have reliable information that missions and similar premises provided "meeting places for the I.W.W. element" but mounting public furor soon made him regret the Hobo Squad's action.

As a Christmas windfall for the newspapers, a better story could scarcely be imagined. As a political sideshow it was even less pleasant but more profitable for the vagrants. The mayor's enemies rushed to attack. The *Record* asked why the police arrested unemployed citizens while arch-criminals lived safely in the city. Ex-commissioner Burge sent $100 to Brother Tom. Chief Pendegast sent $50. Mayor Snyder, claiming that he was "with" the jobless men, founded an Xmas Club to raise money for them.

By December 11, over $400 had been sent directly to the Midnight Mission, allowing Brother Tom to plan a mass Christmas dinner. Thus the administration's insensitive methods produced criticism instead of praise, even though the anti-vagrancy statutes had broad public approval. On April 1, 1921, a suitably ironic date, Pendegast disbanded the Hobo Squad. [21]

Snyder still lacked a feasible campaign issue. The mayor had been a strong municipal socialist during his early days in politics. He continued to proclaim the faith but events belied his words. Not only had he failed to implement proposed municipal garbage collection and street-sweeping departments but the city cement plant had been leased to private interests. He could expect no progressive support on that issue.

The mayor turned to trust busting, Los Angeles style. The "ice trust" monopolized trade and gave short weight most of the time. The "milk trust" controlled distribution and watered the milk to boot. The "paving trust" extracted high prices for low cost roads. The "building products trust" controlled the supply of construction materials. Snyder chose to attack the builders' trust, probably because a recent report mentioned 70,000 persons living in canvas huts because they could not obtain proper accommodation. The mayor promised to "root out" the trust but it was too late for an issue of that sort to be built into a major crusade. [22]

One by one, Snyder's campaign planks disintegrated. Miserly administration, police reorganization, clean government, anti-radicalism, anti-vagrancy, all failed. Vice abatement, master key to the progressives' hearts, was the greatest failure of all. Although Chief Pendegast mounted dozensof vice raids and led many himself, forcing the *Record* to admit that open vice had disappeared, a series of political setbacks overshadowed his success.

While Pendegast waged successful war against vice, two deputy sheriffs were arrested for taking $12,000 to release a bunco swindler. This set the stage nicely for the trial of Everett "Big Hutch" Hutchings for his part in the LAPD bunco scandal. Hutchings had received several continuances. His trial in the late stages of the mayoralty campaign may well have been arranged. Witnesses revealed that ex-chief Home was a personal friend of Hutchings and that in return for seventeen per cent of the gross, LAPD detectives shielded the swindler, informed him of secret indictments and permitted him to continue in business. [23]

Concurrently, the Reverend Gustav Briegleb alleged that certain dancehall proprietors claimed to have influence with the police that allowed them to operate a haven for bootleggers and immoral women. The *Times,* in a rare venture into muckraking, suggested that protected prostitutes were plying their trade in the Mexican district called Sonoratown. Naval authorities complained about the amount of vice available to sailors and particularly the number of diseased women working as prostitutes.

Worse still, Police Commissioner E. Clem Wilson, a conservative businessman who replaced R.T. Burge, resigned his office. Wilson claimed that Snyder knew but tried to hide the extent of protected vice, that he did not cooperate with the police commission and that he appointed and transferred police personnel without consulting other officials. [24]

With a week to go, the desperate mayor broke a rule of politics and publicly mentioned the name of his opponent, George C. Cryer. In a slashing attack, Snyder first accused Cryer of favoring police and fire department unions. He then outlined the curious coalition that supported Cryer's candidacy. On one side, Henry Laub, leader of the liquor interests; on the other, S.T. Montgomery, head of the Anti-Saloon League. On the left, the Central Labor Council; on the right, Harry Haldeman, president of Labor's sworn enemy, the Better America Federation. Add Owen McAleer, president of the board of public works under Mayor Woodman and "mentioned in the indictments," along with Tony Schwamm, a disgraced police commissioner under the deposed Mayor Harper.

Nor was that all. There stood the Reverend Briegleb and Doctor Nelson, head of the Church Brotherhood, in company with Kent Kane Parrot, disgruntled office-seeker and man about politics, not to mention George Brown, Central Avenue vice dealer and his friend the dismissed vice squad sergeant from the Woodman scandal. Include ex-commissioner R.T. Burge, the well known rent gouger and not least, Frank Reese, chief lobbyist of the paving trust. Snyder ridiculed Cryer as one who had always been a deputy —to the city attorney, the district attorney and the U.S. attorney—and implied that he was currently a deputy to Harry Chandler of the *Times*. The mayor closed on a fine traditional note, pointing out that Cryer had never been successfully in business for himself. [25]

George C. Cryer possessed no more program than had Meredith Snyder in 1919. He claimed to be a reluctant candidate, offering himself only so that Los Angeles could have an efficient business administration. An unsuccessful campaigner, previously beaten in elections for city attorney and municipal judge, he preferred to leave the campaign in the hands of Kent Kane Parrot, chief architect of the strange alliance that endorsed him. On June 4, 1921, when the *Record* turned its columns over to the candidates, Parrot spoke for the Cryer campaign.

Parrot employed calm but effective prose. Was not Meredith Pinxton Snyder mayor of Los Angeles from 1900 to 1904, when vice districts flourished under police protection? Had Meredith Snyder changed his policy? The recent accusations by Rear Admiral Welles and Captain Shackleford of the U.S. Navy indicated clearly that he had not. So much for "Pinky" Snyder, the vice crusader. Parrot then managed to imply that Cryer believed strongly in law and order but did not much favor Sunday blue laws. Cryer coasted to a comfortable victory, receiving fifty-three per cent of the ballots cast. [26]

Cryer, hardly a popular hero, owed his victory to an anti-Snyder vote. Three successive "reform" mayors—Sebastian, Woodman, and Snyder—betrayed the public trust and were duly discarded. Many progressives held high hopes for Cryer, based on his unblemished if mediocre record. Cynics waited for results and their worst fears soon were realized. A month after the election, the Church Federation described Los Angeles as a national mecca for gamblers. Six months later, the *Record* portrayed Cryer's administration as "the most abysmal imaginable...in the whole dismal record of many years of corrupt and inefficient policing." As later events revealed, the same could have been said about the public works, harbor, and civil service departments. [27]

The new mayor immediately appointed a new police chief. Lyle Pendegast, saddened by the "the chicane that seems inseparably connected with American police affairs," left office with his personal reputation unsullied. Detective Sergeant Charles A. Jones took command. This surprised many who had predicted the return of John L. Butler but the choice made reasonably good political sense. Although Jones had twenty years of service in the LAPD, his relatively low rank meant nothing; high rank could indicate political preferment, low rank the burden of honesty. As a detective on loan to District Attorney Woolwine, Jones in a sense was outside the department during the Woodman and Snyder years. Association with Woolwine also permitted him to assume the role of vice crusader that the D.A. habitually played. [28]

Knowledgeable progressives denounced the appointment. The *Record* asserted that an unscrupulous cabal chose Jones. These included ex-chief George Home, Milton "Farmer" Page, an ex-newsboy turned gambling czar, and Guy McAfee, a former policeman discharged for running a dice game in the police station and then rehired by Home. McAfee resigned in 1920 to open an illegal casino in the Spring Street district.

Whatever the truth about this appointment, Chief Jones lasted only six miserable months. The progressives complained constantly and with reason about vice conditions. In addition to the usual problems, advertisements of sensational "girly" shows appeared in the newspapers. Prizefighting, banned by statute, returned to the city for the first time in years. Reporters agreed that the underworld expected vast profits when the U.S. Navy Pacific fleet put into port in September. Mayor Cryer ordered Jones to close the vice district or retire. Jones responded with repeated raids, many of which he led himself. Unfortunately, the campaign produced ridicule instead of results. [29]

On one occasion, after a "sweeping" raid against bookmakers along West Third and South Spring streets, reporters recognized Everett "Big Hutch" Hutchings, bunco swindler and horse parlor proprietor, then out on bail while appealing a conviction. They noted that Hutchings "slipped past Chief Jones and a number of officers." Jones found it astonishing that Hutchings, "of all people," should escape. He promised to look into the matter. Most newsmen believed that the gamblers expected the raid because bartenders on the premises had poured all their liquor into the sewers before the police arrived.

Another time, in answer to a reporter's question, Chief Jones made one of the most revealing—and unintentionally humorous—remarks ever to issue from that humorless source. Under the headline "Chief

Warns Underworld," Jones declared his intention to close Chinatown
and the Spring Street area down tight, "next week, after the Elks' convention." As for protected vice, Jones asserted that gamblers planted
misleading rumors to create unrest among the police.[30]

On one issue—increased manpower—Jones enjoyed a measure of
success. The police commission, supported by the business community,
requested an additional 500 policemen. The city council agreed to 100 but
finally authorized 355 after two officers were slain on duty on December
6, 1921. Although this amounted to a fifty per cent increase, Jones and the
Examiner continued to press for a 1000-man authorization. To fund the
increase, the council levied a thirty-three per cent rise in the business
licence tax. This drew immediate criticism from powerful interests such as
the Chamber of Commerce and the Merchants & Manufacturers Association. Nevertheless, a majority of councilmen refused to allow the appropri-
ations of other departments to be reduced. The tax increase stood.[31]

Within the month, half of the newly authorized policemen were on
patrol. The hastily recruited rookies may have allayed the fears of citizens but they came too late to help Chief Jones, again under attack for
vice conditions in the downtown area. John Pelletier, of the Morals Efficiency League, described the disgraceful conditions on North Spring
Street, where gambling, women and liquor were available. Pelletier further asserted that gamblers had somehow arranged the transfer of the
Central Division police commander because he vigorously enforced the
anti-vice statutes.

Pelletier challenged Jones to investigate the charges. Mayor Cryer
intervened at that point, offering Pelletier a squad of detectives whom he
could lead on vice investigations. Pelletier accepted and soon proved to
his own satisfaction what had long been suspected: someone within the
department warned the vice operators prior to police raids. There matters
stood as the year ended.[32]

On January 3, 1922, the progressives received a late Christmas
blessing. Chief Jones resigned. Jones claimed that due to "too many
interfering reformers," the force spent too much time chasing penny-ante
gamblers, too little protecting the lives and property of citizens. Furthermore, H.H. Kinney, secretary to the mayor, continually interfered in
police department and police commission operations. Beyond that, con-
niving and competition among departmental factions corroded morale.
Finally, the 1000-member force was still only one-third the necessary
size. Jones declared that he left the job voluntarily, although the *Times*
and the *Examiner* had predicted his departure, to the day. After discus-

sions with H.H. Kinney and Mayor Cryer, Jones requested retirement. Pointing to his office, he told the *Times'* reporter that "when they decide to get you, they get you there."[33]

Jones' sudden ouster provided a fitting introduction to the short, explosive regime of Chief James W. Everington. The appointment thrilled most reformers. The *Record* described it as a miracle, presaging a "new era of clean government." Mayor Cryer admitted that the police department had been "a storm center for many years past ... one police regime after another has crumbled and fallen." The department lacked internal harmony. The public failed to support the police. Cryer hoped that a change would occur and that apathy would give way to enthusiasm.[34]

The new chief presented a distinct departure from the norm. The forty-two year old retired army colonel had no law enforcement, criminal justice or political credentials. He was, however, vigorous, forceful and accustomed to command. He said that he had no strings attached to him, no axe to grind and only one order: "succeed." He promised no flashy results. He thought it would take six months merely to learn the job but he could say one thing without equivocation: when he closed the town it would be entirely closed. This sounded familiar.

Everington ordered the department to enforce the laws stringently and to be especially diligent at the revenue-producing task of inspecting business licences. He tried to abolish the old tradition of courtesy cards and honorary police badges. Often in the past, officers making arrests or investigations would be shown the personal card of one or another senior officer, bearing the notation that any "courtesy" shown the bearer would be appreciated by the donor. Citations could thus be avoided. Worse misuse perhaps was made of honorary badges handed out by senior officers and police commissioners. Because the honorary lieutenant or captain probably had political influence, arresting officers might find it wiser to let such violators go with only a warning. Next, the chief attempted to stop the "fixing" of traffic tickets, which, according to his estimates, occurred in fifty per cent of the cases. He also abandoned "speed traps" in favor of "showing the uniform."

Everington quickly became notorious for his stubbornness and outspoken manner. He would not accept an assistant whom he could not replace and so refused to fill the post of Assistant Chief, recently certified by the civil service commission. He described new recruits as "brainless" and remarked that good men apparently retired early while the stupid ones remained on the force. He reported the details of disciplinary proceedings in the police *Bulletin,* to the dismay of innocent and guilty officers alike. He also dismissed unsatisfactory policemen at an unprecedented rate.[35]

On January 23, Everington disclosed his intention to close all lotteries, speakeasies, brothels and casinos, including those in country clubs and private houses. He realigned the bureaucracy so that responsibility for vice abatement devolved from himself to the acting assistant chief, thence to the captain of Central Division and finally upon the lieutenant commanding the Central vice squad. The chief then commanded his subordinates to eliminate commercial vice. This order precipitated a major departmental crisis because the three officers asserted that it could not be carried out. Everington then dismissed the captain and the lieutenant and forced the acting assistant chief to retire. The ousted men appealed to the police commission, which scheduled a hearing. This set the stage for a remarkable inquiry into departmental politics.[36]

Prior to the hearings, Everington's opponents struggled for advantage. They applied a variety of strategies, including threats against his life. Embarrassments came from within the force. Officers raided important social events and arrested people for such crimes as "dancing after 1:00 P.M." Others circulated departmental statistics that implied a tremendous increase in crime, concurrent with Everington's administration. Businessmen complained about armed robberies committed while Everington chased prostitutes and gamblers. Rumors passed of "150 pickpockets" working freely in Central Division. The ousted acting assistant chief delayed his pension request until after the police commission inquiry, an ominous portent.[37]

Mayor Cryer's cryptic defense of his police chief revealed other aspects of the anti-Everington campaign. Cryer denounced "bankers and landlords" who, with vice entrepreneurs and "secret societies numbering hundreds," exerted "insidious pressure" to force Everington from office. The mayor suggested that some unknown number of police officers aided the criminal element because they were subject to underworld blackmail for prior indiscretions. He announced his intention to support Everington to the fullest possible extent, to establish whether or not the citizens of Los Angeles really wanted reform.[38]

The hearings began on April 12, 1922, and quickly turned into a general examination of the vice situation in Los Angeles. A parade of witnesses testified to the honesty and vigor of the vice squad lieutenant, "the man the underworld feared most." Former vice squad men claimed that the big hotels all had women procurable through bellboys but could not be caught because they were careful. Gamblers could not be eliminated because the courts would not convict. There was no open vice and no payoffs. One sergeant, after naming the major gamblers and the biggest clubs, said "they don't deny they are gambling and making book. They just say we can't prove it. And we can't prove it, in most cases." Acting against the customers was pointless. After a recent futile raid on Farmer Page's Del Monte Bar, the dismissed lieutenant "vagged" the 78 men found there. All were released on ten dollars bail, which was forfeited. So ended every similar case.[39]

Chief Everington raised the subject of a notorious protected brothel on Main Street between Second and Third Avenues. Police witnesses argued that the Madam admitted no one not personally known to her. No one had ever beaten her surveillance. When pressed, the witness admitted that the brothel was known as "so and so's place," "so and so" being an unnamed police officer.

John Pelletier, of the Morals Efficiency League, asserted that two police judges were corrupt, a charge made earlier by former chief Charles A. Jones. Like Jones, Pelletier declined to name the judges, who worked with a ring of attorneys that handled vice cases. The judges freed prostitutes defended by the ring but convicted women defended by other lawyers. Pelletier recounted how he identified some vice locations, informed the vice squad and then surreptitiously followed a patrolman who visited the intended target places the afternoon before the scheduled raids. Since the raiders later found no evidence of illegal activities, Pelletier deduced that the policeman warned the criminals.

The defense attorney for the two dismissed officers asserted that Everington's mishandling of the department allowed criminals free reign. Burglaries for March, 1922, rose to twice the total for the same month of the previous year, he claimed. Homicides increased 500 per cent over the previous March. Other witnesses reported that vice was only more circumspect, not scarcer, under the new regime. District Attorney Woolwine's deputies claimed that Los Angeles had always been a clean city, suggesting that Everington had created a false issue.

Everington fought back, attacking everyone in view. Police Commissioner De La Monte, he said, wanted to whitewash the whole police force. City Prosecutor Erwin Widney had not conducted a proper cross examination of the witnesses. When Mayor Cryer adjourned the hearings over a weekend, Everington implied that the recess was designed to thwart him. Cryer did not take this remark casually. When the case resumed he refused to say that the chief still had his full support.

The *Record,* supposedly the chief's friend, urged him to keep fighting because the citizens would "rather have an honest bungler than a smart crook." The city council investigated Everington's use of secret service funds because the money had not been spent by the vice squad, as regulations required. As testimony showed, the chief used most of the funds to investigate the police department and certain business interests. This was viewed with alarm.

The proceedings reached their climax on 18 April. A senior captain took the stand and revealed more about the inner workings of the department than had all the exposes published in newspapers over the years. A policeman, he explained, must "play policy....I do myself. If I didn't I would have to look for another job." This meant overlooking certain things if the administration condoned them and permitting them even if the administration opposed them, because the next one certainly would. "I have suppressed evidence before the police commission myself," the captain admitted.

The captain described the dismissed officers as "honest and efficient, according to the standards of the department." The force was totally disorganized, every man concerned only with saving his job. In substance, the captain declared that vice could not be eliminated because the powers that profited from it were too strong. "Bookmakers told me if I didn't quit arresting them I would be transferred. Chief Jones transferred me the next day. He didn't tell me why, and I didn't ask him."

The testimony, which reportedly left Mayor Cryer "gaping in amazement," could not be permitted to continue. The police commissioners ruled that Everington had not substantiated his charge that the men were derelict in their duty. The dismissed captain had considerably less benign testimony in his behalf than the lieutenant and talk passed of a compromise, retaining the lieutenant and letting the captain go. Finally, the commission restored both officers and the mayor admitted embarrassment at Everington's failure to prove his case. This severely rebuked the colonel, who reacted in his usual manner.

The chief of police was a passionate man of a few thousand ill-chosen words. The mayor and the commissioners, he said, were "spineless jellyfish," "weakkneed creatures of expediency" and other things. As for the reformers, "the soft-heads and saps who have showered me with resolutions," they had "fallen down on me at the last minute. I have told them all to go to hell." His prophesy had proved correct: "the present apparent interest on the part of the great, normally apathetic, buck-passing, let-George-do-it mass of voters will die out six months after we accomplish the little we can after the brief spasm of reform."

What more evidence could be required, he wished to know. Policemen, up to the highest ranks, admitted that they obeyed or disobeyed orders as they saw fit. Gamblers called the turn and could have a captain transferred if he pressed them too hard. A police officer either protected or owned a downtown brothel. Unknown persons within the department tipped off vice raids. Yet the police commission restored the two men because Everington had not proved his charges.

With the police department in turmoil and the mayor disenchanted, some reform leaders turned against the chief. The Reverend Briegleb, smarting from Everington's "softheads and saps" remark, criticized him for accusing innocent men without evidence and asked for his resignation. The *Record,* which had so often called for police chiefs from outside the department, denounced appointed police executives and favored men from the ranks. Police Commissioner De La Monte considered the chief "doomed" because he had used secret service funds to investigate "businessmen and pioneer residents." Mayor Cryer claimed to have doubted the legal value of Everington's evidence from the beginning. To help the chief he had required the officers to prove their innocence. Nevertheless, when the verdict went against him, Everington blamed the mayor, the police commission and the city prosecutor.[40]

Everington's unsoldierly attack on his superiors proved his determination to reform the city. He had said that no honest man could be chief. Sooner or later he would be asked to overlook law evasion, to grant special privilege, to protect special interests. A career chief would have to go along. Everington would not. His retention would have pleased most reformers and the general public but powerful interests behind the scenes were working to depose him.

Aside from vice operators and rentiers, Everington had become dangerous to the anti-labor leaders of Los Angeles. Firing two veteran officers as "examples" proved to the department how tenuous were the jobs of policemen caught in political crossfires. The *Times* learned that union sentiment within the force had reached a new peak. An A.F.L. charter had been requested and 400 men were pledged to join. Since the unionization of the police force outweighed any possible benefit Everington might accomplish, the open-shop interests had good reason to destroy him.[41]

The reactionaries' fears soon were realized. The arbitrary dismissals of Chief Everington's term produced organized resistance in the form of the Fire and Police Protective League. Fearing formal union organization, anti-labor leaders arranged a compromise. They joined with the police in support of Proposition 8A, a charter amendment providing improved pensions for policemen and firemen. The new plan allowed retirement on half pay after 20 years of service regardless of the employee's age. The rate payers assumed the entire financial burden. The beneficiaries paid nothing. Reformers, including the *Record,* withheld adverse commentary on police matters until after the amendment passed in November, 1922.

In return, the FPPL made no attempt to affiliate with organized labor and remained ostensibly a patriotic fraternal association controlled by conservative senior officials. Although promoted as a means to attract good men to the police service—a move toward professionalism—8A actually represented a significant advance in the direction of departmental independence. As in 1919, by threatening to unite with organized labor, the otherwise impotent and unpopular police force extracted concessions from the administration. This tactic proved effective on subsequent occasions.[42]

Everington, who spoke often of being "framed," "gotten," "forced out" and of resigning, now refused to quit. Undoubtedly, directing the police department and matching wits with the underworld made a much more satisfactory life for a vigorous man than raising flowers in Glendale. Perhaps the chief thought of this. In any event he did not resign but instead issued an ultimatum. If the citizens wanted reform they had ten days in which to come forward with personal and financial support. If they responded he would fight on.

Mayor Cryer quickly forestalled any such crusade. On April 20 he removed Everington. Captain R. Lee Heath, who said that "under no conditions" would he take permanent command, accepted the position long enough to restore the two dismissed officers and call back the acting assistant chief. The next day, Heath gave way to Detective Sergeant Louis D. Oaks.[43]

Oaks, then forty years of age, was born in Missouri in 1882 and arrived in Los Angeles in 1910. After a stint as a streetcar motorman he joined the LAPD. In twelve years he twice distinguished himself in unspectacular ways. On the occasion of a citizens' presentation for his work in a kidnapping case, Mayor Cryer met him and was suitably impressed. Tall, handsome, modest and apparently competent, Oaks lived quietly with his wife and daughter. He had no reputation as a power in any departmental faction but as a regular police officer, unlike the "outsider" Everington, he had the general goodwill of his fellow policemen. Celebrations began at once. Cheers for the new chief rang in the ears of the old as Everington departed from the police building.

Cryer's action outraged the reformers, excepting possibly the Reverend Briegleb. A mass protest meeting at Trinity Methodist Church under the auspices of the Reverend Robert P. Shuler and smaller meetings elsewhere accomplished nothing. The *Times,* breaking its usual editorial silence on police matters, predicted that Oaks would "bring harmony out of the chaos created by the turbulent reign of Colonel Everington".[44]

Snide newspaper commentary could not disguise the fact that disorder in the police department long antedated Everington's term. The honest and independent colonel, by revealing police complicity in vice operations, only brought an ugly situation into the open. The *Times* editors realized that substantive reorganization of the police department could no longer be avoided. Consequently, they and their counterparts at the *Examiner* sponsored the Community Development Association, a reform organization distinctly separate from the church-oriented progressives.

The CDA directors included the presidents of a large life insurance company, a major oil company, the state labor council and the vice president of a bank. The general membership came from the most prestigious organizations, led by the Men's and Women's City Clubs. The *Times, Examiner, Express, Herald* and *Record* had equal representation on the CDA and the citizens' crime commission. To avoid controversy, each journal could veto crime commission proposals. This narrowed the crime commissions's focus but ensured unanimous support for its program.[45]

The CDA noted that crime rose 300 per cent between 1919 and 1923 while population increased 42 per cent. The association intended to protect the good name of Los Angeles, starting with an investigation of organized protected crime. Walter Tuller, a conservative attorney, became the first CDA crime commission chairman. Buron Fitts, a professional war veteran and a rising star in the district attorney's office, served as Tuller's eager assistant. [46]

During the following year, the Community Development Association exerted considerable influence in Los Angeles politics. It seemed to be a time for stern measures. Police Judge Raymond Chesebro ordered one beggar to avoid Los Angeles for 25 years or serve six months in jail. The city council passed an anti-jaywalking ordinance that permitted $500 fines and 6 month jail terms for the offense. Police Judge Joseph F. Chambers sentenced motorists to jail for going 28 to 30 miles per hour in a 25 mph zone.

The crime commission believed that stiffer jail sentences might stem the crime wave and sent a number of ordinances to the city council for action. The state legislature codified several crime commission suggestions. Armed robbery and night burglary became "first degree" crimes with a five year minimum sentence. Probation was denied to persons convicted of armed robbery or who had previously been convicted of a violent crime, and to former public officials convicted of bribery, extortion or embezzlement. Escaping from custody was made a felony instead of a misdemeanour. If criminals considered the potential penalties for their acts a decrease in armed robbery, burglary and jailbreak might be expected, in addition to an end to the worst excesses of the probation system.[47]

In addition to the citizens crime commission and the Shuler-Briegleb ministerial leadership, a new activism in the mayor's office produced even greater interference in police affairs. Mayor Cryer announced the end of the "no strings" days. Henceforth he would take a direct part in running the department. Chief Oaks could expect plenty of advice. The *Record* interpreted the changes to mean that the old guard still held power. Oaks' appointment appeared to be a "peace move" because he was not expected to issue orders that would be difficult to execute.[48]

Oaks' first public announcement gave substance to the allegations. He described Los Angeles as "one of the cleanest cities in the country." Commercial vice presented no problem, despite newspaper reports that new spots opened after Everington left office. Oaks promised that the department would direct its efforts to "banditry, burglary, and the higher branches of crime." For the CDA's benefit, Oaks analyzed the causes of the recent rise in criminal behavior: first, a breakdown in the moral teachings of home and church encouraged a lust for material things; second, sensational newspaper accounts stimulated crime; third, crooked lawyers, insanity pleas, indeterminate sentences and other judicial foolishness thwarted the forces of justice.[49]

Oaks' remarks fell on receptive ears. The crime commission represented a direct response to the apparent thwarting of justice. So did the Shuler-Briegleb moral reform campaign, beneath its self-serving sensationalism. It would not be surprising if the immense publicity given the prohibition wars, I.W.W. and other labor violence, the clash of "foreign" ideologies with the American way and the national crime "wave" generated a broad, participatory reform movement among the working and middle classes. This is one explanation of the remarkable rise in Ku Klux Klan membership during the early 20's, accompanied as it was in some areas by the physical chastisement of bootleggers and prostitutes by bands of hooded men.

Southern California provided fertile ground for vigilante organizations. On April 22, 1922, a detachment of the Klan raided an alleged bootlegger in the suburban town of Inglewood. In the confusion, one Klansman was killed and several wounded. When the dead man proved to be a police constable and one of the wounded a deputy sheriff, the question of police participation in secret societies became urgent. Chief Oaks at once ordered all KKK members in the department to quit either the Klan or the force and the city council followed with an order forbidding city employees to hold membership in secret societies. Subsequent revelations, nevertheless, established that Klan membership included Chief Oaks, Sheriff William Traeger and U.S. Attorney Matthew Byrne.[50]

The law enforcement officials resigned from the Klan but membership produced no adverse consequences. Some time later a series of attacks on girls and women brought another vigilante group, "the White Knights of Womanhood," thundering to the rescue. The Knights asserted that so many of the police were crooks that "only one or two were left to do the arresting." They threatened to storm the Central Jail and punish the inmates. While the White Knights of Womanhood took direct action, Shuler and Briegleb led mass meetings to protest the lack of police protection and to demand the dismissal of Oaks. In response, police shotgun squads received orders to "shoot to kill" when pursuing molesters, although this was hardly a new policy. The *Record* concerned itself with the imminence of mob rule in Los Angeles and demanded that the mayor assert command of the police and the city.

Oaks made the best possible use of these events. He turned attention away from vice toward felonious attacks on persons and property. Of course, protection within the vast city could only be provided if sufficient policemen were available. As always, manpower was in short supply. The *Record* encouraged the LAPD to forget about vagrants, speeders and petty criminals and "go after the big fellows!" Chief Oaks told the CDA he could reduce crime and eliminate vice if people would "stop knocking" and provide 1000 more men, salary increases and $250,000 for a signal system, police building, jail, garage and receiving hospital.[51]

The city council gave Oaks a sympathetic hearing because the city continued to grow at an astonishing rate and crime seemed about to become pandemic. More to the point, the conservative business and social organizations united in the CDA firmly supported police expenditures. The council therefore authorized a forty per cent increase in personnel and a twenty per cent rise in salaries. Unfortunately, these measures had no significant effects. The new recruits were of low calibre. The crime rate rose. Political factions within the police department continued to disrupt operations. The newspapers remained silent, however, in order to further the police pension amendment, which was passed by the voters in October, 1922.

As the year closed, Shuler and Briegleb attempted to topple Oaks on the ground that he had entirely failed to eliminate vice or reduce crime. A cashier in the city engineer's office embezzled $9,000, which he lost to Spring Street gamblers. Bookmakers operated in city hall. James Everington asserted that the town was wide open. Chief Oaks blamed the presence of gamblers on the race meet at Tijuana, Mexico. Vice raids were mounted. Several hundred found-ins were arrested and released on bail. Rumors alleged protected vice in the Central Avenue area but the mayor seemed uninterested. Sweeping reorganization of the vice squad was made.

Oaks promised to put "every available man" in the field on New Year's Eve to enforce the police commission's stern order: "no dancing after midnight allowed." Chief Oaks' New Year's message praised the "unity and harmony...at present being manifested throughout the whole department," which were the "essential elements of an efficient organization." Oaks had grounds for optimism. With sufficient personnel and increased wages, perhaps a real upgrading of the department could be accomplished.

Mayor Cryer's re-election campaign literature emphasized the police reorganization theme. Cryer supported a charter amendment to make the chief's rank a certified civil service position. He also spoke of removing the mayor from the police commission to further "de-politicize" the force but this proposal did not appear on the ballot.[52]

The primary election was scheduled for the first week in May, 1923. Between January and May, the gamut of crimes—extortion, bribery, white slavery, bootlegging, robbery and murder—were charged against Los Angeles officers. The influence of gamblers, in and out of city hall, was brought forward. The *Record* accused Mayor Cryer, on rather good evidence, of deliberately avoiding a chance to uncover malfeasance in the police courts. Nevertheless, the reformers, including the *Record* and the CDA, supported the mayor in the election. Cryer won easily, receiving more than twice the combined number of votes cast for his four opponents. The "civil service chief" amendment also passed without difficulty.[53]

A week after the election, the LAPD repaid its conservative constituency by breaking a strike by the I.W.W.and the Federation of Marine Transport Workers against the Waterfront Employers Association. Again the progressives, with a few notable exceptions, exhibited indifference to police mistreatment of labor organizations. Anti-labor paranoia antedated the *Times* outrage of 1910 but opposition to social and political radicals became more strident and more violent during the following decade. Initial hostility was directed to vagrants and the I.W.W., between whom the Strong Arm Squad did not discriminate much. World War I added "subversives" to the list but the Bolshevik Revolution and subsequent Red Scare, which coincided with a wave of strikes in Los Angeles, identified communists as the true enemy.

The city council, not satisfied with California's infamous criminal syndicalism act, passed a municipal *Red Flag Ordinance* which, according to the state supreme court justices who overturned it, would have made advocating the direct election of U.S. senators an indictable offense. Chief John Butler, leaving office in 1919, identified the "Red Menace" and exhorted the department to "fight for the sake of our homes and posterity...in the crucial test that must come sooner or later." His successor, George K. Home, quickly formed the "Anarchist and Bomb Squad" and armed his officers with clubs, to "immediately halt all unpatriotic or radical movements."

Nevertheless, the LAPD commitment to the open shop became suspect during the Boston Police strike of 1919. The strike, though unreported in the major Los Angeles journals, provoked full page patriotic diatribes against unidentified traitors who left their posts. Los Angeles police officers, whose salary index (1913=100) then stood at 120 while prices stood at 210, formed an unaffiliated "Relief Association." This moved the city council to authorize forthwith a twenty per cent rise in pay. In 1922, formation of the Protective League produced a generous, fully paid pension scheme.[54]

Between threats to unionize, the LAPD scourged radicals. Perhaps because of the dubious legality of the criminal syndicalism and red flag laws, the department made very limited use of them. Instead, the police formed an alliance with the American Legion, another favorite progressive organization. Lieutenant Buron Fitts of the A.E.F., a demagogic leader of considerable talent, led the Legion in its battle for American ideals, avoiding messy questions of due process and constitutional rights while effecting the destruction of dissident organizations.

Politicians had no qualms about public recognition of the LAPD-Legion "understanding." At a "law enforcement service" in Trinity Methodist Church, in January 1920, attended by progressives and legionnaires, Mayor Meredith Snyder called attention to what "these

boys did in this city to drive out the I.W.W.'s." The mayor stated his
assurance that "none of us would advocate lawlessness," but pronounced
himself "glad that the police had their backs turned when these boys
went after them, and knew enough to keep their backs turned."

The LAPD had undercover agents attempting to infiltrate alleged
radical social and political organizations. William "Red" Hynes, destined to become one of the best known and most widely hated policemen
in the United States, and Luke Lane, made a career of anti-subversion.
The term "radical" was given extremely broad interpretation. The extent
of police harassment was a major factor in the establishment, in 1923, of
the Southern California branch of the American Civil Liberties Union.[55]

The harbor strike of 1923 had a surprising genesis. Oddly enough,
the workers wanted the morning "shape-up" at each dock restored. This
much-maligned system had been abolished by the employers in favor of
a centralized hiring system. The unions, however, claimed that the central bureau, conducted in the appropriately named Fink Hall, operated as
a black-listing agency. This method eliminated "troublemakers" much
more efficiently than could the shape-up.

The M & M and the Shopowners Association issued an ultimatum:
"the I.W.W. must leave the harbor and the seamen and longshoremen
must go back to their jobs at once or the jobs will be given to strikebreak-
ers," of whom one thousand were enroute. The police expected serious
trouble and many arrests when the scabs attempted to move cargo. City
and county officials agreed that a $20,000 stockade, capable of holding
1000 men, should be built in Griffith Park. The president of the M & M,
I.H. Rice, urged haste so that subversive laborers could test the value of
"hard shelled grub and hard labor." The *Times* concurred: "the challenge
to ordered government has been given and it must be met...stockades and
forced labor are a good remedy for I.W.W. terrorism." Chief Jailer John
Shand demolished the stockade idea, however. Griffith Park, being fre-
quented by the public, was an untenable site because "you couldn't shoot
(the prisoners) if they started to run away."

On May 14, police interrupted a workers' meeting on private property in San Pedro and arrested the leaders. A mass protest followed, leading to mass arrests that filled the jails. The *Times* described the day's
events as "an attempt to storm the San Pedro police station." The *Record*
sympathized with the distressed laborers, who were charged not with
attacking a public building but with "standing on a public street to hinder
and obstruct free passage thereon." Upton Sinclair, famed muckraker,
pacifist and Socialist chose this moment to take a stand for the constitu-

tional right of the workers to hold public meetings. Sinclair announced a meeting that very night, on Liberty Hill in San Pedro, at which he would read the provisions of the Constitution that guaranteed free speech.

The attendant thousands witnessed an unusual sight. When Sinclair began to read the U.S. Constitution, police arrested him, as they did three friends who attempted to continue the reading. On hand were Police Chief Louis D. Oaks and Captain Clyde Plummer, commander of the San Pedro division, quoted as telling Sinclair, "you can't hand me that Constitution stuff." This was also the position of Chief Oaks, who hoped that Sinclair did not escape with "just a fine" for reading the Constitution "in violation of my order."

Chief Oaks declared that Sinclair "will not be allowed to read the Constitution. If he carried a copy of it in every one of his pockets I would still be convinced of his insincerity." Sinclair, on the other hand, claimed to be enjoying jail because the newspaper reporters paid attention to what he said instead of ignoring him as they usually did. He requested the aid of the U.S. Army in preserving constitutional government at the harbor, accusing Chief Oaks of rescinding the Constitution and imposing martial law. Nothing came of this. Sinclair and his friends were released on bail; charges were later dismissed.

Nothing significant came of any of it. The police were found to have systematically harassed and jailed labor sympathizers, including ministers. Brutality in the jails and abominable conditions were documented. The Ministerial Union established a committee to investigate the matter but Chief Oaks, subpoenaed by the ACLU in connection with a probe of police brutality against the strikers, escaped official censure.

The strikers were allowed to hold meetings at Liberty Hill but the strike failed. Strike-breakers operated the harbor with little interference. Oaks and the department won praise for their anti-labor activities. In company with the police brass band, the chief set forth for a three week tour of eastern cities.[56]

Nevertheless, Oaks faced serious opposition. Crime rose, vice flourished and the activities of bad policemen were continually revealed. The progressive reformers, both CDA and church oriented, were determined to reduce crime and suppress vice. This required a thorough reorganization of the department, something which Oaks seemed loathe to begin. In fact, Oaks' directives seemed more likely to retard than encourage good police work.

Oaks changed the procedure for handling vice arrests in central division. A vice squad detail was assigned to prosecute all cases, the arresting officer being present only if summoned. While Oaks defended this as a move toward specialization and efficiency, it removed the actual witness from the trial and made it much easier to lose cases when the police, the prosecutor or the judge did not want to win. Another change in policy concerned the payment of rewards to policemen for the recovery of stolen property. After Oaks took over, the *Daily Bulletin* devoted a good deal of space to reward notices, which had not previously been the case. Perhaps this increased efficiency but the chance was equally good that policemen ignored regular duties and instead searched pawnshops and garages for stolen valuables and missing autos.

The chief reinstituted a special narcotics squad. The police action was part of a nationwide revulsion to certain scandalous events in Hollywood. The murder of William Desmond Taylor, a famous director, was thought to be connected with the dope traffic. The death from addiction of the popular star, Wallace Reid, added to the public clamor for action. Attempts by Hollywood leaders to counter the effects of the Taylor and Reid cases, the appearance of narcotics peddlers around high schools and the belief that addiction kept many women in prostitution who would otherwise "reform," meant that police attempts to eliminate the drug traffic would be good politics. Officers periodically arrested "the notorious Tom Wah" for selling opium, but though Tom Wah took many a pinch he spent very little time in jail.[57]

The reformers, therefore, were in full cry when Chief Oaks, resplendent in white dress uniform, returned to the city on June 23. Marco Hellman, banker-politician and "big brother of the LAPD," greeted him as he stepped from the train. Mayor Cryer remained at city hall, signing bonds, but a satisfactory crowd of well-wishers escorted the chief. Eventually, the group arrived at the City Club and joined a luncheon meeting then in progress. Oaks entered the hall just as Fighting Bob Shuler began an all-out attack on the chief's administration, challenging him to investigate the true state of moral conditions in Los Angeles.

Shuler, speaking rhetorically, asked the City Club members if they knew "a man named McAfee who was on the force. He went into business, didn't he? He is a rich man now, isn't he?... it's a dirty shame that with crime all over this city...the chief should take 65 cops...to go play parades all over the country while he tells folks how to prevent crime." Oaks took the platform and tried to change the subject, describing his trip as "advertising Los Angeles as the capital of the world;" the LAPD was "second to none;" compared with eastern cities, local crime was no problem. The audience received the chief's boosterism poorly and he hurried from the club.

After a day's reflection, Oaks accepted Shuler's challenge. He also asked that the preacher be called before the grand jury. Shuler agreed to testify and requested that former chief Everington, Captain Heath, the gamblers and their bankbooks, vice squad men who had been transferred hither and yon over the years and vice operators also be subpoenaed because "we could afterward send a few score persons to prison for perjury." Police Commissioner De Coo took an oblique shot at Mayor Cryer, saying that Oaks could close vice at once if the police force knew the chief had the mayor's backing. The *Record* attacked Cryer, Oaks and Shuler without favoritism.[58]

Events in July illustrated the inconsistencies of selective police reform. The I.W.W. filed an injunction seeking to prevent Oaks and Luke Lane, of the undercover squad, from infiltrating and interfering with their organization. No one worried much; the ACLU was still trying to find out what the police commission meant to do about the brutality charges filed two months earlier in connection with the harbor strike. The commissioners disclaimed responsibility and argued that they could not discipline the chief. Oaks subsequently requested tear gas bombs for use against strikers.

The influential forces of the city thus encouraged brutal, illegal and unconstitutional police work. On the other hand, detectives who connived with swindlers and burglars, policemen who overlooked bootlegging and prostitution and officers who "shook down" erring citizens were considered among society's most debased creatures. Reformers constantly demanded that the chief eliminate these particular departmental miscreants.[59]

On July 28, Chief Louis D. Oaks fired Captain R. Lee Heath. This was big news. Heath, commander of the central division, had 19 years of service. Oaks said it pained him to dismiss an officer so close to pension eligibility but Heath's overt participation in politics in violation of departmental regulations was so blatant and so divisive that no other decision was possible. Captain Heath pleaded not guilty and demanded that Oaks prove his charges before an open hearing of the police commission. The stage was again set for an inside drama of the department.

Robert Lee Heath had the most powerful political connections of any police officer. He was close to Kent K. Parrot and H.H. Kinney, the mayor's advisors, and had also the support of influential leaders of the Ministerial Union. For the June elections he had prepared something called "the Police-Fire Department Slate" of candidates and tried to have members of the two departments deliver political posters. From this point the story depended upon which side told it.

Heath's partisans said Oaks objected because the Police and Fire Slate excluded his younger brother Wallace, a candidate for the city council. Nor was the slate divisive; when Heath found that the fire chief did not want the posters distributed he did not force the issue. Oaks' apologists claimed that Fire Chief Scott destroyed the Heath-Parrot literature and nearly came to blows with Heath because the fire department had been ruined in the past by politics. The fire chief refused to let it happen again. Cryer favored the Heath faction but agreed reluctantly to the discharge after Oaks threatened to resign.

Later events proved that the Oaks-Heath conflict involved actual control and responsibility for vice conditions and police procedures. Mayor Cryer had denied Oaks the power to transfer Captain Heath out of the central division and expressly forbade the chief to interfere with Heath's vice squad. Out of limbo had come Mayor Woodward's disgraced vice squad sergeant, William Hacket, dismissed in 1920 for protecting vice. The police commission restored Hackett at the request of Cryer's secretary, H.H. Kinney. A few weeks later, Hacket again commanded the central division vice detail. This appointment so infuriated Oaks, who bore the brunt of the reformers' ire, that he forced Heath out of the department.[60]

Heath's hearing was scheduled for 2 August. Great revelations were expected but late on the night of 1 August the stunning news passed that Mayor Cryer had dismissed Chief Oaks. Cryer named August Vollmer, famed criminologist and police scientist, as the new LAPD chief. Louis Oaks could not be reached for comment. A lawyer represented him at the Heath proceedings the next day.

Oaks' lawyer tried to introduce affidavits detailing the charges against Heath but Mayor Cryer refused to admit them. Someone tricked the former chief's secretary, Ralph Boyeson, so that Boyeson, taken from the premises on a fictitious warrant from the county grand jury, could not testify in Oaks' behalf. Instead, Cryer revealed that the police had discovered Oaks in his auto in company with a young woman and a bottle of bootleg whisky. This violated several laws, written and unwritten, and resulted in the chief's dismissal.

The trial of Oaks in Heath's place stifled his testimony but the problem of Heath remained. The newspapers all carried the story at length and none defended R. Lee Heath. The public discovered that the mayor and his advisors over-rode the police chief, that a disgraced sergeant again held an important position and that Captain Heath had tried to turn the department into a political machine. The hearing was adjourned while the mayor and commissioners sparred over a solution. Finally, Cryer and De Coo reinstated Heath over the objections of Commissioner De La Monte. They criticized Heath for political activity and excessive participation in outside business but dismissed Oaks' specific charges.

The reinstatement confounded the crime commission. Oaks' correspondence with the crime commission revealed that he requested and was promised support in the Heath matter, prior to the actual dismissal. The crime commission clearly hoped to bag two stormy petrels with a single machination, since the Vollmer negotiations showed that Oaks' replacement had already been planned. Good reasons for change were plentiful, of course. Aside from the large scale fixing of traffic tickets, intervention by police to aid the suspects in gambling and bootlegging cases had reached grave proportions. The number of "bad" policemen had been noted by the newspapers and the county grand jury. The rise of vigilance committees to combat the crime wave and the persistence of organized vice further indicated an inefficient police force.

The reformers led by Shuler and Briegleb had wanted Oaks' dismissal for some time. Passage of the amendment placing the chief under civil service protection placed a brake on ouster proceedings but made possible the best ultimate solution. The civil service examination for the chief's position, scheduled for September 5, was open to every adult male citizen in the country. The crime commission representatives expected Oaks to make a lower score than Vollmer or some other desirable outside candidate. He could then be replaced on the basis of inferior merit rather than politics or corruption. The Heath crisis merely hastened the inevitable.[61]

Vollmer's appointment, the seeming culmination of a quarter-century of increasing professionalism, actually closed a much shorter transition period. Social turmoil attending the end of World War I and the onset of Prohibition placed severe strains on the police service. For a time, under Mayor Snyder and Chief Home, it seemed that frontier vice conditions might be permanently restored. The public favored reform, however, and the progressives appeared to triumph. Henceforth, even machine politicians and police executives became vociferous advocates of professionalism and progress.

The reorganized political machine won the real victory. In the politicians'view, Vollmer was but one of a long line of chiefs. Just as Pendegast succeeded Home and Everington replaced Jones, so Vollmer replaced Oaks. This followed established practice: a corrupt executive gave way for a short time to a genuine reformer. When the situation permitted, the politicians removed the honest chief.

The political-criminal combination could look ahead to the end of Vollmer's term. However, the combination recognized that the repeated removal of chiefs, aside from the obvious political expediency, destroyed police morale and efficiency, widening the progressive constituency and making police reform a perpetual issue. The machine therefore supported the professional ideal of civil service tenure for chiefs. Including John Butler in 1919 and Vollmer in 1923, eight men held the office in four years. After Vollmer, even machine chiefs enjoyed unprecedented longevity.

Notes

[1] *Times,* 5-22-43; *Record,* 9-5-22, 10-4-22, 12-1-22; Isadora Duncan was banned in Los Angeles, *ibid.,* 11-22-22; Police Commission *Minutes,* 4-5-21, 1-24-22, 3-8-22; see also Edmund Wilson's description of Briegleb and Shuler, reprinted in *The American Earthquake: A Documentary of the Twenties and Thirties* (Garden City, N.Y., 1958), 379-396.

[2] *Record,* 10-11-22, 12-6-22, 6-4-23, 6-9-23, 6-13-23. See especially the *Record* front page editorial, "Shuler at the Mob Organ", 6-12-23; Edmund Wilson, *loc. cit.; Times,* 9-12-65.

[3] Carey McWilliams, *Southern California Country* (New York, 1946), 343.

[4] *Evening News,* 3-12-09; *Times,* 4-13-09 through 4-22-09, and 4-18-29.

[5] Willard H. Wright, *loc. cit.*

[6] *Record,* June-July 1915, *passim;* Adela Rogers St. John credited her father, the attorney, Earl Rogers, with persuading Sebastian to seek office. Apparently she participated in the phoney assassination attempt. Rogers, 480-490.

[7] James H. Richardson, *For the Life of Me: Memoirs of a City Editor* (New York, 1954), 94-103. *Record,* 3-1-19 through 7-1-19, also 2-5-20. Trial records are L.A. Superior Court #13160, #14161.

[8] *Record,* 6-1-19 through 6-4-19; *Times,* 4-2-04 through 4-7-04.

[9] *Record,* 6-4-19, 7-4-19, 7-7-19; *Times,* 6-8-25, 6-28-26, 1-5-36.

[10] LAPD *Daily Bulletin,* 6-10-20.

[11] *Record,* 1-28-20, 2-18-20, 2-3-20, 4-20-20, 4-26-20, 6-3-20, 6-8-20; P.C. *Minutes,* 3-9-20, 7-15-20, 5-3-20.

[12] *Times,* 8-21-18, 10-1-18, 10-22-18, 2-4-20; *Record,* 1-28-20, 2-3-20, 3-16-20.

[13] *Ibid.,* 1-2-20, 1-7-20, 1-14-20, 1-19-20, 3-5-20, 3-6-20, 3-7-20.

[14] *Ibid.,* 1-29-20, 2-13-20, 3-12-20, 3-13-20, 3-16-20.

[15] *Ibid.,* 3-22-20, through 3-29-20; James H. Richardson, *Spring Street: A Story of Los Angeles* (L.A., 1922).

[16] *Record,* 4-3-20 through 4-9-20, 5-3-20, 5-6-20, 6-18-20, 7-4-20, 7-12-20; P.C. *Minutes,* 5-3-20, 6-8-20; *Examiner,* 8-15-20 through 9-20-20.

[17] P.C. *Minutes,* 4-13-20, 5-3-20, 8-2-21; LAPD *Daily Bulletin,* 7-10-19, 2-26-21, 7-29-21, 9-26-21, 3-1-22; *Record,* 3-24-20, 4-7-20, 4-14-20, 8-17-20, 8-20-20.

[18] *Ibid.,* 1-29-20, 3-5-20 through 3-25-20, 4-1-20, 4-17-20, 4-22-

20, 4-25-20, 7-8-20 through 7-16-20, 8-6-20, 8-10-20, 8-11-20, 8-12-20; P.C. *Minutes,* 2-17-20, 3-3-20, 3-9-20, 8-17-20, 8-20-20.

[19] *Ibid.,* 9-16-20; *Record,* 9-15-20, 10-8-20; *Times,* 9-5-20, 9-16-20, 9-17-20; LAPD *Annual Report,* 1919-20, 5-6, 7, 42, 46-51; cf. *ibid.,* 1918-19, 14-17, 34.

[20] P.C. *Minutes,* 10-3-20, 11-23-20; LAPD *Annual Report,* 1920-21, 5-7; LAPD *Daily Bulletin,* 11-1-20, 2-26-21, 3-24-21.

[21] *Record,* 9-17-20, 10-21-20, 12-4-20 through 12-11-20, 12-17-20, 1-17-21; for typical anti-vagrant orders see LAPD *Daily Bulletin,* 12-2-19, 1-8-20; Louis B. and Richard H. Perry, *A History of the Los Angeles Labor Movement, 1911-1940* (Berkeley, 1963), 193.

[22] *Record,* 1-8-20, 2-23-20, 2-27-20, 5-9-20, 12-6-20, 4-26-21, 5-14-21, 5-20-21.

[23] *Ibid,* 12-31-20, 1-3-21, 1-8-21, 2-4-21, 2-14-21, 3-3-21, 3-5-21, 3-19-21, 3-23-21, 5-31-21, 6-2-21.

[24] P.C. *Minutes,* 4-15-21, 4-19-21; *Times,* 4-19-21; *Record,* 4-1-21, 4-12-21, 4-19-21, 6-2-21.

[25] *Ibid.,* 6-3-21.

[26] *Ibid.,* 6-4-21, 6-8-21.

[27] *Ibid.,* 8-13-21, 8-22-21, 8-23-21, 8-30-21, 12-10-21.

[28] *Ibid.,* 7-5-21, 6-9-21, 6-27-21, 6-28-21. *Times,* 6-25-21.

[29] *Record,* 6-27-21, 7-5-21, 7-28-21, 7-30-21, 8-31-21, 9-1-21 through 9-10-21, 10-1-21, 1-28-20; P.C. *Minutes,* 8-18-19, 2-10-20, 3-9-20, 5-5-20; for a resume of Page's career see *Times,* 2-4-25.

[30] *Record,* 7-4-21 through 7-12-21, 9-17-21, 9-19-21.

[31] L.A. City Council *Minutes,* 10-18-21 to 12-15-21; *Record,* 10-18-21, 10-20-21, 11-9-21, 11-10-21, 11-15-21; *Examiner,* 12-6-21, 12-8-21, 12-11-21, 12-23-21; the *Times,* 12-7-21, arguing that there existed no single solution to the crime problem, in effect supported the M&M position against that of the *Examiner* and the city council.

[32] *Record,* 10-19-21, 10-21-21, 10-27-21, 11-14-21, 11-15-21, 11-10-21 through 12-21-21; Pelletier's charges did not appear in the *Times* and *Examiner* until December 4, 1921. The *Examiner* then conducted a short expose. *Ibid.,* 12-5-21, 12-13-21, 12-23-21.

[33] *Times,* 1-4-22; *Record,* 1-3-22, 1-4-22; *Examiner,* 1-1-22, 1-3-22.

[34] *Ibid.*

[35] LAPD *Bulletin,* 1-30-22, 2-6-22, 3-9-22; *Record,* 1-5-22, 1-20-22, 1-23-22, 1-28-22, 2-17-22, 3-2-22, 3-10-22, 4-13-22; Los Angeles Board of Pension Commissioners *Minutes,* 2-15-22 to 4-17-22; the Police Commission *Minutes,* 1-6-22 to 4-18-22, record 48 dismissals,

compared with only 53 over the 30 previous months when Home, Murray, Pendegast, and Jones, respectively, commanded the force.

[36] *Record,* 3-17-22, 3-23-22, 3-24-22; P.C. *Minutes,* 3-28-22.

[37] *Record,* 3-25-22, 3-27-22, 3-28-22.

[38] *Ibid.,* 3-29-22, 3-30-22, 3-31-22, 4-3-22, 4-7-22.

[39] The testimony may be followed in the *Record,* 4-12-22 through 4-20-22; see also *Examiner,* 4-19-22, 4-21-22; the *Examiner* deleted certain critical testimony.

[40] *Ibid.*

[41] Memorandum from *Times* reporter A.M. Rochlen to editor Ralph Trueblood, dated 3-24-22, *Times Archive.*

[42] LAPD *Bulletin,* 9-14-22, 10-13-22, 12-30-22; the pension amendment passed; see *Record,* 11-8-22.

[43] *Examiner,* 4-22-22; *Record,* 4-21-22; P.C. *Minutes,* 4-20-22.

[44] *Times,* 4-22-22; *Record,* 4-22-22; *Examiner,* 4-22-22.

[45] The C.D.A. grew out of a chance, streetcorner meeting between rival publishers Harry Chandler of the *Times,* and Max Ihmsen, of the *Examiner. Record,* 3-27-23.

[46] L.A. Crime Commission *Bulletin,* #3, *passim.*

[47] *Record,* 11-2-22, 11-3-22, 11-22-22, 11-23-22, 1-30-23, 2-1-23, 3-7-23, 2-27-23, 5-21-23.

[48] *Ibid.,* 4-21-22, 4-22-22.

[49] *Ibid.,* 1-6-23, 1-9-23, 1-10-23.

[50] *Record,* 4-24-22, 4-28-22; LAPD *Bulletin,* 4-28-22, 5-1-22. P.C. *Minutes,* 5-2-22; the incident is also discussed in David M. Chalmers, *Hooded Americanism* (Chicago, 1968), but the reference to "the Catholic mayor of Los Angeles" is in error (p. 119); however, the D.A. was a Roman Catholic; see also Kenneth T. Jackson, *The Ku Klux Klan in the City,* 1915-1930 (N.Y. 1967), 187-195.

[51] *Record,* 1-6-23, 1-9-23, 1-10-23, 6-9-23, 6-11-23, 6-12-23.

[52] *Ibid.,* 11-8-22, 12-30-22; P.C. *Minutes,* April-December, 1922, esp. 3-14-22, 4-11-22, 5-23-22, 7-18-22; LAPD *Bulletin,* 10-13-22, 12-30-22.

[53] John S. Ealey, a Central Avenue black politician, confessed at length to bribing police officers in return for vice protection, and named H.H. Kinney, the mayor's secretary, as a principal conspirator. Mayor Cryer refused to read the confession. *Record,* 1-27-23, 1-29-23, 1-31-23, 5-2-23.

[54] LAPD *Daily Bulletin,* 7-7-19, 7-15-19, 11-15-19, 11-10-10, 11-22-19, 11-24-19; P.C. *Minutes,* 10-20-19; Ordinance #20,586 (New

Series), (New) Penal Code 1919, *Statutes of 1919*, Ch. 101, Sec. 403-a; U.S. Bureau of Labor Statistics, *Monthly Labor Review* 19 (1924): 88; an organization called the American League for Industrial Freedom, in full page advertisements, asked "Who Is An American?" and posed such questions as "What if Washington had decided to strike at Valley Forge?" *Times*, 6-28-25 and 10-1-19 through 11-30-19, esp. 10-10-19, 10-24-19, 11-15-19; neither the *Times* nor the *Examiner* reported the strike. Unfortunately, no copies of other local newspapers for that specific period have survived.

⁵⁵ Woodrow C. Whitten, "Criminal Syndicalism and the Law in California, 1919-1927," *Transactions of the American Philosophical Society* New Series 59:2 (1969); LAPD *Daily Bulletin*, 12-2-19, 1-8-20; Perry and Perry, 193; *Record*, 1-19-20, 3-17-20, 9-17-20, 10-21,20, 2-17-21, 4-1-21; for the recollections of an ACLU founder, see Clinton J. Taft, *Fifteen Years on Freedom's Front* (L.A., 1939).

⁵⁶ *Times*, 5-14-23 through 5-30-23; *Record*, 5-15-23 through 5-31-23; for unknown reasons, the *Examiner* buried this story and practically ignored the strike. *Examiner*, 4-15-23 through 5-31-23. Taft, *op. cit;* see also Louis Adamic, *Laughing in the Jungle: The Autobiography of An Immigrant in America* (N.Y., 1932), 234-236. see Sinclair's open letter to Chief Oaks in *The Nation* 116 (June 6, 1923), 647; see specific charges of police brutality made by Rev. F.R. Wedge, Rev. C.J. Taft and Rev. C.R. Richmond, *Record*, 5-23-23, 5-28-23. Complaints about inhuman jail conditions, made by the ACLU and the Ministerial Union, were verified by a panel of twelve ministers appointed by R.P. Shuler, but their report had no effect on the authorities. *Ibid.*, 5-25-23 through 5-31-23.

⁵⁷ LAPD *Bulletin*, 4-25-22; *ibid.*, 7-20-22 for an example of reward notices.

⁵⁸ *Record*, 6-23-23, 6-26-23.

⁵⁹ *Ibid.*, 7-16-23, 7-18-23.

⁶⁰ This story made headlines in the *Times, Examiner,* and *Record.* There were daily charges and countercharges from July 28 to August 15. See esp. *Times*, 7-29-23, and *Record*, 7-28-23, 8-1-23.

⁶¹ See *Examiner*, 7-29-23, for a complete text of Oaks' letter to the crime commission; also 8-2-23, 8-3-23; LAPD *Bulletin*, 12-21-22, 1-19-23, 3-15-23, 5-9-23, 5-16-23, 5-24-23, 6-21-23, indicates the nature and extent of administrative problems. See *Record*, 6-22-23, for typical comments; also 8-2-23. P.C. *Minutes*, 7-31-23, 8-2-23, 8-28-23.

CHAPTER THREE

THE YEAR OF AUGUST VOLLMER

It would probably take two generations to produce the
kind of a police department we would like to have. Policing a large city is about the most difficult of government
functions, and it grows increasingly complex and arduous
year by year. With very few exceptions, our archaic system is responsible for deplorable conditions. Our whole
method must be abolished before we can succeed. We
must devise scientific methods and apply them to the
investigation and removal of social, economic, physical,
mental and moral factors underlying crime and vice. Prevention and not punishment must be our ultimate objective. We must develop experts who have intelligence,
training and character, and they must employ the best scientific and professional tools.

> August Vollmer
> *The Police and Modern
> Society*

August Vollmer's year as chief established several significant
facts. First, the police department could be reorganized and the vice
statutes enforced whenever the political leaders, the financial and social
elites, the police executive, and the progressive voters united in a common reform effort. Second, although scandal inflamed the progressive
spirit, the general public lost interest as a particular crisis subsided. Successful reform therefore required immediate response to the initial public
outcry. Third, although a resolute civil service chief could protect his
organization from outside interference, his plans could be neutralized if
either the politicians or the civic elites abandoned him. Both groups
deserted Vollmer, the politicians mainly because of backroom negotiations by various sorts of entrepreneurs, the elites because a transcendent
economic issue far removed from police matters shattered their united
front. Nevertheless, Chief Vollmer achieved a considerable success.

Vollmer avoided the Oaks-Heath controversy and moved quietly into command. The forty-seven year old police reformer had led a pleasant life as village police chief of Berkeley and lecturer in criminology at the University of California. Only the need to test his theories of crime prevention and police administration in a larger laboratory persuaded him to chance Los Angeles. He expected that his system could be installed within one year and had obtained twelve-month leaves of absence from his employers.

Vollmer was a utopian progressive whose ultimate theory engrossed the moral reform of mankind and the creation of a society in which crime would not occur. He believed firmly in the influence of environment on the human. High recidivision rates made him doubt the efficiency of prison reform or prisoner rehabilitation although he recommended separation of first offenders from "hardened" criminals. His hopes lay in crime prevention through the elimination of criminal behavior. He favored the careful examination of school children for signs of antisocial behavior and the segregation, if necessary, of those whose tests indicated aberrant attitudes. For a healthy society he asked sufficient jobs at satisfactory wages for adults and wholesome recreation combined with strong moral training for the young. Neither the crime commission nor the mayor cared much about Vollmer's social theories; they wanted only "scientific" police management.

Vollmer postulated two essential elements for the efficient police agency and the reformed city. First, a professional police force completely free of political influence, staffed by sufficient intelligent, well paid, highly trained, dedicated, respected policemen, utilizing every modern tool that technology could provide. Second, an intelligent, well informed, honest citizenry, willing to be taxed for the public benefit, prepared to obey the law, to report those who evaded it and resolved never to berate, belittle or bribe police officers.[1]

Public respect for policemen, closely related to police morale, was especially vital in 1923. Vollmer hoped to eliminate major problem areas by making vice abatement and traffic control the responsibility of new agencies, separate from the police department and under separate command. He reasoned that liquor, prostitution, gambling and narcotics operators offered substantial bribes. Inevitably, some policemen accepted them. Their sins became known. The public then blamed all policemen for the errors of a few. Moreover, vice squad shakeups and transfers affected innocent and guilty alike. Public disrespect and loss of police morale followed.

Proper enforcement of the traffic ordinances produced a different problem. The department found itself in constant conflict with the auto-owning middle class, whose support Vollmer needed for the revenue bond issue to implement his program. Removal of vice and traffic as police functions would avoid the two greatest deterrents to an honest, self-confident police force and permit the executive and the men to concentrate on catching criminals and protecting property.

Even had Vollmer succeeded in transferring vice and traffic to other agencies, formidable problems remained. Vollmer remarked that "no self-respecting stockman would keep his cattle in the Lincoln Heights stockade," a mild comment in comparison to the municipal prison horror stories then current. The "crime wave" elicited Vollmer's comment that Los Angeles had "even passed Chicago." He estimated that the department had only half the equipment needed to properly police its jurisdiction. Modern methods of identification, communication and record storage were practically unknown. After years of upheaval, public respect for the undermanned, undisciplined, untrained, indifferent and apathetic department was virtually non-existent.

Public opinion could be manipulated, however, and the reversal of the common attitude toward policemen was the second level of the chief's plan. Ludicrous film portrayals, such as the Keystone Kops, enraged Vollmer, who feared the effect of such buffoonery on the tender minds of children. Periodically he demanded that motion picture producers, the directors of plays, newspapermen and other opinion makers "cease to describe the police as numbskulls and crooks as heroes." Remarkably, the newspaper editors agreed to cooperate.

Vollmer spoke often to service clubs and church associations, urging people to organize in cooperation with the police department. He said that about twelve percent of society vigorously upheld the law and an equal number had criminal proclivities. Therefore, the great middle group had to be organized and motivated to battle crime. He requested that the women's clubs each choose a problem—truancy, jails, bail-bonds, probation—investigate it thoroughly and suggest reforms. After reform occurred the clubs should monitor the performance of public officials to ensure that the new standards were maintained.

Vollmer also took it upon himself to defend the force publicly in every conceivable circumstance, supporting his officers while making capital of nasty situations. This permitted him to criticize the department while drawing attention to its needs. He exonerated a patrolman who killed a bystander in a gunbattle with felons, arguing that inaccurate

shooting reflected ineffective weapons training. This he would soon rec-
tify because shooting to kill was the best way to eliminate desperate
criminals. The high rate of crime indicated poor police work, the chief
averred, but blame also must fall on the general public, which refused to
pay for an efficient force: "Can you expect to get intelligent men for
$120 a month when they can make $165 driving a milk wagon?"[2]

The proper selection and training of policemen remained
Vollmer's major interest. He carefully prepared his ideas for future presentation but for the moment he tried to reduce friction between police
and public by reforming the men he already had. His administrative
orders implied rather dreary conditions. He forbade the issuance or rec-
ognizance of courtesy cards and badges. He forbade smoking on the
streets or in the public areas of the station and demanded neatness,
including coat and tie even when in plainclothes. There would be no
more "scoops;" news would be released at the same time to all newspapers. Police, when approached, should record citizen complaints, not
direct the taxpayer to some other division. Officers must obey the speed
limits. A complaint from the Rotary Club that "the police seem to think
the uniform gives not only the power to enforce the law, but also to insult
the citizens" appeared in the *Bulletin* with Vollmer's comments. Police
could not accept rewards even if afterwards donated to the police pension fund. (One idealistic young patrolman refused $2,000 for finding a
lost child, a sum greater than his annual salary).[3]

An order forbidding traffic-ticket "fixing" appeared several times
in the *Daily Bulletin* and policemen having knowledge of this practice
were asked to inform the chief. In response to judicial criticism, officers
received orders to attend court promptly, to answer subpoenas, to be prepared with notebook and facts and to make short, factual answers rather
than general statements. Officers seeking complaints from the district
attorney were ordered to provide forms describing the particulars of the
offense and arrest.

For a policeman of his time, Vollmer exhibited an unusual devotion to constitutional procedures. During his term the ACLU knew that it
would receive a fair hearing. He warned the department against the
undue use of force. He made the officers who guarded or transported
prisoners responsible for safeguarding the prisoners' personal property
and required that such property be kept on the same premises where the
prisoners were held. He demanded quick investigations to avoid the
unnecessary detention of suspects. Considering the prisons, this order
had both humanitarian and practical values.[4]

The city jails presented a serious and continuing problem, due in part to overcrowding of misdemeanants, in part to court delays which kept many technically innocent persons in custody awaiting trial and in part to an official reluctance to finance new construction. To solve the immediate difficulty, Vollmer released 300 vagrants and lesser miscreants. The district attorney freed all minor offenders held without trial for more than thirty days and the county sheriff accepted 100 city prisoners at his rural facility.

The future seemed grim, however, as Vollmer foresaw a doubling of the inmate population before a new country jail could be built. He obtained $50,000 from the city council to pay for four barrack-style dormitories. These sheltered 500 men from the Lincoln Heights stockade. He then forced the rapid completion of a two-storey annex to the Lincoln Heights jail, providing adequate quarters for a further 250 prisoners. Vollmer also urged the immediate establishment of an industrial farm to be directed by a scientific penologist, where minor offenders could be "restored to citizenship, thoroughly rehabilitated...with a kindly feeling toward society and respect for the officers who were obliged to detain them." City councillors and police commissioners praised the idea but refused to provide the money.

To reduce court delay, the crime commission obtained the cooperation of the superior court justices. Studies indicated an average "court-life" of 110 days per felony case from arrest to disposition. The crime commission and the judges assigned five court divisions from which all non-felony court business would be excluded. The judges bound themselves to strive for a thirty day average court life. The crime commission eventually reported a reduction to fifty-eight days, on average, accompanied by a twenty-five percent decline in continuances.

The experiment therefore proved to be a great improvement if not an entire success, and the program was expanded. A concurrent arrangement allowed police officers to obtain search warrants at any hour of the night. The district attorney agreed to speed the process by rushing evidence before the grand jury so that immediate indictments could be returned. Thus, if justice delayed were justice denied, the criminal justice system became for a time more just.[5]

The critical absence of contingency planning and the limited capability for response to emergencies also drew Vollmer's attention. In the event of a bank robbery, patrolling officers could not be alerted and instructed to close escape routes or pursue bandits. Some reserves were held ready at headquarters but traffic congestion in the downtown streets often made pursuit futile. Vollmer obtained twenty mounted traffic officers to facilitate pursuit by sixty-three new autos and sixty new motorcycles.

To warn patrolmen of emergencies Vollmer placed a 300 pound siren with a range of eight miles, atop Central Division headquarters. The council agreed to purchase an additional 70 sirens for installation at other strategic locations. For night signalling, rather than energize the sirens, Vollmer requested that the power and light company blink the streetlights in given areas. These arrangements sufficed until a proper call light and communication system could be installed.

The station-house reserves formed a 300-member, mobile division nicknamed the "Crime Crushers." This became the elite corps of the LAPD. Its members participated in many dramatic exploits. Fierce competition ensued for the few available places. The most efficient performer was Harold K. Freeman, a quiet lone-wolf dubbed "the marvel cop" for his forty-eight "good" arrests in a single month.

The crime crushers operated on hypotheses suggested by Fred A. Knoles, a statistician hired by Vollmer to direct the reorganized Records Bureau. Vollmer demanded the systematic collection of a wide range of crime statistics. From these data, Knoles plotted the time and place where certain crimes were most likely to occur. The crime crushers then flooded the designated area, producing a sudden vast increase in police efficiency.

The division struck different targets on different days, with spectacular success. Auto thefts fell to six per day from an average of twenty-five. Ex-convicts lectured the division on criminal techniques to counteract the criminals' knowledge of police methods. Subsequently, the crime crushers netted fifty-six burglars and thirty hold-up men within a month. The chief reported a twenty per cent decrease in crime during August and September of 1923. A series of gunbattles—fatal to six desperados—emphasized Vollmer's stern warning that "many will die."

The lack of trained personnel presented another difficult challenge. Only an intellectually competent staff could cope with the finger printing, handwriting analysis, lie-detector operation, *modus operandi* classification, Bertillon measurements, data collection and analysis, report writing and other clerical skills on which Vollmer based his administration. Vollmer had Leonard Keeley, a youthful developer of the lie-detector, to introduce its use in Los Angeles but staff for other new positions had to come from within the organization. Special schools had to be organized and qualified instructors found.

Entrance examinations for the new schools, open to all, produced a few surprises. A junior "clerk-female" placed first in the finger-printing class and promptly advanced to fingerprint technician. The number of fingerprint technicians rose from two to nineteen. Other employees studied handwriting analysis. Forty men enroled in the department's initial first aid class; the chief's plans included teaching the skill to all future recruits.

As part of Vollmer's analysis of personnel, the entire department completed the U.S. Army "Alpha" intelligence test, an eight-part, 212 question examination that measured the ability to observe, follow instructions and make logical deductions. Since Vollmer used the test scores to find people for newly created posts, he disrupted regular lines of promotion. One man, after scoring 97.5%, rose overnight from the beat to a key position in the Records Bureau.

Not unexpectedly, Vollmer advocated a liaison between the police and the university, to bring the best minds available to bear on given problems. He arranged for Dr. Aaron Rosaroff to teach abnormal psychology to a beginning class of seventy-five policemen, using lectures and textbooks utilized at the University of Southern California. Dr. Ernest B. Hoag and Dr. Edward H. Williams taught criminology. Judge James H. Pope lectured on Criminal law and R.A. Abbey of the Berkeley police department taught Principles and Processes of Identification. Vollmer lectured on *modus operandi* crime identification. For detectives, the chief strongly recommended a memory course offered by a private expert at $12 for four lessons. Periodically the *Daily Bulletin* listed new books on criminology and abnormal psychology available at the public library.[6]

Preliminary institutional reform began. Vollmer organized a Jails Division, placing all jails under the control of a chief jailer. This encouraged uniform conditions and treatment, and fixed responsibility in one man. Since the escape of prisoners was not uncommon, a new system of receipts eliminated disputes between jailer and arresting officer over whether an individual had actually been incarcerated. A new Vice Division united the vice, Chinatown and narcotics details in one fifty-member squad but this did not relieve division commanders of responsibility for vice abatement in their areas. A new forgery detail battled "paperhangers" and tried to reduce business losses.

The chief also established a personnel division. Given the amount of personal data that Vollmer collected, this may have been inevitable but bad police work provided the impetus. Vollmer observed that a large proportion of reports from George K. Home's detective bureau bore the notation "no clues, no suspects, case closed." He ordered all such files immediately returned for further investigation. Furthermore, an "Officer File," newly created, recorded each man's case work so that superior officers could readily compare individual performances. Understandably, this bureau did not win favor among the less productive men.

Chief Vollmer followed an extremely busy work schedule. To reform the corrupt, instil morale in the demoralized, regain public respect for the disreputable, educate the uneducated, obtain new equipment, upgrade the prisons, rehabilitate the criminal, perform daily executive functions and also develop plans for a major reorganization required more hours daily than Vollmer could safely endure. Spokesmen announced that the chief would make no more speeches (already it took one clerk most of each day merely to refuse speaking engagements). Instead, he applied himself to the integrated system of scientific police administration and crime prevention planned for Los Angeles.[7]

The master plan, presented to the city council in April 1924, fell generally into two parts. The first included reorganization of the divisions, redeployment of personnel and modernization of plant and equipment. The second dealt with the selection, training and promotion of qualified police officers. Part I called for the outlay of large sums of money, which the city council proposed to obtain through a special bond issue that required a favorable vote by the taxpayers. This involved a publicity campaign to ensure passage by an enlightened electorate. It also meant careful scrutiny by whatever anti-bond interests existed. The bond plebiscite was scheduled for May 6, 1924, but debate started in November 1923, when Vollmer opened a drive to get the police bond issue onto the ballot. The general provisions of the first section were therefore fairly well known.

Part I recommended organization of the department in eleven divisions, uniting similar functions under a single head, providing more efficient leadership and clarifying lines of authority. The eleven executives reported to the chief but handled day to day administration themselves. The master plan included most of Vollmer's ideas about "scientific," professional police administration:

1. Uniform, or Patrol Division: Vollmer designed small divisions so that every citizen would reside within two or three minutes of a station. He proposed seven new subdivisions, making sixteen in all. This required seven new stations and expansion of four others at Lincoln Heights, Wilshire, Sawtelle and San Pedro. A new headquarters building also was needed. The Crime Crushers Division acted as Reserve in the event of major crimes, civil disturbances or natural disasters.

2. Property Division became responsible for property found, seized, delivered or held for any reason.

3. Detective Division.

4. Construction and Maintenance Division took responsibility for emergency signal and alarm systems, departmental communications, traffic signals and all other equipment except transportation. Vollmer wanted a common telephone switchboard so that everyone in the city would call the same number for police service. The operator could then extend the call to the correct substation, eliminating jurisdictional confusion for the citizen and providing a truer view of the number of calls for assistance. Vollmer also requested a common teletype system which would deliver information to every division at the same time, keeping every station in touch with events and permitting rapid coordination of manpower. A third requirement was for a complete electrical emergency signal lamp system, complemented by the extension of the call box network to every beat. The application of technology in combination with arrangements to close streets and bridges meant that rapid communication could exist between the chief in central headquarters and the widely dispersed patrol force.

5. Jail Division

6. Crime Prevention Division combined the City Mother's Bureau, the Juvenile Bureau, the male and female parole boards and the female probation unit. Its main purpose was to work with women, juveniles and children in the hope of preventing adult tragedies. The Bureau was directed to form cooperative relationships with schools and welfare agencies.

7. Traffic Division had existed for several years. In addition to enforcing city and state vehicle ordinances, Vollmer expected it to carry out traffic surveys, compare local problems with those of other cities and seek efficient solutions to drastic downtown congestion. Studies by independent agencies in 1924 showed that several Los Angeles intersections were vastly more busy than the busiest Chicago corner. The city also led all others in traffic deaths per capita.

8. Transportation Division was responsible for equestrian and mechanical transportation.

9. Records Division maintained fingerprints, Bertillon, photographs, handwriting, statistics, accounts and correspon-

dence. It included a statistical bureau which issued a monthly report on crime, vice and traffic developments.

10. Vice Division operated from Central Division Headquarters but was directly answerable to Chief Vollmer.

Of the estimated $3,000,000 cost of Part I, about half was for the eleven substations and related signalling and communications equipment, the remainder for a new headquarters building. In Los Angeles, that was a lot of money, not in absolute terms—huge water, school and road construction expenditures were common—but because it was for construction of police buildings. Calling attention to the city's high burglary insurance rates, Vollmer argued that "the very first step necessary to reduce crime to a minimum" was the proper distribution of substations. Once these were built, rapid signals and fast autos could be utilized to the most effective extent. As it was, the city had outgrown its police system and crime was epidemic.

A number of influential persons and organizations rallied to the cause. The city council and the police commission endorsed the plan. The crime commission, the Municipal League, the Better America Federation, the financier Marco Hellman and Louis B. Mayer, a rising power in city politics, all urged the voters to vote "yes" on Proposition Five. Second thoughts prevailed, however. The County had a massive new Hall of Justice under construction. The city council decided to rent five floors of that edifice for a police headquarters, rather than build one.

The bond issue, reduced to $1.6 million, received an overwhelming majority. At Vollmer's request, the council borrowed money in anticipation of bond sales so that work could begin, and construction started late in July. By that time Vollmer had submitted his *Survey of the Los Angeles Police Force 1923-24* to the police commission and the full results of the police intelligence tests were known.[8]

Vollmer claimed that he was "not a politician." The release of the *Survey* proved it beyond doubt. A number of low Alpha test scores and Vollmer's unguarded comments about them were seized upon and blown into a controversy that for a time threatened the entire reorganization program. The *Record,* which made the revelation, described its unfortunate blunder as an "exclusive report." With tiresome facetiousness the newspaper harped upon the police "bean tests." Cartoons, drawing crude allusions to the supposed mental ages of the police, pictured the men in sandboxes, cribs and baby carriages. Defensive comments by police officers were carried on the front pages. A schism developed between the chief and his subordinates.

The Alpha results had been discussed months earlier, after completion of the tests. The LAPD scored higher than its counterpart in Cleveland and a good deal higher than the federal prohibition unit in Chicago. The *Survey* revealed that the department had men who scored as high as 201 of 212, but it also had men who scored as low as 6. A captain scored below 24, a sergeant below 14. Captains, as a group, scored lower than patrolmen as a group.

Many policemen, even some with high scores, argued that "mental gymnastics" proved nothing. Practical experience counted more. Anyone fresh from high school might pass examinations but fail at police work. Critics of the tests alleged that the officers who made good scores usually were not the best men at their jobs. One comment summed up the general attitude of the department: "these tests are OK, but will they catch crooks?"

Irresponsible journalism created an issue where none existed. In the furor, Vollmer's purpose was ignored. No one argued that, of two applicants, one scoring 6 would be a better prospect than one scoring 201, which was the actual range of LAPD scores. The statistics, not meant for public consumption, supported the chief's point that low entrance standards allowed unintelligent recruits to be employed. Men whose performance indicated unfitness for office held important jobs and high ranks. With stringent entrance standards, such men could never be appointed.[9]

Vollmer went further. His plan for selecting and training police officers included individual examinations by trained psychologists and psychiatrists. No officer would be given authority until his or her mental balance was conclusively proven. As the chief said, "our records show that even mentally unstable men have been appointed policemen and their instability not recognized by commanding officers until they killed some innocent person or committed a heinous offense." Vollmer estimated that $100,000 annually could be saved by careful educational and psychological testing of civil service candidates. To illustrate, he pointed out that 294 policemen had been terminated for one reason or another between January 1, 1923 and January 1, 1924. The loss to the city was $183,260.

Furthermore, Vollmer led his critics in recognizing the limits of intelligence tests. His "Officers Rating System" required every commanding officer to measure each of his officers against the best officer in the division in different categories. Thus the most efficient, or most dependable, or most self-reliant person was considered the standard for that category. Others were rated in comparison. From the sum of scores, a composite was developed for comparison with other personnel.

Ironically, Vollmer argued that competitive civil service promotional examinations placed too little emphasis on experience. He suggested changing the regulations to reduce the examination "weight" to fifty per cent. The other fifty percent would be based on the commander's opinion of the candidate's experience and potential.

Actually the low test scores ought not to have surprised anyone. In March 1924, the secretary of the civil service commission released to the *Record* some answers given by patrolmen on a promotional examination. The reporters believed that the official was joking, until he offered to produce the originals. This examination may have been the genesis of several classic American police jokes:

Q. What would you do in the case of a race riot?
A. Get the number of both cars.
Q. Name an act that would constitute reckless driving.
A. Driving without due regard for the presbyterians on the street.
Q. What is sabotage?
A. Breaking the laws of the Sabbath.
Q. What is arson?
A. Mistreating a woman.
Q. What would you do for someone having an epileptic fit?
A. Take him to the doctor and have the bite treated.
Q. What are rabies, and what would you do for them?
A. Rabies are Jewish priests and I would do nothing for them.
Q. To what extent may an officer use force in effecting an arrest?
A. Use commonsense and if not capable, summon help.

This information appeared on the front page of the *Record* but no one complained and no controversy developed. Unfortunately, the Alpha results provoked bitterness rather than hilarity.

During World War I, military authorities administered the test to 1,726,966 men. The distribution of scores showed only 13% above 105 of 212, the point separating men capable from those not capable of college work. Vollmer tested 1918 individuals. The range was from 6 to 201; the mean was 97.9 points. The distribution was quite different from that of the army.

Vollmer analyzed the results according to Yoakum and Yerkes' *Army Mental Tests,* which stated that "men of 'A' intelligence have the ability to make a superior record in college or university; 'B' intelligence is capable of making an average record in college; 'C+' intelligence cannot do so well; 'C' is rarely capable of finishing a high school course; 'D' men are of such inferior mentality that they are rarely able to go beyond the third or fourth grade of the elementary school, however long they may attend. In fact, many 'D-' men are of the moron grade of feeble-mindedness."

Vollmer's own comments were scarcely less pointed. The 272 ranking officers, 7% of whom scored `C-' or less, especially galled the chief. One captain, three detective lieutenants, two lieutenants, nine sergeants and four motorcycle officers (equivalent to sergeant) scored at the level expected of children nine to thirteen years old. A captain scored among the `D's, along with a detective lieutenant, a sergeant and three motorcycle officers. The `D-' group included a sergeant.

Vollmer found it "hard to conceive" of tests that such men could pass. To print this sort of commentary in conjunction with the tables and charts was provocative enough, though the report was not meant for the eyes of police officers. Vollmer compounded the error by revealing the name, rank and score of every officer. Not only did this undermine good order and discipline, it was very bad politics.

Vollmer wanted to create a police department in his own image. As he saw it, police work required the highest mental and moral capabilities. He compared the LAPD with 41,000 commissioned military officers and with a group of college men. Neither comparison flattered the police force. Readers of the *Survey* might easily gain the impression that Vollmer blamed the police for their stupidity, rather than criticizing the system that employed them. The chief's awkward method obscured the validity of his premise.

The data could have been examined in a less abrasive manner. References to mental age might profitably have been dropped. The LAPD scores might have been compared with those of the Cleveland police and the Chicago prohibition agents, placing the local force in a better light. In fact, 72% of the scores indicated mentality above the average. Only 1.3% actually indicated inferior intelligence. Enthusiastic recognition of the 45% who exhibited "superior" intelligence would have been well taken. Then, if the chief asserted that the increasing use of science in police work demanded college-level intellectual performance from all future recruits, few would disagree. Not even the mossiest oldtimer regarded "intelligent policeman" as a contradiction in terms.[10]

The *Survey* revealed incidentally that American-born officers constituted 94% of the police force. Most had previously been unskilled laborers. About 90% came from states other than California. Compared with the Los Angeles population, the west, southeast and southwest were vastly overrepresented while the east, midwest and certain foreign countries were significantly underrepresented. No Asian and only a dozen Spanish surnames appeared on a roster of several thousand officers.

Blacks numbered perhaps two dozen. About twenty females served as jailers and juvenile officers.

Most LAPD officers were Protestant but the force included Roman Catholics. There is inconclusive evidence that American Jews were excluded where possible, although some Jews obtained appointments. Immigrants and non-white Americans undoubtedly were discouraged if not prevented from obtaining police jobs. No data are available that would permit reliable explanations of overrepresentation, underrepresentation or discrimination.[11]

Vollmer intended more than the revelation of weaknesses when he analyzed the LAPD. He hoped to find ways to identify candidates who had the potential to become first-rate officers. Such a discovery would have profound consequences, since manpower was even more important than methodology in the creation of the model police force. He did not succeed. Neither previous occupation, nativity, race, experience nor even educational qualifications could be securely correlated to high quality police work. The only sure criteria, Vollmer believed, were intellectual ability and emotional stability, with perhaps a nod to youth. None of these qualities had enjoyed a formal place in the LAPD selection process.

There was room for modernization of the methods of induction. A residence rule decreed that candidates must reside in the city for one full year before applying to the department. Another rule restricted eligibility to citizens between the ages of 23 and 35 years although much older men sometimes were appointed. Regulations prescribed minimum physical qualification but required no intellectual or educational qualifications. Applicants were assessed on a twenty point scale that allotted more weight to the display of physical abilities than to education, experience, personal qualifications and the written examination combined. The rules failed to specify a mandatory retirement age; patrolmen as old as seventy-two years still reported for duty.[12]

At Vollmer's request, the civil service commission rescinded the residence rule so that any qualified person could join, and reduced the upper age limit to thirty years. The minimum physical requirements remained at the previous levels, five feet, nine inches in height and 150 pounds in weight. A thorough medical examination and the required feats of athletic prowess became preconditions to eligibility rather than weighted parts of the examination. High school graduation or equivalent standing also became a precondition, the first formal recognition by the LAPD of the value of education. The new ten point scale weighted intellectual capabilities significantly above experience or similar factors.

Vollmer's analysis of previous occupations indicated that with the possible exception of policework, no prior experience merited credit toward a police appointment. "Experience" remained a much abused category, however. The ten percent veterans' bonus, which could be added to an applicant's score, also weakened the selection process. (The bonus was abolished in 1954.) Reduction of the upper age limit partially closed this loophole but the bonus still circumvented the requirement that recruits must score in the "A" range of the Alpha test.

A later chief observed that "men who are fitted for police work will not join. We must manage with what we get," but Vollmer envisioned a time when only the "best" people in society would be considered for police service. He insisted upon the most rigorous standards of selection, complemented by the most efficient methods of instruction. To replace the old police school, at which officers spent two or three hours a week in their off-duty time, Vollmer established a ninety-day, full-time police academy. The curriculum included sixty-five subjects, ranging from the laws of the state, county and city, criminal procedure, criminal psychology and police methods to first aid, foot-drill and marksmanship. Professors, judges, attorneys, physicians and police officers from other jurisdictions lectured the students at Vollmer's request. Psychologists and psychiatrists, seeking to eliminate cadets of questionable mental stability, maintained surveillance.[13]

In insisting upon severe uniform entrance qualifications, followed by graduation from a rigorous training school, Vollmer applied a single standard of performance to all police recruits. This followed the common practise of American police departments, whether the standards were high or low, but its inherent contradictions in terms of human nature had been recognized and criticized by Vollmer in the past. Inevitably, the vast majority of police officers spent their entire careers in the rank of patrolman, concerned with the routine duties of the beat, the school-crossing and the traffic intersection. No matter how honorable this calling, individuals of the highest mental capabilities seldom found its rewards adequate compensation for a lifetime as a "harness bull."

Experience indicated that after six or eight years without promotion, when such men realized that their creativity and leadership potential would not be utilized within the department, two tendencies arose. Some officers resigned and found similar positions with rural or suburban law enforcement agencies. Others "protected the pension." The more cautious man, unwilling to throw away the investment of his years, tried to avoid controversy. He offended no one. He "played safe," "kept his nose clean" and "minded his own business." His efficiency declined as his incentive disappeared and when the minimum twenty years was served he was happy to retire.

Both of these tendencies were apparent in the Los Angeles police force for many years before Vollmer arrived. The loss of patrolmen having eight to twelve years of service was less common but the retirement could be predicted of any, even ranking officers, who accumulated twenty years with the department. This may have been a natural response to low salaries, internal politics and continual police scandals.

Vollmer did nothing about mandatory retirement or early retirement. He tried to ease discontent at the bottom by allowing patrolmen to rise to the fourth (and highest) salary level by passing qualifying examinations rather than serving time. Anytime after the fourth step, patrolmen could write the examination for sergeant and, if successful, be placed on the civil service promotion list. At that point the plan foundered, for close to 2,000 patrolmen competed for whatever vacancies occurred among the 135 sergeants. These were unsolvable problems.

The military alternative to the single standard, where higher standards were applied to officer candidates than to enlisted men, never received serious consideration in America because incumbent police officers would not permit it to happen. They considered it crucial to departmental discipline, cooperation and incentive that the patrolmen knew their superiors had started at the bottom. Given this fact, Vollmer insisted upon rigorous entrance and training standards. It was better to replace experienced but dissatisfied officers with excellent recruits than to lower the general quality of the department through less demanding entrance criteria.[14]

The initial results of the police academy pleased everyone. The first of four classes of cadets began its ninety-day training schedule on June 23, 1924. Of 945 men enroled in the four classes, 201 received discharges for various shortcomings prior to graduation. Observers hailed the elimination of so many potential troublemakers as sufficient justification for the cost of the school. The elite status of the men chosen for the academy created an esprit among the 744 graduates that extended to the establishment of exclusive fraternal organizations. The number of men from this group that resigned or was dismissed was significantly below the norm.[15]

Unfortunately, by the time that the first contingent of new-style police commenced its training, Vollmer's career in Los Angeles was nearly over. Luckily for Vollmer, he could fall back on his original agreement to stay only one year. Considerations of personal health and commitments to other organizations perhaps had some bearing on the decision to quit, even though the job was not finished and the fate of the reorganization plan remained in doubt. The most pressing reason was the continued interference of politicians in police affairs. When Vollmer arrived in August, 1923, the influential businessmen guiding the Crime Commission seemed on the verge of separating the police from politics. A contest then began between the crime commission and the mayor's circle of advisors. By June, 1924, the reform movement was in decline and the politicians were triumphant.

Perhaps the issue never was in doubt.The *Examiner* implied as much when it revealed the inside story of Vollmer's appointment. The crime commission sought out Vollmer and received his promise to enter the civil service competition for chief. The commission then informed Mayor Cryer that the famed criminologist was available but when the Oaks-Heath crisis occurred, Mayor Cryer sent his own delegation to Berkeley to assess the candidate. The emissaries included Kent K. Parrot, the Reverend Robert P. Shuler and Dr. Samuel T. Montgomery, head of the Anti-Saloon League in Los Angeles. The choice of this odd trio, the Hearst paper insisted, meant that Cryer "had deserted the cleanup campaign to stick with the politicians." Subsequent events supported the *Examiner's* allegations.[16]

Vollmer expected the crime commission to protect the department against outside influences. This hope was forlorn. The "non-political" chief had no more success than his predecessors in avoiding political entanglements. This might have been expected, since Vollmer was viewed by many as an agent of the crime commission. In turn, the Crime Commission appeared to some observers as simply one more political machine contending for control of the city. Both charges contained a considerable element of truth.

From the beginning, therefore, the new chief had antagonists if not outright enemies. When he asked the city council for a Hollerith tabulator, Councilman William Mushet led the opposition, arguing that Vollmer would be replaced within a few months and his successor would not want the machine. Mushet, Boyle Workman and Edwin Baker blocked requisition of traffic signals at an important intersection. In the wisdom of the councilmen, "if the police can't stop accidents without a flasher signal, it (sic) can't do it with one." Council members dismissed a request that the city offer a reward of $500 in local murder cases as "a bad precedent" but agreed to the reward if a municipal employee were the victim. The council also criticized the department for failing to abolish over-parking and illegal left-turns.[17]

The police commissioners proved even less cooperative than the councilmen. Early in October, 1923, the Crime Commission issued a public rebuke to Mayor Cryer and commissioners Charles H. De Coo and John H. De La Monte, reminding the three officials that they had pledged to support the chief. This promise remained unfulfilled. For example, Vollmer discharged two patrolmen for extortion. The police commission reinstated the men on a technicality. When Vollmer produced new evidence, the commission ruled that the case could not be reopened.[18]

Commissioner De Coo appeared at the center of several other controversies. One concerned "Madison Square Garden," a boxing club built on Central Avenue by George Brown, the black political boss. Since prize-fighting and betting were illegal, only amateur matches could legally be held. The news that Sam Langford and other famous black fighters appeared in Brown's productions caused Vollmer to request an abatement but the commissioners refused to withdraw the club's license. It was known that the materials in the club were bought from Commissioner De Coo, whose official police commission stationery bore the names and addresses of five lumber companies he controlled.

In short order, evidence was produced that De Coo had requested special treatment for a notorious prisoner in the city jail. One of De Coo's companies was under investigation in connection with an issue of stock. A newspaper revealed that De Coo had seriously injured three pedestrians in separate auto accidents over a three month period. Progressives demanded De Coo's replacement. Mayor Cryer complained that his request for the commissioner's resignation had been rejected.

The removal of the police commissioners became a major political issue. The Municipal League, the Greater Los Angeles Improvement Council, the crime commission and various progressive church congregations joined the *Record* in formal demands for the ouster of De Coo. This was an important strategy. Vollmer's friends believed that a plot existed which called for the dismissal of Commissioner De La Monte, leaving De Coo to neutralize the chief's efforts while Cryer remained in the shadows. The mayor's failure to depose De Coo added to their suspicion.

Commissioner De La Monte, who had the support of the Merchants and Manufacturers Association and the Chamber of Commerce but the enmity of the church groups, asked De Coo to resign; De Coo, appointed at the request of the church federations, suggested that both resign. Mayor Cryer broke the deadlock in mid-October by dismissing De La Monte, after which De Coo resigned. Only when new commissioners were appointed would it be clear which side had won.[19]

Opposition to Vollmer was growing because he refused to share his authority with anyone outside the department and he refused to overlook vice operations. A reporter claimed that a bet could not be placed at any odds that Vollmer would be chief six months hence. Ex-commissioner De La Monte declared that indeed a plan did exist to topple Vollmer and replace him with R. Lee Heath. Behind the plot De La Monte saw Kent K. Parrot. Captain Heath, however, after first criticizing "politicians who threw dust in the eyes of the public by setting former Chief of Police Oaks and I against each other," stated that he did not want the chief's job, that he considered Vollmer the top policeman in the country and that he would back the chief to the limit.[20]

The appointments to the police commission were of paramount importance. The crime commission nominated Dr. Rufus Von Kleinsmid, of the University of Southern California. Von Kleinsmid, a criminologist, would be a sturdy buttress to Chief Vollmer. He was not chosen, perhaps for those reasons. Instead, Mayor Cryer nominated Samuel T. Montgomery, a Presbyterian minister and official of the Anti-Saloon League. This satisfied the church progressives. The other nominee, Isadore W. Birnbaum, was a successful investor, a Republican, a Mason, an Elk and a Native Son. Neither man had experience in any branch of law, law-enforcement or penology. They appeared to be perfect progressive choices but they were weak reeds indeed when the political winds blew strong.

The *Record* echoed the *Examiner* in describing Montgomery as "a politician, pure and simple." Birnbaum, a self-made man who wished to dabble in civic affairs, owed his position entirely to the mayor or the mayor's advisors. The choices plainly favored Kent Parrot, not August Vollmer. The chief's friends saw, or thought they saw, a plot in the making. A traditional Los Angeles moral crusade would begin. Old blue-laws would be enforced and new ones devised. The department would be drawn ever deeper into the proscription of public and private amusements. Other duties would be neglected. Crime would rise. Every section of the community would have its grievance. The chief would not be able to function successfully in the constant political cross-fire. He would resign.

When Commissioner Montgomery announced a plan to outlaw dancing in public ballrooms it seemed that the anti-Vollmer moral crusade was underway. Montgomery soon added boxing exhibitions and petty gambling at charity events to the list of forbidden delights. Dr. Briegleb and Fighting Bob Shuler joined the campaign, demanding that Sunday movies and the sale of gasoline and cigarets on the Sabbath be banned. They also sought abatement proceedings against art galleries that featured representations of the nude human body. City councilmen criticized the chief for failing to eliminate vice. Nor could Vollmer trust his own men. In one instance, a man in a Santa Claus suit, collecting for charity, was arrested under the anti-disguise ordinance directed at the Ku Klux Klan. The chief's friends appealed to the public not to let these strange events reflect on Vollmer, who did not personally respond to his critics.[21]

The New Year brought new problems. District Attorney Asa Keyes attacked the "self-appointed" Crime Commission as "an oligarchy of great wealth" devoted to "power politics." The Reverend R.P. Shuler supported Keyes, describing the Commission as a political monolith designed to control the city. The *Record* argued that room existed for many anti-crime organizations and urged Shuler and Briegleb to form one of their own. The struggle was being made to appear a straight political fight between two factions, one of which included August Vollmer. This prevented the chief from appearing in the role he preferred, that of independent, impartial police reformer.[22]

Vollmer at first refused to take part in the quarrel. He hoped to avoid confrontation because his reorganization plan was not getting the full support of the council. The reduction in capital improvement from $3 million to $1.6 million was only the first setback. The councilmen slowly debated whether or not to seek a bond issue or to finance the program from taxes. Bond revenues would be spent as planned but the politicians would have complete control of a tax-supported program and the result would be in doubt. The enmity of Councilman Mushet, head of the finance committee, was formidable, since he pictured the chief as a wild-spending outsider with no care for the taxpayer. Eventually , enough powerful support was rallied to the cause of the police bond issue that it was placed on the ballot for public judgement. Unfortunately, the event was hailed as a victory for Vollmer over the city council.

The chief could not indefinately avoid partisanship. The opposition charged that the *Times* controlled the crime commission and through it hoped to influence all holders of public office. The *Record,* to refute the charge, sketched the crime commission's history, including Parrot's brilliant move in having Vollmer appointed on the advice of Shuler and Montgomery rather than the crime commission. The latter two, happy to have influence in high places, now opposed the crime commission at every turn, presumably carrying their followers with them. District Attorney Keyes, it was asserted, opposed the commission because it revealed corruption in the prosecutor's office. At this time, in answer to a question, Vollmer announced his loyalty to the crime commission. He would not have accepted the mayor's delegation, he said, had the commission not already received his agreement. In taking the side of the commission, the chief in effect set himself against the mayor. [23]

While the political quarrel raged, the *Record* renewed its old campaign against the mistreatment of vagrants. The only result was the further embarrassment of the chief. The crime crushers squad in the course of its duties arrested several blind street musicians and singers. The newspaper issued one or two vague warnings about "interference with the commercial use of God-given talents" and then enlarged the issue. A headline told of "800 Jobless Men Jailed in 70 days." The story revealed the hopelessness of the transients' situation. An example was a youth of eighteen years who received a suspended sentence of ninety days. He had neither money, job nor family but if he were found wandering on private property or in the public parks or begging or hitch-hiking or seeking a free ride on a freight train, he would have to serve the time.

The tragic death of an honored war veteran focused public attention on the plight of jobless men. The former soldier, found asleep at the Third Street tunnel, hurled himself down an embankment to his death to avoid arrest as a vagrant. Chief Vollmer again requested a city farm, where such men could work for food, lodging and a small wage. A twenty-four-hour court was suggested, so that innocent men charged as vagrants could be released at once, rather than spending one or more days in jail awaiting trial. Police Commissioner Birnbaum, with sudden forcefulness, announced that he would ask Vollmer to prevent further arrests for vagrancy. He visited the jails and remarked that he "would rather be in the dogpound." Just as suddenly, Birnbaum lost interest, perhaps because the ideas for reform came from the wrong side of the political fence. Despite newspaper criticism, the commissioner refused to help with the city farm or the twenty-four-hour court.

As always, there was support for the jobless among the general population but the business leaders encouraged the anti-vagrancy campaign. The sergeant of the vagrancy squad described his prey as "the scum of the earth." There were 150 men released from jail every day. That meant that the same number had to go into jail or the city would be over-run. The guiding principle of the vagrancy squad was bluntly stated in an official release approved by Chief Vollmer: "It is not our duty to support people who migrate to California with the idea that they can get rich quick here." The police attitude was applauded by the presidents of the Chamber of Commerce, the Los Angeles Realty Board, the Trades Council and the presiding police judge, Joseph Chambers. These individuals were engaged in forming a new civic booster association. Its device was a plain white lapel button and its motto was "Help Keep the White Spot White."

Public opinion as expressed in letters to the editor of the *Record* laid some of the blame for mistreatment of vagrants on the callous police force, but a good deal was reserved for the civic organizations that constantly publicized the glories of California to residents of eastern states. It was argued that lies were told, that workmen came for specific jobs that lasted only months and that many hard-working people, having lost their jobs, were now considered "scum." Even the *Record* had no sympathy for those who opposed boosterism. Perhaps for that reason the vagrancy issue was dropped, even though no perceptible change had been made. The newspaper fell happily upon the results of the Alpha tests. Again it seemed that with the friends he had, Vollmer needed no enemies.[24]

The sudden furor over the results of the police intelligence tests allowed the city council to harass the chief. When he asked for $25,000 to purchase options for the seven new stations, he was given $1,500. His budget of $5.5 million was reduced twenty per cent without examination. His request for 500 additional men was reduced to 250, although police officials argued that, based on population and area, 3000 extra men actually were needed to provide adequate protection. At every turn, considerations of economy eroded the great reorganization. Even general expenditures were reduced to ridiculous levels. When the chief jailer requested $100 to purchase clocks for the jails, council instructed him to go to a second-hand store and buy $5 worth of alarm clocks, rather than burden the taxpayers with such absurd costs.[25]

Political implications aside, the council's concern with the rising cost of police service was understandable. In the five year period from January 1, 1920 to January 1, 1925, the number of departmental employees rose from 732 to 2364, an increase in excess of 320%. Salaries for all ranks were increased by various amounts. The important item, patrolmen's wages, rose from $100-$120 to $140-$170 monthly. The annual budget, $1.3 million in 1921, rose to 3.9 million in 1923-24. The population increased about 40% but the cost per capita of the police department rose 80%, from $2.21 to $4.00, and would have been higher had the reorganization plan been financed through tax revenues.[26]

The long struggle in the council chambers took its toll of the chief, described as "tired, jaded, his voice nervously sharp." The end was near but one final indignity remained to be experienced. In a vigilante raid on the I.W.W. at San Pedro, six Wobblies were kidnapped, tarred and feathered. Vollmer was outraged, not alone at the perpetrators but at his men. He stated publicly that the commander of the San Pedro division was derelict in his duty. Not only had he failed to protect the I.W.W., he had made no effort to apprehend the criminals. The chief threatened to discharge the captain unless the kidnappers were arrested at once. The response to the chief's determination to enforce the law was a public attack by a delegation of business men for his criticism of the San Pedro commander.[27]

In saying farewell to Los Angeles, Vollmer remained true to his friends. He announced his resignation to a luncheon meeting of the crime commission on June 30, 1924. Not until July 8 did he submit a formal letter to Mayor Cryer. He admitted that the practise of reform was a great deal more difficult than the theory and that in attempting the reform of Los Angeles he had taken on more than he could handle. Nothing he could accomplish as police chief, he added, was as important as his work at Berkeley, training young men to be good police officers. He was not ashamed of his record, however. Arrests for the year increased over the previous year by 90% for burglary, 182% for robbery, 19% for felonies and 30% for misdemeanors. Most significantly, while the population increased about 12% the rate per capita for "hard" crimes was reduced by 10% over the previous year.[28]

By any criterion, August Vollmer had accomplished much. His functional reorganization of the department into separate divisions meant that for the first time in many years the chief commanded the department in fact as well as in law. As branches and bureaus were added haphazardly over the years, they were placed under control either of the captain of detectives or the captain of central division. These two officers became the real powers in the department. For example, vice suppression had been the concern of the central division commander, recently R. Lee Heath. When Chief Oaks forbade Heath to appoint a certain sergeant to the vice squad, Heath ignored the order on the ground that the vice squad was solely his responsibility. Heath's interpretation was concurred in by the police commission. After the reorganization, the chief had undivided power. Moreover, the position was under civil service protection, giving the chief legal tenure. An honest and determined executive, if he chose to do so, could eradicate protected crime in the city.

Second, Vollmer's basic theories of the need for scientific methods of detection, protection, administration, and selection and training of personnel, were accepted. In a relatively short time the city had its new jails and new police station, complete with common telephone, teletype and signal systems. A complete police laboratory replaced the lone chemist Vollmer had hired. The Alpha test became a permanent part of the selection process and the goal was approached of having the entire department within the upper range.

The personnel bureau, which kept records of each man's qualifications and professional performance, was an early victim of departmental malice but was later reestablished. A similar fate befell the police academy, one of the most vital parts of Vollmer's system. After one year of successful operation it was eliminated by the politicians. The school so impressed the policemen themselves, however, that subsequent chiefs continually pressed for its reorganization and eventually their efforts succeeded. Vollmer took over a directionless, unresponsive, inchoate city department. When he left, the foundations of an efficient modern police force had been laid.[29]

Vollmer proved that when the chief was under civil service protection, a rather small group of honest policemen could defeat organized criminals. Once, to refute innuendo about protected gambling, Vollmer led a secret raid. No one was told the destination until the police cars were in motion. The result was the elimination of one of the city's best-known casinos. Captain Clyde Plummer was then given control of the vice division. Plummer exhibited relative honesty and a disregard for constitutions, state or federal. With a picked squad and a strong battering-ram, he made up for years of frustration. Daily raids turned up hundreds of drug addicts and dealers, prostitutes, bootleggers and gamblers.

No enterprise was safe. In a drive against bootleggers, 300,000 gallons of mash was destroyed in a single raid on four adjacent houses on North Wall Street. Even the Ringe Ranch, where thirty miles of coast permitted the safe landing of contraband, was invaded. In the raid, a rum-runner ship was captured with $50,000 worth of liquor aboard. The case ramified into a million dollar scandal involving the Curtis Corporation of Long Beach. Some suspicion was cast toward the Los Angeles Athletic Club as well, concerning the $100,000 worth of liquors found stored in the cellars. It was typical of the times that all federal officers connected with the investigation were immediately discharged. Plummer's campaign went on relentlessly until some vice entrepreneurs actually suspended operations.

Chief Vollmer applied pressure in other ways. Any officer who arrested a known gambler was given two or three days paid vacation. Detective Captain George Home was removed from the parole board, denying criminals one route of escape from punishment. Vigorous complaints were directed at the practise of transferring vice cases from court to court until the "right" judge was found, after which dismissal or suspended sentence could be expected. The bail-bond business was curtailed by requiring the bondsmen to prove they owned the property on which their bonds were based. Nor were bondsmen or lawyers allowed in the jails or police stations unless a specific prisoner requested the services of a specific individual. This interfered with highly remunerative rackets designed to fleece the prisoners.

A double blow was struck at prostitution. The drive against massage parlors was renewed. At the same time, it was announced that those who forfeited bail would be arrested and arraigned. Usually, harlots were arrested, taken before the "right" judge, and released on $10 bail, which was forfeited and the case forgotten. Vollmer's plan meant that if the wrong judge heard the case, a fine and possibly a jail sentence would result. (The "right" judge would probably dismiss the case for lack of evidence, entrapment or similar grounds.) Since Vollmer and Plummer were careful in selecting judges, the prostitution rings faced tripled and quadrupled financial outlays plus the prospect of a reduced work-force.[30]

Going further, Vollmer demanded that the law-abiding citizens who sublet the properties used for vice be held responsible for the conduct of their tenants. He asked that the licenses of legitimate businesses be revoked if it could be shown that violations of the Volstead or other vice acts had occurred there. The chief actually obtained abatement orders and padlocked several hotels, ignoring the owners' pleas that they were unaware of conditions. These actions roused opposition of serious proportions. To defend himself, Vollmer threatened to publicize the name of any citizen or politician who tried to influence him, but he had created another group of powerful, hidden enemies.

Vollmer requested an ordinance that would permit charges to be laid against the patrons of clubs and other places where successful liquor raids were staged. Not only was this at variance with the chief's philosophy, it was aimed at a very broad section of society and would have created tens of thousands of anti-Vollmer partisans. The liberal element was already uncertain of the chief's ultimate goals. His wish to have the fingerprints of every resident on file at the police station and his request to the public to watch their neighbors and report any suspicious activities seemed dubious additions to a free society.[31]

There was a question, too, about police brutality. Vollmer demanded that his men observe the law, yet illegal detention and the "third degree" were standard procedures. Cruelty was so common that a deputy district attorney who visited an interrogation cell was severely beaten by police detectives before he could identify himself. No disciplinary action was reported. In a more tragic incident, a patrolman killed a youth who ran from a penny dice game when ordered to halt. Vollmer was silent. The district attorney refused to issue a complaint. The county grand jury brought an indictment in defiance of District Attorney Keyes, and the policeman was convicted of manslaughter.

The ACLU was in a continual quarrel with the department over brutality to Wobblies in the San Pedro area. All of this meant that while the chief's enemies grew stronger and more unified, his support steadily eroded.[32]

Vollmer's popularity within the department is difficult to assess. It might be expected that his refusal to overlook any crime—except traffic violations—would gain him the respect of all honest officers. The same might be said of his attempts to provide the most modern equipment, plant and training, higher salaries, more men and a reduced work load, not to mention his attempt to encourage public admiration and support for the police. On the other hand, he came from outside the department and his praise for the men in it was modest and sporadic. Small things aggravated them. The chief's refusal to give the band a day off to play on November 11 angered the musicians as well as the veterans. His ban on the acceptance of rewards was not well taken. In addition to these minor irritations there was a number of politically motivated officers whose aim was to demolish the chief, often using ammunition that he himself provided.[33]

Politics, of course, was the rock on which Vollmer's ship broke. He was not without blame. He misread the Central Avenue situation and tried to set up a power base independent of George Brown. This failed, although vice was closed down. His loyalty to the crime commission, while understandable was perhaps too overt. Without the crime commission, the reorganization would not have been possible. Only it could call upon five newspapers, the Chamber of Commerce, the Merchants and Manufacturers Association, the Better America Foundation and the leading service clubs; only it could contend at once with the city council, the district attorney and the Cryer-Parrot ring. At the same time, to give public support to the commission was to do more than snub the mayor who had appointed the chief. It was to raise in the mind of every elected official the suspicion that whatever was accomplished in the way of police reform would be credited to the crime commission, which would undoubtedly back a slate in future municipal elections.[34]

In an excess of zeal for his program Vollmer described the police bond opponents as "crooks, grafters and certain professional politicians." It was not clear whether or not he excluded the city council from the charge. Actually, the vice interests opposed the chief himself, not his system. Therefore, the bond issue passed easily although Vollmer had few reliable allies. The progressive leaders, Samuel T. Montgomery, Robert

P. Shuler and Gustav Briegleb were in the other camp with the vice operators, the district attorney, most of the councilmen and the mayor's circle. Only the crime commission remained, and even the commission made no effort to keep the chief in office beyond the agreed year.[35]

Probably it was known that Vollmer would not stay under any circumstances. Otherwise, the commission's lack of concern would be inexplicable. The commission had been bested in the political arena by the combined opposition but as long as Vollmer was chief, an honest, efficient police administration could be maintained. No doubt Vollmer understood this. He knew also that if he resigned, Mayor Cryer would appoint R. Lee Heath. Politics once again would determine police policy to the detriment of the public and the police. Vollmer was a civil service chief whose friends were extremely powerful; to frame his removal for cause would have been extraordinarily difficult even for Kent K. Parrot. Yet Vollmer chose to resign, or perhaps to escape. Billboards around town told where the victory lay when they announced: "THE FIRST OF SEPTEMBER WILL BE THE LAST OF AUGUST."[36]

NOTES

[1] *Examiner,* 8-22-23. For biographical details of Vollmer's life see Alfred E. Parker, *Crime Fighter: August Vollmer* (N.Y. 1961), Gene E. Carte, "August Vollmer and the Origins of Police Professionalism" (doctoral thesis, University of California at Berkeley, 1972), and O.W. Wilson, "August Vollmer," *Journal of Criminal Law, Criminology and Police Science* 44 #2 (1953) 91-103. His thoughts about police work were expressed in several books, of which the best is probably *The Police and Modern Society* (Berkeley, 1936). Specific police educational programs are described in about a dozen articles published in the *JCCPS.* Vollmer's ideas were expressed in a series of interviews published in the LA. *Record* under the title "The Policeman Today and Tomorrow," 8-18-23 to 1-16-24. See also John P. Kenney, "Administration of the Police Function in California," (doctoral thesis, University of California at Los Angeles, 1963), 42-125 *passim.*

[2] *Record,* 8-14-23, 8-17-23, 8-20-23, 8-21-23, 8-22-23, 8-27-23, 9-28-23, 10-8-23. LAPD *Daily Bulletin,* 8-6-23, 8-9-23, 8-14-23, 8-17-23, 9-4-23, 5-26-24.

[3] *Record,* 1-12-24.

[4] Vollmer was the main speaker at the first ACLU "Open Forum" in L.A. Discussing "The Policeman," he characterized oldtime police forces as "enemies of Society" but asserted that changes were taking place. *Record,* 9-2-23.

[5] LAPD *Daily Bulletin,* 10-5-23, 10-18-23, 10-20-23. *Record,* 9-29-23, 10-8-23, 10-11-23. 10-12-23, 10-13-23, 11-15-23, 11-21-23, 1-12-24, 3-11-24, 1-26-34.

[6] *Times,* 8-7-23, 8-10-23, 8-11-23; *Record,* 8-23-23, 8-28-23, 8-29-23, 10-3-23, 10-6-23, 10-31-23, 11-31-23, 12-4-23, 1-11-24, 1-17-24, 1-23-24, 1-25-24, 2-1-24, 2-7-24, 2-9-24, 2-27-24, 3-11-24; LAPD *Daily Bulletin,* 1-4-24, 1-11-24, 3-27-24, 4-17-24, 6-14-24.

[7] *Ibid.,* 9-23-23, 9-25-23, 12-9-23, 1-10-24, 1-21-24, 2-20-24. *Record,* 9-21-23, 11-6-23, 11-13-23, 11-17-23, 2-18-23, 1-2-24, 1-23-24, 1-24-24, 2-5-24, 2-15-24, 2-20-24, 3-4-24.

[8] August Vollmer, "Reorganization Plan," *Survey of the Los Angeles Police Department, 1923-1924.* The survey consisted of a collection of data and analyses of different parts of the program. The pagination was irregular and page numbers were sometimes non-existent. Vollmer's original copy is in the hands of the Berkeley Police Depart-

ment. Neither the *Survey* nor the *Annual Report* for 1924 were published. Copies are in the Council *Records. Record,* 2-2-24, 2-14-24, 2-21-24, 3-18-24, 3-25-24, 5-13-24, 5-14-24, 7-29-24. Council *Minutes,* 2-13-24, 2-14-24, 2-15-24.

[9] Vollmer *Survey,* "Survey of Intelligence," *passim. Record,* 12-19-23, 1-23-24, 5-21-24 to 5-29-24.

[10] Vollmer *Survey,* 1 and "School for Police" and "Survey of Intelligence," 3-30, esp. "Supplementary Table Showing Numbers of Cases Earning Scores Described;" *Record,* 3-22-24, 5-27-24.

[11] LAPD personnel records are no longer open to examination, as they were during the Progressive era. It seems logical that the relative permanence of the job was its most attractive quality, in L.A. as in other cities. See Richardson, *New York Police,* 172-180; also W.H. Parker, quoted in O.W. Wilson, *Parker on Police* (Springfield, Ill., 1957), p. 20. However, a remarkable sameness characterized police recruits in different cities: cf Vollmer *Survey,* "Occupations of Department Personnel Immediately Prior to Appointment," n.p.; Leonard V. Harrison, *Police Administration in Boston* (Cambridge, 1934), 36, 43; Bruce Smith, *Chicago Police Problems* (Chicago, 1931), 58; This may be due in part to a specific "police mentality;" see John L. Holland, *The Psychology of Vocational Choice* (Waltham, Mass., 1966), 110-111; the relatively low but stable status of policework is also apparent. See George S. Counts, "The Social Status of Occupations," *School Review* (33) 1925, 16-27; John A. Nietz, "The Depression and the Social Status of Occupations," *Elementary School Journal* 35 (1934-35), 454-461; R.W. Hodge, P.M. Siegal and P.H. Rossi, "Occupational Prestige in the United States, 1925-1963, *American Journal of Sociology* 70:3 (Nov. 1964) 286-302; however, police work seems to enjoy relatively high status among non-professional occupations; see J.J. Preiss and H.J. Erlich, *An Examination of Role Theory: The Role of the State Police* (University of Nebraska Press, 1966) 125 and note, 127-128.

[12] At least two men aged 72 were patrolmen in 1923. Requirements for 1921-22 were obtained from the Los Angeles Civil Service Department.

[13] W.H. Parker, quoted in O.W. Wilson, *op. cit.,* 7, 28.

[14] The problem of the single (usually low) standard was pointed out by Fosdick, 217-245. See Vollmer in the *Record,* 8-18-23. During 1922-23, only 17 men retired on pension. The average service was 24.6 years but 10 retired at exactly 20. P.C. *Minutes, passim;* LAPD *Annual Report* 1921-22; *Record,* 3-11-24. See also Preiss and Erlich, 87 and note.

[15] LAPD *Annual Report,* 1924-25, 8.

[16] *Examiner,* 8-3-23.

[17] Council *Minutes,* Oct., 1923 *passim; Record,* 9-5-23, 10-2-23, 10-3-23.

[18] P.C. *Minutes,* 10-7-23; *Record,* 1-15-23.

[19] The charges were true but politically motivated. *Record,* 8-2-23, 10-4-23, 10-6-23, 10-11-23; Commissioner De La Monte's decision to live apart from his wife of many years destroyed his political base among the church groups. *Ibid.,* 10-15-23, 11-2-23, 11-5-12, 11-13-23.

[20] *Ibid.,* 11-15-23.

[21] *Ibid.,* 10-5-23, 10-10-23, 11-14-23, 11-20-23, 11-27-23, 11-30-23, 12-3-23, 12-5-23, 12-8-23, 12-11-23, P.C. *Minutes,* 6-17-24.

[22] The Crime Commission, doubtful of Keyes' integrity,tried to prevent his interim appointment to succeed Thomas L. Woolwine, who retired due to a serious illness.

[23] Mushet's obstructive attitude on the Finance Committee throughout Vollmer's employment is apparent in the Council *Minutes,* esp. 3-17-24, 3-18-24; *Record,* 2-8-24, 2-14-24, 2-20-24, 2-21-24, 2-27-24, 2-29-24.

[24] *Ibid.,* 3-12-24 through 3-21-24, 3-27-24, 4-3-24.

[25] Council *Minutes,* 5-26-24, 5-27-24, 5-28-24; 6-5-24 through 6-17-24; *Record,* 5-28-24, 6-5-24.

[26] LAPD *Annual Report,* 1924-25, 5; *Monthly Labor Review* (1924) Table I, "Salaries of Employees in the Police Departments of Specified Cities," 74; there is some doubt about per capita calculations for Los Angeles during the 1920's. The booster mentality inflated population figures, so that per capita costs may have been higher than reported levels. Also, the police wanted to emphasize their overextended resources and to reduce the crime rate by artificial means. In 1925, the LAPD claimed to protect 1.1 million people and 1.4 million in 1929, but the 1930 U.S. census showed only 1.2 million residents. In 1926, the Bureau of the Census ceased to accept local population estimates from Los Angeles. One source estimated per capita cost at $4.00. See *American City Magazine* (Sept., 1924) 273. The California Taxpayers' Association set the figure at $3.54. *The Tax Digest* VII, 7, July, 1929.

[27] *Record,* 6-14-24, 6-17-24, 6-19-24.

[28] *Ibid.,* 7-1-24, 7-2-24, 7-8-24, 8-5-24.

[29] LAPD *Annual Report,* 1925-26, 8; *ibid.,* 1929-30, 5,15; *Record,* 8-1-24; Los Angeles Civil Service Commission, "Facts Concerning the Personnel of the Los Angeles Police Department," (Jan., 1932).

[30] As chief, Home was involved in curious parole proceedings which apparently he continued while commanding the detective bureau. See *Times,* 10-18-19; *Record,* 8-23-23, 10-9-23, 10-20-23, 10-31-23, 11-1-23, 11-7-23, 1-21-24 through 1-30-24, 2-9-24, 2-11-24, 2-13-24, 2-26-24, 3-13-24, 4-17-24, 4-25-24; *Times,* 7-22-23; LAPD *Bulletin,* 10-8-23, 6-24-24.

[31] *Record,* 9-19-23, 9-22-23, 10-19-23, 11-7-23, 2-27-24; LAPD *Bulletin,* 4-17-24.

[32] Deputy district attorney William J. Clark was the victim. There is no entry in the P.C. *Minutes* bearing on this event, although the *Record,* 9-27-23, asserted that Vollmer knew which officers were responsible. The policeman was convicted of manslaughter but was allowed to resign. The P.C. *Minutes* did not reveal the facts of the case.

[33] Vollmer's emphasis on crime control meant that traffic control suffered, for which he was continually criticized. *Record,* 11-6-23, 2-11-24, 7-2-24.

[34] Although Vollmer used "more spies than the Czar of Russia," George Brown asserted that whoever the chief set up as his Central Avenue representative would be used by Brown or by someone acting for Brown. *Record,* 3-20-24, 5-6-24.

[35] The members of the Crime Commission divided over the issue of control and distribution of electric power and irrigation waters that could be expected to flow from the proposed dam on the Colorado River at Boulder. This became the central issue of Southern California politics and remained so for several years, until the "public power" interests were victorious.

[36] *Record,* 7-31-24; Alfred E. Parker, 164.

CHAPTER FOUR

BOSS PARROT'S LOS ANGELES

Those "good old days." It is true that they were simple
times—the lines were clearly drawn. The police considered
themselves and the public to be separate entities. It was a
case of the police versus the public...They were simple times
but they were also ugly times. I do not remember them with
any great pride in the American police service.

William H. Parker[1]

The combination of conditions that led to Vollmer's departure and
to the subsequent disintegration of the crime commission produced an
important long-term victory for the machine over the progressives. Fifteen
years would pass before a genuine progressive mayor could be elected and
an honest chief appointed. During that period, the progressives continued
to elect "reform" mayors who, as in the past, proved to be either dupes or
willing allies of the combination. George Cryer, reelected in 1925, gave
way in 1929 to John C. Porter, a leading member of the 1928 grand jury
that indicated several important criminals and public officials. During
Porter's term, however, the municipal and police administrations nearly
collapsed due to outside interference in their operations. Frank L. Shaw,
who replaced Porter in 1933, allowed anti-libertarian and criminal interests to dominate the city to the extent that the reform movement burgeoned
and expelled Shaw from office before his official term ended.

Chiefs of police reflected political realities. R.L. Heath undid
much of Vollmer's work while praising him as a great police reformer.
The decline continued during the stewardship of Roy Steckel, Porter's
chief. Under James E. Davis, who served both Mayor Cryer (1926-29)
and Mayor Shaw (1933-38), the police force reached the lowest depths
of its dreary history. The LAPD became known for brutal, unconstitutional treatment of vagrants, "radical" labor and political organizers, and
critics of the municipal administration. However, it was the perennial
progressive crusade against protected vice that brought down the Shaw-
Davis administration and finally overthrew the combination.

Throughout the decade and a half when the so-called "invisible government" dominated the city, Kent Kane Parrot remained its most visible symbol. Parrot produced electoral victories for Mayor George Cryer in 1921, 1923 and 1925, and easily confounded an attempted recall in 1928. After abandoning Cryer in 1929 he continued to manipulate municipal events from a distance and exerted an indistinct but apparently significant impact upon federal, state and county politics in southern California.

Nevertheless, "Boss" Parrot remained a mysterious figure. He gave no interviews. The few available facts were gained second hand. He was born in 1883 and arrived in Los Angeles about 1906, where he obtained a law degree from the University of Southern California and entered local politics as a backstage schemer and influence peddler. Parrot rose to prominence in 1921, when he managed George Cryer's successful mayoralty campaign. Afterward he exploited the lucrative opportunities that control of the city business made available.

Parrot did not lack charm. The *Times*, his resolute enemy, described him as "a swaggering, more or less insolent and altogether colorful personality of imposing physique and personal magnetism." He usually spoke of administrators as "my appointments." "George" (Mayor Cryer) received little credit for the machine's success. Parrot's friends said that he ran the city for the "fun" of it but in the Boss' mind, fun had a clear correlation with profit.

The Boss suffered some minor setbacks. Mayor Snyder perceptively described Parrot as a corrupt office-seeker with designs on the Los Angeles harbor. When mayor-elect Cryer nominated Parrot to the Public Service Commission, the Municipal League and the Clean Government Association protested so strongly that the city council refused to ratify the appointment. A similar fate overtook the proposal to make Cryer's publicity agent, M.J. Daugherty, chairman of the Harbor Commission. Thereafter, Parrot contented himself with informal control of municipal departments.

Harbor Commissioner Charles E. Richards complained that "Mr. Parrot's sinister shadow" fell across the Commission's dealings "at every turn." Richards accused Dr. E.J. Lickley of the Los Angeles School Board of lobbying for Parrot as the Harbor Commission lawyer. The *Times* noted that J. Henry Wood, a civil servant appointed to audit the Harbor Commission books, was discharged when he attempted to do so. The Efficiency Commission had already described the books as "worthless." Parrot alone knew what went on at the harbor.

Even the discovery that Parrot had helped the telephone company to obtain a huge rate increase against the city's best interest did not diminish his power. The *Times* ridiculed Cryer as "Parrot's Puppet" but without effect. The *Times* observed that "the place to get action is the new offices of Kent K. Parrot, at Third and Broadway, overlooking City Hall, where Councilmen, City Hall lobbyists, politicians and citizens seeking administration favors rub elbows in the Parrot ante room."

Chief Louis Oaks asserted during the Oaks-Heath controversy that Parrot often summoned him to discuss police policy and to issue orders. Sometimes Parrot dealt directly with Oaks' subordinates, even transferring personnel without consultation. Finally, Parrot in effect dismissed Chief Oaks by writing out the order and then browbeating Mayor Cryer into signing it. Thus Parrot's protege, Captain R. Lee Heath, faced only a discredited adulterer in the confrontation that followed, not a powerful incumbent chief of police. It followed that Heath became chief of police when Vollmer resigned from the department.[2]

The appointment of R. Lee Heath fulfilled an old prophesy. Wise observers thought him the most powerful politician in the department, without whose cooperation no chief could succeed. They predicted his rise whenever an incumbent chief resigned or was discharged. Heath invariably disclaimed interest in the position. The reorganization under Vollmer altered the situation in fundamental ways. Civil service rules prevented arbitrary dismissal of the chief. The centralization of power in his hands significantly reduced the captains' authority. Control of the chief's office meant control of the police department. These facts, perhaps, plus increased salary and pension benefits, persuaded Heath to accept the post.

Heath's promotion emphasized the decline of the crime commission, which considered him the antithesis of a good policeman. Heath had admitted to the police commissioners that he disobeyed orders when it suited him, that he suppressed evidence when necessary and that he "played policy" in matters of vice suppression. When Heath commanded central division he allocated key vice squad personnel to suit the mayor's political advisers. A year earlier, the crime commission had helped oust Heath, only to see him reinstated and Chief Oaks discharged instead. Now, the commission declared meekly that it would support any honest chief. The promotion also disappointed August Vollmer, who had declined to recommend Heath as his successor.

Nevertheless, Heath possessed undeniable qualifications for the position. Heath was born in Pennsylvania in 1879. He arrived in Los Angeles in 1901, worked as a carpenter's helper and a streetcar motorman, and joined the police force in 1904. He took advantage of his talents and opportunities, gradually gaining a reputation as the most brilliant man in the service. He became a captain in 1918 and also won a law degree at the University of Southern California.

Later Heath practised civil law while commanding a police division. At the same time he was a partner with other officers in an undertaking firm. Prior to Vollmer, Heath directed the rudimentary police school, writing most of the texts himself. In the first civil service examination for chief, only Vollmer scored higher than Heath. Politics aside, Heath was the logical officer to succeed him.

Heath's fatherly appearance complemented his determination that "reason," "harmony" and "cooperation" should characterize his administration. Not over-modest, he accepted credit readily whether deserved or not and his public pronouncements, if less turgid than most police prose, were marked by an unusual hyperbole. (When the men gave him a gift, he remarked that he would rather have it "than receive from some other source the Kohinoor diamond.") Little homilies appeared in the *Bulletin:* "If there were no clouds, we could not enjoy the sun." During his term he continually urged the force to be polite to citizens and to show respect to newspapermen, for the good of the department. Heath's first executive innovation, the bureau of public relations, indicated the method he preferred.[3]

The new chief's term began pleasantly. Members of the force presented a jewelled badge and many floral tributes. The influential Breakfast Club gave a gold badge and conferred the degree of "Regular Fellow." Thomas Foss, named to the police commission when S.T. Montgomery resigned, declared his sorrow that Heath, "the best chief in history," did not receive the appointment in 1923 instead of August Vollmer. From the city council came an increase in secret service funds and the promise of 500 additional men. Heath responded that he would run the department efficiently, "as businessmen run corporations." With regard to vice, he declared the town "permanently closed."

This oldtime rhetoric fitted well with the traditional jewelled badges and floral tributes of the old days, which among other signs indicated a return to abandoned methods. Policemen could again accept rewards. Courtesy cards reappeared. A note in the *Bulletin* reminded officers not to be "careless" about returning recovered property. Orders forbade a host of petty but instructive violations: policemen must not attend public events in uniform to avoid paying admission; they must not congregate around the callboxes; they must avoid pool halls and movie houses while on duty; and they must not examine the pockets of dead or injured persons. One hypocritical order warned that political activism was grounds for dismissal.

Some questionable procedural changes occurred. A new regulation allowed the reduction of felonies to misdemeanors if done before charges actually were filed. Whatever the intention, this invited extortion and bribery. It soon became notorious that prisoners arrested for "felony drunk driving" were finally booked as "drunk," a misdemeanor. Prisoners remained in jail without charge until they raised enough money to have charges reduced. Jailers sometimes persuaded prisoners to hire lawyers or bailbondsmen who worked with police officers. This combination, called "running and capping," was a continuing scandal in the city and county jails.

Heath revealed another typical LAPD procedure when he threatened action against officers who waited so long to file charges that prisoners gained their freedom on writs of *habeas corpus*. The LAPD often held prisoners incommunicado for four, five or even seven days while detectives searched for legal reasons to charge. Heath had no concern for civil rights. If the prisoner's whereabouts became known a writ could be obtained and the individual might be released. Issuing writs required extra work on the part of judges and district attorneys, who then complained to the police commission, which complained to the chief. Conversely, the department was criticized for filing charges without proper evidence.[4]

During Heath's term, the existence of protected commercial vice became more difficult to deny. Although the newspapers ignored the vice issue most of the time, deadly competition between rival gangs for control of the bootlegging, gambling, and prostitution rackets produced a good deal of excitement and a number of corpses. Periodically the outraged reformers forced Heath to "detail every available man" to restore order, a tactic always more shadow than substance.

In October 1924, Councilman Robert Allan denounced Heath's "absolute indifference" to gambling casinos. Allan recalled that Vollmer managed to close vice premises "despite the fact that they pay high rents and wealthy property owners and rent collectors in the downtown districts were howling their heads off." Heath, who could close vice operations "in ten minutes, by telephone," challenged Allan to show him an open casino. The Church Brotherhood, vociferously taking Allan's comments at face value, scheduled an anti-vice crusade to begin in November.[5]

This was the ritual overture to any Los Angeles municipal election but a startling departure from tradition marked the 1925 campaign. The staid *Times* lamented "deplorable moral conditions" while the *Record* dismissed allegations of protected vice as "mere election propaganda." The reversed roles of the old antagonists defined a developing political quarrel which eventually overwhelmed municipal affairs. From mid-1924 until December, 1928, "the Colorado question" dominated Los Angeles and Southern California politics.

The issue was a congressional bill sponsored by Representative Philip Swing and Senator Hiram Johnson of California. The bill allowed the federal government to build and operate a high, water-storage and power-generating facility at Boulder, on the Colorado River. Irrigation water would flow to the Imperial Valley through an "all-American" canal, excluding Mexican farmland from its benefits. The alternative proposal provided for a low, flood-control dam, with power facilities in private hands.

"Public ownership" interests included the *Record*, the Cryer administration, the Municipal League, the California Progressives and similar groups, and the farmers of the Imperial Valley. Potential benefits to the area were so enormous that the capitalist Hearst, Earl and Vanderbilt newspapers also supported "public power." Opposed to the bill stood the private power companies, "anti-socialists" and the *Los Angeles Times*, whose publisher owned and irrigated about 300,000 acres in Mexico. In 1925, the mayor, city council and county district attorney faced the voters, followed in 1926 by the governor, lieutenant governor, U.S. senator and county sheriff. In every case, the candidate's stand on public versus private ownership of the Colorado River project determined his support.

Recognizing the long-term significance of the Boulder development, newspaper editors hesitated to criticize politicians for small failings if they remained "sound" on the Colorado issue. As the *Examiner* put it, "Every Candidate Must Pass the Colorado Test." Kent Parrot and H.H. Kinney disappeared from the *Record* pages. The *Record* became the champion of the Cryer administration, describing the mayor as a "statesman" worthy of the governorship, rather than Kent Parrot's puppet.[6]

The *Record* commenced vicious personal attacks on Harry Chandler of the *Times* and mounted a somewhat less vituperative campaign against the Chandler mayoralty candidate, federal judge Benjamin Bledsoe. Other newspapers preserved some degree of objectivity. Since Bledsoe, the "clean government" candidate, charged that protected vice and other civic corruption existed, condemnation of "those who would blacken the good name of Los Angeles" could be printed without naming Bledsoe or supporting Cryer, and strong support could be given to the Swing-Johnson bill without mentioning Chandler or the *Times*.[7]

The crime commission became the first casualty of Colorado River politics. The schism between the *Times* and other newspapers destroyed the commission's solidarity, although it continued as an effective conservative lobby for harsher state criminal laws. Because the other newspapers forbore direct criticism of the Cryer administration, the crime commission's collapse eliminated the only broad-based, influential and determined civic reform organization. The police department became almost unassailable. The *Record* discontinued its annual attack on police mistreatment of vagrants and unemployed men and printed the basic facts of criminal activities without comment. The other journals seldom printed police news. The *Times* maintained its policy of praising the department, especially the vagrancy and "red" squads, and focused its criticism on the corrupt men who controlled the administration.

The department did not escape entirely without censure. The religious reformers continued their battle against organized vice but without the newspapers they could not publicize their charges. Only the Reverend R.P. Shuler had a forum, an independent radio station provided by his followers. The radio preacher's poor reputation for veracity reduced his effectiveness among thoughtful citizens and his showmanship irked some conservative church leaders and laymen. The public enjoyed his wide-ranging attacks on politicians and police executives. Prior to the 1925 city election, Shuler broke with Parrot and turned against the Cryer machine. At that point he could not—alone or with the *Times*—elect or unseat public officials but his influence grew enormously during the following five years.[8]

The Parrot-Cryer organization maintained four distinct policies, aside from the general pro-business, anti-radical approach that all effective political groups adopted. First, the major criminal interests received protection regardless of threats or promises to eliminate vice. Second, the old, middle class, City Club progressives received unwavering support for public ownership of water and power utilities (at times the mayor suggested adding the telephone and transit systems). Third, the church-oriented, Protestant moral reformers were promised a city free of organized vice. Raids on Negro honky-tonks and Chinese opium dens, which frequently turned up white women, both titillated and pacified the reformers, and incidentally revealed the strong racial-sexual overtones of that kind of "reform." Fourth, the Central Avenue Negro vote was purchased with money and favors, including permissive vice conditions.

The difficult task of balancing the demands of the religious reformers against the needs of the Central Avenue district became impossible due to the Swing-Johnson impasse. The Negro precinct organization alone survived the reforms of 1909-1913, when the progressives abolished wards and established non-partisan election rules. The black bosses controlled the only significant, dependable block vote. With elections every year, fought on the Colorado issue regardless of the office at stake, no"off-years" allowed election promises to be forgotten. Although the new city charter of 1925 reduced the power of the block vote in the council by reestablishing councilmanic districts, its influence in citywide and county elections probably increased due to the influx of Negroes from elsewhere. The black leaders used their new power to extract a significant concession: aside from programmed "pinches," the police must tread carefully on Central Avenue, where illicit operations constituted the major industry and possibly the single largest employer.

Vice interests contributed large sums to campaigns for mayor, sheriff, district attorney and judge. In return, the big operators expected freedom from arrest and advance warning of raids. To protect the police, the vice operators occasionally "took a pinch." Perhaps once a month, police raiders captured a dozen or so players at each gambling location or well-known speakeasy and arrested prostitutes at agreed intervals. Ten or fifteen dollars bail was arranged and forfeited when the arrested persons failed to appear. Certain judges exonerated the bail so that no money was lost. Prostitutes usually received suspended sentences.

Continual raids ruined business, nevertheless. On the other hand, the police needed large numbers of raids and arrests to prove their honesty and zeal. In the past, raids on small-time operations in Chinatown, Sonoratown and especially along Central Avenue produced the necessary statistics. But now the requirements of politics foreclosed the Negro district.[9]

Forced to look elsewhere, the vice squads turned to the foreign neighborhoods, especially "Little Italy." Captain James Davis' men set new records each month as hundreds of "criminals" were brought in to be charged with possession of a pint or so of whiskey, or half a gallon of wine. The squads repeatedly broke into private homes and arrested families for having wine with dinner. The same conditions existed in the county, where the sheriff's men habitually raided the homes of those who obtained permits to make legal wine.

State Senator Joseph Pedrotti denounced the police for discriminatory enforcement. Jack Dragna, a mafia gangster, led the Italian-American Defense League, allegedly protecting his ethnic group from mistreatment by the authorities. Griffith Jones, the League's attorney, charged that bootleggers operated every night in almost every downtown building while the police busied themselves with pointless raids on respectable citizens. Although the county grand jury admonished both the police and sheriff's departments, the law enforcement agencies praised themselves for their record number of arrests. The raids continued.[10]

Periodically the competitive struggle in the underworld erupted into murder. Not only did competitors contend with the local syndicate but a new type appeared who preyed on the illicit rackets by hijacking liquor shipments and robbing gambling casinos. Reports of gunfire exchanged from speeding autos, liquor dealers shot down on the streets and thugs found dead in alleys became rather common, though no newspaper revealed the true extent of the warfare. The fact that the Irvine ranch had replaced the Ringe ranch as the favored spot to land contraband came to light when two would-be hijackers fled to a police station to escape vengeful bootleggers.

As the law enforcement situation deteriorated, Chief Heath admitted to some problems but denied the existence of protected bootlegging, prostitution or gambling. Few progressives believed him. Even before Heath's appointment, rumors foretold an "open" town. Heath responded that a few optimists might have prepared vice premises but "the time when they can open will never come." Large numbers of vice arrests seemed to prove the chief's sincerity. His reorganization of the vice squads clearly indicated a different reality.

Heath replaced Vollmer's vice commander with acting captain James E. Davis, a member of Heath's own central division vice detail during the infamous administration of Chief George K. Home. The most notorious policemen in the department, almost all of whom eventually were discharged for criminal activities, led Davis' squads. Most of their arrests resulted from "hip flask" raids against petty violators of the prohibition laws, penny ante gamblers and freelance prostitutes. The important criminals operated in safety.[11]

Robert Allan, the lone police critic on the city council, first asserted the existence of open vice after Milton "Farmer" Page wounded a patron in a casino on West Third Street. Page, a former newsboy become gambling kingpin, paid the expenses of the victim, who refused to file charges. Another known Page casino on West Sixth Street, and Chief Heath's public threat to file vice abatement proceedings against three dozen downtown premises, appeared to verify Allan's charges but the mayor and council refused to initiate an investigation.

In February 1925, less than four months later, Page killed Al Josephs in "Bert the Barber's" Sorrento Club at Sixth and Valencia. Josephs had opened a rival club but the police immediately raided it.

Josephs blamed Page and followed him to the Sorrento; Page therefore argued that he shot in self-defense. Though charged with murder, he was released on bail. The Ministerial Union demanded thorough enforcement of the laws and stated the Union's complete lack of faith in the city government and the police administration.

District Attorney Asa Keyes added a measure of hyperbole, announcing that he was "not going to temporize any longer." His picked squad would close a dozen well-known premises. He did nothing. Deputy Sheriff Frank Dewar reported that on two occasions when he raided Page's clubs, an LAPD car drove away as the sheriff's auto arrived. Police "tipped off" the gamblers, Dewar believed, since he found no evidence on the premises. Who in the sheriff's office warned the LAPD remained an unasked question.

The Reverend R.P. Shuler continued to slash at Parrot, Heath and Cryer from the pulpit and by radio. The *Times* traced the rise of Farmer Page and implied strongly that the police had protected his operations for at least eight years. Mayor Cryer and the *Record* rejected these allegations as an electoral smoke screen designed to hide the main issue, the Swing-Johnson bill. The police commission voted confidence in Chief Heath.[12]

With time running out, the *Times* accused Cryer of finding an issue "250 miles away" because local conditions would not stand scrutiny. Attacking Cryer's slogan, "Let George Do It," the Chandler paper argued truthfully that George did nothing and invariably left the city during crises. Kent Parrot suffered daily denunciations. Several unsavory developments were traced to his machinations. Reverend Shuler made a final appeal to his followers and to the Ku Klux Klan to ignore fellow klansman Miles Gregory, and vote instead for Chandler's mayoral candidate, Benjamin Bledsoe.

The *Times* and Fighting Bob could not defeat all of the other newspapers and the machine as well. "Shall We Re-elect Boss Parrot?" the *Times* asked, but the voters seemed more afraid of Boss Harry Chandler and the private power interests. Benjamin Bledsoe never overcame Parrot's devastating counter-slogan: "Harry calls him 'Ben.'" Mayor Cryer easily won an absolute majority in the primary election.[13]

The primary and regular elections of May and June, 1925 were the first under the present city charter, devised by the progressives and adopted by the electorate. The charter restored the ward system and raised the number of council members to fifteen from nine. Terms of office were increased to four years from two. The mayor no longer sat on the police commission. The new police commission, five members instead of three, served five-year terms, staggered so that (in theory) only one member could be replaced each year. The commissioners could not be removed by the mayor without consent of the city council, which also approved their appointment.

Old progressives who had eschewed city politics for years participated in the charter campaign. As always, the framers had distinct ends in view. The ward system eliminated their former strength, the bloc vote, theoretically reduced the possibility of a council bloc and provided local representation for a growing metropolitan area. Removing the mayor from the police commission removed politics from the police administration. The police commission structure prevented control of the police from passing suddenly from one political group to another. The four-year term reduced costs and increased efficiency. Perhaps the most revealing aspect of the 1925 charter was the fact of machine support. Whatever the progressives may have intended, the combination apparently had little to fear.[14]

The anti-vice campaign did not end with the election. The dropping of murder charges against Milton Page angered the progressives. Councilman Allan identified eight clubs owned by Page, one in premises owned by the Lankershim estate, another on property owned by a company headed by William Gibbs McAdoo. This seemed to substantiate the old rumor that respectable businessmen had an interest in commercial vice. Then a machine-gun war broke out between the Page syndicate and Tony Cornero, an independent rumrunner who refused to join the combination or to look elsewhere for markets. Bogus federal agents seized one of Cornero's liquor boats. Others hijacked his trucks. Cormero's counterattack left several Page gunmen near death. As usual, the newspapers tried to suppress the story but city officials were forced to act when, inevitably, the details became known.

The authorities responded in an interesting manner. They first released a list of wanted criminals to the newspapers and then mounted a "cleanup" sweep which netted 200 alleged criminals despite the warning. A good deal of aggressive rhetoric followed. The public learned of twenty squads of "hard-eyed, heavily armed detectives" who patrolled constantly, ready to oppose any influx of "eastern gangsters." Chief R. Lee Heath, Sheriff William Traeger and District Attorney Asa Keyes, with their vice and homicide squad commanders, ordered Farmer Page, Tony Cornero and their imported gunmen to leave the city. On August 8, 1925, Milton Page left his hometown forever. In this case, "forever" amounted to sixteen days.

This incident apparently cost Page his place at the head of the gambling rackets. Perhaps he became "too hot" to be allowed to continue. He played a much reduced role in subsequent years. In his place rose Guy McAfee, the former vice squad officer who probably had been the "tip-off man" inside the police department.[15]

Allegations of protected crime introduced the public to two antagonists destined for local fame: Albert Marco, a flamboyant underworld boss, and Carl Jacobson, an austere councilman from the thirteenth district. Marco, an Italian immigrant, controlled a "stable" of prostitutes and several speakeasies. The Norwegian-born Jacobson, a Protestant, Republican insurance salesman, typified the moral reformers.

The facts seemed plain enough. A young patrolman arrested Marco for assault with a deadly weapon. Two detectives then reduced the charge to "disturbing the peace" and released Marco on bail. City Prosecutor Jacob "Jack" Friedlander said he issued no complaint because the officers "wanted more time to think it over." Jacobson claimed that the arresting patrolman faced dismissal if the felony charge was entered, and vainly demanded an explanation from Chief Heath. Some councilmen purported never to have heard of Marco but Councilman Robert Allan quickly provided a review of the vice lord's career and addresses of places he operated. Allan and Jacobson failed to instigate a full investigation by the council, however, and the complaint was filed.

Needless to say, Marco did not stand trial for assault but the case had interesting ramifications. By coincidence, the Internal Revenue Service was then investigating Marco and revealed that he banked $500,000 in the period 1922-1924. It seemed that crime paid, and paid well. The twenty-four year old Cornero also was known as a "millionaire." Rumors passed that two detectives recently sent to "the sticks" were there because they interfered with Marco's prostitution racket.

Furthermore, Marco, an alien forbidden by law to possess a firearm, had a permit to carry a concealed weapon. Investigation showed that Marco, Cornero and others obtained their permits through the county sheriff's office. Sheriff Traeger denied that he signed any permits; that duty fell on the undersheriff, a careful young politician named Eugene W. Biscailuz. Fortunately for all concerned, the original applications for gun permits disappeared mysteriously from the sheriff's files. Whether the applicants perjured themselves or the undersheriff issued permits to aliens and convicted felons in defiance of state and federal law would never be known.[16]

Chief R. Lee Heath, his retirement less than a year away, avoided center-stage as much as possible. Only the absence of relentless newspaper criticism made his position tenable. By any honorable criterion his administration was a disaster. Allegations of protected vice could be denied and the rising incidence of felonious acts by policemen overlooked but serious complaints from influential sources could not be passed off as mere politics. In sum they produced a dismal portrait of the LAPD.

Detective Captain George K. Home, it was alleged, arranged to prevent a fake kidnapping of American's Sweetheart, Mary Pickford, in order to boost his campaign for county sheriff. The county grand jury declared Captain L.L. McClary unfit to hold office and asked that he be dismissed. The Civil Service Commission reached a similar conclusion about Captain Jonathan Finlinson and requested his discharge. Governor Friend W. Richardson severely criticized Captain James Bean for inefficient police work. The Police Commission's investigator, Lieutenant Morris Posner, was removed to alleviate grave misgivings about his conduct in office. None was discharged or disciplined.

Heath's transfers of personnel did little to inspire confidence in the police department. On the other hand, he may have lacked the political authority to reform the upper levels of the department. Early in his term he transferred George Home to Sawtelle, the "graveyard." Home, with the strong backing of the *Times*, returned to central division within two months, commanding a larger unit than before. Chief Heath said the transfers were part of a planned reorganization. Nor could Heath prevent the rise of Captain L.L. McClary, a leader of the equally corrupt opposition faction within the department.

Heath did manage the humiliation of his old enemy, ex-chief Louis D. Oaks. Oaks, on leave of absence since his dismissal by Cryer, applied for a disability pension on grounds of a severe kidney ailment. When Oaks ousted Heath, Heath, "with a wintery smile," had promised that "if ever the wheel should turn, and I find myself in the position you are now in, I shall treat you with equal courtesy." The wheel had turned. Louis Oaks was discharged for chronic alcoholism and repeated adultery.[17]

Heath's political influence outside the department did not match his reputation as an effective politician. In view of his relationships with business leaders through such organizations as the Breakfast Club, his complete failure to expand and modernize the police force is the more remarkable. The council reneged on its promises of more men, money and machines, and the mayor's reduction of departmental budgets removed financial leeway. Because Heath failed to obtain the pay increase promised to Vollmer (from $140 - $170 to $170-$200 monthly), many police recruits resigned shortly after graduation from the academy. Despite periodic praise from

Parrot's appointees, Heath's only accomplishments were the Bureau of Public Relations and the pistol range in Elysian Park.

In 1926, Heath retired to practice law and politics but first he attempted to have his brother, Captain Cleveland Heath, appointed chief. Nepotism failed but the appointment of James E. Davis indicated a victory for Heath over the opposition candidate, Captain L.L. McClary. Heath's farewell address struck the traditional notes, describing the department as "one of the outstandingly honest and efficient police organizations in the world." and wishing to his successor "the same comradely and loyal service and helpfulness that brought such happiness and success to me."[18]

During the first three years of Cryer's final term (1925 - 1929) Parrot managed the political situation with relative ease. An attempted recall early in 1928 failed to gather even a quarter of the signatures needed to put the matter to a vote, as the administration continued to benefit from the still unresolved Colorado question. Although the progressive-machine victories in the 1925 and 1926 elections made the issue somewhat less immediate, newspapers other than the *Times* still refrained from direct, penetrating criticism of the municipal government. When the Swing-Johnson bill finally passed, late in 1928, the journals then joined in a continuing, relentless attack on the Parrot machine and especially the police force.

Cryer's arbitrary twenty-seven percent reduction of the 1926-1927 departmental budget closed the police academy, undoing the most important part of Vollmer's work. Formal recruit training and evaluation stopped. The general caliber of recruits declined. The council refused to authorize personnel increases to match population growth. The number of crimes by policemen increased. The department steadily became worse (although this malady affected most urban police forces during the late 1920's). The character of the chief also was important but here the machine faced an unresolvable dilemma. No one could successfully protect the combination and reduce its competition, provide adequate protection to the general public, and suppress vagrancy and radicalism to suit the reactionary interests.[19]

It is conceivable that "running on the record" of low taxation, frugal administration, devotion to public power and similar issues, Parrot and Cryer might have won again in 1929. Maladministration of the police department, however, compensated for the lack of firm evidence that somehow the machine gathered illegal profits at the taxpayers' expense. The department became embroiled in a series of sensational scandals. Cossackism and corruption eventually alienated almost all of the adult population. More than any other single factor, maladroit police work doomed the Parrot-Cryer organization.[20]

The importance of "public power" notwithstanding, much of Parrot's success undoubtedly resulted from good management. No open scandals occurred while the Boss controlled the city's commercial transactions. Two councilmen convicted of suborning bribes had no connection to the machine. Indeed, the taxpayers received a beautiful, modern city hall from the Parrot-Cryer ring, within the scheduled construction time and at less than the scheduled cost. In contrast, the County Hall of Justice cost about three times the original budget and began to fall apart before the dedication ceremony. In grudging admiration, the *Times* suggested an ulterior motive: Boss Parrot hoped to facilitate a take-over of the County government by impressing suburban folk with his vision and efficiency.

The Parrot-Cryer organization contributed to its own demise by becoming less progressive. Whereas the machine supported the Protective League and the pension agreement of 1922, the Vollmer bond issue and reorganization in 1924 and the city charter of 1925, it subsequently responded to the demands of taxpayers' organizations and drastically reduced police spending. The city council refused even to vote the pay increase promised to Vollmer. In 1926, the Protective League had to sponsor a ballot initiative in order to obtain the salary increase. The machine did not oppose the initiative, which the electorate duly passed. However, the administration imposed a new pension system which required police contributions.

Chief James E. Davis, the first General Manager appointed by the new, "non political" police commission, directed the LAPD through the final years of the Cryer administration. Davis, appointed at thirty-seven, had fourteen years of police experience, most of it as a patrolman. He scored a very respectable 156 on Vollmer's Alpha test and had an Officer's Rating of 88.5 percent. His reputation rested on sporadic but effective vice raids, usually during election campaigns. In 1924, Chief Heath placed Davis in command of the vice details, where he developed some improved reporting techniques. In 1925, although he ranked higher on civil service promotion lists, he stood aside and allowed two older officers to advance.

Davis became chief on April Fool's Day, 1926. By the most significant criteria—policeman, administrator, and "system" man—he had proved himself. Furthermore, his hardshelled fundamentalism suited the dominant religious persuasion. His poverty-stricken west Texas upbringing apparently nurtured a deep admiration for rich and powerful men and encouraged a ferocious opposition to "radicals" who questioned the status quo. His subsequent encouragement of the Red, Vagrancy and Intelligence squads earned him the unwavering support of the *Times*, the M&M and the Better America Federation[21]

Davis, like several other chiefs, wanted the fingerprints of every Los Angeles citizen on file at police headquarters. Captain George Home even proposed a system of local passports, so that migrants could be turned away if their documents indicated a police record or inadequate financial resources. Davis opposed the use of search warrants in liquor cases because police raids often were made on the basis of information that later proved to be mistaken or malicious. Arrests seldom resulted in these cases, which meant that the time spent obtaining warrants had been wasted. City Attorney E.P. Werner eventually ruled that the police were required to obey the state constitution, which repeated federal strictures governing illegal searches and seizures. The Anti-Saloon League denounced Werner's decision as "a backward step in law enforcement."

The chief and police commissioners occasionally published orders in the *Daily Bulletin* forbidding verbal and physical abuse of citizens or prisoners. Fines, suspensions and dismissals were administered for individual brutal acts. On the other hand, the verbal violence of Chief Davis and his general disregard for constitutional guarantees set an example that probably produced more aggressive police behavior than his orders prevented. Given the rugged frontier and seaport traditions of the local police service, the callous attitude toward "vagrants," "radicals" and "criminals" that the *Times* and similar sources encouraged, and the undermining of Davis' disciplinary powers by outside political interests, it can be argued that the cossacks were inevitable.

Davis understood and encouraged solidarity among his men. It was "only natural" that policemen refused to testify against fellow officers accused of brutality. Officers who physically punished persons who insulted them also acted naturally. The populace thus received fair warning: anyone who antagonized a policeman and was beaten for it had himself to blame. Many complaints of police brutality were filed with the notation: "Officer was within his rights."

Brutality in the jails, including the abuse of prisoners during interrogations, received an interesting justification from Deputy Chief Clyde Plummer. According to Plummer, only two percent of humanity turned to criminal activity. Of that portion, however, sixty of every hundred were diseased in mind and body, while others exhibited a very low mentality. The point seemed to be that criminals understood pain and very little else.

Some kinds of criminals suffered more than others. Police arrested known narcotics addicts on sight and charged them with vagrancy. Once in jail, "this particularly worthless type of offender" received no milk, coffee, sugar, butter, tobacco, candy, reading matter, games, visitors or time off for good behavior. They deserved only "beans and abuse," said Davis. "That is my stand and I won't back down on it."

"Eastern gunmen" drew the chief's most bombastic threats. Davis, a nationally famous marksman, had killed one man in the line of duty. He believed that accurate police shooting represented the greatest deterrent to criminals. Announcing the formation of a fifty-member "gun squad," Davis declared that "the gun-toting element and the rum smugglers...are going to learn that murder and gun-toting are most inimical to their best interests." After detectives slew a suspected killer, Davis warned that his men would "hold court on gunmen in the Los Angeles streets." "I want them brought in dead, not alive," he asserted. "If the courts won't eliminate them, I will." He then named one of the Cornero brothers as "next" on the gun-squad's schedule. [22]

The fate of Mileaway Thomas, suspected killer and hijacker, raised grave questions about the gun squad's activities. Police questioned Thomas on a dozen separate occasions but his alibi, that he was "a mile away," proved unbreakable in each case. The hijacker's career ended in a garage at Thirty-Fifth Street and Normandy one April night in 1927. Thomas, confident that the building contained a liquor shipment, received a fatal blast from a shotgun when he opened the doors. Newspapermen believed that Detective Richard Lucas, the "dirty work man" for the Cryer administration who killed Thomas, enticed him there by personally telling him of the liquor cache. Neither Lucas nor Chief Davis denied the allegations. [23]

The chief professed dismay at the lack of public respect for law and criminal justice but openly blamed the courts for the serious crime situation. In return, individual judges excoriated the LAPD. Unfortunately, exchanges that might have been ludicrous, if unbecoming, had grave results. One example involved two officers who committed a residential burglary. The householder identified one offender, who then implicated his partner. Due to the inability of the householder to identify the second man and the absence of a corroborating witness, the judge dismissed the second officer for lack of evidence. The police commission then restored the known felon to duty. The infuriated judge suspended sentence on the convicted policeman. The police commission criticized the judge for releasing a confessed criminal but restored him as well. Thus the department employed at least two known burglars.[24]

A tragic event in the black community had comparable results. A police vice raider fired several shots into a house, accidentally killing the occupant and wounding the officer's partner. The policeman placed a gun near the dead man's hand and accused him of shooting the wounded officer. Two passing patrol officers agreed to corroborate this story. The police persuaded a petty criminal to hide narcotics in the dead man's residence to provide "probable cause" for the raid. Chief Davis commended the policemen, all of whom were black. Negro community leaders forced the administration to reopen the case. The two patrolmen pleaded guilty to perjury, received five-year suspended sentences and were discharged from the department. The wounded officer admitted to perjury, was released and reinstated by the police commission. The commission also reinstated the vice officer who fired the fatal shots.[25]

The most nefarious policemen led details of the vice, vagrancy, radical and intelligence squads, setting an example and maintaining a tradition of brutal, unconstitutional and dishonest law-enforcement. They typified the new definition of policeman: "an official who breaks ten laws while enforcing one." Discounting the jailers and such men as Captain J.J. Jones, about a dozen of the unlovely lot deserved special mention.

Sidney "Sweety-pie" Sweetnam, an Irish immigrant discharged over the Woodman scandal in 1919 for protecting brothels, won reinstatement on a technicality of the sort that so often suited the machine's needs. Subsequently, he was named on numerous complaints of vice-squad depredations. Richard Lucas, indicted in 1920 for violation of the prohibition laws, also won reinstatement. After several mysterious shooting incidents and the killing of Mileaway Thomas, he was forced to resign for his part in the attempted entrapment of a councilman. Later testimony alleged that Lucas participated in a highly remunerative racket while serving as an officer. In time he was again reinstated.[26]

E.D. "Roughhouse" Brown, a huge man known as "the king of East Fifth Street," won early fame due to his singlehanded defeat of a squad of sailors. His effect on vagrants can only be imagined. When Al Capone came to Los Angeles, Brown was sent—allegedly by the Combination—to bid the Chicago gangster a speedy goodbye. Capone left town soon afterward. James Howry and Charles Hoy were less colorful detectives who operated with Sweetnam, Brown and Lucas. Like the others, Howry and Hoy were frequently named in citizen complaints. M.B. "Mose" Sheffield was a fearsome black officer who literally got away with murder. His partners, Frank Randolph and Thomas Washburn, were only somewhat less terrifying.[27]

William "Red" Hynes led the radical, or "Red" squad. Hynes gained a national reputation for blatant disregard for constitutional guarantees. With good reason, civil libertarians believed the squad to be an arm of the Merchants' and Manufacturers' Association, paid to stifle labor union organization and social or political radicalism. In Los Angeles, radicalism appeared to be equivalent to free speech, so Hynes had the help of the city council in limiting free expression. Chief Davis gave Hynes a free hand, which alone ensured the *Times'* powerful support, but Davis held similar ideas. Like many policemen, he accepted himself as an authority on the Red Menace.[28]

Although questions were later raised regarding Hynes' unusual affluence, the red squad leader had no apparent connection with the machine's criminal operations. This could not be said of Earl E. Kynette, reinstated by the police commission after the police trial board voted to fire him for extorting money from prostitutes. Kynette, an alleged agent of the Combination, moved to the intelligence squad, where he searched for scandals in the lives of the administration's critics. Kynette became the most infamous policeman in LAPD history.[29]

Davis also employed irregulars whose conduct shamed the department. Detectives in America traditionally were raffish types whose effectiveness was due to their semi-criminal life-styles. Harry Raymond embodied the old way, an efficient but amoral investigator who resigned in 1920 to save Chief Home embarrassment, returned in the mid-Twenties and resigned again after another scandal in 1928. Max Berenzweig, like Raymond, could not meet civil service requirements but suited the machine. In 1919, Chief Butler dismissed him as "unfit" to be a special policeman. In the early Twenties he continually appeared in newspaper accounts of police news as someone whose avid interest in police work led him to help the force, even to lending automobiles and going on raids. By 1924, reports mentioned "Lieutenant Berenzweig." Captain Clyde Plummer later discharged him but Davis restored him to duty. In 1929, he commanded a vice squad detail.[30]

The story of Captain J.J. Jones and Walter Collins appalled and outraged all but the most adamant defenders of the police. While serving in the Children's Bureau, Jones compelled a distraught woman to accept a strange child as her own missing twelve-year-old son, Walter Collins. After consulting with neighbors and school personnel, she returned the boy to Jones, only to be committed for psychiatric examination because

of her "unnatural conduct." That same day, an eyewitness revealed that
Walter Collins and several other young boys had been murdered by a
sadistic youth. Jones continued to insist that he had Walter Collins in
custody. Mrs. Collins, found sane and released after five days of "obser-
vation," had in the meantime lost the clerical position that was her sole
source of income.

Responding to a public outcry generated by newspaper reports, the
police commissioners reviewed the facts, found Jones guilty only of "hasty
judgement," and dismissed the matter. Fifty business leaders, led by Harry
Chandler, praised the commissioners' action. Popular fury reopened the
case. The Reverend Shuler and the Reverend Briegleb exhorted mass public meetings. Both the grand jury and the city council threatened to investigate. The police commissioners again convened and levied a four-month
suspension on Jones. This stilled the immediate clamor but did nothing to
refurbish the shabby reputation of the city police.[31]

Even more astounding revelations followed the arrest of Councilman Carl Jacobson for a morals offence. The police stated that an anonymous complaint of a wild party led them to a house at 4372 Beagle
Street. As they watched, a man arrived and entered the house, where-
upon the officers entered and found Jacobson in his underwear, lying on
a bed with a nude woman. The councilman allegedly identified himself
and admitted his guilt, describing himself as "only human." Jacobson, a
severe police critic known also as "Marco's nemesis" for his constant
attacks on the vice-lord, described the affair as "a frame-up" and
demanded a jury trial. Shuler and Briegleb convened mass meetings of
Jacobson's allies. The councilman said he was framed because he
accused the police of protecting gamblers. The police said that even if
Jacobson's political enemies had framed him, "the police did not lead
him out there or remove his clothes or those of the woman."

The case had many curious aspects. Usually a vice squad included
a sergeant and three detectives. In this instance, responding to an ordinary "anonymous complaint," Captain Bert Wallis, commander of the
vice division, Captain Frank Williams, commander of the intelligence
squad, Detective Lieutenant Richard Lucas and Special Investigator
Harry Raymond rushed out to make the investigation after informing the
Times' crime reporter that something was going to happen.

After the arrest, the squad went to the home of Rodney Webster,
president of the police commission, who accompanied them to the jail.
There District Attorney Keyes appeared and with Webster elicited an
admission from Jacobson of an immoral interest in the woman, Helen

Ferguson. But the woman was found to be actually Callie Grimes, sister-in-law of Frank Cox of the LAPD vice division. Jacobson claimed that the police offered to withdraw the charge if he gave them an affidavit admitting his guilt, which he refused to do.

At the trial, the police officers repeated their story. Jacobson testified that the woman, a ratepayer in his district, made many requests for a meeting to discuss local improvements. When, enroute home, he visited her residence, she offered him liquor, which he refused. She then left the room, the lights went out and the police suddenly arrived. The jury refused to convict Jacobson of lewd conduct and he resumed his role of police critic.

In November of 1928, Mrs. Grimes went before the county grand jury and repudiated her previous testimony. She said that Albert Marco tried to silence or destroy Jacobson. Through Cox, the vice detective, he offered her a $2,500 cash payment and $100 per month for life if she maneuvered the councilman into a compromising position. According to her information, Marco, Chief Davis, District Attorney Keyes and Police Commissioner Webster were behind the plot. The grand jury quickly indicted Marco, his associate Charlie Crawford and police officers Wallis, Williams, Lucas, Raymond and Cox, on charges of criminal conspiracy.

At the subsequent police trial, the jury divided 11-1 for conviction. Evidence of jury tampering justified a second trial. The prosecution proved that Mrs. Grimes had been seen with Lucas and Raymond before the event, that the squad waited two hours for Jacobson to appear, that they could not provide a single example of a similar raid on an anonymous tip and that the vice squad log showed no entry for the day in question. The judge ruled that the "resorting" ordinance did not apply to private homes, making the arrest illegal in any case.

The defence attorneys, including Jerry Geisler and Grant Cooper, argued that Jacobson paid Mrs. Grimes to testify, but their best witness was Jacobson himself. For the first time he charged the police with hitting him from behind and knocking him unconscious. When he regained his senses, he said his trousers were in Captain Wallis' possession. The issue then rested on whether the councilman's pants were removed willingly or unwillingly. The jury divided 6-6 and was discharged. Another tampering charge started another grand jury investigation but the new district attorney, Buron Fitts, withdrew the charges and closed the case.

The police commission wanted to dismiss the accused officers but the city attorney ruled that they must be reinstated. Wallis, Williams and Cox were protected. Richard Lucas, "the dirty work man," had to resign.

Harry Raymond also departed for the second time. Commissioner Webster, arrested for selling meat to the city jails in violation of law, resigned.[32]

Between the trial of Jacobson and the trials of the police officers, Albert Marco was convicted on two separate charges. Federal officers raided Marco's speakeasy, the North End Pleasure Club, and captured Marco and some illegal liquor. Two LAPD detectives found in the place vainly assured the raiders that Marco sold only "near beer." Marco threatened to "have the jobs" of the raiders. They were in fact discharged but the case was won in federal court. Marco received a six months sentence.

An appeal was entered. While waiting for the decision, Marco wounded two people in a shooting affray in the Ship Cafe at Venice. The vice-lord was captured by Patrolman J.W. Brunty, who refused a proffered bribe of $1500. After much legal maneuvering and two trials in which the prosecution was suspiciously weak, Marco received two "1 to 10 year" sentences. He served four and one-half years before being deported.

In the county jail, Marco received extra privileges. He spent much time in the hospital, where conditions were more pleasant. He went out to lunch, as Undersheriff Biscailuz discovered to his horror one day while dining at a favorite restaurant. Although Marco's hotel was closed under the *Red Light Abatement Act,* he conducted his prostitution business through his assistants, Augusto "Chito" Sasso and June Taylor. In San Quentin he again received the privileges due visiting underworld royalty.[33]

Joining Marco in San Quentin were Asa Keyes, the former district attorney and his chief trial deputy, Harold "Buddy" Davis. Under Keyes, not only did the guilty go free, if they had money and hired the right lawyers, the innocent sometimes went to prison. Those offenders who could not be released through withdrawn charges or lost cases could escape by way of the parole system. Herbert Wilson, a famous burglar who killed an associate in the county jail, said he paid Keyes $50,000 to avoid the death penalty. The Julian Petroleum crash allowed the financial, social and criminal elite of the area to rob the 40,000 stockholders of a sum in excess of $40,000,000. Keyes received $1,650,000 to divide as required to save the looters from the law. Keyes' share amounted to $165,000. [34]

The rogue policemen of the LAPD were equally corrupt. Whether or not Chief Davis controlled them is problematic. He could ignore complaints about the red and intelligence squads but not about vice conditions. Numerous reorganizations of the vice division and extensive reassignments of personnel were pretences intended to satisfy the reformers. A single, central vice squad could protect criminal operations because its members could decide which premises to raid and which to avoid. Separate vice details in each police division tended to eliminate vice except in those areas where "the fix" was maintained.

Chief Davis decentralized the vice division in October, 1926, threatening to dismiss any captain who failed to keep his division "clean." The vice squad was centralized again in June, 1927, divided in May, 1928, reunified in October of the same year and again decentralized in December, 1928. Throughout the period, copies of all vice reports were supposed to be sent to the chief's office, ostensibly so that headquarters could easily discover whether or not action was taken to investigate complaints.

Despite the chief's orders, some policemen declined to submit vice reports. These officers refused to be license inspectors for the machine. They knew that vice reports were used to control or eliminate competition. Vice operators who came to terms with the administration continued to do business; others were raided as soon as they were discovered. Transfers of vice squad personnel failed to reform the division, since the few key men soon returned. The real purpose of the transfers may have been to break up local protection rackets organized without reference to the machine. With so much graft allegedly going "upstairs" it was not surprising that the lower ranks occasionally extorted some for themselves.[35]

Reorganizations and transfers did not silence Davis' critics, especially Robert Shuler and his followers. The chief argued that the city was clean but also praised the vice squads for record achievements. Davis blamed the district attorney and the courts. Three convictions sustained on vice arrests at a given premise required the prosecutor to begin abatement proceedings. Neither Asa Keyes nor Buron Fitts acted on the cases Davis supplied every month. Few premises were padlocked. Vice continued.[36]

The chief also noted that the law set specific penalties for slot machine operations, yet most judges levied fines far below the legal minimum. Davis was correct. Certain prosecutors and judges served the underworld. The police also took a selective approach to slot machine control, seizing some but ignoring others. Perhaps some judges refused to act as a tariff board for the syndicate and returned the independent slot machines to competition.[37]

In 1929, a municipal election year, the department made a perfect target for reformist rhetoric. With the backing of the *Daily News,* Councilman William Bonelli entered the mayoralty campaign, promising to rebuild the police force. John Clinton Porter, foreman of the 1928 grand jury that indicted Asa Keyes and Albert Marco, also ran as a police reformer. Porter, a member of the board of directors of the Los Angeles County Church Brotherhoods, had the backing of Robert Shuler and the

Record. The *Times* supported John R. Quinn, a senior officer of the American Legion. No one backed Cryer; indeed, even Kent Parrot severed his connection with "George." The mayor who had swept every election since 1921 had to withdraw from the race.[38]

Porter won. He made no immediate move against Davis but a series of unfortunate events put the chief in an untenable position. The trial of the Jacobson framers dragged on until July. Two heinous murderers escaped due to blundering police work. Incidents of police brutality received much publicity. At the end of August, Harry "Bathhouse" McDonald, a major bootlegger, revealed that although he paid $100,000 yearly for protection, the police became so greedy that they bankrupted him, taking even his personal effects. The ramifications of this case provided the charges necessary to formally oust a civil service chief.

It seemed that Los Angeles had two vice squads. One, led by Captain Clyde Plummer, made an excellent record against rumrunners, hijackers and bootleggers. The other, headed by Max Berenzweig, supplied the information on which Plummer's raids were based. Thus the syndicate could eliminate unwanted competition by legal means and Chief Davis could point to an honest vice squad producing splendid results. Most of Berenzweig's men were involved in extortions from Bathhouse McDonald. When the bootlegger was arrested, Berenzweig and James Howry fled to escape prosecution.

Mayor Porter, who knew of McDonald through grand jury proceedings, initiated the investigation. District Attorney Fitts mentioned that twenty-five men were implicated but federal prohibition officials argued that at least sixty-two policemen were in league with the liquor interests. Critics asked why Chief Davis took so long to find out about the bootlegger. Davis retorted that two weeks after he learned of the situation he had the culprit in jail. Ten police trials then in session negated Davis' excuses. A public campaign to depose the chief grew rapidly.[39]

The general manager could be removed by the police commission after a formal trial at which he was found guilty of nonfeasance, misfeasance or malfeasance. On October 31, 1929, the commission charged Davis with incompetence and neglect of duty, including the use of non-civil service personnel to lead the vice squad (Berenzweig) and failure to acquaint himself with the vice situation (Bathhouse McDonald). Davis, the first chief appointed under the new charter, stood a good chance of being the first dismissed under it.

The chief faced a difficult decision. He could obtain counsel, subpoena witnesses and prepare to fight the commission. He was clearly the victim of a politically motivated ouster movement. The man pressing the investigation, John A. Quinn of the "Developers' Association," admitted that he owned no property in Los Angeles, had no residence, was not registered to vote and had no bank account. He claimed to operate on borrowed funds. The *Times*, probably correctly, charged that Quinn wanted to legitimize his cause by confusing himself with John R. Quinn, a recent conservative mayoralty candidate.

On the other hand, an inquiry into Davis' administration of the police could ruin the chief. Even complete denial of any knowledge of police misconduct tended to prove incompetence, if not perjury. "Outside influences" could not be blamed because Davis and the police commissioners often had proclaimed their joint authority over the department. Davis was a career officer without other training whose pension eligibility commenced in 1933. A transfer to another post within the police force could avoid a trial, preserve his job and protect his pension.[40]

Over the years, the chief and the police commission had worked together in harmony. Davis and the white, Protestant, Republican commissioners held similar socio-economic views. The businessmen appointed to the commission respected the opinions of the highest-ranking "professional" policeman. Despite some mutually antagonistic behavior in 1928, the commission continued to act as a bulwark of the chief and the department rather than a guardian of public interests. Criticism from citizen groups or other sources including the city council, usually produced an official vote of confidence in Chief Davis.[41]

Unfortunately for Davis, he would not have the machine's commissioners as judges. Within five months of taking office, Mayor Porter placed three of his own men on the police board, evading the intent if not the letter of the 1925 charter. In addition, commission chairman Willard Thorpe, though a Cryer appointee, broke with the administration in 1928 and afterward pressed continually for an investigation of the department. Porter's appointments provoked Thorpe's terse remark to Davis: "There is a new day in the Police Department. Get me?" In the following months, the commission curtailed the chief's authority. He lost the power to appoint or promote personnel, ending his effective control of the department. The third porter commissioner, Edgar T. Wehn, a member of the 1929 grand jury that indicted a score of Davis' men, ensured a majority for dismissal should the chief choose to fight.[42]

Various local chambers of commerce and downtown business associations supported Davis, as did some powerful figures such as Harry Chandler and respected ones such as August Vollmer. The *Times* saw the "scurrilous and offensive allegations" of sundry "prostitutes, bawdy-house keepers, vice exploiters and vicious riffraff" and "vengeful, talebearing, disgruntled subordinates" as part of an horrendous conspiracy. "Dispatches from Chicago", the *Times* reported, "indicate that a crew of racketeers accompanied by gunman and gangsters, associated with lawless union leaders, is plotting to make over the industrial map of this city on the Chicago plan." Apparently only James E. Davis could save Los Angeles from that terrible fate.[43]

August Vollmer praised Davis in letters published by the *Times*. Vollmer, who despised both the Shuler-Briegleb reformers and the Parrot-Cryer ring, well understood the chief's position. His natural sympathy was reinforced by the private reports of two friends, police statistician Fred Knoles and public relations officer Alida C. Bowler. Knoles and Bowler blamed the L.L. McClary-Marco Hellman faction in the department for Davis' problems. Bowler said that Davis'investigation of the Bathhouse McDonald case had opened up the entire police graft ring to prosecution by the district attorney but that Fitts ignored the evidence and indicted only small-fry. Bowler and Knoles believed Kent Parrot to be the instigator of the anti-Davis movement, a charge made repeatedly by the *Times*.[44]

Vollmer publicly asserted that Davis was an honest, efficient policeman, victimized by crooked politicians for corrupt ends. As such, he had nothing to fear. Since Vollmer hoped to preserve the civil service ideal, he urged Davis to battle every step of the way against an old-time, political removal.[45]

No battle ensued. When summoned before the police commission December 30, 1929, Davis accepted a demotion to deputy chief in charge of the traffic bureau, thus avoiding a trial, maintaining high rank and protecting his pension. The *Times* publicly bemoaned the injury done the civil service concept. Privately, Vollmer regretted that at such a critical moment fate should cast James Davis as the champion of principle. "If, instead of Davis, Colonel Everington had been on the job," he wrote, "I feel reasonably sure that there would have been a different story to tell."[46]

With a new mayor and chief safely in office, the Bathhouse McDonald scandal faded away. Only two dozen of the 60-odd policemen involved with the bootleggers were indicted. The district attorney withdrew half of those complaints "for lack of evidence." Of the men tried, several won acquittal by arguing that they were honest cops being framed by gangsters. Eight or nine were convicted but judicial reversals freed them. Appeal courts reversed several verdicts due to prosecution errors. Others were dismissed by the trial judge for lack of evidence after juries found the men guilty. The new police commission restored all of them to duty except James Howry, Roughhouse Brown and Max Berenzweig. To complete the farce, the district attorney dropped all charges against McDonald and his accomplices.

NOTES

[1] William H. Parker, in O.W. Wilson, ed., *Parker on Police*, 135.

[2] For pre-1926 attacks on Parrot see *Record*, 6-4-21, 12-8-22, 8-17-23, 8-20-23, 10-6-23, 11-14-23; see *ibid.*, 11-15-23 for Parrot's clash with Vollmer, and 3-3-24 for Parrot as "de facto mayor;" for Shuler's experience with "the Boss" see 11-15-29; also 6-4-21, 8-1-23: *Times*, 1-7-22, 1-18-22, 7-29-23, 7-18-24, 4-25-25, 4-30-25, 7-18-25.

[3] The Heath testimony is missing from the Council file, but see *Record*, 4-18-22, and L.D. Oaks' letter to the crime commission reprinted in the *Examiner*, 7-29-23; *Times*, 7-2-24. Two other men, G.S. McClary and Chief Kelley of Pasadena, stood higher than Heath when the 10% veteran's bonus was added. See Heath biography, *Times*, 7-29-23. *Record*, 7-1-24, 8-1-24, 8-28-24, 8-1-24. LAPD *Bulletin*, 5-25-25, 8-6-24, 1-5-25, 9-1-25.

[4] *Ibid*, 10-18-23, 8-6-24, 11-28-24, 12-6-24, 1-24-25, 2-13-25, 3-21-25, 3-24-25, 4-1-25, 2-5-26, 3-23-26.

See also 1-4-25. One person, held incommunicado for nine days, won a $25,000 law suit against the city. *Record*, 7-6-28.

[5] *Record*, 10-21-24 through 10-24-24, 2-17-25, 2-18-25; *Times*, 3-8-25 through 4-30-25, *passim*.

[6] The *Examiner* stated its principles daily in black type above the editorial column.

[7]*Examiner*, 2-7-25. See the *Record*, 4-26-25, for typical pro-Cryer statements, and 6-15-25 for the first of R. Borough's series, "Chandler-land is the Land of the Serf". For Swing-Johnson propaganda see *Examiner*, 3-4-25 to 4-5-25; *Times*, 2-23-25 and 4-14-25 for typical vice exposures. The *Daily News* was more overtly anti-Chandler. See 2-9-25, 2-12-25, 2-27-25. See *Times*, 3-8-25, for pro-Bledsoe editorial.

[8]The *Record*, 12-2-25, took some credit for Heath's decision to sacrifice "quantity for quality" in vagrancy arrests. R.P. Shuler's radio sermons were popular and provocative: "Why (D.A.) Asa Keys Does Not Want an Investigation," "What August Vollmer Told Me," "Will Christmas be Booze-Soaked in Los Angeles" and similar fare. *Record*, 12-18-25. By 1929 Shuler was given credit by some observers for electing a mayor and unseating a police chief. See Alida C. Bowler to Mayor John C. Porter, 12-31-29. August Vollmer, *Papers and Correspondence 1898-1945*, Box 1, Folder "Alida C. Bowler." Hereafter cited as Vollmer Papers.

⁹ The L.A.P.D. *Annual Reports* 1919-1931 reveal thousands of days sentence suspended for convicted prostitutes. In addition to burlesque reviews, peepshows, and risque magazines, churchmen received close police cooperation in closing "salacious" plays such as Eugene O'Niell's "Desire Under the Elms." Isadora Duncan was denied permission to dance in Los Angeles. The sex-race aspect of reform was evident from the fact that the discovery of white women in vice dens was worthy of newspaper headlines. The police commission revoked the licenses of taxi-dance halls where Asian and Mexican men were allowed to dance with white women. *Record*, 8-24-21, 11-21-22, 6-11-23, 10-5-23, 8-15-25. P.C. Minutes, 4-23-29, 4-27-27. For a discussion of Central Avenue problems see Don Ryan's interview with George Brown, *Record*, 3-30-23. Carey McWilliams thought Los Angeles was a "good" town for blacks after 1916. The Negro population rose from about 19,000 in 1920 to 31,000 in 1930. McWilliams, *op. cit.* 321-322, 329.

¹⁰ Local police agencies made hundreds of "hip-pocket" raids. *Record*, 3-24-25, 4-1-25, 12-19-25, 3-2-26, 3-6-26; there is some indication that Italian criminals controlled the Protective League; Ed Reid, *The Grim Reapers* (N.Y.: Bantam Books, 1970), 166-170.

¹¹ *Examiner*, 10-21-24, 10-22-24. *Record*, 12-17-25.

¹² The story was suppressed for several days until reported by the *Record*, 10-21-24 through 10-24-24. The *Examiner*, 10-21-24, then printed a full report but the *Daily News* made only a single obscure reference to "the incident," 10-23-25. See also *Record*, 2-7-25 to 2-18-25, *passim; Times* 2-4-25, 2-11-25, 2-17-25, 2-19-25; *Daily News*, 2-9-25.

¹³ *Times*, 3-8-25 to 4-30-25, esp. 4-23-25; *Record*, 3-21-25; The *Daily News* ran a mock contest for "Boss of L.A.," playing down Parrott and emphasizing Chandler; see *Daily News*, 2-27-25.

¹⁴ The John R. Haynes *Papers* contain a wealth of useful materials dealing with the city charter.

¹⁵ *Record*, 7-23-25, 7-24-25, 7-28-25, 8-5-25, 8-5-25 to 8-13-25. *Times*, 8-5-25, 8-6-25, 8-24-25. The *Examiner* story did not name the central figures. Interview with R.L. Heath, 11-3-70.

¹⁶ Jacobson was elected to fill a vacancy when Councilmen C.E. Downs and J. Fitzpatrick were convicted of accepting bribes in connection with city contracts. *Record*, 8-21-25, 12-8-25. *Times*, 12-26-25, 12-29-25, 12-30-25, 1-17-26, 1-20-26, 1-21-26. One astute reporter described Marco as a creation of Eugene Coughlin of the *Daily News*. He argued that Marco's conviction had no effect: "the city's prostitutes continued to operate exactly as before and to split their earnings with the

police executives in exactly the same manner as they had done since time immemorial". C.H. Garrigues, *You're paying For It!* (N.Y., 1936),30-32. Nevertheless Marco exhibited the power to "get the jobs" of federal officials.

[17] *Record*, 10-13-24, 10-23-24, 1-4-25, 1-13-25, 1-14-25, 2-17-25, 2-18-25, 4-1-25, 7—19-25, 1-25-26, 2-2-26, 2-4-26. *Times*, 7-29-23, 19-18-24, 11-14-24. *Examiner*, 7-29-23, L.A.P.D. *Bulletin*, 2-13-26. P.C. *Minutes*, 1-20-25, 10-7-24, 12-9-24. L.L. McClary was one of the disgraced officers reinstated by Chief G. Home in 1919.

[18] For Heath's plans see *Record*, 11-2-25, 11-3-25, 12-31-25. Resignations are discussed in *ibid.*, 5-19-25, 1-28-26, and P.C. *Minutes*, 4-21-25, 4-28-25, 5-6-25. Heath's "accomplishments" were praised at the Breakfast Club, *Record*, 3-19-26. Also LAPD *Bulletin*, 3-31-26.

[19] The salary proposition passed on April 30, 1926. See Davis' budget requests in LAPD *Annual Reports*, 1925-1929. The California Taxpayers' Association complained that per capita police costs rose from $1.80 in 1917 to $4.61 in 1929. *Tax Digest* v. 7, #7, July 1929. *Record*, 3-9-26, 3-23-26, 4-27-26, 5-27-26.

[20] Chapters of the League to Protect the Foreign Born and the Citizens' Protective League were formed in response to police actions. The ACLU, described by Davis as a "radical" organization, vainly requested the abolition of the Red and Intelligence squads. P.C. *Minutes*, 7-10-28, 7-17-28. *Record*, 6-10-28, 10-17-28. See P.C. *Minutes*, 4-1-26, to 12-31-29, *passim*, for disciplinary actions. See esp. Municipal League *Bulletin* v. 6, #4, 12-1-28. Moreover, the National Bureau of Casualty Writers claimed serious burglary losses during Davis' tenure, raising the insurance rate to twice that of other California cities. P.C. *Minutes*, 3-19-28. *Examiner*, 6-8-28.

[21] Details of J.E. Davis' career can be found in the *Record*, 11-29-29 through 12-23-29, esp. 12-3-29; also 3-19-26, 3-22-26, 12-6-24. P.C. *Minutes*, 6-30-25, 6-18-29. *Examiner*, 7-3-29, 7-4-29.

[22] LAPD *Bulletin*, 3-22-27, 4-27-27, 12-3-27, 6-5-28, 3-28-29. P.C. *Minutes*, 10-1-29, 4-6-27, 2-21-28, 7-13-28, 10-15-29. *Record*, 8-5-26, 4-22-27.

[23] Thomas' attorney, S.S. Hahn, claimed that Lucas "tipped" the hijacker. *Record*, 8-4-26, 2-14-27, 2-23-27, 4-22-27, 8-19-29.

[24] P.C. *Minutes*, 6-3-29, 6-18-29.

[25] *Ibid.*, 5-4-27, 5-17-27, 6-14-27, 7-27-27, 8-10-27, 8-23-27. *Record*, 4-27-27, 5-31-27, 6-13-27, 7-8-27, 7-11-27, 7-13-27, 7-18-27, 7-25-27, 9-28-27.

[26] Davis dismissed at least 248 men for cause during his 45 month first term. P.C. *Minutes*, 4-1-26 to 12-31-29, *passim*, for disciplinary actions; also 5-3-20, 6-1-20, 1-4-21, 3-7-23. *Record*, 9-1-28.

[27] Matt Weinstock, *My L.A.* (1947), 55; J.H. Richardson, *For the Life of Me: Memoirs of a City Editor* (1954), 213; *Record*, 8-29-26, 12-13-27, 12-14-27. Howry and Brown were indicted and dismissed in 1929. Hoy, present when Lucas killed Mileaway Thomas, was not ousted until 1939. Sheffield was convicted, Superior Court #38241, 38432. Randolph and Washburn were eventually discharged.

[28] Clinton J. Taft, *Fifteen Years on Freedom's Front* (L.A., 1939); Hannah Bloom, "The Passing of `Red' Hynes," *Nation*, 175: 91-2, August 2, 1952. Hynes persuaded the Council to forbid public speaking, especially in Pershing Square. Ordinance 13182. P.C. *Minutes*, 2-1-28, 3-6-28. *Times*, 3-23-25.

[29] J.H. Richardson, *op. cit.*, 222. P.C. *Minutes*, 5-25-27, 11-15-27, 11-29-27, 12-13-27, 12-20-27.

[30] Roger Lane, *op.cit.*, 142-157. P.C. *Minutes*, 5-27-19, 5-13-24. *Times*, 9-8-22, 5-21-24, 11-21-19.

[31] See the Collins story in the *Record*, 9-15-28 to 10-15-28, esp. 9-17-28, 10-15-28. *Times*, 10-30-28. P.C. *Minutes*, 10-9-28, 10-16-28, 10-18-28, 10-23-28, 10-30-28, 11-19-28.

[32] All L.A. journals reported the Jacobson case, but the most thorough account is in the *Record*, 8-6-27 to 10-1-27 and 11-5-28 to 7-7-29 passim; also 5-5-28. Municipal Court #30200. Superior Court #36216. P.C. *Minutes*, 7-2-29, 11-26-29. D.A. Fitts replaced Asa Keyes, convicted of accepting bribes. Withdrawal of charges proved to be Fitts' favorite method of cooperating with the Combination. Interview with former Chief A.H. Hohman, 8-15-70.

[33] *Times*, 7-28-27, 10-3-27, 11-16-27, 5-22-28, 6-27-28 to 9-15-28, passim, 11-15-28, 5-28-31, 11-5-33. James Spencer, *Limey: An Englishman Joins the Gangs* (London, 1957), 212. Spencer worked for a vice operator forced out by Marco through prosecution by Keyes.

[34] For Keyes' trial see Superior Court 29422, 35226, 35231, 35361, 35362. Some of Keyes' dishonest subordinates were prosecuted and some discharged, while others were retained and continued to market their services. For three examples of "fixing" see *Record*, 1-7-28, 1-9-28, 2-25-28; also 1-30-28.

[35] For honest vice squad organization see Chief A.H. Hohman, LAPD *Bulletin*, 8-24-39. Interview with H.B. Sansing, 2-16-29. *Record*, 4-1-26, 7-2-26, 10-15-26, 6-7-27, 2-4-28, 5-31-28, 6-1-28. P.C. *Minutes*, 1-31-28, 2-4-28.

[36] *Record*, 6-11-29, 12-19-29.

[37] Machines owned by Robert "Bob" Gans were believed to be safe from police action. *Record*, 12-21-29.

[38] *Times*, 1-27-29, 1-29-29. *Record*, 1-20-29.

[39] Porter received 151, 710 to Bonelli's 106, 511 votes. *Record*, 6-8-29, 6-14-29, 6-19-29, 7-27-29, 8-26-29, 9-12-29, 10-10-29, 11-20-29, 11-26-29. Hohman interview, 8-15-70. J.E. Davis to grand jury foreman E. De Garmo, 9-12-29. Vollmer *Papers,* Box 1, File "Alida C. Bowler".

[40] Los Angeles City Charter,(1925), Sec. 79; P.C. Minutes, 10-15-29, 10-31-29. *Times*, 10-12-29, 10-25-29, 11-12-29. Davis thought his ousted rival, Captain L.L. McClary, supported Quinn. J.E. Davis to August Vollmer, 10-15-29. Vollmer *Papers,* Box 1, File "LAPD." McClary was believed to have amassed a fortune while a member of the LAPD. For an attack on an unnamed "police politician" that is obviously McClary, see *Daily News,* 6-5-28. Also *Record*, 8-9-26, and LAPD *Bulletin,* 6-5-28. Mayor G.E. Cryer to the Board of Police Commissioners, 5-28-28, and the Board of Police Commissioners to Chief J.E. Davis, 6-1-28.

[41] *Times*, 7-14-28. *Record*, 7-16-28. P.C. *Minutes,* 7-26-27, 2-4-28, 2-28-28, 6-1-28, 1-2-29.

[42] *Record*, 7-2-29, 7-23-29, 8-7-29, 10-2-29, 12-2-29. J.E. Davis to A. Vollmer, 11-26-29. Vollmer *Papers,* Box 1 File LAPD; P.C. *Minutes,* 7-10-28, 4-4-29, 6-3-29, 6-11-29, 6-18-29, 7-2-29, 8-20-29, 9-10-29, 9-25-29, 10-1-29, 10-2-29, 12-10-29.

[43] *Times*, 10-15-29, 10-24-29, 10-25-29, 10-29-29, 11-12-29.

[44] A. Vollmer to J.E. Davis, 10-18-29, Vollmer *Papers,* Box 1, File "LAPD." A Vollmer to A.C. Bowler, 3-3-30, *ibid.*, File "Alida C. Bowler." *Times*, 8-2-29. *Record*, 11-14-29.

[45] Vollmer urged Davis to fight for the civil service principle. A. Vollmer to J.E. Davis, 12-4-29. Vollmer *Papers,* Box 1, File "LAPD."

[46] Davis said the Commission offered him every compromise, even to demoting him only one rank, to Assistant Chief. J.E. Davis to A. Vollmer, 11-26-29. Vollmer *Papers, ibid.,* but his telegram of 12-31-29 asserts that four commissioners would have voted for his dismissal; *ibid.* Also A. Vollmer to Fred A. Knoles, 1-7-30. *ibid.;* P.C. *Minutes,* 10-31-29.

CHAPTER FIVE

THE CHURCH BROTHERHOOD AT CITY HALL, 1929-1933

Los Angeles is a "racket" infested city, almost as much so as Chicago. But here the "racket" wears the cloak of police authority, and many of the "racketeers" wear police badges.

Thomas H. James,
former Chief Investigator
for the Los Angeles Police
Commission

The reformers worked hard to elect John C. Porter, assuming that the eminent Protestant layman and grand jury foreman would establish an honest police administration and suppress organized vice. Again they were disappointed. While Porter and the council cooperated in tax and municipal wage reductions that kept the city solvent through the depths of Depression, on all other counts Porter failed. He was guilty of serious abuses of authority. Furthermore, the mayor's ineptitude and rampant bigotry brought ridicule upon the city and seriously reduced the efficiency of the municipal departments. The police red squad made Los Angeles a byword for denial of constitutional liberties. War in the underworld produced anarchic conditions that the combination could not control. Porter's corrupt, arbitrary and indifferent administration fell far short of the ideal so often proclaimed by the Church Brotherhood.

The regal disregard for civil service rules and city charter provisions evident in the overthrow of James E. Davis and the Cryer police commission might have proved beneficial had a Vollmer-style chief been nominated. Instead, Porter chose Roy E. "Strongarm Dick" Steckel, a "system" man without illusions who had earned an unsavory reputation on the Chinatown vice squad, and for rough handling of prisoners.

Steckel's career resembled that of James Davis. He made no progress for a decade after joining the force in 1911 but rose rapidly through the vice division during Cryer's regime. Steckel had completed

four years of high school, well above the LAPD average. He scored
148/212 on the Alpha test but his officer's rating was only 49/100. In
July 1929, after Porter's election, he rose from detective lieutenant to
deputy chief although finishing fourth on the civil service examination.
The third man withdrew, allowing Davis to promote Steckel over the
first two. Rumors immediately foretold his rise to the chief's office.[1]

Steckel presided over some technological advances during an otherwise undistinguished stewardship. In 1931, the LAPD air patrol commenced operation. Ten pilots received certificates. Steckel asked for custody of an airplane seized by the city in lieu of unpaid airport fees, to
speed the delivery and return of extradited prisoners. In 1931, the police
radio station began transmissions. The use of "two-way" radio increased.
The new Lincoln Heights jail alleviated some of the worst abuses of the
city penal system. The Hollywood division moved to a new headquarters. By happy chance, the U.S. Olympic Committee chose the police
range in Elysian Park as site for the 1932 olympic pistol matches and
brought the facility up to world standards.

The city council rejected requests for additional policemen. The
police budget, largest in history in 1930, declined annually until 1936.
Officers "on the streets" rose to 68 percent from 51 percent of the total
manpower. The records, vice, jails and administrative details were
stripped to supply the extra patrolmen. In April 1930, Steckel announced
a six percent decrease in crime; in July he asserted that Los Angeles had
fewer crime problems than any other large city. Thereafter, crime and
anti-police criticism increased relentlessly year by year.[2]

Porter kept his police commissioners subservient to himself. Their
resignations, submitted prior to appointment, insured against maverick
impulses toward autonomy. The commission kept Steckel under close
supervision, passing on reinstatements, promotions and transfers, reorganization plans and budget policies. Suddenly, the police commission
announced a police reorganization scheme that promised the gravest
consequences for the department and the city. The commissioners decided to reconstitute the police force as the Bureau of Public Safety, commanded by Charles A. Burke.

Burke, a notorious private detective, planned to realign police divisions to coincide with councilmanic districts, allowing each council member to supervise police activities in his or her own district. The chief,
already subservient to the mayor in fact if not in law, would see his authority further divided by a factor of fifteen. Burke's appeal to councilmanic
vanity would isolate reform police chiefs from the precincts, should a

councilman-commissioner favor permissive vice conditions, and reverse the effects of Vollmer's centralization of authority in the chief's office.

Practical politics and the city charter blocked the reorganization. Charter revisions required the consent of the electorate and posed definite dangers. Unquestionably, an initiative campaign on the bureau of public safety issue would produce a penetrating investigation of Burke and the police commissioners. For the time, the commission retained Burke as a special consultant at a salary equivalent to Steckel's, and placed his son in the police secret service.

The commission's inexplicable determination to force Burke on the department in some independent capacity provoked questions, especially from newspaper editors. Burke's arrest for grand theft resolved the issue. He avoided conviction but his influence vanished as suddenly as it had appeared. The administration repudiated Burke and the chief dismissed Burke, Jr. from the LAPD. Young Burke claimed, rightly, that the secret service existed mainly to aid the mayor's friends.

Alida C. Bowler, former secretary to Chief James E. Davis, asserted that Burke used a certain affidavit to blackmail Mayor Porter. Materials in the Joseph Shaw *Papers* suggest that Porter used his authority as grand juryman to silence a woman who threatened a paternity suit against a well known churchman and auto-parts supplier. The affidavit in question referred to this matter. Bowler alleged that persons opposed to Burke and his "gang of racketeers" arranged Burke's indictment. To save himself, Burke paid over the affidavit to district attorney Buron Fitts. Fitts then used it to obtain Porter's support for his unsuccessful 1930 gubernatorial campaign.[3]

Chief Steckel accepted the severe restrictions on his authority. He took no action without consulting the mayor and the police commission. Porter ensured consultation by moving Steckel's office from central jail to a room adjoining his suite in city hall. The existence of a buzzer to summon the chief to the mayor's office generated considerable levity concerning callouses on Steckel's forehead from kowtowing to Mayor Porter.

Real power often resided in inferior officers or civilians outside the department. Deighton McDonald Jones and Thomas H. James, though official members of the force, operated outside the chief's authority. So did William S. Hynes of the red squad. Hynes' headquarters were in the Chamber of Commerce Building, close to his actual superiors. The Hotelmen's Association "contact man" had a desk inside Chief Steckels'office. Events making for unfavorable hotel publicity were handled directly from the top. Odd characters such as Wells Mosher, Harry Light and the Reverend Martin Luther Thomas held police badges but answered to no one inside the department. Criminals such as Charles Burke received special appointments beyond Steckel's control. Hundreds of people carried honorary police badges connecting them somehow to powers behind the scenes, enough influence to avoid arrest in minor cases. The chief's impotence reduced police morale by undermining discipline.[4]

Mayor Porter organized his own vice and investigative bureau. Deighton McDonald Jones, a violent detective discharged by Chief Davis, led the mayor's intelligence detail. Jones, a favorite of the WCTU ladies, served as the public watchdog over the disgraced police department. Chief Steckel's authority did not extend to Jones. Going further, perhaps to spy on Jones, Porter employed a group of amateur detectives known as the "super snoopers". Wells Mosher, the Reverend Martin Luther Thomas and Harry Light carried police captains' badges to facilitate their investigations. Ellis Eagan observed the internal workings of the city attorney's office until ousted by the incumbent, Erwin P. Werner. Thomas H. James used his position as investigator for the police commission to conduct private investigations for the mayor. Porter also used the city prosecutor's bureau as a patronage and spy depot until the city council abolished the office.

The mayor's spies demoralized the city departments. Their work consisted largely of political and religious surveillance and intimidation. Veteran civil servants, mainly Catholics and Jews, lost their jobs for no apparent cause. "Shulerism" seemed the most likely reason. The blame fell upon Thomas H. James for the dismissal of a popular Catholic captain only one year from pension eligibility. The captain's drunken peccadillo, which included damaging a police auto, seemed trivial in view of worse escapades suppressed by the department. The captain's partisans considered the incident a clear case of official religious discrimination. Eventually the police captain won reinstatement but the events ravaged the department and reduced Porter's chances of re-election.

Officer James, a patrolman raised to acting captain because of close family ties to the WCTU leadership, investigated the religious background and activities of possible commissioners. The mayor's flat refusal to appoint a Catholic, Jew or Negro to the police commission verified charges of official bigotry made by the Serra Association, the Young Men's Civic Organization (a Negro group), spokesmen for the Jewish community and the Municipal League.

After three chaotic years the council defeated Porter's snoopers by cutting their salaries from the budget. Harry Light lost his badge for some shady dealings along Central Avenue. Thomas H. James ran afoul of the mayor. A bargain was struck with regard to D. McD. Jones. Surveillance of the police department stopped. Captain Jones returned to the central vice squad, where the former watchdog soon became the departmental apologist.

In eliminating Wells Mosher, the council responded to a typical Los Angeles scandal. In 1930, persons unknown conspired to entrap Police Commissioner Thomas J. Walkup, using a young woman as decoy. The plotters intended to coerce Walkup's consent to certain changes in the vice division. Walkup sensed the situation and summoned detectives. The girl's testimony convicted a taxi company executive. His confederates escaped. The coincidental disappearance of Mosher's assistant raised questions that received an embarrassing answer in mid-1932. Police found him in Texas; the former assistant got the greater part of Mosher's salary as the price for silence. Mosher's indictment for the attempted entrapment of Commissioner Walkup further illumined the seamy underside of the church in politics.[5]

The scheme to coerce Commissioner Walkup emphasized the extensive powers delegated to governing commissions under the city charter. Normally, police commissioners concerned themselves with granting or withholding business licenses and passing on contracts for police department supplies. Enterprising commissioners could turn such mundane duties to highly lucrative account because the charter placed the chief under the commission's control. Reformers and police professionals opposed day-to-day decision making by commissioners. Viewing "nonprofessional interference" as a serious hindrance to efficient administration, the experts preferred that the chief be granted complete discretion within broad guidelines of policy laid down by the commission.

Porter's commissioners reversed the professional ideal. They made few major policy decisions but they meddled in everyday administration. August Vollmer, visiting the city in 1930, suggested that the department be placed under a single commissioner responsible directly to the mayor. Vollmer observed that no chief could serve five masters. Ergo, Steckel's tenure would be short. Nothing came of Vollmer's idea but the farcical trials, reinstatements, snooper squad scandals and other indiscretions produced further reform recommendations. The city council's legislative committee proposed a single, salaried commissioner to replace the five-member board. Councilman Roy Donley proposed a commissioner and a deputy commissioner to be responsible to the council. Both amendments failed.

The commission showed little concern for the department's declining standards, nor did the mayor or the chief. The city council reimposed a residence requirement restricting recruitment to residents of the city. The commission raised the upper age limit for recruits to 35 from 30 years. Formal recruit training fell below the primitive level of 1918. Steckel's reappointment of numerous disgraced officers belied his dismay over the demise of the police academy. Police automobiles carried political advertisements. Under orders, policemen campaigned for city bond issues. Chief Steckel took to the hustings in support of Mayor Porter, a gross violation of regulations.[6]

The Wickersham Commission, the first great national crime survey, described the Los Angeles situation in 1929-30 as "the antithesis of proper policing." Jerome Hopkins, a Wickersham Commission investigator, printed his own findings under the title, *Our Lawless Police: Unlawful Enforcement of the Law*. Again the LAPD fared badly. A former officer, forced out for political reasons, produced an expose of Chief Steckel. Both the local and national bar associations published contributions to the attack, repeating for a national audience what the ACLU, the People's Lobby and other organizations had been saying for years.

The Wickersham Report, the Hopkins book and the bar associations attacked illegal use of force and denial of constitutional liberties, the commonplace transgressions of American police. In Los Angeles, however, violent and unconstitutional police work accurately reflected community mores. Certain kinds of unlawful police activity had judicial sanction. Important newspapers and financial interests strongly supported anti-vagrancy and anti-racial operations that violated state and federal constitutions. Denial of the rights of guilty parties was accepted almost by acclamation.

In 1922, the California courts ruled that the fourth amendment to the federal constitution did not bind local police. If competent evidence were introduced the state would not ask how it was obtained. Though raids without warrants were illegal under the state constitution, evidence seized during such raids would be admissible. The court's "door kicking" decision encouraged aggressive, arbitrary and illegal police procedure.

The courts also allowed police officers to hold prisoners incommunicado for 48 hours without preferring charges against them. This contravened a state law requiring that prisoners be arraigned "forthwith" or "as soon as possible" after arrest. The illegal practice was so well established that the public defender complained only if a prisoner were held longer than two days without access to a lawyer, judge or other assistant. Chief Steckel considered the 48-hour rule a police "right," to be extended as necessary. The police frequently held prisoners four to seven days without charges.[7]

The LAPD insisted upon its right to violate state laws. It was a misdemeanor to record or reveal the arrest records of minors. Former juvenile offenders could deny juvenile arrests and convictions. The department routinely recorded the photographs and fingerprints of arrested juveniles, compiled dossiers and passed the data to other police jurisdictions and to employers who requested information. Though forbidden by state law except in felony cases, the department fingerprinted all adults arrested, whatever the charge.

A "good" felony arrest won its maker two or three days vacation with pay. Some officers arrested on the slightest pretext, hoping that fingerprint comparison would reveal a wanted felon. Police "dragnets," sparked by some current sensation, caught many innocent men. In most cases, charges were dropped or thrown out of court. The damning arrest records remained, a constant threat to innocent victims of inefficient or capricious police work.

For Chief Steckel, utility superseded legality: "Suppose it is against the law; is that any good reason why it shouldn't be done? It's practical. It gets results...we have no intention of stopping." Adverse publicity forced Steckel to repudiate the practice but the department then evaded the law by arresting suspects for federal felonies. After "mugging and printing" the prisoners, charges were reduced to reflect the actual offence.

Attempts by the courts to inhibit illegal police methods seldom succeeded. For the sake of efficiency the department sent a single officer to court as witness against many minor offenders, usually vagrants. The police "witness" relied upon the arresting officer's report and could not be cross-examined. Judge Hugh Crawford generally dismissed the case when the complaining witness was absent but other judges cooperated in the mechanical arrest-sentence-jail sequence by which vagrants were processed.

The departmental attitude toward judicial intrusions received a thorough exposition when a vice squad captain defied a judicial restraining order. Describing the injunction as "just a bunch of paper," the captain raided a production of "Lysistrata" and arrested the players for lewd conduct. The irate judge sentenced the policeman to pay $100 or spend 50 days in jail. The officer chose jail "as a matter of principle" and served nine days before the WCTU paid the fine. This earned the captain no official censure.

Until 1923, the *Los Angeles Record* was the only enduring opponent of police malpractice. Then the Reverend Clinton J. Taft organized a chapter of the American Civil Liberties Union, primarily to defend political and economic radicals. In 1928, the Los Angeles Bar Association formed a constitutional rights committee to investigate illegal police methods, especially third degree interrogations. In the early 1930's the *Citizen-News* and the *Daily News* joined in the opposition to unlawful enforcement of the law. With rare exceptions, the libertarian advocates confined themselves to the innocent. Anti-third degree commentary stressed the idea that innocent people suffered. Frightful descriptions of the city jails followed the same line; innocent people and technically innocent people awaiting trial were imprisoned in pestilent hellholes. The guilty received no sympathy.

The bar association justified the dragnet and the "stop and frisk" tactic, arguing that "citizens ought not to complain of slight delays and casual examination" by police. The public submitted. In some respects the city still exhibited a frontier mentality. In 1930 a crowd tried to lynch a careless motorist. In 1931, during a heated jury deliberation, the jury foreman confiscated and unloaded all the guns in the jury chamber to forestall violence. Apparently a willingness to evade, subvert or override the law imbued most judges, policemen, civic leaders and ordinary citizens.[8]

The report of the 1931 grand jury committee on public safety illustrated middle class official tolerance of police brutality. Fifty separate cases were presented, involving ruptured kidneys, broken bones, clubbings, kickings and shootings. During the hearings a huge policeman accused of gross brutality ran amok in the Hall of Justice outside the grand jury chamber. A photographer was beaten and his camera destroyed before bystanders subdued the officer. The grand jury took no notice. Its report argued that aside from a few uncivil officers, criticism of the LAPD was "unjust and unmerited."

Public indifference to unlawful law enforcement was most evident when the police attacked economic and political radicals. Radical violence, epitomized by the International Workers of the World, the McNamara Brothers and the Mooney-Billings case, led to the passage of criminal syndicalism and red flag laws. Middle class opinion sustained official oppression of social misfits and dangerous anarchists who criticized the American system. The ban on public speaking in parks allowed the LAPD to silence radical speakers. Accusations of "bolshevism" from the police were met by cries of "fascism" from the tiny though vociferous radical minority.

The depression added a note of immediate fear to the social conflict. The secular god, Business, had failed. Thousands of confused, hungry, unemployed people roamed the country or huddled in the cities, potential proselytes for prophets of a new order. In Los Angeles, the friends of the status quo took the offensive. William F. Hynes' red squad, after years of *sub rosa* encouragement, suddenly found aggressive public champions. The Ku Klux Klan, the Chamber of Commerce, the *Times* and the *Examiner*, the Central Labor Council, the county grand jury and the Porter administration praised violent police raids on "subversive" organizations. Police Commissioner Mark A. Pierce enthusiastically stated the official position: "The more the police beat them up and wreck their headquarters, the better...Communists have no constitutional rights and I won't listen to anyone who defends them." "Red" Hynes could not ask more.

Hynes named about a dozen organizations as Communist fronts. The Friends of the Soviet Union, the John Reed Club, the League for Repeal of the Criminal Syndicalism Law, the League for the Protection of the Foreign Born, the Workers Ex-Service League, the Young Socialist League, the Young Pioneers, the Peoples Lobby, and to a lesser extent the Socialist Party of California, were obvious examples. The ACLU received similar treatment, including physical assaults on Union lawyers.

In addition to raiding and wrecking the radicals' headquarters, the red squad prevented public discussion in the parks, streets and vacant lots, stopped leaflet distribution (even from the air), disrupted radical meetings in rented halls and denied the streets to protest marchers. The squad harassed individuals by raiding their homes, by arresting them frequently on specious charges and by verbal and physical abuse. As the depression worsened and unemployed thousands organized to extract concessions from the city and county administrations, the squad increased its efforts to suppress dissent. Hynes extended his power in every direction, at one point demanding that all Young Pioneers be expelled from high school, at another requesting newspaper censorship to eliminate Communist-inspired criticism of the police department.

Sometimes the radicals played directly into Hynes' hands. The Communists, regular victims of police misconduct, showed little respect for democratic processes. They repeatedly disrupted anti-Bolshevik Russian and Democratic Socialist meetings, provoking police violence against themselves. In a real sense the police preserved freedom of speech on these occasions. Upton Sinclair, jailed in 1923 for reading the U.S. Constitution, enjoyed police protection in 1930 when he and Morris Hilquit spoke. Actually the police made little if any distinction between Communists and Socialists. Police Commissioner Willard Thorpe described the California Socialists as "outrageous, deplorable, appalling, un-American, and uncivilized."

Great street demonstrations occurred, with hundreds of radicals and police battling amid clouds of tear gas. Though the police always won, they suffered casualties, including Hynes himself on several occasions. One serious confrontation developed out of a proposed "hunger march" to city hall by 3000 unemployed men. William Busick, executive chairman of the California Socialist Party, applied for a march permit. Hynes argued that Busick's previous allegations of police brutality were, per se, attacks on duly constituted authority. Furthermore, Busick was a likely candidate for city council and should not reap the publicity a successful march might yield.

Council members had personal reasons for rejecting the permit, aside from Busick's political ambitions. One councilman, after praising the colorful and exciting Shriner parades, ridiculed the notion of "a bunch of bums in ragged clothes" cluttering the streets. Another offered to obtain apples for the jobless men to sell, provided that they did not march. Finally, and remarkably, the true reason was stated: the hunger march could not take place because the people were too hungry. The situation was too dangerous.

Subsequently, Busick was arrested, beaten and jailed for distributing leaflets. Deputy City Prosecutor D.M. Avery asked Municipal Judge C.E. Hollopeter to disregard "the theoretical, so-called rights these people are forever hollering about." Busick's lawyer introduced Avery's remark that "we've been trying to get Busick for a long time." (The leaflets were legitimate campaign literature. Busick ran unsuccessfully for council in 1931.) Judge Hollopeter dismissed the case but could not intimidate the red squad. Among others, the squad arrested Meyer Beylin, an official of the League for Repeal of the Criminal Syndicalism Law. Beylin, charged as an illegal alien, had to prove what Hynes undoubtably knew: that he entered the country legally with his Russian immigrant parents. Hynes used the incident to emphasize the "foreignness" of the radical leadership.[9]

Late in 1931, when the red squad began to threaten middle class liberties, "respectable" voices questioned the worst features of the anti-radical campaign. The fruitless efforts of these civic organizations revealed the extent to which anti-Communism, whether true hysteria or merely political tactic, influenced the Porter administration. A committee consisting of one rabbi, two ministers and one Daughter of the American revolution met with the mayor and the police chief to discuss the red squad's disruption of public meetings. Chief Steckel called the group "a bunch of Communists." Mayor Porter ventured that the organizers of disrupted meetings must be at fault; he himself held many meetings without incident. When the bar association criticized the red squad's denial of civil rights, Hynes replied "they haven't any rights. I'm going to keep right after them."

A joint committee sponsored by the Los Angeles Bar Association, the Los Angeles Ministerial Association, the Methodist Ministers Association and the Municipal League, called upon the mayor. The committee argued that the police department, acting unlawfully as judge, jury and censor, habitually abrogated civil rights in four specific categories. First, the police neglected to obtain search warrants before raids on radical headquarters. Second, men, women and youths were wantonly beaten without cause. Third, the police denied the right to peaceful assembly. Fourth, they denied the right to petition government.

Porter, echoing Steckel and Hynes, accused the committee of abetting a plot "to overthrow the United States Government." By the end of 1932 the Southern California Methodist Ministers Conference openly expressed fear that the red squad represented the vanguard of fascism in Los Angeles. That the organized Protestant clergy—defenders of the status quo—should question the police campaign against "godless" Communism augured poorly for Porter's political future.

The red squad could be restrained only by a separate legitimate force. This happened first in Pasadena, after the squad provoked a riot at a political meeting. On later occasions the Pasadena police physically barred the red squad from the vicinity. Peaceful meetings followed. County Sheriff William Traeger took similar steps. The police, arriving to disrupt a radical meeting, found the path blocked by deputy sheriffs. After a brief scuffle, Hynes angrily departed.

Libertarian hopes, briefly raised, quickly died. Traeger withdrew his men. Hynes agreed to raid no future meetings unless the organizers' Communist affiliations were definitely proven beforehand. The meetings of William Z. Foster, the Communist presidential candidate in 1932, and his Negro vice presidential colleague, James Ford, provided good targets. By closing assembly halls at the last minute, leaving hundreds of angry, chanting radicals milling about the streets, Hynes ensured sufficient cause for police action. [10]

The federal courts, in a very few cases, defeated the red squad by enjoining police actions against specific meetings but granted no permanent injunctions. Several small cash judgments against Hynes persuaded him only to use more search warrants. The significance of occasional procedural victories by the ACLU and the bar association (allied but not allies) paled beside the strident support of the Better America Federation, the *Times* and the county grand jury. The 1932 and 1933 grand juries swept aside all criticisms of the red squad and forced the sheriff to institute a similar anti-radical detail.

The red squad's popularity seemed highest early in 1933, after a melee in the city council chamber. Attorneys for the ACLU and several dozen members of the John Reed Club of Hollywood appealed to the city council after a destructive police raid on their headquarters. A heated debate ensued, causing the council president to order the chamber cleared. The ever-present red squad fell upon the Communists and drove them from the room. Police administered beatings to the Reverend Clinton J. Taft and attorney Leo Gallagher. Gallagher, an old Hynes enemy, had his clothes ripped, his glasses broken, both eyes blackened and received other contusions and abrasions. The red squad earned high praise for saving the council from radical violence.[11]

The civic reformers' campaign against protected criminal enterprises provided the most colorful political issue. Vice control and police corruption, the traditional foci of political reform movements, contributed heavily to Porter's eventual defeat. Oddly enough, Central Avenue raised no controversy. For political reasons not entirely clear, "downtown" ceased to exact the weekly payoff from the Negro district. In underworld vernacular, "the line was off." Covert vice operations continued, allowing individual policemen to set up private extortion rackets. Some payoffs could be traced to "Newton Street" (the police station) but the old system temporarily ended.

Political considerations caused the change. Hugh McBeth, a black attorney and reformer, Mrs. Charlotta Bass of the *California Eagle* and George Brown, the vice boss, formed a strange alliance to halt exploitation of the Central Avenue situation. During Porter's mayorality the usual east side vice scandals gave way to well publicized jazz reviews, complete with music, dancing, "blue" humor and semi-nude women.

Elsewhere in the central city and in Hollywood, old methods continued. Captain John A. McCaleb charged that his transfer from Hollywood to Highland Park division, on January 21, 1930, signalled the beginning of open vice in Hollywood. City interests cut into the crowds that patronized gambling casinos and speakeasys on Sunset Strip, a wide open section of county territory surrounded by Los Angeles. By mid-1930 citizen reform groups were again complaining of widespread gambling, prostitution and bootlegging. *Hollywood Citizen-News* editorials specifically alluded to police protection of the vice operators. Chief Steckel denied the allegations.

At the same time, Porter and city prosecutor Lloyd Nix asserted that the gross annual product of so-called "minor, "unorganized" vice in Los Angeles amounted to $75,000,000. Porter organized a citizens commission to investigate. The committee met once but produced no recommendation. It served briefly to deflect criticism from the mayor and the chief. The police arrested some underworld figures. Homer "Slim" Gordon and Milton "Farmer" Page had their establishments temporarily closed, and headlines warned "twenty-three Chicago gangsters" that the LAPD was on their trail.

Violent clashes between criminal factions belied Chief Steckel's soothing assertions that Los Angeles had no vice and no gangsters. Murders, attempted murders, kidnappings and disappearances were common. The list of missing men included such "legitimate" businessmen-bootleggers as Frank Baumgarteker and Jacob Silverstein. Someone bombed the home of black politician George Brown. Outside competitors were blamed. This charge was supported by the arrest of six members of George "Bugs" Moran's Chicago gang.[12]

The most significant and dramatic underworld event occurred in May 1931. C.H. "Charlie" Crawford, a close associate of Kent K. Parrot, and Herbert Spenser, editor of a political scandal sheet, were shot in Crawford's office at 6655 Sunset Boulevard. Spenser died almost instantly. Crawford lived for several hours but refused to reveal the identity of the assassin even to his "old friend," Chief of Detectives Joseph Taylor. Rumors hinted at a violent upheaval in the underworld that would "tear the city to pieces." District Attorney Fitts speculated that the scandal would cost Mayor Porter and Chief Steckel their jobs. No further killings occurred and no officials lost their positions but Crawford's death significantly reordered the political and criminal situation.

Crawford, fleeing an earlier scandal, arrived from Seattle sometime after 1910. His saloon, the Maple Bar, soon became a hangout for gamblers and other "sportsmen." When prohibition began, Crawford moved into the bootlegging industry. Reports alleged that he brought Albert Marco to the city, incidentally running in the first shipment of Canadian liquor to arrive by land. Later Marco handled bootlegging and prostitution locations and himself gained a reputation as an underworld boss. At some point early in the 20's, Crawford became closely allied with the Kent Parrot-Marco Hellman-Judge Gavin Craig triumvirate that ran the city during George Cryer's eight years at city hall.

Crawford retained some direct vice interests (in 1930 his hotel was padlocked under the *Red Light Abatement Act*) but rose to central broker of police protection. "See Charlie," was Parrot's reported answer to requests for favors in the police department. The syndicate rationalized competition. Only Bob Gans'slot machines, Albert Marco's and Augusto Sasso's brothels and speakeasys, Guy McAfee's and Milton Page's casinos, Zeke Caress' handbooks, and a consortium of bootleggers received protection for a fee. Others were raided.[13]

When Crawford visited Europe in 1927, Parrot called upon U.S. Senator Hiram Johnson, the soul of Progressivism, to ensure that American embassies and consulates extended every aid and courtesy to this "very prominent citizen." Crawford's power declined abruptly when Parrot abandoned Mayor Cryer but failed to elect William G. Bonelli in his place. Crawford, deeply involved with Parrot and others in looting the Julian Petroleum Company, then "retired" from politics after undergoing a remarkable religious conversion.

The transformation occurred in Gustav Briegleg's St. Paul's Presbyterian Church. Crawford tossed an enormous ruby into the collection plate. A new chapel in honor of Crawford's mother and about $35,000 in cash donations followed. "Fighting Bob" Shuler proclaimed that he "would as soon baptize a skunk as Charlie Crawford." Briegleb had scripture on his side, however, and made the best of passages extolling charity, forgiveness and the prodigal son. Briegleb used Crawford's money to make political broadcasts in support of district attorney Buron Fitts and other machine favorites. More importantly, Crawford intended to build a private radio station in Briegleb's church.

Briegleb asserted that Crawford's generosity had no cynical political motives. Guy McAfee, the former vice squad policeman who had become the leading underworld power, would have disagreed. McAfee meant to rally "liberals" who wanted an "open" town but through Briegleb's radio, Crawford could capture "the church crowd." Crawford hoped to control 60,000 to 100,000 votes, enough to swing the coming mayorality election.

The police made McAfee the leading murder suspect. Contrary to his protestations of having made peace with Crawford two days before the shooting, McAfee was Crawford's deadly enemy. Crawford intended to regain his former preeminence in vice operations. McAfee would be attacked constantly by means of Briegleb's radio station and by pamphleteers such as Herbert Spenser. Spenser received considerable financial assistance from Crawford. The most recent issue of Spenser's magazine, the *Critic of Critics*, showed McAfee in the form of an octopus, his tentacles wrapped around city hall and the county hall of justice and extending eastward to encircle Las Vegas.

Crawford also intended to use the county grand jury to pursue a vigorous investigation of McAfee and other vice operators. A list of potential jurors found in Crawford's pocket had certain names underlined. The first name underlined came up first on the wheel when choice of the jurors began. By that time the story was known and the "Crawford men" asked to be excused. The incident did not end there. Crawford's correspondence included a warm letter from the presiding judge in charge of appointing the grand jurors, thanking the him for a $10,000 deposit in a shaky bank directed by the jurist.

Another letter revealed Kent Parrot's plan to elevate harbor commission president Walter Allen to the mayor's chair. This news ruined Allen's chances. His indictment soon afterward for stock fraud permanently eliminated him from politics. The most astounding revelation occurred when deputy district attorney David H. Clark, a candidate for the municipal bench, surrendered to the police and asked for an immediate trial on the charge of killing Charles Crawford and Herbert Spenser.[14]

Having first pled innocent, Clark then admitted both killings and pleaded self-defense. Clark purchased the murder weapon the day before the incident, indicating premeditation, but the defense established that both Crawford and Spenser usually carried guns although no weapons were found at the scene. Clark asserted that Crawford stated his intention to "get" Chief Roy Steckel, whom Clark claimed as a friend. A violent argument ensued. Crawford attempted to throttle Clark and Clark shot him. Then, thinking Spenser intended to attack him, Clark shot and killed the editor. Afterwards, due to a sudden panic, he fled.

No living witness could refute Clark's account of the events in Crawford's office. The Reverend Briegleb denied that Crawford, having been instrumental in appointing his "warm personal friend" Roy Steckel, would want the chief removed. Briegleb found few listeners. Rumors hinted that the prosecution wanted acquittal. District Attorney Fitts, having described his former aide as a "racketeer," avoided personal involvement by having Joseph Ford, a friend of Clark's, appointed special prosecutor.

Presumably Ford made every effort to convict his young friend. He tried to prove what was rather generally believed, that Clark was Guy McAfee's candidate for judge. He questioned the idea that the flabby, middle-aged Crawford assaulted the tall, athletic 32 year old Clark. He noted that Crawford was so determined to survive that he had handed over $75,000 in cash to an *Examiner* reporter to keep certain unspecified information out of the newspaper. He emphasized Clark's premeditated gun purchase and subsequent flight.[15]

The defense ignored allegations that Clark had underworld connections. The newspapers repeated a romantic tale that Clark, innocently enjoying himself at the border resort of Calexico, had been doped and photographed in compromising circumstances. Subsequently, to preserve the sanctity of his home and the faith of his wife, the agonized young prosecutor "went along" with the underworld. This accounted for his deficient record of prosecutions. Such emotional fare made good reading and good sense in Los Angeles, given the recent attempts to entrap Councilman Carl Jacobson and Police Commissioner Thomas Walkup.

Clark's defense counsel vigorously prosecuted and easily convicted Charles H. Crawford. In addition to constant references to Crawford's past, unsupported allegations were made that his secretary was also his mistress and that his private secretary had removed Crawford's and Spenser's guns from the murder scene to deprive Clark of a self-defense plea. The jury divided (11 for acquittal, one for manslaughter) and was dismissed. A remark by the jury foreman, Mrs. Alice Thomas, expressed the majority's sentiments: "David H. Clark is one of our noblest Americans." Two days later a bomb, fortunately a dud, was thrown at the house of the juror who had held out for a conviction.

A second jury, eight women and four men, found Clark innocent. The remark of a female juror, "I was sure from the moment I saw you," indicated the wisdom of the defense's jury selection. Clark was a hero. Spring Street gamblers had offered four to one against a murder conviction. Although he lost the election, Clark polled over 67,000 votes for a judgeship while awaiting trial for murder.

Crawford's death caused important changes in underworld power relationships. Notwithstanding his reported fall from power and consequent retirement, his influence in the police department had remained strong. With the central protection broker gone, protection broke down. Confusion replaced tranquillity. Police raided Crawford's previously untouchable protegee, Lee Francis, keeper of the town's most famous bordello. The madam later claimed that the number of "juice" collectors immediately tripled. The price of protection eventually drove her out of business.[16]

North end shopkeepers complained of police harassment by surveillance and interrogation of passers-by, justified as legitimate investigation of bootlegging. The merchants reported that the officers were bent on extorting money to make up the reduced take from protection. The police knew the identity and location of the major bootleggers. If money were needed, let the officers go there. This reiterated a point made time and time again by judges and reformers. Even the *Times* joined a general attack on the police administration.[17]

For the first time since 1925 the syndicate seemed vulnerable to competition. The police no longer automatically eliminated "outside" entrepreneurs. Men died violently in struggles to organize "protective associations" among the cleaners and dyers, theatre owners, barbers, service stations and broom makers. The thugs utilized stench bombs, acid, bullets and dynamite. Foolhardy young gunmen robbed Robert Gans of his slot machine receipts. Others held Zeke Caress, the "betting commissioner," for $50,000 ransom. Enroute to a gambling ship to cash Caress' checks, the kidnappers engaged in a gunbattle with police and were captured. Caress later paid $20,000 to another gang to save his wife from mutilation. Competitors killed Marvin Hart, a leading bootlegger, because he refused to divide his territory. The youthful Hart left $500,000 to his wife and family. Competitors shot Augusto Sasso, successor to Albert Marco, but failed to kill him.[18]

Disaster struck the gambling ships. The *Mon Falcone* burned to the water line. The *Johanna Smith* burned, was refitted and burned again. Aboard the *Rose Isle,* gunplay eliminated several persons. Piracy closed more than one boat. Competitors pushed in regardless of danger. The most profitable boat, the *La Playa,* escaped. By steaming under its own power the foreign-registered boat could evade U.S. laws against gambling, prostitution and beverage alcohol, while the moored gambling boats were devoid of liquor and drugs because those involved federal laws.

Guy McAfee emerged as the putative "boss" of the underworld but not without competitors. Police files suggest that mafia leader Jack Dragna forced McAfee to accept him in partnership, although crime reporters made no mention of the merger. In addition to Dragna, "Bugs" Moran joined McAfee in the syndicate. Underworld gossip indicated that Moran had gained control of the fake bottle and label industry, important to bootleg operations. He attended meetings with Gans, McAfee and others to seek solutions to the deteriorating business situation.

The ramifications of Crawford's death apparently reached the Federal Prohibition Bureau. Without significant changes in personnel the previously moribund bureau suddenly became the only effective anti-vice agency in the country. The federal organization spared neither Bob Goldie in the county nor Guy McAfee in the city. Clubs were raided that had never been hit before even as part of a protection "program." The Maier Brewery, owned by a respectable local family, had its doors broken in and its employees arrested. Reporters hinted that illegal beer had been issued from the premises since the start of prohibition.

The number and importance of the federal raids suggests that rival gangs informed the agency of one another's breweries, although proof is unavailable. Protection did not entirely disappear. Clubs opened in competition with the syndicate and were closed the same day by police. By the end of Porter's term the underworld began once again to exhibit a surface unity similar to the old days. Police Captain J.A. McCaleb charged that the underworld supported Porter. The mayor's opponents tried hard to get a grand jury investigation of his finances.[19]

In response to continued criticism, the vice squad mounted a campaign against petty gambling by ordinary citizens in their own homes. "Penny ante" raids in which police confiscated such sums as one dollar, two dollars fifty cents and ten dollars, after creeping about private residences peering through windows, contrasted poorly with newspaper accounts of the "famous no-limit Casino at 1057 La Brea," where $25,000 might change hands on the turn of a single card. Councilman Robert Allan ridiculed the police in several speeches to the city council. Councilmen James Hyde and George Baker suggested that vice suppression be forgotten and the vice squad put to work fighting crime.[20]

The *Citizen-News* noted that when competition in the county grew too fierce, the syndicate member, Bob Goldie, moved his casino inside the city limits. Then the sheriff's vice squad swept through the district in a well publicized vice crusade. Occasionally the city operators moved to the county for similar reasons, returning when the situation stabilized. Evidence that ordinary vice squad detectives had assets in excess of $100,000 supported Captain McCaleb's charge that 1700 "joints" operated in Los Angeles and an alleged admission by Mayor Porter that Guy McAfee actually ran the city. Newspaper reports implied that Porter's campaign funds came from underworld contributors.[21]

Porter's failure to encourage the growth of the municipal water and power system earned him the enmity of progressives and socialists. The public power interests, lead by water and power commissioner John R. Haynes, wished to expand the city-owned utility, especially its electrical distribution system. Porter and certain councilmen interfered, first by appointing advocates of private power to the water and power commission and then by blocking the issuance of power bonds for expansion. Porter went so far as to dismiss Commissioner Haynes, the most revered progressive in the city.

The city council refused to oust Haynes. The progressives attacked the mayor and five "turncoat" councilmen who favored private power advocate Frank Brooks for the water and power commission. The Progressive Committee encouraged the recall of the five councilmen, until another strategy was devised. A political machine, the Municipal Light and Power Defense League, appeared suddenly to contest the 1931 council elections.

On one side stood the private power companies, Mayor Porter, "Power Trust Bob" Shuler, Harry Chandler's *Times* and E. Manchester Boddy's *Daily News*. Boddy asserted that "Tammany" controlled the public power forces, accusing John R. Haynes and Judge Harlan Palmer of the *Hollywood Citizen-News* of machine politics. On the other side, the Defense League and the *Record* endorsed the progressive campaign for expanded public utilities. The election in May, 1931, was a smashing defeat for Porter. Ten councilmen endorsed by the *Record* were elected, sufficient to override the executive veto and to block unsatisfactory appointments to municipal commissions.

Shuler and the *Daily News* both congratulated the *Record* on its victory and urged the editors to run the city in a nonpartisan manner. The losers' sarcasm was not without reason. The Light and Power Defense League immediately issued crude threats to the effect that it had "made" and could "break" certain councilmen if their support for public power should weaken. An anti-Porter recall election was scheduled for May 1932. Conservative opinion opposed the recall. Even the *Record* suggested that Porter's removal could wait until his term ended in 1933.

The recall failed. Ten candidates contested the election. The issues ranged from prohibition to public welfare, not simply public versus private power. Two major candidates emerged. State Assemblyman William Bonelli, former president of the city council, had close connections with Kent K. Parrot. He took a "wet" stand on the liquor question. Most progressives therefore supported Assemblyman Charles Dempster, a relatively unknown public power advocate. The multiplicity of candidates and the diversity of their goals helped the mayor, who maintained the backing of the Ku Klux Klan, the Anti-Saloon League, the WCTU, the leaders of organized labor, the LAPD, the private power interests and everyone opposed to political recalls.

Porter defeated the combined opposition by 18,000 votes. Invoking the theory of divine right, he proclaimed that "the people have spoken and I believe it to be the voice of God, who still rules over the destinies of men." Again he dismissed John Haynes and two other water and power commissioners but the council again rejected the ouster. Porter threatened to campaign against the ten uncooperative councilmen in 1933. On second thought, he authorized the water and power commission to build a $12 million dollar generating plant at the Los Angeles harbor. This attempt to regain support among municipal socialists failed. Dr. Haynes and his followers transferred their allegiance to Frank L. Shaw.[22]

Porter's feeble attempts to deal with the depression made few friends among the unemployed. Some politicians believed the local situation to be less severe than elsewhere. Others argued that, with more unemployed people per thousand than any other section, Los Angeles was among the very worst places. The city council's fear of the hungry masses reinforced the latter interpretation. The jobless found little to praise in Porter (who campaigned for Herbert Hoover in 1932) but commercial interests including the *Times* supported his economic policies. Los Angeles did not go bankrupt. Drastic reductions in taxes pleased the business interests. The Chamber of Commerce recommended that the rockpile be reintroduced to punish vagrants and received sympathetic consideration from Porter.[23]

The dishonesty of public officials and civic leaders was much in evidence during Porter's term. Spot zoning, patent paving, streetlighting and other sources of councilmanic income were as lucrative as before. Judges were recalled. Councilmen, county supervisors, the city attorney and dozens of major business figures were indicted. Though few convictions resulted, continual allegations of official dishonesty probably reinforced a desire among the voters for a new deal and new faces in the city government.[24]

Criticism of the Porter administration and the police increased. The *Record*, Porter's sole newspaper ally during his first election campaign, attacked the mayor for weakening the municipal power and water system, and the police department for inefficiency and corruption. The *Hollywood Citizen-News* revealed the location and ownership of gambling casinos in a series of potent editorials. The *Daily-News* criticized the police for brutality and inefficiency. The *Examiner* and the *Times* continued to praise the police red squad but both complained of the department's inability to protect persons and property. Even the faraway *New York Times* carried stories of increasing gangster control of California.[25]

In the mayorality election of 1933, only the *Times*, the private power agencies, a few diehard prohibitionists and possibly some criminal interests supported Porter. The Ku Klux Klan endorsed Frank L. Shaw, the city's latest "reform" candidate. Temperance was good politics but insulting the presidents of France and the United States was not; as the guest of France, Porter stalked out of a banquet rather than toast the two political leaders with wine. Religion also was good politics, but ordering the police to stop traffic exactly at 3:00 P.M. on Good Friday so that all could ponder the significance of Easter on the exact anniversary of the crucifixion appeared extreme even to good Christians. Porter narrowly avoided elimination in the primary but winning a place in the regular election merely postponed the inevitable.[26]

NOTES

[1]. *Times*, 9-17-29, 12-31-29, 1-2-30, 11-15-50. *Record*, 6-3-24, 11-9-26, 1-1-30, 6-26-31. Thomas H. James, *Chief Steckel Unmasked* (L.A., 1931).

[2] LAPD *Annual Reports*, 1929-30, 5-6; 1930-31, 26; 1932-38, passim. *L.A. City Employee*, 4-8-30. P.C. *Minutes*, 4-1-33. LAPD *Bulletin*, 2-13-31. L.A. Citizen's Tax Committee *Report*, 1945, Table II, 84. *Daily News*, 2-1-30, 3-3-30, 6-20-30, 7-16-30, 7-25-30, 8-13-30, 2-9-32, 4-6-32, 5-11-32. *Record*, 8-6-31, 8-21-31, 8-25-31. *Times*, 4-18-30.

[3] *Record*, 1-24-39, 1-6-30, 1-7-30, 1-15-30, 2-22-30, 3-18-30, 3-19-30, 8-12-31. *Daily News*, 1-1-30, 1-2-30, 1-9-30, 2-21-30, 5-27-30, 8-6-30. *Examiner*, 1-1-30. A.C. Bowler to A. Vollmer, 2-25-30, Vollmer *Papers*, File "Alida C. Bowler".

[4] L.A. City Charter, 1925, Sec. 78-80. For example of dubious commission acts, see *Daily News*, 1-9-30, 1-15-30, 1-15-30, 7-1-30, esp. 10-19-32; also 1-8-30, 3-29-32, 5-3-33. Vincent Ostrom, *Water and Politics*, p. 68. Marvin Abrahams, "Functions of Boards and Commissions in the Los Angeles City Government" (unpublished Ph.D. Thesis, U.C.L.A., Dept. of Political Science, 1967), 232-233. P.C. *Minutes*, 1-1-30 to 7-1-33, *passim*, esp. 3-4-32. F. Knoles to A. Vollmer, 12-31-29, Vollmer *Papers*, Box I, File "L.A.P.D."; *Record*, 7-2-29, 12-26-29; LAPD *Bulletin*, 3-25-31.

[5] Municipal League *Bulletin*, V.9, #3, 12-20-31. *Daily News*, 4-22-30, 5-7-30, 7-1-30, 6-25-32, 12-30-32. *Record*, 12-30-29, 1-11-30, 2-3-31, 4-29-31, 6-10-31, 6-23-31, 6-26-31, 6-30-31, 7-13-31, 7-22-31, 8-8-31, 8-26-31, 8-28-31, 10-22-31, 5-6-32. *Times*, 11-22-30.

[6] Municipal League *Bulletin*, 11-1-30, 10-20-31. LAPD *Bulletin*, 7-12-30, 10-26-30, 2-20-31, 10-22-31. *Daily News*, 2-27-30, 4-25-32, 6-1-32, 9-20-32.

[7] The National Commission on Law Observance and Enforcement (Washington, 1931); Jerome H. Hopkins, *Our Lawless Police: Unlawful Enforcement of the Law* (N.Y. 1931); Thomas H. James, *Chief Steckel Unmasked* (L.A., 1931); American Bar Association, Committee on Lawless Enforcement of the Law, *Report*, 8-19-30. *The People vs. Fred A. Mayen*, 1922. For a discussion of this decision see *Record*, 2-7-30. American Bar Association, *op. cit.*, fn #41, p. 40, for testimony of J.J. Pope, Los Angeles public defender.

[8] LAPD *Bulletin*, 1-1-30 to 7-1-33, *passim*. J.L. Kimbrough to the

author, 12-10-71. *Record,* 3-13-31, 3-31-33, 4-17-31, 6-4-31, 8-24-31. *Daily News,* 2-4-30, 7-3-30, 1-6-32, 1-8-32, 1-26-32, 2-6-32, 7-26-32, 12-15-32. Clinton J. Taft, *Fifteen Years on Freedom's Front* (L. A., 1939), 3; L.A. Bar Association Constitutional Rights Committee, *Annual Report,* Dec. 22, 1933, 2.

⁹ Committee on Public Safety of the L.A. County Grand Jury *Report,* 3-4-32, 1-4. P.C. *Minutes,* 8-1-32. LAPD *Bulletin* 2-13-31, 8-2-32. Taft, 23-24. Perry and Perry, 229. *Record,* 3-7-30, 3-12-30, 3-19-30, 3-31-30, 2-4-31, 5-28-31, 7-13-31 through 8-5-31, esp. 7-28-31, 7-29-31, 8-21-31, 9-22-31, 10-2-31, 10-30-31. Compare reports of events at the Los Angeles Plaza in the *Times, Examiner, Daily News* and *Record.*

¹⁰ *Record,* 10-10-31, 11-7-31, 11-26-31, 11-30-31, 12-3-31, 12-4-31. Hannah Bloom, "The Passing of Red Hynes," *Nation,* 8-2-52, 92. *Daily News,* 10-18-32. For examples of an extended conflict, see *Daily News,* 5-17-32, 6-27-32, 9-21-32, 10-4-32, and the *Times* and *Examiner* of the same dates.

¹¹ Taft, 25-26-41-42. L.A. Bar Association Constitutional Rights Committee *Annual Report,* 1933, pp. 1-3. Acceptance of Red Squad activities can be seen in 1932 council files 58, 421, 540, 547, 549, 867, 2804, 4245, 4539, 3091; 1933 files 499, 811, 3062. Bloom, 91-92. LAPD *Bulletin,* 2-23-31, 8-2-32. *Daily News,* 2-14-33, 2-17-33, 2-17-33, 2-25-33, 2-25-33, 7-5-33.

¹² See the testimony of Sebe Hendricks against M.B. Sheffield, L.A. Superior Court No.38432; cf., J.L. Kimbrough, black former detective: "There was no widespread vice program as in former years," to the author, 12-30-71. *Record,* 1-31-31, 2-3-21, 2-6-31, 2-9-31, 2-10-31. Citizen News editorials in Biscailuz *Papers,* Scrapbook No.1. *Daily News,* 1-10-30, 1-14-30, 1-21-30, 4-22-30, 4-24-30, 5-1-30, 5-3-30, 5-15-30, 5-17-30, 5-22-30, 7-2-30, 8-13-30, 4-29-33. *Record,* 11-17-30, 1-31-31 through 2-10-31. See the LAPD's "Gangland Killings, Los Angeles, California Vicinity, 1900-1951", for discussion of 58 murders deemed to be the work of the mafia. Other gang murders were not included. For a few of many examples in a single year (1930), see *Record,* 5-23-30, 7-18-30, 9-8-30, 9-9-30, 10-14-30, 11-16-30. There were at least sixteen more in 1931.

¹³ The best account is the *Record,* 5-21-31 through 10-19-31, *passim.* Also R.P. Shuler, *The Strange Death of Charlie Crawford* (L.A.,1931), *passim.* See the *Record,* 5-11-15, for Crawford's early campaign as "a friend of organized labor." Lee Francis, famous Hollywood madam, said Crawford started her business as the machine's "official"

brothel the night George Cryer won election in 1921. Lee Francis, *Ladies on Call* (Holloway House, 1965), 88.

[14] Shuler, *Death of Charlie Crawford,* 5. Weinstock, 54-55. Remi Nadeau, *Los Angeles: From Mission to Modern City,* (1960), 258. William F. Bonnelli, *Billion Dollar Blackjack* (Beverly Hills, 1954), 54. See K.K. Parrot telegrams to U.S. Senator Hiram Johnson, esp. 3-8-27. Hiram Johnson *Papers,* Part III, CB 581. Keim, 19. Clark trial is Superior Court #44743. *Times* 4-8-30, 7-1-30, 7-7-30, 11-30-30, 5-28-31, 9-8-31. *Record,* 3-11-30, 5-19-31 through 5-23-31, 6-5-31, 9-7-31, 9-8-31.

[15] The reporter implicated Crawford, Parrot and State Corporations Commissioner Jacob Friedlander in the Julian Petroleum crash. A bribe of $330,000 was demanded; $75,000 was paid while police observed. The city clerk's assistant stole the cash and lost it in the stock market. *Record,* 3-11-30.

[16] Francis, 173-175, 187. *Times,* 6-20-30. *Record,* 6-2-31, 8-24-31, 8-25-31, 10-19-31.

[17] *Record,* 6-2-31, 6-18-31, 7-18-31, 9-29-31. *Times,* 9-30-31. LAPD *Bulletin,* 2-6-31, 10-22-31. *Examiner,* 9-28-31, 1-4-32. *Daily News,* 8-16-32.

[18] For examples, see *Record,* 3-23-31, 3-25-31, 8-18-31, 9-25-31, 10-5-31, 12-12-31, 12-18-31, 12-23-31. *Daily News,* 1-16-32, 3-29-32, 7-16-32, 8-11-32, 10-29-32.

[19] *Daily News,* 3-9-32, 5-4-32, 6-20-32, 7-11-32, 7-20-32, 7-22-32, 4-12-33. LAPD Gang Killings. *Record,* 10-21-31, 11-12-31, 12-24-31.

[20] See city council File 8857. *Record,* 10-7-31, 11-23-31. *Daily News,* 5-24-32, 8-16-32, 10-20-32, 10-29-32, 12-14-32, 5-6-33.

[21] Biscailuz *Papers,* Scrapbooks No.1, No.2, *passim. Record,* 7-23-31, 7-25-31, for a discussion of vice squad bank accounts and connections with organized crime. *Daily News,* 1-30-32, 6-2-33, 6-26-33, 6-27-33.

[22] Municipal League *Bulletin,* 12-20-31, 4-20-31. P.C. *Minutes,* 5-6-31. Ostrom, *passim. Daily News,* 1-21-30, 5-7-30, 7-1-30, 7-17-30, 7-25-30, 2-16-32, 3-12-32, 4-9-32, 2-16-32, 3-12-32, 4-9-32, 4-30-32, 5-3-32, 5-4-32, 5-5-32, 8-13-32. *Record,* 12-23-29, 12-27-29, 12-24-29, 1-7-30, 1-11-30, 1-20-30, 3-7-30, 6-3-31, 7-2-31, 7-4-31, 7-17-31, 8-11-31, 9-14-31. The best short analysis of the recall is Stanley Rogers, "The Attempted Recall of the Mayor of Los Angeles:, *National Municipal Review* No. 21 (July, 1932), 416-419.

[23] For an extended discussion see Leonard Leader, "Los Angeles in the Great Depression" (unpublished Ph.D. thesis, U.C.L.A., 1972). Gover-

nor C.C. Young remarked: "Unemployment? I think it's exaggerated." *Record*, 3-11-30, 6-29-31. Reuben W. Borough, "Reuben W. Borough and California Reform Movements" (U.C.L.A. Oral History transcript), 115.

²⁴ A number of enormous business failures, many due to speculation, led in turn to corruption in the dealing out of receiverships. T. Beverly Kiem, "The Recall of the Judges in 1932" (unpublished M.A. thesis, U.C.L.A., 1936). For other civic scandals, see the *Record*, 3-13-20, 4-30-31, 5-27-31, 7-1-31, 8-27-31, 9-8-31; see also the *Daily News*, 3-23-32, 7-9-32, 2-23-33, 3-1-33, 3-10-33, 3-31-33, 4-26-33, 6-10-33.

²⁵ *Record*, 1-12-29, 1-1-30, *passim*. See *Citizen-News* editorials in E.W. Biscailuz Scrapbooks. For examples of Hearst's criticism see *Examiner*, January 1932 through March, 1932, during the campaign to recall Mayor Porter, esp. 1-4-32, 4-27-32, 5-24-27, 5-24-32. The *Times* often combined an attack on Steckel with a defense of the deposed Davis. *Times*, 4-1-30, 9-30-31. See also *New York Times*, 4-5-31, 5-31-31, 10-18-31.

²⁶ Grand Dragon T.S. Moodie to John Roberts, 4-24-33. Joseph Shaw *Papers*, Box 11. Also Box 8, File "Correspondence, 1933-35."

CHAPTER SIX

IDEALS AND SACRED THINGS; THE LAST REFORM CRUSADE

The purpose of any political organization is to get the money from the gamblers.

Wilbur LeGette [1]

We will fight for the ideals and sacred things of the city.

Motto of CIVIC

The election of Frank L. Shaw added one last name to the inglorious list of "reform" mayors who cooperated with the criminal combination. The mayor, assisted by his brother, Joseph E. Shaw, presided over the final degradation of the municipal government. The police force was especially affected. To protect themselves from arbitrary superiors, the officers managed through diligent efforts to isolate the internal disciplinary process from the legal control of the chief and mayor. Concurrently, the department became so corrupt and undisciplined that denial of civil rights and liberties became almost systematic. Open vice operations flourished. The reformers fought hard but in vain to elect honest men and women to city and county offices. Eventually, an attempted assassination by the police intelligence squad united all the diverse reform elements in a final effort that overthrew the machine and the combination and placed a genuine reformer in the mayor's chair.

Frank Shaw exactly fitted the Los Angeles political mold: a small businessman of white, Protestant, Masonic, Republican convictions. He ran as "a friend to business" because as a city councilman he had helped to reduce taxes and to block a "ratproofing ordinance" directed at landlords. As a county supervisor he supported a "three-year indigent law" to keep migrants off welfare and fostered Mexican repatriation for similar reasons. He eagerly endorsed Roosevelt's recovery program, leading Porter to accuse him of "trading on human misery to buy votes." Two other charges were more serious. Robert Shuler alleged that Shaw took bribes while in office. The *Times* asserted that Shaw was not an American citizen and could not legally hold office.

Shaw had a inadvertent reputation for honesty when he left the corrupt city council for the even more notorious county board of supervisors. A lobbyist for the Southern California Gas Company testified that Councilman Shaw received none of the $200,000 his utility had paid to city officials. Shaw ran on this ready-made program at a time when supervisorial boodling had reached horrendous proportions. The new County Hall of Justice, budgeted at $2.5 million, cost between $6.5 and $8.0 million. Two million dollars disappeared from the County General Hospital Building fund before ground was broken. Taxpayers got only a frame of rusting girders for their initial five million dollar appropriation. Shaw easily defeated Jack "King Bean the First" Bean, the man most responsible for fiscal disarray in the county. Another supervisor resigned and several indictments were returned but the corrupt district attorney, Asa Keyes, refused to prosecute.

According to one witness, supervisors Shaw, Sydney Graves and Fred Beatty often held illegal secret meetings to dispose of county contracts and sometimes received immediate bribes. Supervisors apparently received one cent per yard for concrete used by county contractors. Supervisor Graves went to prison in 1932 for taking $80,000 in connection with San Gabriel Dam contracts. A second $80,000 remained untraced because District Attorney Buron Fitts dropped the investigation. Rumor had it that Frank L. Shaw received the money. Shaw's campaign manager and field secretary, James Bolger, was closely involved with H.H. Merrick, a businessman jailed for peculations involving county contracts. And Shaw had been heard to say, "where the money goes, I go".

The *Times* asserted that the Canadian-born Shaw was an alien. Shaw claimed U.S. citizenship on the basis of his father's alleged naturalization. Since only citizens could legally claim federal land, he offered the elder Shaw's homestead deed as proof. Former state senator George Rochester eventually obtained evidence from Washington which a federal judge accepted as proof of Shaw's U.S. nationality. The "New Deal Republican" Shaw then defeated the "Hoover Republican" Porter, receiving 54 percent of the votes.[2]

Shaw began well. He established a "free speech zone" at the Plaza. The red squad reduced its activities. "Red" Hynes took leave of absence to serve as consultant to various anti-communist groups. The reduced and reorganized vice squad raided several exclusive and previously immune gambling clubs. Chief Steckel was told not to ask the politicians for instructions because he alone commanded the force. Shaw asked the Porter police commissioners to resign because he wanted a commission in harmony with the mayor and chief, to "give our people a just and equitable enforcement of the law." When they complied, he ordered his five new appointees to "run the racketeers and gangsters out of town and put a stop to commercialized vice." If the commissioners found fault with Chief Steckel, they—not the mayor—were to choose a replacement.[3]

Talk passed of a new chief, although Steckel argued that he held a civil service rank and would keep it until proved incompetent. On August 5, 1933, the *Daily News* proclaimed the return of James E. Davis, noting that "local political figures, none of whom are police commissioners, reached the decision at a secret meeting." The *Times* noted "the growing police chief mystery." Commissioner Martin C. Neuner suggested that James E. Davis and Chief Steckel should exchange jobs. The *Examiner* stated that "Chief Steckel has until noon tomorrow to decide how he is going to retire." On August 10, Davis became chief, Steckel a deputy chief. Shaw assured the public that he would pull no strings from his office to direct Chief Davis.

Davis asserted that he had reduced crime by 50 percent during his first term, and promised to "not only continue that decrease, but add to the total." He praised Steckel for giving his best during a period when the mayor did not support the police. The *Examiner* applauded Davis' proposal to fight crime rather than attempting to regulate private morals. The *Times* doubted that the administration would hold to its policy of non-intervention in police matters but endorsed the Davis appointment. Unlike 1929, the *Times* happily concurred in the illegal removal of a civil service chief.

Some political sophisticates believed that Davis replaced Steckel at the request of *Times* publisher Harry Chandler. In return, the *Times* dropped the issue of Shaw's citizenship and suppressed documents indicating that the mayor had claimed Canadian citizenship in 1917 to avoid war service. The substance of these allegations is difficult to ascertain; however, Shaw's most powerful and implacable enemy inexplicably became his most resolute and unwavering apologist.[4]

The bright new administration quickly tarnished. Lt. Joseph E. Shaw retired from the U.S. Navy to become his brother's personal secretary. Joe had a touch of iron in his soul that Frank Shaw seemed to lack. The influence of "the Sailor" soon reached every corner of Los Angeles politics. The Shaws set out to control all profitable aspects of the city's affairs by placing their men in strategic positions. In the police department they assigned James "Sunny Jim" Bolger as personal secretary to Chief Davis.

The police commission soon overturned the stringent new employ-ment regulations announced by the civil service commission. The Depression made it easy to sell places on the police appointment list, at prices ranging from $300. Promotions also were sold. Illegal changes in records were made to hide illegal appointments. Many disgraced officers returned, including "Roughhouse" Brown, "Dirty Dick" Lucas and the alcoholic ex-chief Louis Oaks. Physical and mental standards were effectively non-existent; in 1937 Chief Davis had to ask that a medical examination be a condition of employment.[5]

The Depression seriously affected police working conditions. The 1926 monthly wage-rate ($170-$200) was frozen by charter amendment. In 1932, the officers were persuaded to petition for reduced tours of duty, thus providing a legal framework for a ten percent wage reduction. In 1934, the council proposed a further reduction of 12.5 percent. The dis-mayed officers also learned that the police commission had secretly voted Chief Davis a $1200 annual increase. The bitterness of the rank and file convinced local communists that the first rupture had occurred between the capitalist system and its protectors. Their use of the revolt of Tsarist sailors as an historical parallel allowed Davis to expound on the Red Men-ace and to imply that only communists opposed his pay raise.

One bold officer, Lloyd O. Enloe, refused to sign the 1934 petition for reduced hours and sued the city for the wages withheld following the 1932 petition. The Protective Order of Police threatened to file a sup-porting suit. The administration immediately dismissed the eleven-year veteran for failing to have a telephone in his house and refusal to buy a new revolver. The commission refused a public hearing and the courts denied his suit for unpaid wages. Enloe's disastrous example was not lost on his fellows. The determination grew to obtain effective, charter-protected disciplinary procedures.[6]

The movement toward independent internal trial procedures had been underway for several years. Section 202 of the city charter granted the power to punish erring subordinates exclusively to the chief. The commission could overrule the chief but could not legally initiate pro-ceedings nor assign punishment. The charter provided no specific trial mechanisms. Most often a panel of three captains sat as a trial board. On the basis of the trial board's finding the chief made a decision and pre-sented the case to the police commission for final determination.

At various times during Chief Davis' first term an appointed panel of captains, the personnel bureau and the chief himself served as trial board. The possibility of favoritism or discrimination made these methods suspect. The police commission and the courts overturned several illegal dismissals. Chief Davis' correspondence noted the frequent reinstatement of men discharged for cause, without the introduction of new evidence. Some won reinstatement as many as three separate times. Davis appealed to Porter to make no departmental regulations without granting the power to enforce them.

During Steckel's term, the commission established a board of three captains to sit as permanent trial board but abolished it when the board exonerated a policeman the commissioners wanted to punish. Then the discharge of several veteran captains demonstrated again the tenuous nature of civil service protection when outside influences controlled the chief and the commission. Just as James Davis ousted his powerful rival, L.L. McClary, in 1927, so Steckel eliminated W.L. Hagenbaugh in 1931. Hagenbaugh and McClary received pensions but another captain, discharged after nineteen years of service, forfeited his eligibility.

To lose pension rights, the holy grail of the police service, could scarcely be imagined. The possibility served as a powerful disciplinary club. Men with fifteen or more years made great efforts to avoid such a disaster. They neither saw, heard, nor spoke things that superiors might construe as evil. The circumstances of the captain's case convinced the department that religious bigotry and personal animosity rather than guilt dictated the extreme punishment. True or not, the idea carried the weight of fact among policemen. Racial, religious and political factions within the department united in the movement for impartial trial procedures.[7]

The reinstatement of men previously dismissed for cause furthered the campaign. Though drunks, thugs, rapists and extortionists made up the majority of the reinstated men, others had connections with criminal organizations. Neither mayor, commissioners nor chief could escape responsibility. Porter had pledged to scrutinize all reinstatement applications. The police commissioners had access to all personnel records. Each petition included a personal recommendation from Chief Steckel.

Many cases involved the repeal of "illegal" removal orders. City charter Section 202 required that a copy of discharge orders be served on the individual or delivered to his last known address. The dismissed men had 15 days in which to appeal the order. Many successfully argued that they had not received their discharge orders. The alleged violation of the charter presumably justified reinstatement, although the men had not appealed their dismissals, and months, even years, had passed since they had worked for or been paid by the city.

The commissioners made no attempt to undo their work. Chief Steckel blandly asserted that the city urgently needed "experienced" policemen. The scandal nevertheless convinced police executives and other city officials that better procedures were needed to prevent future disputes over dismissal and reinstatement. The combination of a department determined to protect itself from arbitrary political and religious discrimination, the willingness of anti-labor forces to grant the department's wishes in lieu of labor organizations and a general wish to avoid illegal removals and reinstatements ensured the success of the police-inspired ballot initiatives that established charter-protected police trial procedures.

Earle E. Cooke, a policeman-lawyer, designed the initiative and the new procedures. The most important section granted duly-sworn policemen a substantive right to their positions. The amendment created a board of inquiry to investigate any suspension or removal upon written request from the individual involved. The board could subpoena witnesses and examine them under oath. The accused received the legal right to counsel. The board submitted its findings to the chief, who then affirmed, rescinded or amended his original punishment orders.

As events quickly proved, the amended Section 202 provided no more protection than did the original. Nothing bound the chief to accept the board of inquiry's opinion. A dismissed officer could not compel the chief to reverse his decision even if the board found the officer innocent. The chief and police commissioners ignored the charter. When a citizen charged brutality against Captain Deighton McDonald Jones, an administration favorite, a special panel of three inspectors exonerated him. Some critics quoted Mayor Porter's comment that he would "step in to protect any officer unjustly accused" and blamed him for intimidating the police commission

Chief Steckel's dismissal of Captain John A. McCaleb, night chief and commander of Highland Park division, involved a more serious breach of the charter. A panel including Chief Steckel, former chief James E. Davis, Deputy Chiefs Jonathan Finlinson and Homer Cross and Chief of Detectives Joseph Taylor, ousted the twenty-two year veteran for neglect of duty, pernicious political activity and unbecoming conduct. "Political activity" was the key phrase. McCaleb refused to support Mayor Porter's re-election and worked to elect Frank L. Shaw. Shaw's police commission reinstated McCaleb but the obvious need for further reform of Section 202 occupied the minds of police professionals.

Lt. William H. Parker, another rising policeman-lawyer, amended Cooke's work. The revised Section 202 was placed on the municipal ballot in November, 1934. Proposition 12A established departmental autonomy over internal discipline. The trial board became a legal entity. Accused officers gained the right to counsel and to a public hearing. No officer could be discharged unless found guilty by a trial board of three captains chosen by lot. The chief could decrease but not increase the severity of the trial board decisions. A one-year statue of limitations on departmental offenses protected officers from reform administrations and the officer's vested right in his position was codified.

Proposition 12A passed by an extremely narrow margin. The *Daily News* accused the police hierarchy of designing a self-perpetuating organization to serve its own ends, beyond the control of machine or reform political administrations. Sharp curtailment of the chief's disciplinary powers had a different rationale, however. Despite the extension of civil service tenure to the chief during August Vollmer's term, the examples of James E. Davis and Roy E. Steckel proved that the mayor still controlled the chief. By extension, every officer served at the mayor's pleasure, as patrolman Lloyd O. Enloe and others could testify.

To free themselves from the politicians, the police had to restrict the chief's discretion in disciplinary matters. Thus the purely utilitarian basis for the charter amendment. Usually, the progressives could be found firmly behind any move to reduce political influence in police affairs but Proposition 12A divided the city. The police fashioned the victory. Not only did they devise, underwrite and campaign for the measure, they also passed it. The final ballot tally showed 89,391 in favor, 89,216 opposed. This *de jure* independence (extended in 1937 to include the chief) provoked subsequent unsuccessful demands that the public be granted greater control over police discipline.[8]

Charter amendment was much more acceptable to progressives than formation of a Protective Order of Police local would have been. In any case, the P.O.P. was as much a racket as a labor union. Its main concern was said to be the sale of $100 memberships to Hollywood personalities, to "strengthen local police agencies." Presumably, membership ensured preferential treatment in the matter of traffic violations. On the other hand, the P.O.P. was controlled by police officers, unlike the usual rackets that victimized policemen.

The charge that Patrolman Enloe refused to purchase a certain make of .38 caliber pistol having a six-inch barrel arose from Davis' decision to eliminate both the .45 decreed by R. Lee Heath and the short barrelled .38 common in detective work. C.H. Garringues, a perceptive reporter for the Daily News, described the deal as simple extortion and predicted an uproar that would spoil the plot to require new tan-colored summer uniforms. Twenty-five dollars per firearm, multiplied by 2500 officers, meant $62,500 to the seller, "not bad for an off year" even when $6,250 was "kicked back" to the officials who enforced the purchase. Chief Davis denied any motive other than efficient shooting but remarked that officers could carry whatever pistols they liked, as long as they bought the new weapons.

Garrigues asserted that "all of the interests" took part in the secret meeting at which Davis was chosen to head the police department. Joining the *Los Angeles Times* were the "badge, gun and uniform" interests, the "meat for the city jails" interests, the "furniture for `rooming houses' and `massage parlors'" interests and the commercialized vice interests. Absent, however, was George Rochester, who obtained Shaw's evidence of citizenship and had expected the presidency of the police commission in return.

The *Daily News* also exposed the "official" garage racket. Officers sent abandoned, over-parked, stalled or damaged vehicles to favorite garages. Subsequently, the owner paid a stiff towing fee and in the worst cases suffered the loss of spare tires, tools, accessories and even gasoline. Chief Davis' list of "official" garages could be defended as a quasi-licensing system for the public benefit. Critics insisted that it was a further rationalization of the graft system.[9]

In February 1936, the spotlight of adverse national publicity fell on the LAPD. "Oakies" and "Arkies," folk heros of John Steinbeck's *The Grapes of Wrath,* were migrating in thousands to California. Texas-born Chief Jim Davis, long an opponent of "the refuse of other states," planned and carried through a program to prevent Dust Bowl refugees from reaching the Golden State. The embargo, or "bum blockade," required officials of border counties to deputize Los Angeles police, establishing their authority outside the city limits. The dubious constitutionality of the program raised serious opposition. Sheriff Eugene Biscailuz restricted his efforts to the Los Angeles area and withdrew his men at the first opportunity. Davis, who recommended the "deportation" of native born Americans from other states to relieve California welfare systems, relied on an opinion rendered by the city attorney.

The *Los Angeles Times* supported Chief Davis. To those such as the Municipal League, who wanted the "foreign legion" brought home, the Chandler journal answered: "Let's Have More Outrages." The newspaper praised "136 of this city's finest—and there are no finer," who were "on the job at every railway...turning back undesirables." Those who got past the police, estimated by the *Times* at 50,000 in the previous 6 months, would "produce rock and sand for Los Angeles." Although state courts ruled that the embargo was unconstitutional and the police-men returned to the city, the anti-vagrant campaign continued through the year. Chief Davis proclaimed the border patrol a successful move which reduced petty crime by twenty percent.

The "Langan Case" became the most notorious of many incidents involving the border patrol. John Langan, after a trip into the Arizona desert, was stopped at Blythe by Los Angeles policemen. Langan questioned the policemen's right to accost him. He then returned home to Los Angeles and filed suit against Chief Davis and the city.

The police intelligence squad intervened. Langan's liberal lawyers were denounced as communists. His employer was threatened with a suit for violation of city ordinances. The employer's customers exhibited reluctance to deal with a supplier who harbored communists. The police threatened to deport Langan's foreign-born wife if he did not withdraw his suit.

Langan's lawyers persuaded him to continue. The suit began in federal court on March 30, 1936. Langan was absent. His frightened wife reported that he had left home the previous day with Lt. Earl Kynette of the police intelligence squad. Late in the afternoon a message withdrawing the suit arrived from Langan but Judge A.L. Stephens decided to proceed with the hearing unless Langan appeared in person to request dismissal.

After several hours Langan appeared, dishevelled and distraught. He withdrew his suit, without explanation. Judge Stephens asked the U.S. Attorney to investigate the possibility of intimidation but Langan refused to cooperate. Kynette was promoted to captain for his "fine work" on the case. Some years later, photographs of the Langans and biographical information ostensibly prepared by *"Time Magazine* reporters," was found in Kynette's files.

The border patrol illustrated Chief Davis' belief that the constitution should not interfere with the police function as he defined it. Hynes and the red squad returned from limbo. Using teargas guns and projectiles supplied by companies being picketed or struck, the squad broke up demonstrations and picket lines. Employers frequently paid for the squad's meals, accommodations and overtime during labor conflicts. Hynes apparently had a hidden source of funds and bet sizeable sums at the Santa Anita race track. The squad's actions, especially the acceptance of money, raised grave questions. Since criticism of the police was rebutted as Communist propaganda, however, progressive candidates hesitated to ask them. Reform politics was difficult enough as it stood.[10]

The political wars of the mid-Thirties were waged mainly for control of the county grand jury. The power of the jury to probe the crannies of municipal and county politics made it a weapon of enormous potential but one that the reformers seldom wrested from the grasp of the machine. Because tradition held that twelve affirmative votes were needed to indict, each grand jury included among the nineteen members at least eight who were subservient to the combination. Moreover, since the district attorney usually obtained complete control over the jury, it could be turned against his political enemies with devastating effect.

The reformers knew this from bitter experience, gained after they asked the 1933 grand jury to investigate City Attorney Erwin Werner and his wife, "Queen Helen." Helen Werner controlled the appointment of tax assessors. Both Werners were closely associated with District Attorney Buron Fitts and the *Los Angeles Times.* "Queen Helen" dispensed patronage in curious ways. One assessor received $100 per diem, based on a 456-day year. Large, unexplained sums of money passed through her bank account, leading to allegations of tax irregularities.

Fomenting the Werner investigation were three members of the new, semi-secret, Los Angeles Minutemen, or Minuteers. The Minutemen supported an unsuccessful resolution by State Assemblymen Lawrence Cobb and Kent Redwine to have the state supreme court direct a probe into Los Angeles politics, financed by $100,000 of state monies. Raymond Haight, recently state corporation commissioner, led the amorphous group, assisted by attorney Carl Kegley and special investigator Edward Otto. The majority of the Minuteers remained anonymous for self-protection and to increase their chances to obtain relevant information.

Not only did District Attorney Fitts prevent an investigation of the Werners, the grand jury indicted Haight and his associates for attempted bribery of a juror. The three men won acquittal but the blunt display of power illustrated the possible consequences of continued opposition. The Minutemen declined to proceed with an investigation of the police and sheriff's departments. Haight, summoned before the grand jury to substantiate allegations that protected vice operations continued in the city and county, balked at testifying while Fitts or his deputies were present. After a juror admitted transmitting information to the district attorney, the Minutemen refused to reveal their evidence of police corruption.

It fell to Judge Fletcher Bowron to choose the 1934 grand jury. This was Bowron's first overt role as a reformer. Bowron had a broad understanding of local politics. While studying for the bar, he worked for the *Record* as a police reporter. On the bench, he served through a decade when many of the political and financial elite came to trial, only to escape punishment through bribery of a prosecutor, jury or judge. He had observed the "runaway" 1928 grand jury that indicted vice boss Albert Marco and District Attorney Asa Keyes. By eliminating the machine's candidates, Bowron hoped to empanel a similar body that would defy District Attorney Fitts and investigate political corruption in the city and county.

Although Bowron's selections gratified the progressives, the *Daily News* warned that certain unnamed jurors would prove untrustworthy. The machine charged that Bowron had created a star chamber to conduct personal vendettas against his political enemies. Subsequent investigations were denounced as politically-motivated smear tactics. This was a realistic possibility in view of recent Los Angeles experience, as both the Minutemen and District Attorney Fitts could testify, but the public disagreed. Bowron easily won re-election to the superior bench during his stewardship of the grand jury.

The "Bowron" grand jurors pursued inquiries without the permission or even the knowledge of the district attorney but they failed to obtain any part of Fitts' $60,000 secret service fund. The *Daily News* charged that James Bolger, Chief Davis' secretary and Mayor Shaw's campaign manager, District Attorney Fitts and Sheriff Eugene Biscailuz arranged with county supervisors to throttle the grand jury by withholding funds. An underworld figure reportedly boasted that "we have the grand jury stopped. They'll never get a dime." To add to the progressives' dismay, a committee of prominent citizens that had pledged to underwrite jury expenses withdrew through fear that the grand jury might actually have a secret political motive. Other reformers held impassioned protest meetings. Public subscriptions raised about $10,000. Jury Foreman Wayne Fisher apparently financed investigative costs beyond that sum from his own pocket.[11]

As events proved, the county supervisors, the district attorney, the sheriff and the mayor had personal reasons for stifling the grand jury inquiries into local politics, as did the city councilmen. A probe into the patented paving, street lighting and trash collection rackets led to the indictment of two former councilmen and the general manager of the public works department. As usual, the officials escaped convictions. The public learned that some councilmen demanded $10,000 to $50,000 for a city contract, that "patented paving" cost as much as $7.20 a ton compared to $2.30 per ton for equally good unpatented paving and that street lights sometimes were installed and working before contract bids were requested.[12]

The inquiry produced no indictments but smudged the reputations of all recent county supervisors. Although the convicted supervisor Sidney Graves refused to testify, the grand jury learned that Supervisor John McClellan had amassed a $500,000 fortune. Supervisor Hugh Thatcher's persistent efforts to have the county purchase worthless real estate at inflated prices ruined his chance for re-election. Frank Shaw's close association with Supervisors McClellan and Harry Baine blighted their political future. Supervisor John R. Quinn's alleged misuse of federal welfare programs to build a political machine aimed at the 1934 Republican gubernatorial nomination blemished his hitherto impeccable record.

Another scandal came to light in the city health department. Shaw's health commissioners planned to attract funds from major poultry dealers by eliminating their small competitors through licensing regulations. Health Commissioner S. "Sammy" Gach represented the administration in the "chicken deal," which would have eliminated eighty percent of the dealers. W.A. Schwartz of the Los Angeles Poultry Association asserted that the program called for $5,000 down and $500 monthly delivered to the mayor's brother.

The Daily *News* charged that health commissioners had used this tactic for many years to exact tribute from flower sellers, electric appliance dealers, laundrymen, trash collectors and similar businesses. Often the commissioners' agent then canvassed the small dealers for contributions to a "war chest" to defend their interests. For example, flower seller licence fees rose several hundred dollars without warning. Shortly afterward, the fee was reduced to its previous level. Councilman E.L. Thrasher agreed that throughout his term there existed "a dirty mess in the health department. Some (commissioners) develop into political chiselers and shakedown artists."

Testimony in the poultry case went beyond mere chickens. Commissioner Fred Frank, named as the administration's collector from the brothel interests, apparently dealt directly with Augusto "Chito" Sasso, the coordinator of prostitution. Former deputy district attorney David H. Clark, the slayer of Charlie Crawford, served as coordinator of gambling interests. The collectors from liquor dealers and gamblers were not identified. The police commission decided to investigate the health department, possibly to avert suspicion, since an arrest warrant specifying a charge of bribery was out for ex-commissioner Fred Gollum.

Vice operations stopped while the health commission scandals made headlines. The vice situation remained unsettled. The city "opened" and "closed" for no apparent cause. Observers could provide no answer other than the appointment of the "reform" grand jury, which as yet had not investigated vice conditions. The purveyors of vice were equally bewildered because the administration still collected protection fees, even from those who were temporarily out of business. *Daily News* columnist C.H. Garrigues claimed that the political machine and the criminal syndicate suspected the existence of a secret reform group modeled on the famous Chicago "secret six." The reporter suggested that the situation had eliminated unemployment among detectives because the police secret service, the district attorney's office, the grand jury, the Minutemen and the underworld all had operatives following one another.[13]

Garrigues, himself a secret investigator for the grand jury, came close to the truth. The Shaw administration feared an expose that would provide impetus for a recall election in the summer of 1934. In the context of Los Angeles politics, neither the Minutemen's avowed determination to depose corrupt officials nor the grand jury's refusal to admit the district attorney to its confidence guaranteed the sincerity of their reformist rhetoric. Both public and private civic bodies were traditional political tools. Rumors that former mayors George Cryer and John Porter were leading candidates to oppose Shaw in a recall election supported a cynical interpretation of the reform movement.

The administration had its own spies. John S. Ward, one of the men involved in the entrapment of Police Commissioner Walkup, was employed by the grand jury but also reported secretly to Joseph Shaw. How much Ward knew of the grand jurors' plans is uncertain. His secret memoranda to Joe Shaw revealed the underworld's dissatisfaction with the "on-again, off-again" vice schedule and supported the interpretation that Joe Shaw made the syndicate subservient to the political machine. This reversed the old order, when Kent Parrot and Charlie Crawford ran city hall.

The predicted vice investigation never got underway although the city remained "closed" for much of the year. The grand jury lacked funds. Attempts to subpoena important criminals failed because process servers could not find them. Lawyers for the combination argued that the grand jury, convened to investigate felonies, lacked jurisdiction over vice misdemeanors. Their clients usually refused to testify. Guy McAfee's lieutenant, Homer Gordon, stated that he had paid $2500 that week to bail out the employees of his casino. If he were buying police protection, he was not getting it. Most reporters considered the police raid and Gordon's testimony mere window dressing to protect the administration.

Neither did the proposed recall of Mayor Shaw get started. Grand jury inquiries barely touched the mayor's office. City vice operations seemed to be suppressed. The grand jury failed to press an investigation of two LAPD detectives involved in the sale of stolen bonds. (The men retired several years later with clear records.) The police commissioners explained their part in licensing "Tango," a "chip-and-circle" game that resembled roulette. Revocation of the licenses satisfied the jurors since the city attorney had "mistakenly" declared the game a legal test of skill and science.

Curtailed schedules produced further rationalization of vice operations as well as fiercer competition. E.V. Durling, another *Daily News* columnist, complained that racketeers had taken over even the small-time punchboards, policy handbooks and pools once run by small shopkeepers, druggists and poolhall owners. A quarrel between "Boss A and Boss B" (Guy McAfee and Robert Gans) led to at least one shooting, "hushed up between editions" to avoid a grand jury investigation. The *Citizen-News* quoted Gans' boast that he controlled Chief Davis, Sheriff Biscailuz and District Attorney Fitts. The *Citizen-News* believed that the power struggle subjected vice operators to police raids even though they brought protection.

The stakes appeared to be worth a struggle. The *Citizen-News* estimated the gross returns of a "wide open" city and county vice program at $2,000,000 monthly, of which twenty percent reached selected policemen, politicians and newspaper men. The newspaper asserted that 1100 locations "ran" in the summer of 1933, each paying $50 to $750 weekly for protection. The *Daily News* figured Guy McAfee's income at $100,000 per month during the"hard times" of 1934. The estimated gambling "take" for Los Angeles city was $200,000 per week. The only reliable figures referred to the short experience with legal Tango. Based on the amount of amusement tax paid by the score of Tango parlors, gross declared income for 6 weeks amounted to $1,596,123.

The grand jury made scant progress in police graft and vice investigations. Indifferent prosecutions stymied the indictments of corrupt officials but the long series of exposes had beneficial results. In November, 1934, progressive reformers John Anson Ford, Gordon Legg and Gordon McDonough won seats on the county board of supervisors. With incumbent John R. Quinn, the new supervisors gave the five-member board its first honest majority in memory. Although honest prosecution and vice suppression depended upon the district attorney and the sheriff, two elected officials beyond supervisorial control, the reformers could look optimistically toward 1936 when both would stand for re-election.[14]

The 1934 grand jury scored one tremendous coup over district attorney Fitts. The jury had earlier ruined Fitts' reputation for controlling events by indicting his brother-in-law for stock fraud. It then returned 21 indictments against Fitts himself, including one of perjury. Fitts had let a rich man avoid trial on a morals charge and then sold property to him at an inflated price. Before the 1931 grand jury, Fitts denied culpability but careful work by the 1934 jury proved otherwise. A pamphlet by C.H. Garrigues, "So They Indicted Fitts!" explained the complicated transaction in detail. Following publication, thugs severely beat the *Daily News* reporter.

Fitts denounced the grand jurors as a gang of political hatchetmen. Clever legal work kept the stock fraud case out of the courts until 1937, when the indictments were dismissed. Fitts avoided trial until 1936. The petit jury then accepted his explanation that an honest mistake occurred when, due to overwork, "his brain was paralysed" and he forgot the details of the real estate deal. In late 1934, however, as rumors of Fitts' impending resignation persisted, the reformers foresaw a splendid future. It seemed unlikely that the district attorney could survive the election of 1936 whether or not he resigned or was convicted. Furthermore, the incoming 1935 grand jury might uncover more evidence of malfeasance in the county prosecutor's department.

A struggle began for control of the 1935 grand jury. Reformers wanted the new veniremen to complete the investigations of the outgoing panel. The machine wanted the jury subservient to Buron Fitts. Both sides considered it vital to obtain a sympathetic presiding judge. John P. Buckley, foreman of the 1934 grand jury after illness removed Wayne Fisher, asserted that seventeen of the fifty superior court justices were tools of "the lawless element." The *Daily News* thought the number too low if judges were included who accepted campaign funds from dubious sources. Lacking admissible evidence, Buckley ignored furious demands that he specify the corrupt jurists. An opportunistic Democrat pointed out that all but two of the fifty were Republicans.

Precedent required the selection of Judge Walter S. Gates. Gates, exonerated after indictment for bribery in 1933, was viewed as an enemy of reform. After a stormy meeting at the Elks Hall, the judges passed over Gates but progressive joy was premature. Judge Reuben Schmidt was given charge of the grand jury. George Rochester, serving himself through serving the machine, became grand jury foreman. The 1936 panel also served the machine, wittingly or not. Not until the minority of the 1937 body issued its report did the county grand jury again function as an instrument of reform.

For the three years from January 1935 through January 1938 the political machine and the underworld combination maintained almost total control over city and county law enforcement. Nevertheless, "reform racketeers" successfully extorted money from vice operators by threatening to expose them regardless of protection bought elsewhere.

The most successful to these bore the elegant name, California Republicans Incorporated. An odd trio made the CRI successful. Andy Foley, an obscure but determined criminal, supplied the "muscle" to withstand syndicate retaliation. Orville Forester, a bootlegger, narcotics dealer and brothel keeper, acted as Foley's collector and agent. Rheba Crawford, the Salvation Army's onetime "Angel of Broadway," supplied a respectable front and a popular radio program with which to scourge the merchants of sin.

One of the best descriptions of Los Angeles politics issued from a CRI agent:"The purpose of any political organization is to get the money from the gamblers, and the California Republicans figure that same way." Small slot machine operators paid the CRI as much as $600 weekly to avoid publicity. Foley, in addition to extorting money from slot machine, pinball and liquor law violators, planned to cut into gambling profits in direct competition with Guy McAfee and Bob Gans. According to Orville Forester, the CRI also expected a share of the graft from city contracts approved by the board of public works.

The combination took what steps it safely could to counterattack the reform racketeers. The demolition of pamphleteer Lindon "Red" Foster's apartment provided a dramatic example. In some quarters, the explosion was considered a reminder to Foster not to engage in reform extortions through his broadsheet, the *Los Angeles Equalizer*. The bombing, officially an unsolved crime, was widely believed to be the work of the police intelligence squad.

In another skirmish, police arrested Orville Forester for narcotics possession. The syndicate wanted a conviction but so low was the jurors' regard for the officers' veracity that they accepted the word of a notorious criminal over that of sworn public guardians. Forester accused the detectives of "planting" evidence and won his freedom.[15]

With unquestionable proof of large vice operations in both city and county and the misconduct alleged by the 1934 grand jury, reformers hoped to oust Fitts at last from control of county prosecutions. Unhappily for the progressives, in November of 1936 Fitts defeated the progressive Judge Harlan Palmer of the *Hollywood Citizen-News*. Palmer had excellent reform credentials. Over the years his scathing editorials identified specific police, criminals and protected premises. He also supported Dr. John R. Haynes and the municipal water and power programs.

Palmer had equally significant disabilities. In the "Markham Will Case," an aged man disinherited his daughter and left his estate to a female friend of Palmer, under the judge's trusteeship. Opponents railed at the alleged miscarriage of justice. Moreover, Palmer believed in "the right to work." His adamant free enterprise paternalism provoked labor opposition. In fact, organized labor, represented by J.W. Buzzell of the Central Labor Council, invariably supported the machine candidates.

Palmer also suffered the ailments common to reform campaigns: little money, weak volunteer associations, diffuse aims, divided loyalties, indifferent discipline and poor political theory. Worse, until the last stages of the campaign he refused to use his own journal to promote his candidacy. Only the *Daily News* supported him. Nevertheless, he polled 502,498 of 1,040,884 votes cast. A change of two percent would have given him the victory.

The city administration gave Fitts its entire support. George Rochester, again denied the police commission presidency by the Parrot-McAfee-Gans combination, asked the Shaw machine to support him for district attorney. A Shaw investigator said Rochester wanted to "program" but if he won without the Shaws' support he would drive them from office. Joe Shaw nevertheless spent four months working full time on Fitts' behalf, as did Parrot's lieutenant, William G. Bonnelli. Fitts may have purchased his 36,000 vote majority. A third of it came from the Central Avenue district where rumors of vote buying accompanied every election. Fitts' campaign manager admitted that the underworld supported Fitts because he was "a practical man, not going out to start things".[16]

If the reformers drew hope from the narrowness of Palmer's defeat, it was dashed six months later when Mayor Frank Shaw defeated the progressive challenger, County Supervisor John Anson Ford. Ford, a Protestant Hoover Republican turned Roosevelt Democrat, had broad reform support. Indeed, the self-employed advertising agent would have been an archetypical mayor. However, his defense of the constitutional rights of vagrants and radicals and mild support for "self-help" cooperative relief programs gave the machine an issue. Ford, a sincere Christian apostle of Bruce Barton, found himself described as a dangerous radical. *The Police Patrol,* published by the Police Officers Association of America, warned its readers in huge type that "Reds Back Anson Ford".

In acknowledging Shaw's victory, the *Citizen-News* editor sounded a sombre note. A mere 171,415 citizens, one quarter of the city's 696,119 eligible voters, had re-elected the "invisible government"; only 144,522 supported reform. Thousands of votes were purchased. The underworld, having spent about $2,000,00 to re-elect Buron Fitts, and a further $1,500,000 to re-elect Frank Shaw, now had a clear field for the coming four years. (The dramatic difference in reform voting between

November 1936 and May 1937 which provoked Palmer's understandable pessimism was probably due to F.D.R.'s huge 1936 vote.)[17]

Ford's defeat was more likely due to voter confusion and lack
of information than to apathy or cynicism. The chaotic state of city politics made confusion inevitable. Many voters perhaps viewed Ford's
campaign as another chapter of "Ins versus Outs," an old political farce.
Ford and Shaw were as Tweedle Dee and Tweedle Dum on every point
but one—who should hold office. Not a single economic, political or
ethnic division clarified the issues. Respected leaders of each religious
denomination, political party and significant racial group could be found
in either camp. The Reverend Gustav Briegleb and his followers supported Shaw. The Reverend R.P.Shuler's forces backed Ford. Republican and Democratic progressives supported reform. The old guard of
both parties stayed firmly behind the city machine.

Campaign strategy forced the reformers to take positions on social
welfare, public power, tax reform and racial progress but the brunt of
their attack fell always on political corruption and commercial vice conditions. Yet every mayor, district attorney and sheriff for twenty-five
years past had campaigned as a moral reformer. Buron Fitts was the honest successor to Asa Keyes. Frank Shaw deposed the discredited John
Porter, who overthrew the corrupt George Cryer regime. The reformers,
including Harlan Palmer and John Anson Ford, were "Porter men" in
1929, "Fitts men" in 1930 and "Shaw men" in 1933. Given these circumstances, moral reform was a bankrupt political issue.

Furthermore, the *Daily News* had eschewed overt partisanship due
to severe advertising losses during the Palmer campaign. Not a single
major metropolitan daily newspaper supported Ford's candidacy. This
was a severe blow, especially since the *Daily News* publisher, Manchester Boddy, was a sincere capitalist whose advocacy would have helped
restore public confidence in Ford. On the other hand, the machine apparently had little difficulty in convincing people that Ford's liberal Christianity masked a "godless Communist." Even some progressives thought
him too radical, for he had once suggested that everyone had a right to
eat. With the *Daily News* muzzled and the treasury empty, reformers
could not reach the uninformed public to declare Ford's virtues or to
refute the red smear.[18]

At the moment of defeat, however, events were in motion that
would accomplish in a short time all that the reformers had striven for in
forty years of sincere effort. In retrospect, the Palmer and Ford campaigns would seem necessary preliminary steps. City and county

machines would topple. The "invisible government" would remove to Las Vegas. An "independent," "impartial," "professional" police force would be established. New civic heroes would emerge. The government of Los Angeles would be profoundly and permanently altered.

The 1937 grand jury was remarkable for two reasons. Though dominated by the machine it began investigations that toppled the city government and it propelled Clifford Clinton, an obscure restaurant owner, to national prominence as a civic reformer. Clinton did not lack resolute associates in the stirring years that followed but he was the only irreplaceable man in the reform movement. Without his energy and wealth the final campaign might not have commenced, let alone triumphed.

Clinton, the son of Salvation Army missionaries, operated the "restaurant of the golden rule," where customers need pay as little as they chose, or pay nothing. During the Depression he sold "five course meals," consisting of soup, salad, bread, jello and coffee, for five cents. He sold a simple repast for one cent and simply gave away thousands of meals to destitute people. His analysis of the county hospital food services showed Supervisor John Anson Ford the way to considerable savings through the elimination of graft. Ford then recommended Clinton to Judge Fletcher Bowron, who placed Clinton's name on the 1937 grand jury list.

By chance or collusion, Clinton was included in the jury convened by Judge William Tell Aggeler in February, 1937. Nine jurors—enough to block indictments—had connections to the machine, important in an election year. Six others heeded the advice of the outgoing jury foreman: "Be a mill and grind up what they bring you." Only Earl Kelly, Harry Ferguson, John Bogue and Clifford Clinton disturbed the composure of Deputy District Attorney Eugene Blalock, a trusted Fitts aide assigned to the grand jury.

The four men interviewed gamblers and harlots and collected evidence, including photographs, but the jury majority refused to examine it. Juryman Bogue asserted that 1800 bookmakers, 200 gambling houses and 600 brothels blighted the area. Mrs. A.A. Blatherwick, the socially-prominent leader of a women's church group, called on Mayor Shaw to explain Bogue's allegations. Shaw denied the existence of protected vice but committed a tactical blunder. He promised to invest his personal authority in any sincere citizen organization that would undertake a vice investigation.

Hearing this, the progressives chose a committee to accept Shaw's challenge. The committee included Dr. A.M. Wilkinson, Wendell Miller of University Methodist Church, Mrs. Blatherwick and Mrs. U.S. George, John P. Buckley, the 1934 grand jury foreman, the Reverend R.P. Shuler and James B. Agnew, a 1936 grand juryman. The committee named Clifford Clinton as chairman, with headquarters in his cafe at 618 South Olive Street.[19]

Clinton's group requested Mayor Shaw's official blessing. The mayor had not expected Clinton; worse still, a recent attempt to assassinate George Lester "Les" Bruneman, "king" of Redondo Beach gamblers, buttressed Clinton's earlier charges. Police, "with machine-like precision," were rounding up "scores of bookmakers." Over the opposition of Chief Davis, Shaw approved the reform association. The group then styled itself the Citizens' Independent Vice Investigation Committee, causing Shaw to withdraw his endorsement. With some justification, Shaw accused CIVIC of "attempting to destroy public confidence in the officials of this city."

The administration struck at CIVIC through Dr. Wilkinson. While serving as a county welfare commissioner, Wilkinson managed "The Last Days of Pompeii," a charity pageant promoted by the Church Brotherhood. Instead of profit it produced a deficit. Into the breach stepped underworld bosses Guy McAfee and Bob Gans with donations of $4,400 and $400, respectively. Then, in a strange tableau, McAfee at Wilkinson's request went to his knees and joined the minister in prayer. Presumably this sanctified the brothel, casino and slot machine profits. Painful publicity resulted.

The grand jury later indicted Wilkinson's assistant for reform racketeering in Hollywood. The man pleaded guilty to extortion and received a short sentence. Other picaresque characters, after convincing Clinton of their reformist zeal, went over to the machine and denounced CIVIC as a political racket. CIVIC's underworld informants were often open to defamation. The Shaw administration frequently pointed out that a rabble graduated from prisons and mental hospitals dared to malign respectable public officials.[20]

Grand juryman Clinton demanded the right to call and examine witnesses. After one day, Deputy D.A. Blalock stopped the procedure. Clinton then applied for a writ of mandamus to the effect that political considerations made certain jurors unfit to serve. Two were related to slot machine operators. Another was the wife of Bob Gans' accountant. A fourth was known as a bagman for Central Avenue vice operators. Sworn affidavits alleged that foreman John Bauer improperly obtained lucrative city paint contracts.[21]

The paint contract affidavit led to more vicious conduct. The grand jury indicted Leo Flowers, a competitor of Bauer's, for perjury. Foreman Bauer, District Attorney Fitts and Deputy Blalock raided the home of Pat

Angellilo, the notary public who had witnessed Flowers' affidavit concerning Bauer. In the skirmish that followed, Fitts struck one of the Angellilo brothers with a pistol. Mrs. Angellilo laid Blalock's scalp open with a stick of firewood. Two policemen also suffered slight injuries. The fight was abandoned but furnished CIVIC with an exploitable example of cossackism. Bauer's misconduct in organizing and voting on the Flowers indictment led to his own conviction for contempt. The judge ejected a deputy district attorney sent by Fitts to defend Bauer.

In the meantime, Clinton was refused a permit to operate a second restaurant after spending large sums to renovate it. The taxes on his first cafe rose dramatically overnight without explanation. At the restaurant, complaints of food poisoning became commonplace. Patrons "fell" on the steps and floors. Clinton opened an aid station and warned customers that they entered at their own risk.

On October 29, 1937, a bomb destroyed part of Clinton's home. Fortunately, no one was injured. The police made a cursory investigation. Someone suggested that Clinton dynamited his own house to gain publicity. Most reformers suspected the police spy squad. An auto seen speeding from the scene was identical to one assigned to the intelligence section. An investigation several years later revealed that the spy squad maintained a full surveillance of Clinton, including dictograph recordings of his private meetings. Since the recordings revealed Clinton's knowledge of police corruption, the spy squad may have hoped to intimidate Clinton by threatening his family.

Included among the spy squad recordings was a conversation between Clinton and David Hutton, the recent husband of Aimee Semple McPherson. The interview took place after the two female evangelists quarrelled over Rheba Crawford's alleged shakedown of the machine. McPherson apparently believed that Crawford sold her political support for $130,000. This cannot be proven. Crawford, however, turned suddenly from berating the Shaw machine and accused Clinton of "fronting for the most notorious band of political racketeers that ever attempted to move in on any decent American community."[22]

It appeared that the 1937 grand jury term would expire without serious embarrassment to the machine, notwithstanding Clinton's diverting tactic of picketing protected brothels as "unfair to organized police," and the assassination of Les Bruneman in the Roost Cafe on West Temple Street. Other killings followed, part of a battle between competing bookmakers' race wire services that the police seemed unable to control or mediate. In late December, the grand jury majority reported that "no evidence of corruption has been presented to this grand jury...Public enemy number one in this country is not the gun-toting racketeer, the confidence man, or the business shylock...He is the malicious, unbridled, reputation-smearing gossip."

Clinton, Kelly, Bogue and Ferguson submitted a minority report. Judge Charles W. Fricke, successor to the deceased Judge Aggeler, ordered the unprecedented report kept secret. The four then presented it to Judge Fletcher Bowron, who pronounced it a legal public document. CIVIC quickly distributed thousands of small pamphlets that included the minority report and a statement of CIVIC's purpose and principles.

The minority report, though impassioned in terminology, spoke directly to the point: "a deplorably bad influence is being exerted over local government by a powerful, greedy, ruthless underworld political machine supplied with an abundance of funds from the growing profits from illicit operations." Beginning with Guy McAfee and Bob Gans it named more than thirty local gang members. It explained how the syndicate supported and controlled politicians. It declared that "the three principal law enforcement agencies of the county, the district attorney, the sheriff, and the chief of police of Los Angeles, work in complete harmony and never interfere with the activities of important figures in the underworld."[23]

The most bizarre event in the city's political annals occurred on January 14, 1938. A bomb wired to the ignition of a CIVIC investigator's auto exploded with tremendous force, destroying the machine and its garage, shattering distant windows, riddling the detective with twelve dozen shrapnel wounds but leaving him miraculously alive. The investigator was the notorious Harry Raymond, returned to play his last role in Los Angeles police history.

Few were better qualified to investigate vice than Raymond. His experiences as police chief of Venice, two stints with the LAPD (interrupted by service with District Attorney Asa Keyes) and his most recent duty as San Diego police chief, all terminated in scandal. He apparently was involved in a shakedown of ex-police commissioner Harry Munson when he became acquainted with Clinton. Clinton employed Raymond to get evidence against his old associates in the police force and the combination.

The Munson Case originated during Frank Shaw's 1933 mayoralty campaign. Campaign assistant Munson failed to pay $3,000 owed to one Ralph Gray for political services. Gray sued Munson, forcing his resignation from the police board. Gray charged that Munson attended a meeting with Kent Parrot, Guy McAfee and Bob Gans, where a huge

Shaw campaign fund was raised. The case was scheduled to be heard January 22, 1938, one week after the bombing occurred. Subpoenas had been issued for McAfee, Gans, Parrot and others. CIVIC hoped for a great expose of the Shaw machine. The attempt on Raymond's life was clearly meant to eliminate the most dangerous witness.

All evidence pointed to Captain Earl E. Kynette, commander of the LAPD Special Intelligence Section. Kynette, nevertheless, was for a short time engaged in investigating the crime. He offered the opinion that Raymond himself constructed the bomb for publicity but misjudged the amount of explosive. Chief Davis, rushing back from pistol matches in Mexico City, proclaimed Kynette's innocence from afar, before examining the evidence. Even after public opinion forced Kynette's suspension, he continued to direct the spy squad.

Kynette, the most infamous "dirty-work man" in LAPD annals, had joined the department in 1925 as an agent of vice boss Albert Marco. In 1927, a police trial board convicted him of extorting money from prostitutes but he won a mysterious reinstatement and a promotion to sergeant. Kynette's influence declined when Marco went to prison but he regained favor under the Joe Shaw-Chief Davis regime. The Langan case demonstrated his ruthlessness. He also operated a reform racket, having seized control of Robert Noble's "ham and eggs" movement.[24]

Following the bombing, a new reform club, the Federation for Civic Betterment, united church, labor, business and social groups (including CIVIC) in a single organization determined to overthrow the machine and the combination. A "committee of twenty-five" directed the campaign. Although recall of the mayor seemed the most obvious strategy, the *Times* and many progressives believed recalls too expensive, too democratic and completely ineffective. Not until March did the circulation of recall petitions begin. The machine also circulated recall petitions, which were then destroyed. Finally, Clinton hired a commercial agency to collect the required 62,000 genuine signatures. The recall election was scheduled for September 16, 1938. The incumbent would be on the ballot and could be re-elected by a plurality of votes, even though a majority might vote to recall him.

The reformers had an issue—good government—but no candidate. Conservatives still found John Anson Ford too radical. Harlan Palmer received no serious consideration. Assemblyman Samuel Yorty had strong radical support and wanted the nomination. Yorty had once stumped the state in company with Dorothy Healy, a known communist. Yorty's attack on "the kings of capital and the princes of power" made him unacceptable to most progressives. Fletcher Bowron, the one man upon whom all parties might agree, refused to run.

Although radicals in the reform coalition feared that the conservative Bowron might retain the red squad, the communist leader, Donald Healy, finally swung the liberal block from Yorty to Bowron. Bowron accepted the draft on his own conditions. No promises would be made and no money not clearly accounted for would be accepted. Scarcely a month remained before the election. [25]

The machine overlooked nothing in its drive for re-election. Vice raids began. The *Citizen-News* noted that even the famous joint at 732 North Highland had been raided by Lieutenant Hoy, "under whose able protection it has operated all these years." Chief Davis made speeches on Shaw's behalf. Physical and verbal harassment of Bowron campaign workers occurred. WPA workers were warned of lost jobs if Shaw failed to win. The police commissioners and other city officials issued thousands of letters praising the mayor.

Clinton and Bowron were denounced as communists and as fascists, as radicals and as anti-labor, as bluenosed busybodies and as political racketeers. In black neighborhoods, callers identified themselves as Klansmen and asked for Bowron votes. In Catholic areas, machine literature announced that "Fighting Bob Shuler asks your vote for his candidate—Fletcher Bowron." In Jewish areas, large billboards portrayed Clinton and Bowron as Nazis, while radio broadcasts warned of their Communist sympathies. Rheba Crawford and Aimee Semple McPherson endorsed Mayor Shaw. Publicists distorted Clinton's remark that a legal vice zone might reduce police corruption. The Reverend Briegleb published a false roster of "ministers for Shaw." Spurious American Legion endorsements also appeared. [26]

The machine had certain obvious advantages: control of the city government, underworld financing, and the *Los Angeles Times*. The Raymond bombing, however, provoked two significant defections from the Shaw camp. First, the Hearst newspapers embraced reform. It has been suggested that Hearst's manager, Nicholas Van Ettisch, feared that Joe Shaw was about to take over the county too. This aided Bowron directly and also removed the pressure from Manchester Boddy's *Daily News*. The *Examiner, Herald-Express, Daily News* and *Citizen-News* gave the Bowron campaign powerful and effective support.

Second, District Attorney Buron Fitts abandoned the city machine. His prosecution of Captain Kynette and two subordinates kept the corrupt police department and its blundering chief constantly in the public eye from February until July. Former state senator George Rochester turned up as one of Kynette's attorneys and correctly pointed out that under the Los Angeles system of justice an innocent man could quite easily be convicted, but the jurors refused to believe that Kynette was "framed." The convictions of Kynette and Patrolman Lloyd Allen greatly aided the reform campaign.

During the trial, Chief Davis explained that Kynette investigated "criminal and criminal-political elements... attempting to destroy confidence in the police department." Asked why the squad spied on Sam Yorty, Carey McWilliams, Clifford Clinton, Fletcher Bowron and other leading citizens, Davis said that all had been arrested. This charge proved to include traffic citations. The trial judge described Davis' testimony as "a debris" and the police records as "a rubble."

Doubt arose that Davis actually controlled the intelligence squad. Kynette's second in command told the grand jury that he "had heard" that Kynette reported directly to Joseph E. Shaw. Kynette asserted that he often sent reports directly to prosecutor Fitts. Other intelligence squad members declined to testify for fear of incrimination, even to tell how long they had served or whether they had ever made arrests. One veteran suspected a political witch hunt: "Mr. Fitts has his problems, and we have ours." A juror asked whether the officer believed that public officials did "dishonorable, criminal things?" "Yes, I do," he replied.[27]

During the Kynette trial the LAPD also was connected to a bribery system at the Santa Anita race track that allowed bookmakers to operate. Police Commissioner Charles W. Ostrom found it expedient to represent syndicate member Milton "Farmer" Page in a suit involving Signal Hill oil properties. Mayor Shaw deplored the fact that a member of the "policy-making board for the police" would represent a gambler but Ostrom replied that the board had no control over the police department. Ironically, only days after Kynette and Allen were convicted of attempted murder, the LAPD celebrated "Law Observance Day."

The progressives received the support of organized Protestantism, the Merchants and Manufacturers Association, all the newspapers except the *Times* and perhaps the most potent weapon, Clifford Clinton's radio broadcasts. The programs literally opened with a roar. A short reenactment of the Raymond bombing preceded Clinton's scathing attacks on machine politics and personalities. The Roper Poll estimated that 300,000 listeners heard each of the four daily broadcasts.

Money, organization and publicity, plus a clear issue, carried the day. Bowron soundly defeated Shaw. Although the voter turnout, 46.6

percent, did not differ significantly from the 46.4 percent of the Shaw-Ford election, Bowron carried every district and received almost two thirds of the votes. Shaw's strongest support came from the Central Avenue wards.[28]

The progressives had captured the highest municipal office. While the new mayor set himself to the practical aspects of reforming the city, Clinton and the CIVIC organization turned their attention to the county district attorney. Only with the defeat of Buron Fitts could they savour the full delights of victory. They looked forward with confidence to the 1940 county elections.

NOTES

[1] "Transcript between Wilbur LeGette, Helen LeGette and Others, Joseph Shaw *Papers,* Box 8, File "David Clark"; Motto chosen by Clifford Clinton for the reform organization.

[2] Shaw, Box 8, File "Correspondence, 1933-1935"; *Record,* 5-20-31; Perry, 227-241, *passim.* Shaw, Box 6, miscellaneous file including Shuler's allegations. *Record,* 6-25-25, 8-21-25, 3-22-26, 6-3-26, 8-28-26, 10-4-26, for examples of county government scandals; also 8-16-28, 8-17-28, 8-24-28, 7-24-29, 8-10-31, 8-11-31. *Daily News,* 5-10-30, 6-30-30, 8-16-30. See Arthur E. Briggs memoirs (U.C.L.A. Oral History typescript), 523, for example of payoffs to councilmen through "poker winnings." Others covered bribes by selling insurance to the briber. Shaw, Box 11, File "Frank L. Shaw Campaigns, 1925-1938." See the memoirs of former County Supervisor John R. Quinn (U.C.L.A. Oral History typescript), 84-100, *passim;* also the recollections of former Supervisor John Anson Ford, *Thirty Explosive Years in Los Angeles County* (1961), *passim.* See especially the affidavit dated 11-7-30, Shaw, Box 8, unidentified file, for assertions that Shaw took bribes. Also Box 11. Superior Court No. 51454. *Times,* 6-1-33.

[3] *Herald,* 6-2-33. Shaw, Box 6, miscellaneous file. Box 11, File "Frank L. Shaw Campaigns, 1925-1938," Box 8, File "Correspondence, 1933-1935." Robert P. Shuler, *Silenced* (L.A.,1931). *Record,* 11-13-31. In 1931, E.A. Dickson's *Express* was combined with the *Herald,* another former E.T. Earl journal taken over by W.R. Hearst. The *Record,* between issues on 11-7-32, switched its support from W.G.McAdoo to R.P. Shuler for U.S. senator. The editors resigned and the paper quickly deteriorated. The *Daily News* remained neutral due to advertising considerations; the *Hollywood Citizen-News,* by itself, had little influence. Bloom, *op.cit.* P.C. *Minutes,* 11-13-33, 9-21-34. *Daily News,* 6-30-33, 7-5-33, 7-14-33, 7-19-33.

[4] *Daily News,* 6-6-33, 7-4-33, 7-6-33, 7-28-33, 8-3-33, 8-5-33, 8-9-33, 8-10-33. *Examiner,* 8-9-33, 8-10-33, 8-12-33. *Times,* 8-8-33, 8-11-33; cf. *Times,* 1-1-30, 1-2-30, 1-3-30. See Shaw, Box 9, File "Correspondence, 1933-1935" for transcripts of secret dictaphone recordings of conversations among underworld figures. See also J. Ward's report to J.E. Shaw of conversation with Miles Dempster about Frank Shaw's claim to Canadian citizenship.

[5] *Daily News,* 7-22-33, 8-5-33. P.C. *Minutes,* 4-18-33, 8-15-33,

passim; 1-15-34, 1-29-34, 3-13-34, 8-27-34, 3-18-35, 7-30-35. The P.C. *Minutes* do not record Lucas' reinstatement. *Times,* 10-13-33, 1-23-37, 5-5-37. Shaw, Box 6, File "Correspondence, 1933-1935."

⁶ LAPD *Bulletin,* 7-16-33, 9-6-33, 9-13-33, 9-19-33, 10-24-33, 7-7-34, 9-14-34. P.C. *Minutes,* 8-10-34. *Times,* 6-2-34. *Daily News,* 3-28-34, 3-29-34, 6-1-34, 6-2-34, 6-27-34, 7-6-24, 7-11-34, 8-27-34, 9-29-34.

⁷ City Charter, 1925 Art. IX, Sec. 202. J.E. Davis to Mayor J.E. Porter, 10-9-29, Vollmer *Papers,* Box I, File "L.A.P.D." P.C. *Minutes,* 5-16-30, 1-20-31, 4-13-31, 7-2-31. A.H. Hohmann, *loc.cit. Daily News,* 1-30-30, 2-26-30, 5-7-30. *Record,* 7-2-31; cf. the Municipal League *Bulletin,* 4-31-26 and 4-20-32 for discussion of police unions as a tactic.

⁸ *Record,* 7-23-31 daily through 8-31-31; 9-4-31. P.C. *Minutes,* 1-1-30, 9-1-32, passim. LAPD *Bulletin,* 1-30-30. *Daily News,* 12-29-32, 4-27-33, 5-16-33. P.C. *Minutes,* 5-1-33, 6-21-33. City Charter, 1935; Halstead, *loc.cit.*

⁹ Shaw, Box 6, "Correspondence, 1933-1935". See also *Daily News,* 8-1-33, 12-30-33, 3-27-34, 3-30-34, 4-5-34, 7-13-34, 10-25-34.

¹⁰ See the rebuke of Steinbeck in *Collier's Magazine,* 9-2-29. Municipal League *Bulletin.* V. 10, No. 72, 3-15-36. For an extended discussion of the blockade, see Leader, ch. 10; *Daily News,* 12-22-33, 12-8-34. LAPD, "Transiency in Southern California" (L.A. 1937). *Times,* 2-5-26, 2-9-36, 2-20-36. The Langan case received local newspaper coverage. A good short account is Dwight McKinney and Fred Allhoff, "The Lid Off Los Angeles," pt. 3, *Liberty* (12-25-39). The six part series contains much valuable information but is so distorted by errors of fact and of interpretation as to be useless to the general reader. On the basis of these articles, Mayor Frank Shaw won a settlement out of court for an undisclosed amount. Perry and Perry, 399-415. Bloom, *passim.* Council files 4-88 (1936), 3287 (1935).

¹¹ See the remarks of George Bush, Fitts' campaign manager, in the *Daily News,* 7-21-33. An impassioned but factually correct account by a Minuteman is Guy W. Finney, *Angel City in Turmoil* (L.A.: American Press, 1945). Also Raymond Haight's story "Indicted: How a City Political Gang Got Its Man," *Scribner's* 44 (March, 1934), 195-198. William G. Bonelli, *Billion Dollar Blackjack* (Beverly Hills: Civic Research Press, 1954), 56. Over $372,000 flowed through Helen Werner's secret account during 1929-1933. *Times,* 7-20-33. Daily News, 7-21-33 to 8-3-33, passim; 1-19-34, 2-10-34, 2-17-34, 3-6-34, 4-19-34, through 4-26-34, 5-9-34, 5-10-34, 5-21-34, 8-27-34. *Examiner,* 8-28-34. *Times,* 8-29-34.

¹² Reuben W. Borough (U.C.L.A. Oral History transcript), *passim;*

Finney, *passim; Daily News,* 1-22-34, 2-1-34, 2-5-34, 2-23-34, 2-24-34, 3-5-34, 3-17-34, 3-21-34, 4-5-34, 4-20-34, 5-31-34, 11-10-34, 11-27-34, 12-24-34.

[13] *Daily News,* 1-25-34, 1-19-34, 2-9-34, through 1-17-34, 2-22-34, 3-29-34, 4-21-34, 5-17-34, 5-25-34, 6-15-34, 10-1-34. See E.S. Ward reports to Joseph Shaw, Shaw, Box 18.

[14] Shaw, Box 8, File" Correspondence, 1933-1935." *Ibid.,* File "LeGette." Finney, 87-95. *Citizen News,* 11-29-33, 12-23-33. *Daily News,* 4-19-33, 8-29-33, 8-30-33, 8-31-33, 9-8-33 through 9-15-33, 9-26-33, 10-5-33, 12-23-33, 2-1-34, 2-12-34, 3-13-34, 4-14-34, 4-26-34, 5-3-34, 5-7-34, 5-10-34, 6-30-34, 7-11-34, 7-18-34, 7-30-34, 9-13-34, 11-10-34. Grace Featherhoff, "An Authentic Detailed Record of the First Supervisorial Campaign of John Anson Ford, July-December, 1934" (unpublished manuscript, Special Collections Department, U.C.L.A.), *passim.*

[15] *Ibid;* Quinn, *passim. Daily News,* 7-6-34, 8-9-34, 9-12-34, 9-20-34, 9-22-34, 11-6-34, 11-7-34. L.A. City Charter, 1935. Finney, 44-50. *Examiner,* 2-26-35, 2-27-35. Shaw, Box 9 File "LeGette"; File "Correspondence, 1933-1935." *Daily News,* 6-2-33, 8-15-33, 6-20-34, 6-21-34, 7-3-34, 7-5-34, 11-2-34, 12-5-34, 12-6-34, 1-4-35, 1-8-35.

[16] Council File 229 (1936). E.W. Biscailuz Scrapbook No.2, *passim.* June E. Hallberg, "The Fitts-Palmer Campaign for District Attorney in Los Angeles County, 1936" (unpublished M.A. thesis, 1940); see also Terrys T. Olender, *For the Prosecution: Miss Deputy D.A.* (N.Y. 1961), for an insight into conditions in Fitts' office.

[17] Shaw, Box 8, File "1936-1937." Arthur E. Briggs, Memoirs (U.C.L.A. Oral History typescript, 1970), 605. Hallberg, 39-40, 102-106, 141-142. Borough, 199-210, especially 200. *American Police Patrol,* V.1, No.3, 3-1-37. See also *Civil Service Monitor,* V.7, No.11, April 1937. *Citizen News,* 5-5-37.

[18] *Times,* 5-1-39. Jerry Saul Caplan, "The CIVIC Committee in the Recall of Mayor Shaw" (Unpublished M.A. thesis, U.C.L.A., 1947), 90,97. Harold H. Story Memoirs (U.C.L.A. Oral History typescript, 1967), 696-740, passim. See the series of campaign statements by Ford and Shaw in James Bolger's "Campaign Scrapbook, 1937"; Shaw, Box 11, File "F.L.S. Campaigns, 1925-1938." Hallberg, 114. Borough, 219.

[19] See "The CIVIC Committee of Los Angeles, Its Background, Activities and Accomplishments" and "The Revolt of the Angelinos," in E.R. Chamberlain Collection, U.C.L.A. Special Collections. Of several dozen articles in national magazines, the most informative is a three-part account by Mrs. Nelda Clinton, published in *True Story Magazine* in

December, 1940, and January and February, 1941. See also the newspaper accounts collected by Joe Shaw, Shaw Scrapbooks, *passim.*

[20] Shaw, Box 8, File "Statements of Frank Shaw, 1937"; File "1936-1937"; Box 11, unidentified file, secret report alleging Coyne's guilt.

[21] See Clinton's affidavits in his mandamus suit No. 420607, copy in Shaw, Box 7.

[22] Chamberlain, "CIVIC", 44-46, 50-55; Nelda Clinton, ii, iii. C.M. *Monitor,* 10-9-37, copy in E.W. Biscailuz Scrapbook No.3. See E.E. Kynette's appeal in the Second Criminal No. 3136, especially 504-513.

[23] Chamberlain, "CIVIC", 55-72. Photos in *Evening Herald and Express,* 4-7-39. Verne St. Cloud, "What's Behind the Bruneman Slaying?" *Official Detective,* 1-1-38 through 6-1-38 (the best popular account of the underworld conflict). L.A. County Grand Jury Summary *Minority Report;* also CIVIC Committee's Purpose, Plans, Organization, 1937. Clinton Papers.

[24] Shaw, Box 11, File "Raymond." The best narrative of this central event is a series of articles titled "Who Bombed Harry Raymond?" *People's World,* 2-2-38 through 2-12-38. The Kynette trial is Superior Court No. 71338. See Shaw, Box 11, unidentified file for Munson case documents. Kynette grand jury transcript, 275 and 342, Shaw, Box 7. James Richardson, *For the Life of Me,* 222-223.

[25] Chamberlain, "CIVIC", 61-75. Caplan, 73-85, 90. Borough, 226-230. Clinton Papers, File "Fletcher Bowron."

[26] *Citizen-News,* 4-6-37. Chamberlain, "CIVIC", 68. See the police commission's letter and attached propaganda directed at W.P.A. workers, Chamberlain Collection; also the Shaw campaign materials, especially the *Herald of Decency,* 3-19-38 and the *Allied Democrat,* 9-7-38, in the Clinton Papers. Caplan, 97; Clinton Papers, photograph file; also Shaw, Box 11, File "L.A. Boosters."

[27] J.H. Richardson, *For the Life of Me,* 213. H.H. Story, Shaw's personal secretary, quoted by Caplan, 62-63, also 109-110. Kynette appeal transcript 204, 217; Kynette grand jury transcript, 261-262, 334, 339. Shaw, Box 7. Chamberlain, "CIVIC", 62. *Times,* 6-25-38. LAPD *Bulletin,* 7-12-38.

[28] Chamberlain, "CIVIC", 74-76. Caplan, 95-96, 111-116, 124-128. G.A. Briegleb remained loyal to Shaw. Shaw, Box 11, unidentified file contains transcripts of Briegleb's pro-Shaw broadcasts. Clinton radio scripts are in Clinton Papers. After two years, Shaw's wife divorced him in Nevada. See her letter to Shaw promising to remain silent. Shaw, Box 14, File "Miscellaneous Correspondence, 1940-1950".

CHAPTER SEVEN

A GENERATION OF REFORM

It would probably take two generations of reform to produce
the kind of police department we would like to have.
                                                    August Vollmer

Progressivism as a movement expired during Mayor Bowron's
long tenure. The old progressives departed, some rejected by the voters,
some into retirement, some taken by death. So too with the vice entrepreneurs, corrupt politicians and venal policemen. Perhaps some went willingly, but many, especially the remnants of the combination, fought on
for years, hoping to overturn the reform administration. Bowron's ability
to win elections, long after the reform coalition collapsed, prevented
both the old and the new generations of criminals and opportunistic
politicians from turning back the clock. The police department made significant progress in the direction of professionalism but not without
struggle and occasional defeat. The days of scandal and disgrace were
not yet past.

The Bowron administration found the municipal departments in
the expected sorry state. The reformers soon uncovered evidence of
gross misconduct, patronage and graft. Some officials lost their jobs but
very few prosecutions ensued. Water and Power commissioner Alfred
Lushing was convicted of extortion in the cleaners and dyers organizational battle. Civil Service commissioner William Cormack and Joe
Shaw were convicted of sixty-six offenses in connection with the sale of
jobs and promotions. General Manager Glen Gravatt escaped indictment
by testifying for the prosecution. Police Lieutenant Pedro Del Gado,
involved in selling police appointments, fled to Mexico.

Bowron ousted nearly 100 commissioners, including the entire
police board. Clyde C. Shoemaker, Raymond Haight, Henry Bodkin,
John P. Buckley and Van M. Griffith took office. The new commission
followed three broad policies: the elimination of every aspect of vice, no
matter how insignificant, the enforcement of rules for proper conduct and
the elimination of unsuitable officers. Each policy met strong opposition.

The California Amusement Machine Operators Association (CAMOA) raised large sums to lobby for its interests. Charles Craddick and Kent Parrot represented CAMOA, to which successful slot machine operators paid "dues" of $1.80 per machine per week plus $25 per machine per election. A small decal signified good standing. Police usually confiscated coin machines not bearing the current CAMOA seal. The commission requested that coin games be forbidden by charter amendment. CAMOA fought hard but its five-night festival of chorus girls and free liquor for city officials and prominent citizens proved inferior to photographs of youths and children playing the machines. The reformers won an easy victory.

Race bookmakers presented a different problem. A legal decision that bets could be placed directly at the track by telephone produced a number of "legal" betting shops. The decision failed to stand and bookies again went underground. The Pacific Telephone Company received considerable criticism for installing telephones in bookmaking locations. Determined police work drove most bookmakers into county territory.

The commissioners struck hard at so-called "escort" services. They limited massage parlors to the service of a single sex and required attendants to be of the same sex as the patrons. Licensing and police surveillance of "B-girl" cabaret hostesses in Main Street bars proved unsatisfactory because a state agency controlled the owners' liquor licences. The city government could not exert real control over disreputable premises. The commission wanted property owners warned and punished but the problem remained. Going further, the Reverend John Kingsley, replacing Commissioner Haight, asked that entry to nightclubs and bars be denied to unescorted women and to women clad in slacks whether escorted or not. Prudery emerged again when the health department obtained "The Condemned," a film dealing with venereal disease and "sex hygiene." The police commission refused to permit the film to be shown.

The new board restated all the old rules against policemen loitering around pool halls, "mooching" from merchants, drinking liquor while on duty and acting as agents for lawyers and bailbondsmen. The commissioners proscribed the sale of raffle or other tickets by policemen, warned against seeking personal newspaper publicity, eliminated most special badges and revoked the police band's privileges. They also proposed a monthly statement by each officer of the sum and sources of his income.[1]

The progressive commissioners then turned their attention to the departmental personnel. Even before the new board took office, some of

the more vulnerable officers retired, among them Captain Monte Thorn-
burgh, head of the vice division, and Lieutenant Sydney "Sweetie Pie"
Sweetnam, the reputed boss of Central Avenue vice. Though taunted for
running away, Chief Davis wisely followed, forestalling any possible
disciplinary proceedings. Then, since charter section 181 permitted the
commission to retire anyone eligible for pension "for the good of the service," the commissioners ousted twenty-three senior officials, including
Assistant Chief George Allen, Deputy Chief Roy Steckel and Chief of
Detectives Joseph Taylor. Eleven captains and nine lieutenants completed the list. A dozen more followed shortly afterward.

Inspector D.I. Davidson assumed temporary command while the
unwilling pensioners battled for reinstatement. The *Times* and the Reverend Briegleb deplored the "premature" loss of so many experienced
officers but the reformers intended to rid the force of many more such
men. Several hundred men whose physical disabilities unfitted them for
duty nevertheless clung to their positions. An eighty-one year old patrolman still served as jailer. Councilman Roy Hampton proposed that fifty
percent of the personnel be replaced over a five-year period.

Unsuitable policemen eligible for pension were eliminated
through a process later called "Biffleizing." Armed with facts and
rumors concerning breaches of regulations, the newly promoted Inspector Biffle visited men who could be ousted under section 181. His vague
remarks usually resulted in a pension application. Approximately 150
officers retired during the following two years. Many accused the administration of a "purge." Although the city council held extensive hearings,
the "Biffleized" men did not return.

The mass exodus had two profound results. First, it removed
almost all of the senior officers who cooperated with the combination
and the machine. Veteran officers have asserted that no corrupt faction
ever again controlled the department, although dishonest officers
remained on the force. This was a giant first step toward reform. Second,
removal of the rogue policemen broke the syndicate's power in the city.
James H. Richardson, city editor of the *Examiner* and a Bowron confi-
dant, asserted that wire tappers obtained crucial evidence against the
police and the criminals by monitoring the police telephone lines. A spy
in the mayor's office informed the syndicate of the content of the recordings and the "invisible government" departed overnight. Guy McAfee,
Tudor Scherer and Wade Buckwald bought casinos in Las Vegas. Tony
Cornero, Farmer Page and others moved onto gambling boats in the harbor or over the city limits into the county. The *Times*, long indifferent to

vice and opposed to reform, noted the absence of "the former crap dealers, wheelmen, and card dealers who a year ago could be found up and
down Spring Street."

Venal officers with less than twenty years of service could not be
summarily retired nor discharged. City charter section 202 protected
them. The Shaws had encouraged the police amendments to section 202.
After the Raymond bomb incident, however, the administration
bemoaned its inability to interfere. While Kynette and two aides faced
criminal charges, the police trial board exonerated the other intelligence
squad detectives. The Shaw police commission ruled that refusal to
answer grand jury inquiries would in future constitute "conduct unbecoming an officer." The Bowron commissioners further forbade officers
to invoke constitutional provisions against self-incrimination when testifying in court. These measures did not affect the internal administration
of discipline under charter section 202.

During the recall, CIVIC strategists carefully ignored the new
police autonomy, although they planned to restore public control. They
saw no reason for a police disciplinary process separate from regular
civil service procedures. The new commissioners suggested rescinding
the 1931, 1934 and 1937 amendments to section 202 in favor of the original provisions of 1925. Then disciplinary power would again reside in
the chief, under police commission direction.

The reformers quickly learned the limitations of an honest mayor's
power to govern the city. The charter supposed a "weak" executive. General managers of municipal departments answered to appointed, nonprofessional commissioners. The mayor might nominate men he trusted to implement his policies and might demand signed resignations beforehand but he
retained no legal power over the commissions. He could neither appoint nor
depose commissioners without the concurrence of the city council.[2]

The progressives proposed a new charter to strengthen the mayor
at the expense of the council and the commissions. The new constitution
would include adequate public control over the police department, eliminating the need for an "anti-police" movement to overturn section 202.
The plan required a council pledged to Bowron and charter reform. In
1939, therefore, the progressives commenced a campaign to defeat
"reactionary" councilmen.

The strategy failed. Some reform councilmen won election but
strong dissident elements remained. The existing police disciplinary regulations remained in force. Sometimes they worked well. Departmental
infractions usually provoked quick, sure punishment. Occasionally, sec-

tion 202 saved an officer from being sacrificed to outraged but misinformed public opinion. At all times, however, the section shielded officers from the consequences of verbal and physical abuse of citizens—actions often viewed sympathetically by the policemen-judges on the trial board.[3]

The importance placed by Bowron's progressive adherents on petty acts of vice, as opposed to their social causes, has often been noted. Bowron has been accused of being more interested in scandal than in anything else. His relationship with the police department provided a case in point. During the recall election, Bowron promised to protect the department against "shakeups," "snooper squads" and pension reformers. Once elected, he invited the men to report one another's misdeeds to him, using anonymous letters sent to a post office box. Police Commissioner Kingsley continually demanded reduction of police pensions to a maximum of $150 monthly. The mayor and commissioners proposed to revise charter section 202. Once Bowron even ignored a trial board decision and demanded the suspension of an errant officer. He promised impartial application of civil service regulations but often acted like the traditional arbitrary political boss.

To establish that sales of appointments and promotions antedated the Shaw administration, Joe Shaw's defense attorneys proved that Inspector Davidson's score exceeded that of Roy Steckel on the 1930 chief's examination. Someone later lowered his grade. Machine favorites such as Captain D. McD. Jones and Earl E. Kynette had their scores revised upward while those of other men were reduced. The Bowron civil service commission, suspicious of all previous test scores, revoked existing promotion lists and opened new competitions. The administration restricted competition for the chief's job to LAPD veterans having ten or more years of service; 171 candidates entered. Bruce Smith and A.J. Cavanaugh, nationally known police administrators, designed the examination and conducted oral questioning of the eleven men who passed the written test. For the first time since Vollmer's arrival the name of the new chief was not known in advance, although Mayor Bowron favored Captain R.R.McDonald, a graduate of the FBI academy who had J. Edgar Hoover's approval. Acting Chief Davidson scorned the post because "the chief of police is pushed around every time a new administration takes office."

The examination results surprised everyone except, possibly, Lieutenant Arthur H. Hohmann. Hohmann's 94 percent grade exceeded the next highest score by ten percentage points, a huge margin in police civil service examinations. Hohmann was a forty-three year old Protes-

tant Republican from San Francisco, a former army lieutenant and truck-
ing contractor, who had attended Vollmer's original police academy. He
was appointed early in 1925. After fourteen years in the uniformed division, where he exhibited considerable administrative talent, his record
was unblemished but he had few important friends and was practically
unknown. Moreover, he was a man of strong, independent nature.

The *Times* wondered idly how Bowron would avoid appointing
Hohmann. Reason for suspicion existed. Several officers complained about
the grading. The civil service commission turned over the examinations,
grading keys and charts, and allowed the policemen to question the examin-
ers. The consequent adjustment of grades, though raising Hohmann's score,
changed the succeeding places on the list. By rising to third place from
sixth, R.R. McDonald became eligible for selection. Finally, after three
weeks of controversy and mounting concern that an old-time machination
was in progress, the police commission appointed Hohmann.[4]

Mayor Bowron promised Hohmann a free hand in the police
department. Time and events proved otherwise. The chief denied that the
police commission directed his affairs but the commission made all the
important promotions. Almost from the day of his appointment, rumors
alleged that Hohmann's tenure would be short. Cynics expected R.R.
McDonald or another Bowron favorite to assume command. The mayor,
the chief and the CIVIC newsletter denied the stories.

Hohmann intended no traditional "shake-up." Nevertheless, his
organizational reforms provoked considerable unrest and opposition. He
divided the police job in three parts—operations, investigations, functions—and planned to rotate all personnel through each duty on a 90 day
schedule. This inevitably involved extensive changes in living patterns
and work habits. Hohmann favored a military model with line and staff
functions clearly identified and separated. He divided the city into four
semi-autonomous zones. Each division took responsibility for patrol,
investigation and vice suppression. Only when a situation demanded
special expertise would central headquarters personnel be sent to help.

The chief disbanded most of the precinct detective bureaus (the red
and intelligence squads were already reassigned). He centralized other
functions, disbanded the vice division, maintaining only a small squad to
keep himself informed of vice conditions in the patrol divisions, stopped
the use of police cars and chauffeurs by city councilmen and abolished
about 400 acting ranks. There were 272 acting detective lieutenants and
only 107 holding substantive rank. Nine of the 24 detective captains, ten
of 28 police captains and 40 of 80 police lieutenants held only brevet

appointments, as did 28 of the 172 sergeants. The elimination of acting ranks opened promotional opportunities to honest officers. Hohmann believed that his most important accomplishment was the replacement of the night chief, assistant chief, detective chief and most of the detective inspectors, detective captains and detective lieutenants, in favor of comparable ranks in the uniformed division.

The police purge reduced but did not eliminate protected vice. In a sense, vice was more open than before. The gambling boats, ostensibly outside county jurisdiction, were advertised constantly in newspapers, on radio and by skywriting. By dissolving the central vice squad and making patrolmen and sergeants responsible for "clean" beats, Hohmann did all that a single executive could do to eliminate vice protection. The reformers advised citizens who learned of vice operations to find a patrolman and accompany him to the suspected premises. If the officer refused to go or first made a telephone call, the citizen should so inform the chief and the mayor. Impressed by the reformers' sincerity, ex-chief Davis offered advice about stamping out bookmakers.[5]

Mayor Bowron proposed to oust 170 corrupt policemen who still dishonored the department. Bowron learned of them from Wallace N. Jamie, head of the secret wiretap squad that monitored police telephone lines. Hohmann knew of the wiretappers but claimed never to have seen Jamie's evidence. He doubted its existence. He refused to punish anyone unless shown sufficient proof to warrant charges. The misconduct, moreover, must have occurred within the previous twelve months. Otherwise it was outside the statute of limitations set forth in charter section 202.

Here was a classic reversal of roles. The police, habitual violators of state and federal constitutions, demanded the full protection of the charter. The progressives, bitter opponents of the Davis-Hynes gang of cossacks, would override the charter to punish men whose guilt they learned of through questionable means. Here was a "reform" administration. Regardless of the charter, the mayor controlled the police. Regardless of civil service rules the chief was turned out if he refused to take orders.

Bowron's anger at Hohmann reflected the reformers' frustration. Their enemies were escaping unharmed. Witnesses in Joe Shaw's trial mentioned $500,000 smuggled into Mexico by Shaw and Police Lieutenant Pedro Del Gado. Shaw and Del Gado probably took money into Mexico, since both later had investments there and Shaw had a secret strong box welded to the underside of his automobile. The enormous sum was not necessarily excessive. W.L. Robertson, an unknown detective on the LAPD robbery squad, who resigned rather than discuss his assets, garnered more than $200,000 from vice operations during the four previous years. An appeals court ruled that the state's chief witness, civil service manager Glen Gravatt, was Shaw's accomplice, and reversed the convictions of Shaw and William Cormack. They were free in Los Angeles, as was Del Gado in Mexico.

After two years of reform, vice interests still assumed that protection could be arranged. Baron Lawson, a Central Avenue figure during Shaw's term and later a CIVIC informant, tried to arrange a program through deputy chief R.R. McDonald. The police installed dictaphones, recorded details and made arrests. Lesser figures agreed to pay Lawson $50 or $100 weekly to operate while "The Baron" handled the police. Operators of the Little Tokyo Club offered Sergeant Guy Rudolph $500 weekly to allow gambling to resume.[6]

Recorded telephone conversations presented problems of evidence. Sometimes the statute of limitations had expired. The use of wiretap evidence in state courts remained controversial. It was illegal in federal courts. Deputy City Prosecutor Grant Cooper knew that grand jury indictments based on wiretap evidence might result in federal prosecution of the wiretappers. Again, dishonest policemen escaped punishment, further frustrating the reformers. Even when the facts were new and unchallengeable the culprits escaped. Paul Loeb, a felon arrested in the county by deputy sheriffs, offered to identify a corrupt police captain in return for his own immunity. Loeb, a "three-time loser," faced a possible life sentence as an habitual criminal. Loeb told Deputy Prosecutor Cooper that Captain Mailheau, head of the LAPD robbery squad, took bribes to reduce or withdraw charges against forgers, pickpockets and swindlers.

Cooper arranged to trap Mailheau. Since Loeb also faced less serious charges brought by Los Angeles police, he asked Mailheau to tamper with the evidence. He made the arrangement from a telephone in Clifford Clinton's office. A dictaphone attachment allowed witnesses to record the details. At the rendezvous Loeb passed marked currency to Mailheau, observed by hidden witnesses. The grand jury refused an indictment because of the dictaphone but the police chief signed a complaint and the case went to trial. Judge A.A. Scott heard the testimony. Scott and his father, the political attorney Joseph Scott, invariably supported the Fitts machine. Reformers rightly feared a political decision designed to embarrass the reform administration. Judge Scott denounced the wiretapping, ignored the bribe and directed the jury to acquit the captain. Mailheau's immediate retirement did little to pacify the thwarted, vindictive progressives.[7]

Hohmann gathered little publicity and built no personal machine. His reforms had sound bases. His methods closed vice as tightly as it had ever been closed. He exhibited enlightened political and racial sentiments. He actively opposed unconstitutional police acts. He took pride in the police service and the LAPD. He informed his subordinates that they need never fear to do their duty, because "the days of `Big Shot' political influence in the police department are over." Nevertheless, when Hohmann failed to respond to important politicians they forced him out, although they withheld the coup de grace until Fletcher Bowron had been safely re-elected.[8]

Clinton and CIVIC pursued two related objectives: the defeat of district attorney Buron Fitts in 1940 and the re-election of mayor Fletcher Bowron in 1941. With the powerful reform organization and the city administration against him, Fitts was vulnerable as never before. The D.A.'s inability to expunge vice in the county provided the main reform issue, closely followed by his alleged predilection for allowing Hollywood celebrities to avoid trial for escapades fraught with tragic consequences. Certain valuable gifts from film personalities reinforced the reformers' suspicions but ridicule proved to be the most devastating weapon against the still-powerful county prosecutor.

Fitts posed in public as a conservative, moralistic prohibitionist but had earned a private reputation as a tippler and Casanova. Clifford Clinton and his son Edmund ridiculed Fitts four times daily over radio station KEHE, reading scripts prepared by Ernest Chamberlain that were hilarious, thinly disguised episodes from Fitts' life. Threats against the station management failed to prevent the broadcasts. Fitts filed no lawsuits, during or after the campaign.

Most progressives supported John Dockweiler. Dockweiler, although a veteran of four terms in the U.S. House of Representatives, was a Roman Catholic Democrat in a Protestant Republican ocean. The Dockweiler family, influential among reactionary Democrats, usually supported the county machine. John Dockweiler's candidacy divided Fitts' adherents, however. His probity and family position precluded Fitts' usual smear campaign, nor could his religion be made an open issue. The formal Protestant church organizations stayed in the reform camp. Even the antipapist Robert P. Shuler could not support Buron Fitts.

Fitts posed Dockweiler as a well-meaning innocent, too concerned with his failing health to overthrow the corrupt political adventurers who controlled him. The district attorney attacked Clinton, CIVIC and Fletcher Bowron, pressing charges of communist subversion and fascistic dictatorship. Dockweiler, though only 42, spent much of the campaign in sick-bed. His advisors disclaimed any friendship or allegiance involving Clinton, CIVIC or the mayor of Los Angeles.

CIVIC's attempted purge of uncooperative city councilmen and Mayor Bowron's nomination of a socialist (Reuben Borough) and a communist (Donald Healy) to city commissions, underlay Fitts accusations. The past national commander of the American Legion delivered a pro-Fitts speech at Patriotic Hall on the topic, "Stalin and Clinton Over Los Angeles." He began on a sensational note: "I have in my hand a list of nearly every Communist in Los Angeles." "Commissar Clinton" was the "hub of this vicious wheel of Communism" that included the mayor and most of the council.

Clinton responded with a broadsheet proclaiming "I challenge Buron Fitts." He offered to underwrite a public cross-examination of his own moral character and patriotism in Philharmonic Auditorium, the proceedings to be broadcast. Seven judges would assess the evidence. If found guilty on any charge, Clinton would donate $10,000 to the Legion's charitable fund. No one accepted the challenge.[9]

Fitts tried to tie Clinton and Bowron to the Shaw machine and the vice combination. The reformers invited these charges. Clinton allowed all comers to speak on his radio program and accepted information from any source. Underworld informants used their connection with "Boss Clinton" to set up small vice programs. Their arrests and convictions hurt CIVIC's reputation. Mayor Bowron interceded for a notorious madam who had supplied important information. This also discredited the administration. Even CIVIC's strongest adherents had misgivings when Clinton invited Joe Shaw to speak for Dockweiler against Fitts.

The district attorney's inability to control either the political or criminal situation undermined his efforts to "stand on the record." George Stahlman, the most respected deputy D.A., resigned after 11 years of service, charging that Fitts often conspired to defeat justice. Although the grand jury stifled Stahlman's proposed investigation, the defection hurt Fitts among "respectable" voters. Former city councilman William G. Bonelli, then on trial in a $10,000,000 state liquor license scandal, testified that as Fitts' financial manager he dispensed $300,000 collected from the underworld during the 1936 election. He added that Fitts often attended meetings with Bob Gans, Guy McAfee, Kent Parrot and others to discuss syndicate operations.

The crime situation also reduced Fitts' chances. The bookies' wire service war produced corpses but no convictions. Edward Nealis, allegedly the new Boss and coordinator of protection, operated in the county, apparently immune to the district attorney and sheriff. Newsreels showing Los Angeles' gala floating casinos produced sensational publicity. State Attorney General Earl Warren finally raided Tony Cornero's ships and destroyed the gambling equipment. Warren denied Fitts' claim that the gambling boats lay outside county jurisdiction.

Only the *Times*, the disorganized county machine, the Reverend Gustav Briegleb and some older progressives remained loyal to Fitts. Kent Parrot retired from politics. Charles Craddick and CAMOA could not deliver the city vote. In November 1940, Dockweiler crushed Fitts, receiving 60 percent of the votes cast. While the *Times* expressed surprise at the "upset," the reformers rejoiced. Dockweiler justified their efforts by appointing Grant B. Cooper to the post of chief deputy.

Cooper, a member of Mayor Bowron's informal cabinet, served as a city health commissioner. His mother-in-law was Bowron's secretary and future wife. The thirty-five year old former deputy district attorney and deputy city attorney probably had political ambitions. In 1938, he managed the local phase of Earl Warren's successful campaign for the state attorney general's office. In 1939, he received consideration as CIVIC's choice to replace Buron Fitts. Cooper's vigorous harassment of vice syndicates could be predicted.[10]

Cooper's appointment repaid Dockweiler's debt to CIVIC. Though Clifford Clinton could not control the mayor or the district attorney, both men owed their positions primarily to him. Clinton spent whatever was necessary to defeat corrupt officials. Clinton could not yet rest, because Bowron's first term had six months to run. Only the mayor's re-election could preserve the earlier victories.

Issues and candidates abounded. CIVIC continued its drive to defeat city councilmen opposed to Bowron and charter reform. The "Dictator Clinton" theme seemed even more useful after Dockweiler's election. The "communism" tactic remained fresh because Bowron repeatedly, if unsuccessfully, nominated Reuben Borough and Donald Healy to city commissionerships. Disgruntled ex-policemen asserted Bowron's destruction of the department's morale and efficiency. Gambling interests and elements of the defeated political machine struggled to restore the old conditions.

Bowron's opponents included former mayors Frank Shaw and John Porter and Councilman Stephen Cunningham. With 49 percent of the vote, Bowron narrowly missed total victory in the primary. Shaw received 24,000 and Porter 28,000 votes. Cunningham alone survived to be soundly beaten in the regular election. Bowron's decline from 64 percent of the vote in 1938 to 55 percent in 1941 probably reflected Cunningham's reputation. Although for lack of alternatives he was the candidate of "the interests," he was also a progressive of unquestioned integrity.[11]

C.B. "Jack" Horrall took charge of the police department after Bowron's re-election. The Protestant, Republican Horrall was forty-six, a native of Indiana who joined the LAPD in 1923 after service as a lieutenant in World War I. His bachelor of science degree marked him as an unusual recruit. He scored 99 percent on the civil service examination and 146/212 on the Alpha Test but his Officer Rating was only 52 percent. Horrall exhibited good intentions, moderate ambition and poor judgement. He preferred to influence a circle of cronies and sycophants rather than command an impersonal civil service bureaucracy. His faith in his friends blinded him to their imperfections. This failing accomplished Horrall's ruin.

Horrall willingly deferred to Mayor Bowron. Accepting the mayor's enemies as his own, he commenced an unseemly quarrel with ex-chief Hohmann. The administration suffered another defeat and displayed again the hypocrisy of the progressives in power. Horrall tried to reduce Hohmann from deputy chief to lieutenant. Beset by the problems of reorganizing a demoralized force, opposed by the corrupt faction, made ridiculous by penny-ante vice raids and blamed for every patrolman's blunder, Hohmann had stepped aside without a fight when the tragic death of his son made the burden of responsibility unbearable. Now he instituted a civil suit and won. The city paid his back salary plus interest. Restored as deputy chief and made a ward of the court, he survived to see his tormentors disgraced and defeated.[12]

Police Commissioner Van M. Griffith encouraged and may have been responsible for the attack on Hohmann. Griffith, a wealthy political dilettante, served on city commissions as early as 1920. Astute observers saw him as the successor to Joe Shaw and Kent Parrot as "the man behind the mayor," notwithstanding election rhetoric about "Boss Clinton." Griffith's irascible nature and single-mindedness kept the police commission in turmoil. John P. Buckley, describing his former colleague as "a barnacle on the ship of state," averred that he, Haight, Shoemaker and Kingsley resigned from the police commission because of Griffith's dictatorial tactics. Henry Bodkin also resigned when Chief Hohmann was removed. Griffith established an office in city hall and spent his days there perusing departmental files, questioning officers and conducting investigations. Chief Horrall acquiesced.[13]

Horrall took over in the midst of a rising controversy over wiretapping. Charles Craddick, CAMOA's lawyer, found a microphone in his office as did Bowron's mayoralty opponent, Councilman Stephen Cunningham. Criminal counsel Sam Rummel traced wires from his office to the adjacent quarters of Clinton's attorney and discovered a police listening post. District Attorney Dockweiler and deputy D.A. Cooper admitted knowledge of the Rummel investigation but denied connection with a tap found on Buron Fitts' telephone line.

The dictaphones produced sensational testimony. Cooper's men placed one in the apartment of Augusto Sasso, the prostitution coordinator. Detectives claimed that Captain George Contreras, head of Sheriff Biscailuz' vice squad, frequently visited Sasso and maintained an extensive wardrobe there. Contreras allegedly asserted that after "seventeen years building up an organization" he would not allow the reformers to destroy it. Contreras had directed vice operations for the corrupt district attorney, Asa Keyes. When Keyes went to prison, Contreras moved to the sheriff's department. He was frequently named in vice trials as a member of the combination but dismissed the charges as underworld attempts to smear an honest cop.

The surveillance of attorney Sam Rummel probably concerned his client, Deputy Sheriff Charles Rittenhouse. Rittenhouse was indicted for protecting bookmakers along the Sunset Strip. One bookmaker, who handled a $20,000 daily volume of bets, claimed to have paid Rittenhouse $100 per week for 61 weeks to protect the 99-telephone establishment. Rittenhouse denied the charge, asserting that he thought the bookmaker was just a small time stool pigeon. Discovery of the thriving horse parlor was "a blow to my pride," said Rittenhouse. The place was successfully raided only after Undersheriff Arthur Jewell got Rittenhouse safely into his automobile and away from telephones before revealing the squad's destination. Rittenhouse claimed that Grant Cooper offered him immunity in return for evidence against Captain Contreras. The jury acquitted Rittenhouse but minor vice figures continued to assert that the sheriff's department sold protection. The trial also revealed a noteworthy telephone company policy: bookmakers deposited $50 per instrument to cover damage incurred during police raids.[14]

In December, 1941, the discovery of a large monitoring station in city hall seriously threatened the Bowron administration. The grand jury, politically opposed to the reformers, indicted Mayor Bowron, Clifford Clinton, Grant Cooper, Wallace Jamie, Chief Horrall and four other policemen. Bowron stood accused of "wilful misconduct" for encouraging public officials to commit illegal acts. Felony wiretapping charges were filed against Clinton, Cooper, Jamie, Horrall and the policemen. Bowron faced expulsion from office if convicted. John Dockweiler repudiated Cooper before the grand jury and disqualified himself as prosecutor. State Attorney General Earl Warren appointed two former presidents of the state bar association as special prosecutors. Judge Raymond McIntosh, of Sierra County, received a special assignment to hear the case in Los Angeles.

In April, 1942, Judge McIntosh dismissed the charge against Bowron and quashed the felony indictments. Section 653-H of the state penal code permitted the use of dictagraphs under the direction of the district attorney when necessary to detect crime. Section 640 forbade unauthorized connections to a telephone line. Two ambiguous words—"unauthorized" and "connection"—required clarification. The indictments rested on monitored conversations from Clifford Clinton's telephone. Clinton agreed to the practice. In the absence of more specific law this "authorization" satisfied Judge McIntosh. Cooper and Jamie used an induction coil device that required no physical connection to the monitored line. McIntosh ruled that since the law allowed eavesdropping by dictagraphs it did not forbid the induction coil.

The happy reformers celebrated a pyrrhic victory. CIVIC had won its last victory. Reform as a movement was dead. Whatever the purity of the ends, the means were those of the Shaw, Porter and Cryer machines. The organization collapsed. Clinton and Jamie joined the armed services. Dockweiler discontinued Cooper's surveillance program. Shortly afterward, Dockweiler died. In appointing the machine politician Fred Howser to replace him, the board of supervisors ended the progressives' short-lived control of county prosecutions.[15]

World War II placed severe strains on the police force. Los Angeles was a major port, a center of the growing aircraft industry and a magnet for the personnel of a dozen nearby military posts. Men thronged the streets in search of liquor, gambling and women. The council refused to enlarge the department, which actually decreased in size. Hundreds of police officers joined the armed services. Other hundreds retired. "Emergency" appointments filled most vacancies but employing large numbers of men unable to meet the mental and physical standards created serious problems. Police brutality replaced corruption as the focus of criticism. Veteran officers blamed "badge happy" wartime policemen.

In 1943, the infamous "zoot suit riots" occurred. White servicemen responded to reports that gangs of oddly dressed Mexican youths had set upon soldiers and sailors. For several days, mobs roamed the downtown streets, stripping and beating "pachucos." The police avoided intervention, placing "zoot suiters" literally outside the law. Subsequent investigations accomplished little. Edward Duran Ayres, Sheriff Biscailuz' "ambassador" to Latin American residents, reported that Mexicans were genetically prone to crime and vice. Chief Horrall agreed. This satisfied the official conscience and terminated the inquiry.[16]

Labor unrest reappeared in 1943. A group of LAPD officers organized Local 665 of the Los Angeles Police Employees Union. An "outside agitator" from the American Federation of Labor advised the policemen and took the brunt of anti-labor criticism. P.E.U. spokesmen praised the Four Freedoms and the rights of free working men; Mayor Bowron described the union as "contrary to the very thing we are fighting for." The local was actually formed because the mere threat to organize no longer produced results. The union relied for its legal existence on an opinion by City Attorney R.L. Chesebro, that city employees could not be penalized for "taking part in the social, religious, economic and political activities of the community." Although Bowron openly accepted the ruling and promised that no one would be punished for union activities, Chief Horrall denied access to bulletin boards, teletypes and similar facilities freely available to the Fire and Police Protective League and several other organizations.

The P.E.U. had an undeniable case. The wage scale of 1926 ($170-$200) remained static, although between 1939 and 1943 food prices had risen by forty-seven percent and clothing prices by thirty-four percent. The number of police personnel had fallen about fifteen percent below the authorization for 1925, although the population had risen about sixty percent during the period 1926-1943. The war brought further throngs of transient servicemen and vastly increased security responsibilities. The officers worked ten hours overtime per week but were paid only four-fifths of the regular hourly rate.[17]

Among other things, the union requested that the city pay for uniforms and equipment, provide a cumulative sick-leave plan and create a promotional system based on merit. Many officers believed that once past the written examination, advancement depended more on Chief Horrall's whim than on ability. The administration offered wage increases that discriminated against jailers and matrons, although police officers held these posts, reduced the annual vacation by one day, limited overtime rates to "straight time," eliminated existing disability pensions in favor of workmen's compensation and confirmed the forty-eight hour work week.

The Protective League accepted the administration proposals but the P.E.U. rejected the offer and struggled to obtain its original requests. Early in 1945, the mayor and council agreed to all the union proposals except those concerning purchase of uniforms and equipment. The politicians faced an election, which perhaps aided the department's cause more than the justice of its requests. The administration also hoped to attract good recruits from among returning servicemen, and this necessity was undoubtedly a factor in the final decision.

The Police Employees Union claimed an exaggerated share of credit for the labor victory. Union spokesmen exulted over the merit provisions, which included open hearings prior to demotions. (The demotion of a number of police officers was laid to their union membership.) The union accused the Protective League of opposition to merit ratings because the senior officials who controlled the League enjoyed their power to make and break subordinates. Demotion hearings would protect independent policemen from Chief Horrall, the worst offender. The department's most important advance, nevertheless, was the Jacobs salary-setting formula, which kept wages competitive with private industry. By the late 1950's, administrators annually computed police salary increases in accordance with the formula and the council automatically approved them.

Unfortunately for the union, its executives openly endorsed the AFL slate of municipal candidates and actively opposed Mayor Bowron. The voters re-elected Bowron at the primary election, 147,273 votes to 126,025 for his 13 opponents combined. The mayor then turned on the PEU and destroyed it. The police commission ruled that no officer could belong to an organization affiliated with the AFL, CIO or similar "outside" interests. In March, 1946, Chief Horrall ordered members to resign from the PEU within 30 days or be discharged from the force. So ended the police labor union.[18]

The 1945 mayoralty election also marked the final breach of the reform coalition. Clifford Clinton had long harbored a desire for office. He presented himself as a liberal progressive Democratic alternative to Bowron, but finished far behind and retired from politics. Bowron then returned Van M. Griffith to private life. Griffith quarrelled with the mayor over nondepartmental matters and the council quickly approved his removal. Neither progressives nor police mourned the going of the last original reform police commissioner.

As 1945 ended, Bowron and the police department could look backward with satisfaction and forward with confidence. Both had accomplished much. Bowron had become the candidate of private business and the *Times* and was "mayor in his own right." Vice seemed to be a dead issue. Furtive small scale operations continued but even the progressives expected that. The department seemed well on the way to professional status. United actions had preserved charter section 202 and the pension system. To these benefits were added a formula for automatic salary increases and a merit promotional system that also hindered arbitrary demotion. Brevet ranks were curtailed, opening the promotional ladder to the more ambitious and intelligent officers. The manpower allotment was raised, decreasing the workload and again increasing promotional opportunities. Only members of the LAPD were eligible to become chief.

The police academy functioned again. A state ordinance of 1936 underlay the return to formal schooling. Faculty members at the University of Southern California trained policemen to instruct their fellows. The first class, styling themselves "the Dedicators," graduated in 1938. Even during World War II, a six-week training school continued. After the war, unqualified wartime policemen were released as fast as returning veterans could be trained. A full-scale program was instituted to train the postwar recruits.

New officers accepted the idea of "professional" police work. The chief's tenure appeared secure. The public, though outraged by occasional brutal incidents, no longer considered the police to be venal lackeys of criminal bosses. Most of the older, corrupt officers had retired. The department appeared to be progressing slowly toward the conditions envisioned by the reformers of 1938.[19]

Unpleasant surprises were in store. During the late 1940's a series of state, county and municipal vice scandals exploded. State and national crime commissions investigated, moralized and suggested remedial action. By 1953, almost all of the people connected with the scandals were out of office, in jail or dead. At the state level the chief actors seemed to be Attorney General Fred Howser (the former Los Angeles district attorney) and Arthur Samish, the infamous "hidden governor." Howser and some ex-LAPD vice officers tried to organize the state for protected gambling. The estimated monthly return from punchboards alone was $500,000.

Samish blocked an anti-slot machine bill endorsed by the police, sheriffs' and district attorneys' state associations. Samish's influence in the state legislature flowed from his control over the statewide liquor dealers' lobby. The California crime commission smashed Howser's operation, although only one ex-LAPD officer went to jail, and then convicted Samish on a different charge. Afterward the anti-slot machine bill was passed and the bookmakers' race wire service was terminated. Attorney General Howser was refused renomination by the Republican party.

The sheriff and the district attorney shared law enforcement duties in the county. Both were elected officials and needed campaign funds, for which they turned to the vice operators. Restricting vice to specific small areas limited voter retaliation. Residents of outlying areas cared little for conditions on the Sunset Strip. The district attorney, although nominally responsible only for prosecutions, maintained dozens of detectives, including a vice squad, "to root out eastern gangsters." This could easily have been done by the grand jury. The D.A.'s vice squad actually existed to extort money from criminal enterprises. According to one source, to prevent jurisdictional quarrels, the sheriff controlled vice in unincorporated areas; incorporated towns belonged to the district attorney.[20]

Bookmaking on horse races and other sporting events constituted the most lucrative illegal business in Los Angeles county. Ruthless men contended for the rich prize. In the decade following the murder of George Bruneman in 1937, at least a dozen unsolved gang killings occurred, incidents in the war between the Continental and Trans-America wire services. Politicians of law enforcement blamed the violence on eastern gangsters and declared that the incumbent sheriff, district attorney or mayor must be retained to meet the underworld threat.

Notwithstanding the claims of police and politicians, "organized" crime had existed in Los Angeles for decades. A change occurred in the mid 1930's. Whereas the McAfee wing of the combination eschewed publicity and tried to avoid violence, newcomers freely exerted "muscle" to force their way into the cartel. After the recall of mayor Shaw, McAfee and others departed for Las Vegas to conduct legal gambling operations. Benjamin "Bugsy" Siegel remained behind to batter his way into control of local bookmaking.

Verifiable information is scarce where important criminals are involved but it appears that the New York and Chicago gangs allotted California to Siegel in 1931, to be organized for their mutual benefit. He lived quietly in Beverly Hills as early as 1934. In 1937 he was implicated in gambling, jewel robbery and perhaps the narcotics traffic. His major interest was the Trans America Wire Service. It was alleged that national criminal groups financed Trans America to compete with James Ragen's Continental service. Charges to bookmakers varied but by 1946 the charge was $150 per week, paid unwillingly to each wire service.

Siegel's chief lieutenants, Jack Dragna and Michael "Mickey" Cohen, served as enforcers. They required bookmakers to use Trans America's service or suffer grievous bodily harm. Students of the mysterious mafia assert that Dragna ruled the local chapter until his death in 1957. Cohen is usually described as a small-time thug and hired gunman.

The Capone organization in Chicago allegedly took over the Continental wire service after its owner was murdered in 1946. Siegel's assassination in Beverly Hills in 1947, allegedly for refusing to dismantle Trans America, ended the national phase of the wire service war. Mickey Cohen then became preeminent although local competition remained fierce. Reporters counted seven attempts on Cohen's life. Many of his employees died violently or disappeared without trace. The scandals of 1949 linked the Los Angeles sheriff's department with Cohen, the wire service and Attorney General Howser.

LAPD vice squad sergeant James Fisk discovered a large bookmaking establishment at 1747 East Florence Avenue, an unincorporated area. Ostensibly the Guarantee Finance Corporation, the business financed the operations of more than 160 bookmakers. It also supplied a loan service for losing bettors. The sheriff's vice squad declined to act. In fact, Sheriff's Captain Al Guasti delivered a letter to LAPD Assistant Chief Joseph Reed, demanding an end to police activities in the sheriff's jurisdiction. When Sergeant Fisk raided the bookmaking establishment, it developed that Guarantee Finance did $7,000,000 annual business in bets, and paid possibly $450,000 for police protection. About $247,000 went to police officers. The California crime commission asserted that Sheriff Biscailuz and vice squad commander Captain Carl Pearson refused to aid an earlier investigation of Guarantee Finance by the State Corporation Commission. Sheriff's Inspector Norris Stensland, informed by the telephone company of Guarantee's operations, did nothing. The crime commission censured the sheriff for "actual resistance" to the LAPD investigation. Captain Guasti foolishly denied the letter to Assistant Chief Reed and received a two year sentence for perjury. The crime commission observed that "the sheriff's authority is less feared than that of the city police," and that most gang killings occurred outside the Los Angeles city limits.

The commission also exposed what it considered "a small coterie" of lawyers, bail bonders and judges engaged in supplying "quickie writs" of habeas corpus to arrested bookmakers. The commission named attorneys Joseph Forno, Harry Margid and Phillip Burg, the Glasser and Nardoni bailbond agencies and superior court judges Walter S. Gates and

William R. McKay as the participants in a process that it would be "absurd to believe" was innocent or coincidental. Police, arriving at the jail with arrested bookmakers, literally found attorneys waiting with completed writs of *habeas corpus.*

Experienced judges suggested two hours as the minimum time required to obtain a writ. Judge McKay, on the other hand, issued three within 30 minutes. Of 159 writs examined, Judge Gates signed 95, McKay 36 and the other 50 judges 28 among them. Irving Glasser's bail-bond license, revoked because of his criminal record, had been renewed, thanks to Sheriff Biscailuz. Glasser was a recent partner of Eddie Nealis and Benjamin Siegel in the Clover Club, and of ex-deputy district attorney David H. Clark in the Cotton Club. These were the most specific, irrefutable charges yet levelled against the administration of Sheriff Eugene Biscailuz. Fortunately for him, he had been re-elected some months prior to the disclosures.[21]

On the other hand, Sergeant Fisk's exploit struck a fine opening note for Mayor Fletcher Bowron's 1949 re-election campaign. Ten opponents, including Joe Shaw, entered the field. Bowron campaigned "on the record." He sounded much like his old enemies, Frank L. Shaw, James E. Davis and the *Times.* "We have met the onslaught of gangster-ism," Bowron asserted. "It was planned in New York and Chicago and westward to take over this city...We have saved a decent police force and a fine civil service." Bowron and City Engineer Lloyd Aldrich survived the primary. Bowron easily won the general election.

On June 1, 1949, the day after Bowron's victory, the grand jury began an investigation of vice in the city and corruption in the police force. The *Daily News* made the probe a major, continuing news item because *Daily News* reporters uncovered much of the evidence that the grand jury reviewed. Since the central events occurred a year earlier, it was clear that the *Daily News,* the district attorney and the grand jury refrained from embarrassing the mayor by investigating police corruption until assured of his re-election.

Chief Horrall "welcomed" the investigation. The police commission quickly voted "complete confidence in the integrity and efficiency of the entire Los Angeles police force." Fletcher Bowron took a wiser and less optimistic view. Complaining that he had no way of knowing what occurred in the city, Bowron asked the council to establish "a little FBI" under his control. Then he could be kept informed of his subordinates' activities. Remembering Wallace Jamie's spy operations, the council demurred.

The alleged protection of a call girl and brothel operation by Sergeant E.V. Jackson of the administrative vice squad led to the grand jury inquiry. Vice squad sergeant Charles Stoker testified that while monitoring the telephone of a known prostitute, early in 1948, he overheard discussions that established a business relationship between the woman and Sergeant Jackson. Jackson ignored Stoker's warning to disassociate himself with the prostitution racket. Stoker told his commander, who informed Captain Cecil Wisdom, head of the personnel bureau. Wisdom arranged to monitor the vice squad's telephones and to record suspicious conversations.

Sergeant Jackson told the grand jury that he dealt with the madam to obtain information about eastern gangsters. His superior, Lieutenant Rudy Wellpott, agreed, claiming that the system was just going well when Stoker's unwise arrest ruined it. Wellpott blamed "malicious officers" for the grand jury investigation. Chief Horrall blamed Mickey Cohen. Horrall stated that he was unaware of Stoker's allegations against Jackson but knew of a continuing investigation of the prostitution operation by police.

Other witnesses contradicted Horrall. Deputy Chief Richard Simon said the call girl investigation had been dropped months before the grand jury meeting. Captain Wisdom asserted that he informed the chief immediately after hearing Stoker's recordings. Sergeant Guy Rudolph, Horrall's assistant, himself accused of protecting Main Street B-Girls and Chinatown gamblers, supported Wisdom's testimony. A *Daily News* reporter swore that Horrall was given information about Jackson and the madam a year earlier, when Jackson was being hailed as a hero for killing a holdup man. The *Daily News* found that Jackson's female companion on that occasion was the madam in question. The dead bandit's partner thought they were after the vice payoff, reported to be $900 per week.

Daily reports of the supposedly secret grand jury proceedings appeared in the newspapers. Questions of the chief's tenure arose at once. On June 18, Mayor Bowron announced that Horrall would remain. Bowron told newsmen that "of course" he had no power to depose the chief and would not do so if he could, but admitted that even some police commissioners had asked him if rumors of a new chief were true. On June 28, four days after Deputy Chief Simon's appearance before the grand jury, Horrall retired. The city charter and civil service rules notwithstanding, the reform mayor had again dismissed a police chief.[22]

Horrall was not the first to go. George Bowman, head of the gangster squad, retired the day the grand jury inquiry began. Florabel Muir, a nationally known columnist and crime reporter, accused Bowman of selling transcripts of recordings made inside Mickey Cohen's new Brentwood residence. Police technicians had wired the building for surveillance prior to its completion. The transcript price ranged from $1,500 to $3,000. The existence of the transcripts supported a rumor that Cohen paid a large sum, possibly $30,000, for the original wire spools, only to find that duplicates existed. The facts implied that policemen got the money.

Horrall's aide, Lieutenant Clyde Tucker, resigned one day later. Tucker commanded the new red squad, which dealt with labor problems. Rumors passed that Tucker hired the squad out as a strikebreaking force at the Los Angeles harbor and other locations. While the taxpayers met the squad's expenses, a few officials divided the employers' payments. The grand jury became concerned as the Horrall administration began to dissolve. The jurors requested that some way be found to keep the police in service until the investigation ended.

Before leaving, Horrall suspended three of Sergeant Stoker's former partners on the Hollywood vice detail. In each case, senior officers had known of the officers' misconduct for six months or more. The men did not deny the charges but pointed out that the department condoned their behavior until Stoker testified before the grand jury. In this sense, their belief that their superiors "framed" them was justifiable. All were discharged. Stoker charged that he was being made a victim of guilt by association with brutal, corrupt policemen.

Stoker himself was tried for burglary. The jury rejected the strong circumstantial case against him, perhaps because of the obvious departmental vendetta. The chief prosecution witness, a policewoman and Stoker's former vice squad partner, admitted to perjury, forgery, burglary and adultery. (The policewoman was the daughter of Deputy Chief Homer Cross and the granddaughter of vice boss Charlie Crawford, which could explain Cross's rise from patrolman to deputy chief in seven years.) The departmental trial board, however, found Stoker guilty and discharged him.

The grand jury indicted Chief Horrall, Assistant Chief Joseph Reed and Captain Cecil Wisdom for perjury, and Lieutenant Wellpott and Sergeant Jackson for extortion. The jurors exhibited more exasperation than good sense. Whatever the truth of their charges, the evidence was scanty or inadmissible. All of the indicted men were exonerated. Those with twenty years completed took retirement. A few others, involved in various kinds of misconduct, received suspensions but returned to obscure posts in the uniformed division.[23]

William Worton, a retired Marine Corps general, replaced Horrall. Mayor Bowron assumed that anyone charged with departmental reorganization would make numerous enemies. It seemed better to have an outsider undertake this task. The charter allowed temporary appointments from outside the department. Although Worton would not be eligible for the permanent position, he could complete two consecutive sixty day terms. In this as in other things the charter could be circumvented. The general actually spent 13 months in office.

Worton commenced with energy and determination. Because he knew nothing of the city or its police force, presumably he acted on the advice of others. He denied plans for "a wholesale shakeup" but ordered repeated multiple personnel transfers. It required considerable time and effort to dismantle completely the associations developed during Horrall's eight year tenure. The effect on esprit de corps is difficult to assess in fact; in political terms it was inconsequential. The mayor simply repeated at intervals that Chief Worton had restored morale.

The new police administration instituted important organizational reform. After studying Vollmer's 1924 reorganization plan, Worton reestablished the 90-day curriculum at the police academy, doubling the existing program, and invested the new bureau of corrections with responsibility for jails and prisoners. He separated the personnel and training division into two bureaus and divided the detective bureau between two inspectors. Special administrative services, a new section within the technical services bureau, placed the vice and robbery squads under Arthur Hohmann's command, along with the planning detail. Worton eliminated the office of assistant chief and banned the acceptance of rewards.

Worton's most significant innovation was the bureau of internal affairs, commanded by Inspector William H. Parker. The new bureau's sole concern was trial boards, boards of inquiry and other special boards. The bureau harbored the "headhunters" who investigated departmental misconduct. For the first time, responsibility for good order and discipline became a separate, distinct function rather than a sideline of the personnel bureau. Inspector Parker, something of a headhunter himself, was the natural choice to initiate the new bureau's operation.

The bureau of internal affairs represented another successful defense of charter section 202. When the grand jury learned that the department could not try Sergeant Jackson because the twelve month statute of limitations had elapsed, demands for charter amendment again were heard. The mayor again requested a personal detective bureau. The newly elected Mexican-American councilman, Edward Roybal (the city's first non white councilman) proposed a paid, fulltime citizen review board that would have investigative and disciplinary powers. The public seemed receptive to some sort of external "watchdog" apparatus. These issues posed a serious threat to departmental autonomy.

Worton's new internal affairs bureau satisfied most critics of the existing system. It was a separate division. Its sole interest was police discipline. It established a formal method for processing complaints against officers. It included detectives assigned specifically to the investigation of police misconduct but it did not serve as a personal spy squad for the mayor.

More importantly, from the police view, it included no civilians. Thus it institutionalized the self-policing norm prized by such professions as law and medicine. Politicians could assert that something had been done to reform the department, while police could praise their own strict trial system. The bureau of internal affairs became the LAPD's most publicized institution.

Leaders of racial minorities responded less enthusiastically to the new bureau. Their complaints indicated the gravity of a problem that concerned black and brown inhabitants but received little newspaper attention. To allay criticism, Mayor Bowron appointed the first black police commissioner, Charles Matthews. Chief Worton gave black leaders his personal assurance that brutality and overt racism would not be tolerated. He also proposed to integrate the department. The minorities had to be content with the chief's promise and whatever redress Councilman Roybal and Commissioner Matthews could provide.[24]

Chief Worton perceived the bureau of internal affairs within a larger context of police reform. Worton suggested that Los Angeles adopt his modification of the New York, Chicago and Detroit police executive systems. Under Worton's plan, a fulltime, paid, non-civil service civilian commissioner-manager would direct the department. The commissioner, appointed by the mayor with concurrence of the council, would serve a three-year term. He would be responsible for the bureau of internal affairs and the planning, accounting, records and identification, public relations, communications, transportation, inspection, and supply bureaus. The police chief would still direct the department's law enforcement activities.

The chief pointed out that his plan placed control over police trials and punishment in civilian hands. He believed that the system could be installed without amending the city charter. The general hoped to be the first commissioner-manager. Legal experts asserted that the proposed organization required extensive charter reform. At the completion of his term, Chief Worton accepted an appointment to the police commission. The electorate rejected charter reform, however, and with it Worton's plan.

While Bowron and Worton reorganized the police force, questions concerning the department's link with criminals were overlooked. That was true also of county and state law enforcement officials. The rise of a streetwalker to coordinator of hundreds of other prostitutes needed only the permission of the administrative vice squad. The reported $900 per week payoff seems insufficient to justify the police chief's failure to act against his subordinates or the district attorney's reluctance to issue a complaint against the woman. Some other network of relationships, as yet undisclosed, may explain the senior officials' malfeasance.

The entire story is not known nor likely to be known. From the available facts, astute observers could infer a conspiracy to obstruct justice. The activities of Mickey Cohen provided one perplexing example. The sudden emergence of a smalltime hoodlum to pre-eminence in county vice operations defied conventional explanation. Rumors did not support straightforward violence, as when Bugsy Siegel organized the county. A voluntary, efficient coalition seemed beyond Cohen's modest capabilities. He may have been the coordinator for others. The LAPD's wire recordings established Cohen's involvement with the amorphous national crime syndicate. Other events proved his association with the state attorney general's office. The squad of ex-LAPD vice detectives, working under Howser's authority to organize the state for gambling, undoubtedly started in their own bailiwick.

The attempt on Cohen's life, in July, 1949, provides an interesting study. Transcripts of the LAPD tapes were on the market. Cohen's accusations of extortion by the police were well known. Cohen was due to appear before the grand jury. On July 19, Attorney General Howser sent an operative to guard Cohen's life. Oddly enough, at the same time, Howser asked the LAPD to "leave Cohen alone" for a few weeks. The assassins struck the next day. Cohen and four others were wounded, Howser's detective among them. One of Cohen's bodyguards died.

Sheriff Biscailuz also maintained surveillance over Cohen. Unfortunately, on this night the two deputy sheriffs left their posts a few minutes early. Not only did they miss the action, they were unavailable to pursue the killers. Sergeant Charles Stoker blamed unidentified members of the police force who feared Cohen's grand jury testimony. Mayor Bowron blamed Frank Costello, a New York gang "czar." Florabel Muir ridiculed Bowron's idea, pointing to six bungled murder attempts. If the mafia wanted Cohen dead, she insisted, Cohen would be dead.

Attorney General Howser refused to explain his interest in Cohen's welfare. The *Mirror,* without pursuing the issue, pointed out that Arthur

Samish travelled to Los Angeles to inform Cohen of the official body-guard's appointment. There was some outraged newspaper comment about the impropriety of Howser's act. Rumors passed that Howser's detective was sent to "finger" Cohen and that the assassins meant to kill both Cohen and the fingerman. The case remains unsolved.[25]

As the police trials progressed, Lieutenant Wellpott admitted possession of the original recordings made of conversations in Cohen's house. No official use had been made of the secret information. Chief Worton asked critics to "look at the boy's side of this thing. These...may prove useful to him in combatting this (extortion) indictment." The chief proved equally permissive in other cases involving proven as well as alleged misconduct. Presumably, his attitude toward police malefactors during the last half of his term would have carried over into his tenure as commissioner-manager, effectively negating "civilian control" of the disciplinary procedure. Efforts by the ACLU to conduct a dialogue with the chief were fruitless.

As the year ended, it appeared that the scandals of 1949 would result only in a minor reorganization of the LAPD. Actually, though the Municipal League, CIVIC and the Federation for Civic Betterment were dead, an inchoate but broadly successful state-wide reform movement was underway. The California crime commission investigations and the federal Kefauver committee's subsequent hearings provided a firm basis for reform action by the state legislature, which banned the use, possession, or manufacture of slot machines. Telephone companies cut off service to bookmakers. Western Union discontinued the racing wire service. These acts had beneficial consequences for law enforcement.

In 1950, the Republican Party returned Attorney General Howser to private life. District Attorney Simpson died suddenly. Mickey Cohen and Arthur Samish went to jail. A sudden campaign to recall Fletcher Bowron failed, in November 1950, as much for lack of time as for lack of organization and a candidate. Bowron again saw the hand of the underworld. In 1953, the voters finally turned him out.[26]

With the passage of laws and the passing of politicians, an era ended. Commercial vice operations as the state, county and city had known them, were permanently terminated. Once before, during the 1909-1913 period, a sincere reform administration succeeded, moving Willard H. Wright to denounce "Los Angeles, the chemically pure." By 1916, the moral reform was over. Much of the early charter reform was dismantled in 1925.

The reform victory of 1938 differed from that of 1909 because the movement perpetuated itself. During a decade of constant struggle, the criminal interests met defeat. A complex of factors made the long-term victory possible. The establishment of legal gambling and prostitution in Nevada drew both vice operators and customers to Las Vegas. California state laws destroying the pinball, slot machine and racing wire industries also played an important role, as did state suppression of the gambling boats off shore.

Clifford Clinton and Fletcher Bowron cannot be discounted. Each in his way was irreplaceable. Clinton's religious fervor and generous purse made possible the defeat of Shaw and Fitts. Bowron's ability to convince the voters that only he could save the city produced five consecutive election victories. Maintaining himself in office for nearly fifteen years allowed almost the "two generations" Vollmer spoke of to pass through the city departments, transforming them from patronage depots to professionalised bureaucracies. The men who succeeded Attorney General Howser, District Attorney Simpson, Sheriff Biscailuz, Mayor Bowron and Chief Worton found the political balance permanently tipped in the progressive direction. The immediate beneficiary was William H. Parker, who assumed command of the department when General Worton retired.

NOTES

[1] The Lushing case is Superior Court No. 72613. See also H.H. Story, 747. The Shaw-Cormack case can be followed in the transcript of their appeal, 2nd Criminal No. 3249, Shaw, Box 14, File "Pedro Del Gado," and Del Gado's affidavits in the Clinton Papers. The Kleinbergers sold used furniture and were believed to be the "furniture interest" involved in the appointment of Chief Davis. See chapter 6, above, and T.T. Olender, 39-49. *Times*, 5-5-39, 5-7-39, 6-27-39, 12-19-39, 1-8-40, 5-29-40. "Bombing the Lid Off Angeles," *Official Detective Stories* (5-25-38) 49-50. P.C. *Minutes*, 9-15-39. *Examiner*, 1-30-40, 4-30-40. P.C. *Minutes*, 11-29-38, 12-13-38, 2-28-39, 8-8-39, 1-9-40, 1-16-40, 4-15-40, 5-15-40, 7-30-40, 4-25-41, 7-15-41.

[2] P.C. *Minutes*, 5-11-38, 6-28-38, 7-5-38, 8-2-38, 10-4-38, 11-12-38, 11-17-38, 1-24-39, 3-3-39, 3-7-39 through 4-30-42, *passim*. L.A. City Charter, sec. 181; sec. 202. *Time* v. 32, no.2, 12-5-38, 14. Interview with Deputy Chief Ervis Lester, LAPD. Muir, 167. J.H. Richardson, *For the Life of Me*, 227. Council file 1437 (1940); council file 10380 includes the council investigation of Biffle's actions. *Times*, 1-31-39, 5-1-39, 5-5-39, 6-1-39, 3-3-40. See Shaw, Box 11, File "F.L.S. Campaigns, 1925-1938", for copy of Amendment 14A. LAPD *Bulletin*, 4-13-39. Lawrence W. O'Rourke, "The Office of Mayor in Los Angeles" (unpublished M.A. thesis, U.C.L.A., 1954), 51-56; 114; Marvin Abrahams, "The Functioning of Boards and Commissions in the L.A. City Government" (Ph.D., U.C.L.A. 1967), *passim*. Royle A. Carter, Memorandum re Certain Major Factors of Police Administration (L.A., July 30, 1940).

[3] Interview with A.H. Hohmann. *People vs. Joseph E. Shaw*, 2nd Crim. No. 3249, opening brief, passim, and closing brief, 89. *Examiner*, 10-27-38; *Herald*, 2-17-39; *Times*, 6-38-39, 9-13-39.

[4] Bowron press releases, 9-7-38, 2-10-39. Shaw, Box 12, File, "1940-1941." J.H. Richardson, 227. P.C. *Minutes*, 4-15-40. *People vs. Shaw*, opening and closing briefs, *passim*. *Examiner*, 6-3-39; *Times*, 6-3-39, 6-10-39, 6-12-39, 6-16-39, 6-17-39, 6-24-39, 9-29-39, 3-9-40.

[5] *Times*, 6-25-39, 6-27-39, 6-28-39, 6-29-39, 7-1-39, 7-21-39, through 7-27-39, 8-17-39, 9-1-39, 10-10-39. P.C. *Minutes*, 3-14-39, 5-9-39, 5-17-39, 2-25-41. LAPD *Bulletin*, 4-13-39, 8-24-39.

[6] Interview with A.H. Hohmann. Shaw, Box 14, File "Miscellaneous Correspondence, 1940"; Clinton Papers, File "Del Gado." In 1973, Del Gado was allowed to return to the U.S.A. *Times*, 12-4-38, 12-

11-40, 12-30-40, 1-9-41, 3-8-42, 3-17-42.

[7] *Ibid*, 1-9-41, 7-31-41, 8-5-41, 12-6-41

[8] *Times*, 6-24-39, 7-13-39, 7-14-39,, 7-17-39, 9-14-39, 10-17-39, 3-7-40, 3-13-40. *The CIVIC Challenge*, 9-19 (1939?) in Clinton Papers, File "CIVIC Challenge." P.C. *Minutes*, 10-17-39. *CIVIC Digest*, Dec. 1939, 29-30. LAPD *Bulletin*, 4-25-41.

[9] Muir, 124-134. *CIVIC Digest*, Nov. 1939, Jan.-Feb. 1940, CIVIC files and broadcast transcripts, and Clifford Clinton, "I Challenge Buron Fitts," n.d., are among the Clinton Papers. Interview with E.R. Chamberlain. Hallberg, 106-110. Fitts speech, n.d., Shaw, Box 12, File "Buron Fitts." Dockweiler pamphlet addressed to city employees, 10-23-40. Box 11, unidentified file. Doyle's speech is in Box 12, File "1940-1941."

[10] See Marshall Stimson's pro-Fitts speech and draft of Shaw's anti-Fitts speech on Clinton's program. Shaw, Box 12, File "Buron Fitts." Also *Hollywood Life*, Aug. 1943, an anti-Bowron broadsheet, in Clinton Papers. Shaw, Box 12, File "Buron Fitts" for charges and countercharges that Joe Shaw or Eddie Nealis instigated the murders of Les Bruneman and Ducky Irwin. Shaw said Nealis was responsible; Fitts blamed Shaw. See also Dean Jennings, *We Only Kill Each Other: The Life and Bad Times of Bugsy Siegel* (N.Y., 1969), 171-172. *Examiner*, 11-9-40. Forabel Muir, *Headline Happy* (N.Y., 1060), 163-174; *American Liberty News*, 12-28-40, Shaw, Box 6. Chamberlain, "Revolt of the Angelinos," 28 and *passim*. *Times*, 1-7-39, 7-27-39, 11-38-39, 1-9-40, 9-11-40, 12-6-40.

[11] Borough, 247; S.W. Yorty; see anti-Bowron campaign materials in Chamberlain Collection, File "Fletcher Bowron." *Daily News*, 2-15-41. Shaw, Box 12, File "Earl Warren."

[12] Interviews with Deputy Chief Ervis Lester, Ex-Chief A.H. Hohmann, and former Dt. Lt. J.L. Kimbrough. P.C. *Minutes*, 12-15-41, 12-16-41, 12-23-41, 8-26-42. *Times*, 3-9-40, 6-6-41, 6-7-41, 8-1-42, 8-20-42. Hohmann retired 9-1-60 to assist in the reorganization of the Chicago police department. Webb, 170-174.

[13] Story, 844; "The Great Van Griffith," Shaw, Box 12, File "L.A. Police Union League, 1944-45," 4-9-40; Address of Martin Mooney, 7-2-40. *Ibid. Herald*, 4-12-39; *Citizen-News*, 3-4-39; *Times*, 3-5-39, 5-29-40; Abrahams, 66-85.

[14] *Times*, 1-9-41, 4-22-41, 5-5-41, 5-15-41, 7-15-41, 7-16-41, 8-15-41, 3-18-41, 6-24-41, 7-3-42, 7-8-42, 7-9-42, 7-25-42.

[15] *Ibid.*, 1-13-42, 2-30-42, 2-27-42, 2-28-42, 4-9-42. Clinton Papers, *passim*.

[16] Solomon Jones, "The Government Riots of Los Angeles, June 1943" (M.A. thesis, U.C.L.A., 1967); Ralph Guzman, "The Function of Anglo-American Racism in the Development of Chicanos," *California Historical Quarterly* L. No. 3, Sept. 1971: 321-337 and fn 25; *Times*, 6-8-43.

[17] The city population rose above 1.5 million in 1940, but the police force had fewer officers than in 1925 when the city held about 981,000 people. LAPD Information Processing Section. See P.C. *Minutes,* 1-1-42 through 4-1-43, *passim,* especially 6-22-43, and 2-9-42, 2-23-43, 3-16-43, 3-23-43. Ltd. William King to J.E. Shaw, 3-30-45; Shaw, Box 12, File "Earl Warren", Box 14, File "Miscellaneous, 1940-1950". Solomon Jones, "The Government Riots of Los Angles, June 1943" *passim.* Ralph Guzman, "The Function of Anglo-American Racism in the Development of Chicanos", 321-337 at footnote 25. *Times*, 5-5-39, 11-29-39, 12-5-39, 5-28-40, 1-19-43, 6-8-43.

[18] P.C *Minutes,* 1-1-42 through 4-1-43, esp. 2-9-42, 2-23-43, 3-16-43 and 6-22-43; Lt. Wm. King to J.E. Shaw, Shaw, Box 12, file "Earl Warren," and Box 14, file "Miscellaneous, 1940-1950"; Chamberlain, File "F.B. Speeches - Police;" Shaw, Box 12, File "L.A. Police Union League"; *Ibid.,* File "Congressman Harry R. Sheppard"; U.S. Dept. of Labor *Bulletin* No.879 (Wash., D.C.: U.S. Govt. Printing Office, 1946), 48-49. Demotions became commonplace. P.C. *Minutes,* 1-1-42 through 6-29-43, *passim,* especially 5-18-43, 6-8-43. LAPD *Union Bulletin,* 12-14-44, 1-11-45. E. Jacobs devised the plan. LAPD *Bulletin,* 2-2-44, 4-25-45. *Times,* 3-14-46.

[19] Clinton's campaign materials stressed the expansion and beautification of the city. Clinton Papers, 1945. Abrahams, 189, 232. John P. Kenney, *The California Police* (Springfield, Ill., 1964), Pt. III, 73-103, *passim.* LAPD *Bulletin,* 4-28-38. *Times,* 10-17-39.

[20] California Special Crime Study Commission on Organized Crime, *Second Progress Report* (Sacramento, Calif., 3-7-49), 16-52. *Ibid., Report* 11-15-50, 17,23,43. *Ibid, 3rd Progress Report,* 1-31-50, 18-21. *Ibid.,* (Hunt) *Report,* 5-11-53, 12 and *passim.* "The Secret Boss of California," *Collier's,* 8-13-49, p.13; *ibid.,* 8-20-13. Arthur Samish, *The Secret Boss of California* (N.Y., 1971), *passim.* Reid, 177. Charles Stoker, *Thicker 'n Thieves* (Santa Monica, 1951), 48-49.

[21] A number of authors have written about the L.A. crime situation in the thirties and forties. Besides Jennings and Reed (note 10, above), see Florabel Muir, *Headline Happy* (N.Y., 1950), 125-200, Hedda Hopper, *The Whole Truth and Nothing But* (Garden City), 1963), 200-210; James H. Richarson, *For the Life of Me* (N.Y., 1954), 16-18, 81-166,

200-289. There is a useful chronology of "mafia" murders, 1900-1951, prepared by the LAPD and reprinted in California Crime Commission (The Hunt Commission) *Report,* 5-11-53. Florabel Muir, in L.A. Mirror, 8-8-49, 10-13-49, 2-15-50. Cal. Crime Comm. *3rd Report,* 1-31-40, 11-16, 34-75. Interview with former Deputy Chief James Fisk.

[22] Charles Stoker, 74-145, 179-182, 196-201, *passim.* Stoker is a special pleader but his account of the vice scandal is useful. His knowledge and interpretation of L.A. history must be used with caution. Citations noted here have been verified by comparison with newspapers, court records and interviews. *Newsweek,* 7-18-49, 19; *ibid.,* 2-20-50, 21-22. *Daily News,* 6-1-49. The reformers had grave doubts about Aldrich as early as 1939. See Clinton Papers, File "Lloyd Aldrich." "Brenda Allen Threatens L.A. Graft Expose," *Daily News* (headline) 6-2-49. *Ibid.,* 5-6-48, 5-10-49, 6-3-49, 6-9-49, 6-11-49, 6-15-49 through 6-21-49, 6-24-49, 6-28-49. Interview with A.H. Hohmann.

[23] *Mirror,* 8-16-49, 8-26-49; *Times,* 8-17-49, 12-13-49. *Daily News,* 6-23-49, 6-29-49, 6-30-49. P.C. *Minutes,* 7-6-49, 7-13-49, 7-20-49, 10-26-49, 11-16-49, 11-30-49, 12-7-49, 12-28-49, 4-18-50.

[24] *Daily News,* 6-30-49; *Times,* 7-2-49, 10-2-49; P.C. *Minutes,* 8-9-50. On arrival, Worton promised no shakeup, but made at least thirteen major personnel shifts in 90 days. Cf. *Times,* 6-7-49, 10-8-49; P.C. *Minutes,* 10-19-49. *Ibid.,* 8-9-50. *Times,* 7-2-49, 7-22-49, 9-23-49, 10-2-49, 11-17-49, 12-10-49. *Daily News,* 6-20-49, 6-21-49, 6-30-49, 7-13-49.

[25] Stoker, 131-134, 230-232. Carey McWilliams, "Big Fix in Los Angeles," *The Nation,* 8-20-49, 170-172. *Daily News,* 6-20-49, 6-21-49. Florabel Muir was with Cohen when the attempted murder occurred. She received a slight wound. *Mirror,* 6-21-49, 7-27-49, 8-16-49, 8-29-49.

[26] *Times,* 8-17-49, 8-18-49, 11-17-49. A.A. Heist, Director, A.C.L.U. to W.W. Worton, 8-23-49, 9-7-49, 9-12-49, 9-28-49; Worton to Heist, 9-8-49, 9-16-49. Copies in the author's possession. Cal. Crime Comm. (Hunt) *Final Report,* 5-11-53, *passim.* The issue in 1953 was tax-supported low-cost housing, not vice. For discussion of Bowron and his administration see Caplan, 136-137. Arthur E. Briggs, Memoirs (U.C.L.A. Oral History transcript, 1970), 495-501; Chamberlain, "CIVIC," 82. The Hohmann ouster, the wiretap scandal and the complaints of Bowron's resigned police commissioners indicate some significant departures from reform ideals. See Story, 844-869,

CHAPTER EIGHT
THE AGE OF PROFESSIONALISM

The future of America may well rest in the hands of the police.[1]
William H. Parker

William H. Parker, the right man in the right place at the right time
in history, transformed the department's statutory autonomy from theory
to fact. In so doing, he gained a national and an international reputation
for bureaucratic competence and became, with J. Edgar Hoover, August
Vollmer and Orlando Wilson, one of America's best known policemen.
Circumstances contributed greatly to his success. In the aftermath of
scandal, Parker's probity, stiff moralism and long service as departmental prosecutor made him a logical candidate. No hint of impermanence
attended the appointment. Mayor Bowron cared only about his own re-
election. He sincerely wanted an end to police scandals and had no intention of replacing Parker once "the heat" abated.

Parker had legal training as well as a spotless reputation. He knew
that he could not be ousted except for cause, which he never provided,
and he would not resign without a trial and full public hearings. These
factors made him nearly invulnerable, a position aided by the gradual
decline of the police commission, the legal head of the LAPD. Every
year in office added to Parker's legend. Longevity made it almost impossible for mayors or police commissioners to challenge him. When he
died in 1966 he was, in the opinions of some observers, the single most
influential public official in Southern California.[2]

In addition to an overweening ambition to command the force,
Parker possessed the requisite credentials: twenty-three unblemished
years of service, most of it in executive positions; graduation from
Northwestern University Traffic Management School; teaching experience at the California Technical Institute of Police Officer Training; a
law degree and membership in the state bar association; wartime experience in developing military and civilian police systems; and first
place on the civil service promotion list. Even so, he became chief by
historical accident.

Three police commissioners, Mrs. Curtis Albro, Henry Duque and Bruno Newman, favored Thaddeus F. Brown, the personable chief of detectives. Brown had maintained an excellent reputation during twenty-six years of service. He was a Protestant and a Mason, like previous chiefs. Parker, a somewhat unpopular Roman Catholic, had the support of Irving Snyder and the black commissioner, Dr. J. Alexander Sommerville. On the eve of decision, Mrs. Albro died. According to Thaddeus Brown, he then requested one of his backers to vote for Parker because Brown did not want to be chief "with Bill Parker behind me with his knife out." In any case, the appointment of ex-chief William Worton to complete Mrs. Albro's term probably ensured a 3-2 majority for Parker. The commission voted unanimously for Parker, indicating solidarity behind the new chief.

Parker, the first practising Catholic among twentieth century LAPD chiefs, was born in South Dakota, where his grandfather had been a frontier lawman and his uncle a prosecuting attorney. While in high school, Parker worked as a hotel detective, expelling prostitutes from Deadwood hotels. He arrived in Los Angeles in the early 1920's and found work as a taxi driver. In 1927 he joined the LAPD and in 1928 married a Los Angeles policewoman. Concurrently, he worked his way through the Los Angeles College of Law, being graduated and admitted to the state bar in 1930.

The worsening depression enhanced the small but regular police salary, persuading Parker to forego law practice in favor of law enforcement. His career included the most violent and corrupt period in LAPD history but he avoided personal involvement in scandal. It became part of departmental folklore that "the machine" inhibited Parker's professional advancement but, as with C.B. Horrall, the facts proved otherwise. After joining in 1927, he became an acting sergeant sometime before 1930 and received the permanent rank in 1931. He was an acting lieutenant by 1934, receiving the substantive appointment in 1937. During that period he served as departmental prosecutor in trial board proceedings and spent three years as administrative assistant to Chief James E. Davis. In 1939, in honest civil service competition, Parker advanced to captain but finished out of contention for the chief and deputy chief positions.

Ironically, Parker found his path barred by Fletcher Bowron's ill-fated reform chief, Clemence B. Horrall. Although Parker stood first on several promotional lists during the early 1940's, Horrall promoted other men. Parker's appeals to the police commission for redress made interesting news but achieved nothing. Chief Horrall, himself a college graduate, blandly observed that "scholastic achievements do not necessarily make the best policemen." The disgruntled Parker then joined the army and served abroad, where he organized police services for several German cities. He became Inspector Parker in 1947, in charge of traffic division.

Later, Parker's obvious exclusion from the inner circles of power stood him in good stead. General Worton charged Parker with finding and prosecuting dishonest policemen. The *Times*, among other wise observers, then predicted Parker's promotion to command the department. Within a year he fulfilled the prophesy. He quickly became a controversial figure inside and outside the department. Some officers believed that while he was administrative officer to Chief J.E. Davis and later as internal affairs "headhunter," Parker collected gossip and other private information about the shortcomings and peccadilloes of his fellows. This he kept against the day when it might yield some advantage in departmental politics. True or not, the rumor inspired real fear; indeed, it expanded after he became chief. Newspaper reports implied that Parker knew dreadful things about one or another public figure and that his secret files made him and the department invulnerable to political interference. Again, the truth is unknown but at least one former city official so feared Parker that he had his own premises periodically inspected for listening devices.[3]

The chief's popularity among his officers also was problematic. Religious issues provoked some uneasy feelings. Parker, a devout man who thought that Catholics had less excuse for wrongdoing because of their superior moral training, held a favored place in local Catholic society. Critics asserted that the arch-conservative chief involved the church hierarchy in police operations in Roman Catholic areas (usually Mexican-American), not because it reduced police problems but to feed his own ego.

Parker also interested himself in the advancement of the Catholic police minority. He pledged himself to appoint the top men on every promotional list but he liked to have Catholic aides if possible. When Catholic officers fell upon hard times, he assisted them in legal but perhaps unsuitable ways. In a traditionally and overwhelmingly Protestant organization, where even post-World War II recruits learned the value of membership in the Masonic Order, a very few incidents could produce allegations of religious preference.

Chief Parker eagerly but vainly sought elective post in the International Association of Chiefs of Police, which would in time have led to the chairmanship of that respected body. On the other hand, his persistent and undeniably effective service on behalf of the rank and file, prior to becoming chief, brought him the presidency of the Fire and Police Protective League. He also led his chapter of the American Legion. As the years passed, experts, administrators and civic officials almost without number and without regard to religion or race paid him the personal tributes due the architect of America's most modern, efficient and professional police agency.

Next to God, Parker revered the police service. That circumstances forced him to abjure an accepted profession perhaps underlay his determination to make law enforcement recognized as a high and honorable calling. From a combination of religion, nationalism and the classic police perception of social disorder, Parker created an ideology of Americanism. The forces of evil—consisting both of habitual criminals and dissenters involved in "a revolution against constituted authority"—would, unless stopped, eventually destroy the increasingly soft and permissive American society. Into the vacuum of power would step agents of "godless" communism, the supreme evil. So would vanish American freedom. In Parker's view, a peace officer's career represented nothing less than a patriotic dedication to preserving American liberty.

Parker was the ideal chief for the McCarthy era but his extreme anticommunism, so typical of Los Angeles policemen, continued long after the Wisconsin senator faded from prominence. Taken at face value it explained much of Parker's subsequent career. Were not the communists disciplined? Then the chief had a clear duty to denounce flabby America, "the most lawless nation on earth," for its refusal to accept the rule of law. Did not the Kremlin hope that Americans would destroy themselves through avarice? Clearly, "a nation founded upon the weakness of its people (could) not stand." What better reason to eliminate legal as well as illegal forms of gambling, including church bingo? If only "the thin blue line" preserved American freedom then mayor, city administrative officer, civil service bureaucrat or anyone else who hindered departmental expansion deserved a public tongue-lashing for his errors.

If courts and legislatures set out to bind the hands of police officers and destroy their will to act, ought not someone speak out? If a federal bill meant "the end of law enforcement in this country," if a state law constituted "a bill of rights for prostitutes," if fools suggested that juveniles had the same legal rights as adults, if subversive elements accused police of brutality toward racial, social and political minorities, should not someone come to the defense of the law enforcement officers? And who better than lawyer-policeman William H. Parker, whose reputation spanned the globe? In fact, by what right did anyone dispute him, on any subject?

Parker's massive ego added an unfortunate dimension to his character. A most contentious man, he could not abide the same quality in others and his abrasive manner when questioned alienated potential allies. He brooked no criticism of himself, his policies or his subordinates. Even legitimate inquiries from civic officials concerning his annual budget projections could provoke furious outbursts. Parker's description of society provided a concise analysis of the chief himself. Americans, he said, were "emotional people, responsive to stimuli administered to us through communicative media; we are immature and subjective about problems, and there is an unwillingness for us to accept our mistakes." His enemies could not have said it better.

Parker, a shrewd politician, had a much more secure initial base than A.H. Hohmann and was a great deal more alert than C.B. Horrall. He did not plan to take orders from politicians. Nor did he bestow loyalty, he demanded it. Unworthy subordinates would never cause his fall. Any policeman, who by dishonoring his trust harmed the reputation of William Parker, could expect the most severe penalty the charter permitted. For culprits who escaped dismissal there remained the lost promotions and daily harassment by which "the system" tormented its outcasts.

Chief Parker's acceptance speech, broadcast by radio in August, 1950, sounded two traditional notes. First, though crime presented a serious problem, in comparison with other cities Los Angeles remained "the White Spot of America." Second, the citizens soon would have a police department in which they could take pride. Unlike past machine chiefs, Parker meant what he said; unlike past reform chiefs, he possessed the determination, the ability and the power to achieve his stated goals.[4]

As a police reformer, Parker faced classic reform problems. The city grew rapidly but the crime rate rose even faster. This placed a relentless strain on the police and required the chief to lobby continually for more men, money and machines. Vice, both as a matter of civic hygiene and as an exploitable issue, continued to excite churchmen, newspaper reporters and political opportunists. A minority of brutal, corrupt officers abused their authority, casting doubt on the integrity of the entire department. The best men still avoided the service, in part due to the small salary and in part because of the policeman's low social status.

Parker, like the earlier reform chiefs, achieved his greatest success in reorganizing the police bureaucracy. His first innovation, the bureau of administration, simplified the command structure and reduced the number of executives reporting directly to the chief from fourteen to eight. The bureau combined the business, public information, internal affairs, intelligence and administrative vice divisions under one head, along with the newly created planning and research divisions. The administrative bureau supplied its special services to the existing bureaus of technical services, corrections, detectives, traffic, patrol, juveniles, and personnel and training.

Aside from the anonymous business unit, the administrative bureau included some interesting and sensitive divisions. The public information division spent much of its time praising the LAPD but also produced the 1950 annual report, which broke with tradition as had Glass in 1897 and Vollmer in 1924. Parker used the report to introduce his administration to the public. Photographs and bright colors enlivened the once dreary publication. Tabular material appeared in attractive modern format rather than the previous tedious presentation of unintelligible statistics. The report included a brief sketch of the departmental history, stated current problems, explained the bureaucratic structure and described divisional functions. The stylish document provided further indication that a fresh wind was blowing away the musty traditions of the past.

The planning and research division represented real innovation. Parker believed that "management research" could help achieve his goal of maximum service per tax dollar. He assigned the PRD three tasks: to analyze the workload with a view to the most efficient personnel allocation; to develop a comprehensive system of police training manuals; and to seek ways to save time and money. The division's immediate success pleased the chief mightily and it quickly became one of the LAPD's most publicized "professional" tools.

One of the PRD's earliest, most inexpensive studies produced an annual savings greater than the division's budget. A method of maintaining permanent booking information on "repeaters" arrested as common drunks reduced the booking staff by 9 officers per 24 hour period. LAPD training manuals, when published, became the national standard and produced much favorable publicity. The division's first commander bragged that PRD research enabled a single police district to increase its patrol calls by 19 percent, juvenile cases by 24 percent, field interrogations by 31 percent, and to recover 32 percent more stolen automobiles than during the previous year, without an increase in personnel.

Traffic control presented the professional department at its best. Police executives found pedestrian and vehicular traffic much more amenable to rational planning than control of crimes against persons and property. Between 1941 and 1950, Parker and other graduates of Northwestern University Traffic School installed methods that reduced annual accident fatalities from 533 to 274. The death rate fell from 32.9 to 13.7 per hundred thousand residents, raising Los Angeles from last to first place among cities larger than one million population, despite increases of 400,000 residents and 350,000 registered vehicles. In 1950, the traffic bureau included 879 officers (21.1 percent of LAPD strength) and 43 civilian employees. By 1966, the bureau required only 678 officers (13 percent of strength) and 50 civilians, although Los Angeles had grown by about 800,000 persons and 900,000 registered vehicles. Success became routine.[5]

Personnel selection and training became the keystone of Parker's administration. Recruitment standards with respect to age, height, weight, scholastic achievement and intelligence approximated those of the Vollmer period. Psychiatric examinations, honored usually in the breach after Vollmer's departure, became again an integral part of the induction process when an experimental program found a significant proportion of recruits psychologically unsuitable for police work. The authoritarian chief applied military analogies wherever possible. Recruits experienced thirteen weeks of training in a "spit and polish," Marine Corps bootcamp atmosphere. Less than seven percent of men who passed the civil service examination reached the academy. The rigorous training schedule and probation period winnowed out a fifth of those. The curriculum included several dozen subjects, mostly manual police skills, but included criminal law and other difficult courses. The intense sincerity of the chief and the instructional staff won the academy a reputation as "the West Point of police training."

The chief demanded "academy" standards of physical condition, deportment and personal appearance, regardless of age or type of duty performed. The department became famous for its imposing physical appearance, a reputation enhanced by the *Dragnet* television program developed by Jack Webb. The "professional" manner of Webb's calm, polite, neatly dressed, physically fit, intelligent, efficient, humorless detective and his equally admirable associates reflected Chief Parker's vision of the department. Until the 1970's, most police screenplays followed the *Dragnet* model. A fictional Los Angeles policeman might on occasion be corrupt but never raucous, untidy or obese.

Recruitment became a long-term LAPD problem. Parker continually demanded more men to battle the rising crime rate, the nation's declining moral values and the communist menace, although the public was repeatedly assured that the country's best chief and its most professional police force protected the city. In election off-years, politicians ignored the crises and accepted the flattering view of police efficiency. The department annually added only a handful of new men, after allowance for resignations and retirements but the city continued to grow at a rapid pace. The International Association of Chiefs of Police and the International City Managers' Association agreed that three police officers per thousand population was the minimum safe ratio in urban areas. In 1950 the LAPD ratio stood at 2.1; by 1960 it had declined to 1.8 because the population increased by about 600,000 persons.[6]

Parker evidently preferred that every LAPD employee be a sworn police officer. Post World War II recruitment raised departmental strength by 2000 men (83 percent) to 4442 officers. In 1950, Parker requested that 2000 regular officers be hired to replace 700 unpaid reserves. In 1956 he asked for 2300 extra man and raised the request to 5000 in 1957. His rationale for the added manpower ranged from increased youth violence to supression of vice. Opponents argued that Parker created artificial shortages of manpower by restricting the reserves to parades, eliminating the deputy auxiliary police (a youth group) and cancelling a proposed police cadet program. He refused to reduce physical standards in order to enlarge the pool of eligible men because he believed that shorter officers were more subject to assault while on duty.

Oddly enough, while the mayor and council argued with the chief over his requests for huge personnel increases, the civil service department tried vainly to attract sufficient qualified men to fill the available vacancies. Although post-war reform and professionalization brought about a modest rise in the social status of police work, the LAPD continued to operate below authorized strength. Parker demanded that the recruitment campaign be widened. The city administrative officer and the civil service general manager argued that a pilot program throughout the eleven western states had produced meagre results at high cost. The chief won this battle. The initial program became a permanent, nationwide search for recruits.

He lost the battle over "civilianization," however. Traditionally, police chiefs developed programs manned by officers, then asked council for civilian employees to staff the "essential" program so that the officers could be released for street duty. In 1954, the city administrative officer, Samuel Leaske, Jr., charged that Parker could release 700 men for police duty by assigning routine clerical tasks to civilian employees. Leaske forced the issue. The percentage of civilians in 1954 (21.5%) rose to 25.4% by 1966. More significantly, between 1954 and 1966 regular police personnel increased by 698 officers, or 13.3 percent, while civilians increased by 553, nearly 45 percent. Parker therefore made civilianization a hallmark of professionalization and used the high LAPD ratio for its publicity value.

Parker also saved money in other areas. Most motorized patrol districts were assigned one officer per car in place of the traditional two member team. He forced the county sheriff to assume his full constitutional responsibility for housing city prisoners. This saved several million dollars annually and also released 210 police officers assigned to jail duty. An initial attempt to pass freeway traffic control duty to the California Highway Patrol failed but State highway patrol officers eventually replaced the LAPD on freeway patrol.

Broadening the recruitment area failed to alleviate the shortage of officers, which allowed Parker to reiterate a favorite maxim: until police wages and benefits allowed officers to provide a middleclass living standard for their families, good men would not joint the LAPD in sufficient numbers to properly protect the city. The Jacobs salary-setting formula, though an adequate indicator of "proper" police wage levels, had no binding force. The tax-conscious councilmen rejected wage increases in 1949 and 1950 despite a rise in living costs. Departmental spokesmen in turn proposed a municipal income tax to fund higher salaries and expenses. The city council heeded the warnings, authorizing a ten percent increase in 1951. In subsequent years the council and mayor granted increases of 5.5 percent; by 1956, the LAPD received the highest police salaries in the United States.

The generous wage scale reflected an important fact. In a "reformed" city, where a popular civil service chief acted as unofficial spokesman for the police union, the police department had again become a political issue. Elected officials feared the allegedly influential Protective League. Though city administrative officer Leaske warned the council not to repudiate its right to determine salaries, the politicians concurred when the Protective League requested that the Jacobs salary formula be inserted into the city charter by means of a ballot initiative. Parker opposed the 1958 proposition, which included an eleven percent pay rise, because "police management," meaning himself, had not been consulted. The successful initiative effectively removed police wages and pensions from the control of responsible elected officials and made the LAPD, in a sense, fiscally autonomous. Henceforth the council approved whatever annual wage increase the Jacobs formula required.

Unfortunately for the taxpayers, the Jacobs formula affected more than wages. Municipal law required that for every tax dollar allotted to police wages, the city must set aside an additional sum to fund the retirement plan. Mayor Norris Poulson denounced that superannuation system as "a financial nightmare." Due to improper financing during the depression, an infusion of $169 million would be required to make the pension actuarially sound. Furthermore, the deficit increased each year.

Despite Mayor Poulson's outraged cries, the Protective League sponsored a series of ballot initiatives to increase benefits that increased the long-term threat to the city's financial structure. Retired officers whose wages never exceeded $200 monthly got pensions equal to half a serving policeman's stipend (in the early 1970's, a former chief received close to $20,000 per annum after 45 years on the pension rolls, although his pension at retirement was only $3,000 per annum). Not surprisingly, the LAPD made "adequate" pensions one of the marks of a truly professional police force.

The ballot initiative, however, allowed elected officials to escape responsibility either for higher taxes or for thwarting the wishes of the policemen's union. This also pertained to capital improvements. A notable building program, the first since the Vollmer period, commenced after the voters ratified a special police bond issue. The new, nine story police headquarters (now the Parker Center) was described modestly as the most modern and efficient public building in the nation. Overall, the police budget increased from $21.5 million in 1950 to $81 million in 1966.[7]

Public acceptance of police-related charter amendments and bond issues implied considerable goodwill toward the department and increased the political capital of the Fire and Police Protective League. Politicians grew reluctant to express disapproval of the League's proposals after the defeat of Councilman Ransom Callicutt, an outspoken critic of departmental expenditures. The Protective League's political success coincided with important changes in the city and the police force. The population continued to undergo disproportionate increases in the percentages of black and Hispanic residents. The reported incidence of crimes committed by minority group members provided the white community with one rationale for supporting its local police. The department ceased to be an arm of the Merchants and Manufacturers Association, removing an old source of conflict and bridging the chasm between the police and the white working class.

Traffic policemen no longer systematically operated "curbside court," extorting bribes from erring motorists. The patrol bureau, still the major source of bad publicity, though no longer described as a gang of thugs, gradually rebuilt public confidence in its integrity. This perhaps was due more to a general absence of adverse commentary than to demonstrated efficiency, although the patrolmen benefited from the publicized glories of the traffic, personnel and training, and planning and research units.

Chief Parker did not escape entirely without scandals but he usually managed them so that they redounded to his credit, rather than undermining the department's reputation. A prime example, an incident known as "Bloody Christmas," occurred in December of 1951. Drunken officers and jailers at the Wilshire station viciously and repeatedly beat seven young hispanic prisoners who were wrongly believed to have maimed a policeman. Rumors of the outrage began to circulate early in the New Year. Councilman Edward Roybal accused the police of systematic brutality and cited fifty incidents known to him. Newspapers, especially the *Daily News* and the *Mirror,* carried huge banner headlines reporting Chief Parker's denial of the charges and his invitation to the police commission to investigate police conduct.

As the inquiry widened, Chief Parker revealed that a departmental probe had already begun. Parker used his television program (titled "The Thin Blue Line") to denounce his critics. In his opinion, bad publicity arising out of the Bloody Christmas incident hurt the LAPD by undermining public confidence and providing the Communists with a propaganda message. Florabel Muir, the *Mirror's* generally "pro-police" crime reporter, retorted that had Parker trained his men properly, there would be no basis for communist propaganda and no need for an FBI investigation.

After extensive hearings, the county grand jury indicted eight policemen, four of whom later served prison terms for assault. Chief Parker, unable to block an outside investigation, intensified the internal audit. Eventually he dismissed half a dozen men after trial board proceedings and meted lesser punishment to about three dozen others. The county grand jury criticized Parker for apparent weaknesses in the command structure and deplored the "lack of military discipline" that their inquiry made evident. The chief rejected the grand jury's "nebulous" criticism, made typical remarks about the deleterious effects of newspaper commentary, and ignored Mayor Bowron's implied charge that Parker, though an excellent executive, delayed the departmental probe until the threat of an outside investigation forced him to act.

The ultimate significance of the Bloody Christmas incident went well beyond the expulsion of a few bad policemen. The officers' felonious conduct threatened nothing less than departmental self-government through self-policing, the hallowed "professional" ideal enshrined

in city charter section 202. The *Daily News,* a reliable progressive journal that consistently supported Mayor Bowron and Chief Parker,
demanded again that section 202 be repealed. The department's enormous investigative effort, however, once the grand jury forced Parker's
hand, allowed the chief to go well beyond anything that the public body
might discover and by punishing men whose guilt could not be proved in
court, to justify the police court-martial system. In Parker's view, the
internal affairs division investigation and subsequent trial board proceedings proved his maxim that "the department not only should discipline itself, it would do so."

Bloody Christmas offered the last realistic chance for repeal of
section 202 during Parker's term. As the civil rights movement burgeoned, anticommunist and racist sentiment could easily be provoked
whenever political or racial "radicals" demanded that the police disciplinary process be returned to public control. Finally, Bloody Christmas
presented the last and perhaps the only realistic opportunity to oust Chief
William Parker through legal, civil service means. Notwithstanding his
vigorous investigation of the incident, the chief's initial attempts to suppress a public inquiry probably constituted nonfeasance if not misfeasance. No responsible official, organization or newspaper suggested
such drastic action, however. The invulnerable chief handled later developments in a similar fashion, including the discovery of a police burglary
ring, some minor vice scandals, considerable brutality and a number of
apparently unjustified civilian deaths by police gunshot.[8]

Parker eventually preempted the administrative functions of his *de
jure* superior, the police commission. Beginning in 1949 with the
appointment of the first non-white commissioner, Charles Matthews, the
commission gradually became "controlled by minorities," in that blacks,
hispanics, Jews, Catholics and women were regularly appointed. Parker,
however, often refused to comply with the suggestions or even the direct
orders of the commissioners. Several commissioners issued furious
denunciations of Parker to no discernible effect. Reform-minded commissioners soon resigned, since the mayor and city council usually supported the chief. Critics, if they considered the police commission,
referred to it as "a rubber stamp."

On the other hand, the chief's dealings with the city council
became somewhat more difficult. Edward Roybal and Charles Navarro
of the ninth and tenth districts, the first twentieth-century councilmen of
hispanic descent, were critical of LAPD practices in the extensive Los
Angeles barrio. The council majority refused to elect either man to the

Fire and Police Committee. The youthful councilwoman, Rosalind Wyman, was the sole liberal voice on the committee, although Roybal and Parker engaged in several impassioned arguments. In 1963, the first black councilmen were elected. Billy G. Mills, Gilbert Lindsay and Thomas Bradley of the eight, ninth and tenth districts, ensured a strong black voice where none had been heard before. The council majority still sided with Parker.

The mayors of Los Angeles invariably praised the Chief. Bowron and Parker differed over the merits of public housing, Norris Poulson and Parker clashed over budget estimates, Samuel Yorty chided Parker for clumsy public relations, but all gave him undeviating support against "outside" critics, including the governor, the state attorney general, the ACLU, the NAACP and other organizations. From this impregnable position, the conservative Parker directed the municipal police force according to his apocalyptic personal vision in which crime, the civil rights movement and the so-called "counterculture" all were parts of a communist plot.[9]

The political maturation of the non-white communities presented an opportunity and a challenge that Parker failed to meet. The Asian, black and Spanish-speaking groups, insignificant in 1927 when Parker joined the LAPD, by 1966 exceeded thirty percent of the population. Although blacks numbered about seventeen percent and hispanics about thirteen percent of the population, their representation on the LAPD remained at five percent and six percent respectively, despite a sincere recruiting campaign by the civil service department. Many among the racial minorities viewed the police almost as an army of occupation. Complaints about insensitive and racist police activities were heard more often as the 1950's progressed. Charges of discriminatory law enforcement were heard even from the superior court bench. Parker successfully stood off his critics, usually by questioning their motives and their patriotism, until the civil rights movement finally engulfed him.

Parker admitted that he commanded an ultraconservative department. He, Inspector Edward M. Davis and Sergeant Norman Moore were prolific critics of what they seemed to believe were communist-inspired minority organizations. Rumor held that many officers were members of the John Birch Society. One well-known story involved the defacement, by white officers, of photographs of the "nigger lover," Eleanor Roosevelt. Several LAPD officers attempted to unseat the liberal Republican U.S. Senator, Thomas Keuchel, by fabricating an arrest for homosexual behavior. Predictably, the department adamantly opposed the idea of a civilian review board when it was put forward in 1960 by the NAACP and ACLU.

The old, traditional civil rights organizations asserted that charter section 202 shielded officers who were guilty of brutal, racist and unconstitutional behavior. A civilian review board could circumvent section 202 and restore public control over the police. During the struggle, the department suffered a few minor setbacks. The practice of laying charges against citizens who made "unfounded" complaints was declared unconstitutional, in that it threatened the right of the citizen to petition for redress of grievance. The mayor successfully opposed Parker's proposal to open the arrest records of civil rights activists (as opposed to conviction records) because it raised the possibility of harassment by arrest. The state legislators revoked the law of "sovereign immunity," thus allowing petitioners to sue the city for redress of illegal acts by civic employees. In the end, the NAACP and ACLU entirely failed to convince municipal legislators of the merits of civilian review.[10]

The newer, more radical minority groups occasionally fought the police in the streets. In April, 1962, a gunbattle between police and Black Muslims left one Muslim dead, six wounded, three policemen injured, and the city in an uproar. Black leaders urged Parker to modify LAPD methods in the ghetto, for fear of inciting an insurrection, but the chief refused. He insisted that the sensible part of the black community supported him; the other part was misled by white radicals. The chief ruthlessly excised such potentially liberalizing influences as Michael Hannon, a white officer who joined the Congress of Racial Equality and sometimes attended demonstrations during off-duty hours. Hannon received a long suspension and soon afterward resigned.[11]

Only two weeks after Hannon's trial, the most tragic event in Los Angeles history occurred. Despite Parker's many confident assertions, the racial conflagration predicted by black leaders broke out. Between ten thousand and fifty thousand of the half-million blacks engaged in looting and burning white-owned businesses, or joined in assaults on white citizens, firemen and police officers. Thirty-four people died violently as a direct result. An unknown number received injuries. About 4000 were arrested. The area suffered property damage amounting perhaps to $40 million. The seven days of fury, finally suppressed by a combined force of over 13,000 Los Angeles police, sheriff's deputies, California national guardsmen and U.S. Army personnel, became known as the Watts Riot.

Again as predicted, a simple arrest touched off the uprising. Two California Highway Patrol officers followed two young black men off the freeway to arrest them for traffic violations. The officers stopped the pair not far from the men's home. Their mother hurried to the scene and engaged in an altercation with the officers, who then attempted to arrest the woman as well as her sons. The crowd of onlookers forced the policemen to radio for help. The battle had begun.

Ghetto residents hurled rocks, bottles and other debris at unsuspecting whites in transit through the district. Police soon blockaded the streets leading into the riot area, forestalling certain death or injury to unwary motorists. Inside the perimeter, looting and burning began. One street, gutted on both sides for several blocks, earned the name, "Charcoal Alley." Some black militants may have seized the opportunity to urge their "soul brothers" to ever more violent deeds. Certainly the television stations did their part to inflame and terrify both whites and blacks. Into the city's living rooms came "live" coverage of widespread criminal behavior, arson and pillage, over-excited threats by blacks to carry the blaze to white neighborhoods and undeniable, overt police brutality. Sniper bullets and "molotov cocktail" firebombs endangered firemen as they struggled to contain the conflagration. Policemen, answering supposed calls for assistance, ran into ambushes. Every patrol car that entered the area, 103 in all, was damaged.[12]

Massive force quelled the riot. By that time, politicians, police officials and notable individuals from every level of society had found firm positions and prepared to argue their own virtue at the expense of other participants. White liberals and the minority communities almost uniformly blamed Chief Parker, not only in the matter of previous, systemic police brutality but for his conduct of the police in suppressing the insurrection. They thought that Parker should have withdrawn the police and let community leaders deal with the rioters without bloodshed. Their consensus required Parker's resignation and the establishment of a civilian review board to investigate police brutality.

Chief Parker said that he drew the police back, rather than striking hard at the center of the disturbance before the crowds grew to unmanageable size, at the request of men who proved to be "pseudo leaders who can't lead at all." Black congressman Augustus Hawkins concurred, accusing the news media of "making more Negro `leaders' than you have sand on the beach." Parker accused the Black Muslims of provoking race hatred and keeping the riot going when it might have died out. He refused to make any effort to halt gun sales in the white districts, as Governor Pat Brown requested, and noted that the police found over 1000 "criminals" among arrested rioters. The chief refused to quit because his resignation "would result in a deterioration of the public security." Mayor Yorty announced that the white community would not permit Parker's replacement. The chief admitted that a problem of "verbal brutality" existed and promised to "redesign" the police vocabulary.

Whites, especially conservatives, gave the chief broad support. The *Times* and the *Examiner*, the mayor and the city council, the county board of supervisors and many writers of letters to newspaper editors praised the chief and the department. The Democrat-controlled California Assembly withheld a Republican-sponsored vote of thanks to Parker but the Republican assemblymen praised him. The Governor's Commission on the Los Angeles Riots (the McCone commission), official investigator of the unhappy event, both praised and criticized the chief and the LAPD. For liberals, the commission's praise far outweighed the blame; they immediately labelled the report "a whitewash."[13]

Whitewash or not, the McCone report verified almost every charge made against the LAPD during the previous decade. The report admitted that blacks hated Chief Parker and feared the LAPD, although in 1964 the Urban League had named Los Angeles the nation's "best" city for blacks. The McCone commission agreed that the ghetto suffered serious deprivation in schools, housing, jobs, transportation and welfare. The commissioners observed that the police commission existed as a mere figurehead, controlled by Chief Parker; that the citizens' complaint procedure did not satisfy public needs; that the department unwisely abandoned its juvenile crime prevention operation; and that its community relations program had lapsed. McCone proposed a city human relations commission to deal with these problems. (A county human relations commission already existed.) Though couched in inoffensive language, these remarks constituted a grave indictment of Chief Parker's administration.[14]

The McCone report served the useful function of stating, from an unimpeachably conservative "pro-police" source, that Parker controlled the department. Good or bad, its policies were his policies. The commission made two recommendations. First, a revitalized police commission should exert its legal powers, providing an open and influential forum for dissatisfied citizens. Second, the internal disciplinary system ought to be modified and placed in the hands of an inspector general, outside the regular police hierarchy. Chief Parker argued that it would cost an additional $108,000 annually to have the internal affairs division investigate every single complaint; furthermore, it reduced the authority and responsibility of divisional commanders. Councilman Bradley fought hard but proved no match for Parker on this issue.

The McCone commission actually criticized Parker's vision of police professionalism when it chided the LAPD for discontinuing its crime prevention work among juveniles. Presumably, Chief Parker equated crime prevention work among youths with selling tickets for fraternal events, accepting rewards and gratuities and other conduct banned as "unprofessional." Seeking ways to decrease police costs, Parker eventually eliminated department-sponsored youth programs, which further deprived the poor. After the riot the LAPD strengthened its community relations program.[15]

In some respects the post-Watts period found Chief Parker at the height of his influence. He had the white majority behind him. He continued his undeviating campaigns against the civil rights movement and the implementation of programs designed to increase the numbers of minority policemen. Parker especially condemned U.S. Vice President Hubert H. Humphrey in connection with a government proposal to lower physical and educational entrance standards and to train physically and educationally unqualified minority candidates to pass the civil service examination. The chief claimed that the Progressive Labor Party and the Communist Party worked to stir unrest in the black area and asked the city council to double police strength to 11,010 from 5,342 officers. He also needed $50,000 worth of new shotguns, so that each patrol car could carry two.

"G2's" discovery of "communists" in the ghetto provided evidence of Parker's continuing misuse of the intelligence division. In theory, the squad fought organized crime; in practice, it seemed always involved in political activities. Policemen, possessing no more expertise than a highschool diploma, appointed themselves judges in a political inquisition and then convicted of heresy anyone they chose—civil rights activists, political dissenters, "hippies," homosexuals, anti-war protesters or any critic of the police.

By 1963, the LAPD had become so militantly anti-radical that members formed a special unit, the Fire and Police Research Organization, to engage in political terrorism. In 1965, several officers had to resign and at least one went to jail for a politically motivated crime. Mayor Sam Yorty, himself a victim of the old intelligence squad, made no recorded complaint about the actions of the FPRO. Perhaps he did not care to remember, or have publicized, his earlier place in the police files as a subversive radical.[16]

Suddenly, Parker died. The sixty-four year old police executive expired of a heart attack on July 16, 1966. His corpse lay in state in the city hall rotunda. Many mourners attended a Requiem Mass at Saint Vibiana's Cathedral. Loudspeakers carried the service to those waiting in the downtown streets, who had been unable to obtain places in the church. Liberals and conservatives, blacks, whites and hispanics, joined in posthumous praise of the deceased chief. Old antagonists emphasized Parker's personal integrity and his devotion to the city. Newspaper editors and other conservatives gave him credit for making Los Angeles the "best policed city in the nation," in spite of "phony" charges of police brutality, designed to undermine the department. A commercial publication noted Parker's opposition to "disrespect for law and order which eventually could destroy the economic climate which has made Los Angeles."[17]

They praised too much. A good portion of fiction quickly became incorporated in Parker's legend. Even before his death, the tale of the chief's deeds surpassed the truth. Perhaps social conservatism, political expediency or the demands of good manners blinded the chief's friends and enemies to the realities of life in Los Angeles. The social and political Right lauded in Parker characteristics that were deplorable when exhibited by the Left. Conversely, some liberals viewed Parker as the main obstacle to social progress and assumed that his removal alone ensured significant change.

The *Times* remarked that Parker made Los Angeles the best policed city in the nation. This claim, made by local newspapers since at least 1892, nurtured the "good business climate" of the White Spot. The FBI annual *Uniform Crime Reports* consistently placed Los Angeles among America's most crime-ridden cities but Chief Parker accused other police administrations of falsifying their records, an old police strategy well known in Los Angeles. Parker chided J. Edgar Hoover for compiling and publishing statistics for which he took no responsibility. The subsequent unworthy competition that characterized the LAPD-FBI relationship interfered with necessary interdepartmental cooperation.[18]

Even admirers felt the chief's lash if their praise fell below the required fulsome level. Bruce Smith, one of the most respected judges of police standards in the United States, once named Los Angeles the fifth best force in the nation, behind those of Milwaukee, Detroit, St. Louis and Cincinnati. Parker immediately attacked Smith, quoting Orlando W. Wilson, another esteemed expert, who placed the LAPD first among American municipal police forces. Yet Parker, in more reflective moments, suspected that the crime rate bore little if any relationship to the activities of law enforcement agencies. He admitted that the police department must be deemed a failure because crime continued to rise despite massive expenditures for men, training and equipment.

Parker vociferously opposed what he called a nationwide "revolt against legally-constituted authority." Yet he publicly and repeatedly blamed the crime rate on the decisions of federal and state courts. On numerous occasions he stated plainly that, consciously or not, the makers of "the judicial revolution of civil rights" aided the communist conspiracy. He challenged the U.S. and California attorneys general, the director of the FBI, the California governor, the mayor and the council, and reduced his superior, the police commission, to a cipher. In short, above all other men in Los Angeles, William Parker led the attack upon constituted authority.

Parker accepted awards from conservative groups for his achievements in "human relations" but the racial minorities disliked and distrusted him. As he said after the Watts Riot, "We're on top and they're on the bottom." He deplored the high rate of crime among blacks and hispanics but discontinued youth oriented crime prevention programs in minority areas because such programs were "nonprofessional." Though he and his men were "not sociologists," he considered himself competent to discuss eugenics and the importance of heredity in human behavior.

The Watts Riot and its aftermath demonstrated the serious deficiencies of Parker-style professionalism. Parker's interpretation, which developed only a single dimension of August Vollmer's multi-faceted vision, emphasized the bureaucratization of the administrative function, seeking the most police function per dollar spent while reducing discretion at the lower echelons to the smallest possible measure. Parker's military model, buttressed by many regulations, could and did produce an honest, obedient, physically fit, neatly dressed police force but his emphasis on power and authority alienated the department from significant portions of the community it protected.

By 1965, generally, the Parker model had become the national model and its shortcomings were being debated in every city where angry confrontations took place between citizens and policemen. Some critics viewed policework as unskilled labor. They suggested that the regular force be removed from ghetto areas in favor of "community control," an odd idea that involved the designation of a few neighborhood residents as police officers. Proponents assumed that a local person, living in the district, would not be brutal or unsympathetic toward citizens or miscreants. Presumably, in difficult situations the community-controlled officer called upon fellow ghetto residents to form a posse to pursue criminals as in frontier days.

Other critics demanded more professionalism. To some, this meant more of Parker's methods: more men, better riot control training, more powerful weapons, massive retaliation. Calmer experts, including many within the police service, preferred the progressive panacea: more education for police officers. Deliberately or not, they followed in August Vollmer's footsteps, maintaining the police force as an efficient, aggressive peacekeeping tool but seeking intellectual solutions to human problems. The upper echelons of the LAPD harbored numerous such men, who had served their entire careers in the reformed, progressive atmosphere of the post-1938 city administrations. They accepted police professionalism as fact but their ideas went far beyond the bureaucratic dogma of William Parker. In life, he stifled their efforts to deal pragmatically with human problems. [19]

Chief Parker's demise, however, signalled neither the end nor the beginning of an era. His successors, though forceful, independent men in their own right, devised some innovative programs but did not transform the department. Tradition ruled. Indeed, the more things changed, the more they remained the same.

NOTES

[1] W.H. Parker, "The California Crime Rise," *Journal of Criminal Law, Criminology and Police Science,* 47:6 (1957) 721-729.

[2] This opinion re Parker's influence was expressed in 1953 by Police Commissioner H.C. Irey, a white, and again in 1972 by former Police Commissioner E.M. Porter, a black. Interview with Judge E.M. Porter, 11-1-72. *Mirror,* 7-13-53.

[3] Biographical details are from several sources, especially the memorial issue of *The Los Angeles Police Beat,* Sept., 1966, and the *Times'* file "William H. Parker," Box 289. Most details of Parker's career as chief are from the LAPD Public Relations Division Scrapbooks, 26 vols., 1948-1966, in the LAPD Archives. In most cases the *Times* is cited. See also Jack Webb, *The Badge,* (Englewood Cliffs, N.J.: Prentice-Hall, Inc., 1958), 241-274; William W. Turner, *The Police Establishment* (N.Y.: G.P. Putnam's Sons, 1968), ch. 5, "Los Angeles: Parker's Legacy," 85-106; Ed Cray, "The Governor and the Police," *Frontier,* May 1962, 5-11; Wesley Marx, "Parker: The Cop as Crusader," *Los Angeles Magazine,* Aug. 1962, 19-20, 47-48; the author has also discussed William Parker with former chief A.H. Hohmann, Deputy Chief Thaddeus Brown, Deputy Chief Ervis Lester, former departmental advocate J.B. Williams, Mayor Samuel W. Yorty and former police commissioners Everette Porter and John P. Kenney. Insight can be gained from the articles in W.H. Parker, *Parker on Police,* edited by O.W. Wilson (Springfield, Ill.: Charles C. Thomas, 1957), and Donald McDonald, "An Interview with William Parker," *The Police* (Santa Barbara: Center for the Study of Democratic Institutions, April, 1962). *Times,* 7-3-39, 6-12-40, 8-21-40, 3-9-41, 2-4-43, 2-9-43, 2-10-43, 2-17-43, 4-14-48, 7-15-49, 7-11-50, 8-3-50, 8-4-50. *Daily News,* 5-14-52. *The Beat,* (L.A., Sept. 1966).

[4] Marx, *passim.* Interview with J.B. Williams. *Daily News,* 9-18-54. Interview with George Wilson, departmental historian. E.M. Porter, *ibid.* "Police Philosophy," *Parker on Police,* 23-32, 49-65, 95-131. Also W.H. Parker, "The California Crime Rise," *JCLCPS,* 47 (1957), pp. 21-29. *Times,* 7-22-50, 2-21-51, 2-8-57, 10-5-57, 2-8-58, 6-17-58, 4-17-59, 12-6-61, 12-28-61, 1-31-63. See speech in *Parker on Police.* Interview with former deputy chief Ervis Lester.

[5] Cf. LAPD *Annual Reports,* 1897, 1924, 1950. Deputy Chief Richard Simon, "The Planning and Research Division of the Los Ange-

244 The Age of Professionalism

les Police Department," *JCLCPS*, 44 (1953), 365-373. *Times*, 8-10-51.
LAPD *Annual Reports,* 1950-1966, *passim.*

[6] *Times*, 9-23-52. See James H. Rankin, "Psychiatric Screening of
Police Recruits," *Public Personnel Review*, 20 (July, 1959), 191-196.
Marx, 47. Also Stephen Marcus, "Police Academy, Los Angeles,"
Leatherneck: The Magazine of the Marines, Apr., 1954, 21-26. *Times*,
9-14-50, 9-18-50, 12-15-50, 9-23-52. See also discussions of recruit-
ment in *Annual Reports,* 1950-1966.

[7] Parker, "California Crime Rise," 722. See *Times* editorial 12-24-
53; ibid., 8-21-58. City Administrative Officer, "Fire and Police Salary
recommendations for the Fiscal Year 1956-57," 11, 21-22 and *passim.*
As of June 30, 1971, the unfunded liability was $888,164,533. See John
Kendall's front page article in the *Times*, 3-13-72. City Council files,
especially 54030, 88060, 130081, 130340. *Times*, 5-24-58, 3-20-61, 6-
8-61, 10-3-61.

[8] Jack Webb, *The Badge*, 170. Marx, 47. For brutality investigation see *Daily News* or *Mirror*, 2-28-52 through 6-17-52. *Citizen-News*,
3-13-52; *Mirror*, 4-1-52, 4-2-52, 4-8-52. *Times*, 3-2-52, 3-28-52, 4-9-
52, 4-34-52, 4-24-52, 5-1-52, 5-27-52, 6-17-52. *Daily News*, 5-14-52, 3-
26-53. Parker merely reprimanded a lieutenant who changed the arrest
record of a patrolman "found in" at a gambling raid. This constituted a
felony. *Herald Express*, 6-17-53, 10-25-55. J.B. Williams. *Mirror*, 1-
12-53. "B-Girl Crackdown," *Newsweek*, 41 (June 15, 1953), 26.

[9] For typical remarks by and about the commissioners, see *Times*,
2-27-52, 2-28-52, 4-11-52, 4-17-52, 6-10-59, 6-19-59, 6-30-59, 3-10-65.
Herald-Express, 4-22-52. *Mirror*, 7-13-53, 7-14-53, 7-15-53. *Daily
News*, 6-25-53. *Sentinel*, 5-10-51. *Tribune*, 7-28-51. William W. Turner, *The Police Establishment* (N.Y., G.P. Putnam's Sons, 1968), 91-92.
Also *Times*, 4-25-61, 6-6-61. *Herald-Express*, 3-16-61, 3-27-61, 4-27-
61, 5-24-61, 6-8-61, 6-9-61. *Mirror*, 6-21-61. Interviews with former
commissioners J.P. Kenney and E.M. Porter, 11-1-72.

[10] The 1960 convention of the liberal California Democratic Coun-
cil (C.D.C) endorsed the review board concept, as did the A.C.L.U.—
N.A.A.C.P. "Committee For A Los Angeles Police Review Board." *Her-
ald-Express*, 2-15-60. "Los Angeles Needs a Police Review Board,"
A.C.L.U. press release, 6-9-60. Review boards were created in Philadel-
phia and New York, but determined police opposition destroyed both.
Documents re publication of arrest records are in council file 90861.
The proposed ordinance is reprinted in a special edition of the Fire and
Police Protective League *News*, 4-15-60. Norman H. Moore, "Police

Review Boards," *California Peace Officer,* 11:2 (November-December, 1960), 5-6. *Parker On Police,* 151; Edward M. Davis, "Move Over, Chief," address to the Police Chiefs' Section, League of California Cities, 10-23-62. "Notes on Police Practices Committee," A.C.L.U., 3-4-60. Ordinance No. 114,852. *Times,* 10-2-63. The court acted in May, 1961. Ed Cray, "The Police and Civil Rights," *Frontier,* 13 (May, 1962), 6. See especially council file 89512, and *Times,* 8-4-65.

[11] See Parker Scrapbooks, 1-27-60 through 4-4-65, *passim. Times,* 6-5-65, 6-17-65, 7-13-65. W.W. Turner, 89-92. Trial records can be examined at the Internal Affairs Division, LAPD.

[12] In June, 1962, black clergymen warned that unless the police changed their overbearing, racist attitude, violence would "tear the town apart." Again in 1964, James Farmer, of C.O.R.E., predicted police-community violence. At that time, the United Civil Rights Committee requested Parker's retirement and the establishment of a civilian review board. *Times,* 6-30-62, 4-27-64. Estimates of the number of rioters are guesses at best. Conservatives, upholding the theory that only "riffraff" participated, hold to the lower figure. Liberals, arguing that violence equalled social protest, prefer a higher number. For an extended discussion see Robert M. Fogelson, *Violence as Protest: A study of Riots and Ghettos* (Garden City: Doubleday & Co., Inc., 1971) *passim,* especially 171-216.

[13] See the remarks of black Assemblyman Mervyn Dymally (Dem., L.A.), *Times,* 8-14-655, 8-15-65, 8-20-65. See the *Times* editorial praising the police as "The First Line of Community Defense," and Parker's gratified response, *Times,* 10-1-65, 10-7-65, 10-17-65, 1-24-66; also Robert Blauner, "Whitewash over Watts," *TransAction,* 3:3 (March, 1966), 3-9-54.

[14] Transcripts of the McCone Commission are deposited in the Graduate Research Library at U.C.L.A. The commissions's brief report is titled *Violence in the City: An End or a Beginning?* (L.A., 1965). For discussions of the riot, its causes and its results, see Robert Conant, *Rivers of Blood, Years of Darkness* (N.Y., 1967); Jerry Cohen and William S. Murphy, *Burn, Baby, Burn!* (N.Y.: E.P. Dutton & Co., Inc., 1966); Paul Jacobs, *Prelude to Riot: A View of Urban American From the Bottom* (N.Y.: Random House, 1966); also Fogelson, *Violence as Protest;* Turner, op.cit.

[15] Parker phased the juvenile bureau into the patrol bureau in his first year in office. He eliminated youth gang supervisors, deputy auxiliary police, police cadets and police-sponsored sports programs, against

the opposition of mayors and newspaper reporters. He opposed the extension of constitutional rights to juveniles. See the discussion of juvenile work in the *Annual Reports,* 1950-1966. Also *Times,* 3-10-52, 4-8-52, 8-23-60, 2-28-63, 9-21-65, 10-16-65, 12-9-65, 1-7-66, 4-22-66, 11-20-66. *Mirror,* 8-24-60. The post Watts community relations section rose to five persons from one.

[16] *Ibid.,* 6-29-66, 7-24-66; Bruce Bollinger, "Police Unions in Los Angeles County," for the Institute on Law and Urban Studies, Loyola University Law School (Los Angeles, 1962).

[17] *The Beat,* 21:2 (Sept., 1955), 3. *Times, Examiner,* and *Southern California Business* editorials, reproduced in *ibid.,* 6.

[18] The Parker-Hoover feud began in 1950, the last year until Parker's death that LAPD officers attended FBI training schools. It worsened through the years, as the *Uniform Crime Reports* annually contradicted the chief's crime statistics. Parker faced his own dilemma. He enjoyed national publicity, such as "'Best' Police Force vs. Worst Crime Wave," *Newsweek,* 43 (Feb. 3, 1954), 50-54, that underplayed crime and emphasized the preeminence of Parker and the LAPD. He had a strong negative reaction to such headlines as "F.B.I. Says L.A. Crime Center of Nation," *Times,* 9-2-58. Parker had good reason to suspect under-reporting in other jurisdictions because it was an old trick. Yet he could not deny the rising L.A. crime rate. His own statistics, used to refute Governor Brown, showed that L.A. rates far exceeded that of the rest of the state. Ed Cray, "The Governor and the Police," *Frontier,* 12 (May, 1961), 5-7. The kidnapping of Frank Sinatra, Jr., marked the worst point of the quarrel. Parker said that the FBI held back important information from the LAPD, a charge that Hoover "refused to dignify" with an answer. Newsmen, not the federal agency, informed Parker when the culprits were arrested. See *Times,* 12-12-63, 12-13-63, 12-15-63; *Mirror,* 12-5-52; O.W. Wilson is quoted in "'Best' Police Force vs. Worst Crime Wave," 52.

[19] From early in his career, Parker exhibited a strong suspicion of potential successors. A number of senior officers departed for other jobs, some with the California Highway Patrol or other police agencies, others to organize police services in foreign countries. See *Herald-Express,* 11-4-54; also Thomas H. Reddin, quoted in Los Angeles *Times West Magazine,* (June 6, 1968), 13.

CHAPTER NINE
THE LEGACY OF WILLIAM PARKER

Thomas H. Reddin was appointed chief of the LAPD in February, 1967. He immediately set out to improve the department's unpleasant relationship with the black community. Reddin increased the community relations section from less than half a dozen to more than a hundred persons. He ordered the police to fraternize with minority citizens and to wear name-tags for easy identification. The chief met in frequently acrimonious debate with militants and radicals as well as moderate blacks. He increased the recruit training period to five months and included "racial sensitivity" classes. He returned some officers to foot patrol, used black ex-convicts in police community liaison work and reinstituted a broad variety of youth-related programs cancelled by Parker. Police issued warnings instead of citations for "mechanical" violations of the vehicle code that were common in poorer districts.

After the murder of Dr. Martin Luther King, Jr., Reddin ordered that police vehicles proceed with headlights on as a mark of respect to the black community and its slain hero. He increased efforts to recruit black officers and established the post of inspector general, as both ex-chief Worton and the McCone Commission had recommended. The inspector general directed the internal affairs division but reported directly to Reddin rather than to the commander of the special services bureau. The intention was to make the internal affairs division more professional and more accountable, and less likely to undervalue the testimony of complaining citizens.

Reddin suppressed the Watts Community Alert Patrol, an abortive attempt to achieve neighborhood control by surveillance of police operations in the black ghetto, because some members armed themselves and threatened citizens' arrests of overly aggressive officers. This reduced CAP support among moderate blacks but Reddin's determined opposition prevented a reorganization along more sensible lines. Chief Reddin also organized a broader intelligence network than that which Parker directed.

Reddin served less than twenty-seven months. He resigned in May, 1969, to accept a position as a news commentator with a conservative local television station. The nature of his going was controversial because of the mayoralty campaign, then in its last stages.[1]

The 1969 campaign revolved around a single overriding issue: the racial origins of the two contenders. Councilman Thomas Bradley, a black retired police lieutenant, challenged third-term candidate Mayor Samuel Yorty, once praised by Chief Parker for his refusal to interfere in departmental matters. Bradley, a critic of police misconduct in the ghetto since his election in 1963, essayed the lofty role of statesman, concerned with broad problems of business expansion, urban renewal, ecology, rapid transit and social harmony. Yorty charged that a Bradley victory would result in mass resignations from the police department.

A white retired patrolman, known for his association with the ultra-conservative police "research" group, polled the department and predicted that most white officers would quit if Bradley were elected. Chief Reddin's sudden resignation, shortly before the poll, seemed to justify the alleged findings. Reddin's new salary, reputed to be $100,000 per year, was sufficient reason for changing jobs. Nevertheless, his refusal to deny that the possible election of a black mayor caused him to retire, aided Yorty. Reddin's "law and order" positions were well known. His speeches, reminiscent of William Parker at his most florid, left no doubt about his political sentiments. Yorty won.[2]

Chief Edward M. Davis was appointed to replace Reddin in August, 1969. Davis, like Reddin before him, was appointed over Deputy Chief James Fisk, who finished first in both competitions. It was said that Mayor Yorty preferred Davis. Fisk had headed the LAPD minority relations program after the Watts Riot and was feared to be too liberal.

Davis followed Reddin in introducing innovative crime prevention programs intended to draw the police and the community closer together. In this regard, Reddin and Davis did not resemble Parker. Davis' "Basic Car Plan" assigned the same officers to the same patrol districts for extended periods. They were expected to park their cars, walk the streets and meet the people. Citizens were encouraged to meet officers in small groups to discuss local problems and get to know "their" police.

Other forms of "team policing" were developed, such as the Team 28 Project, in which a "mini-department" was set up in a given area to deal with local problems. It was tried first in the Venice district and then expanded across the city. A city management audit concluded that the program was "of significant benefit to the department and the community." Neighborhood Watch and other community crime prevention programs also were promoted. Chief Davis credited a drop in certain crime rates to increased citizen involvement with the police in crime prevention.

On the other hand, Davis took an extremely negative approach to academic police research that was intended to improve police operations or make them more cost-effective. He published a scathing criticism of a famous motorized patrol study, although he had not read it. He refused to cooperate in a nation-wide study of gambling, underwritten by the National Institute of Law Enforcement and Criminal Justice, because the NILECJ had previously funded an influential study of detective work that he did not like. He rejected participation in a national survey of criminal justice personnel resources because Pat Murphy, director of the Police Foundation and former chief of the New York City police, did not in Davis' view adequately represent the police community.[3]

The recruitment of minority officers lagged. After four years in office, Davis could count only 366 black officers, or five percent of strength, although the city was then about seventeen percent black. He made little effort to fill positions set aside for the recruitment of female officers. Racial minorities, "hippies" and homosexuals continued to suffer verbal and physical abuse and harassment. White liberals also were victimized. A police riot on the UCLA campus, in 1970, gave the white middle class a lesson with the nightstick and revealed how fragile was the "professional" police veneer. The excesses of the uniformed civil servants generated international publicity but the LAPD received only praise from most local officials.[4]

These events emphasized the department's political independence. For at least a decade, observers had marked the growing influence of the police force. The Protective League illustrated its power through a series of charter revisions, passed by the voters, that placed severe strains on the city's financial structure because of the costs of wages and pensions, gave the department title to parkland privately donated for public use in perpetuity, and exempted section 202 of the city charter, the police disciplinary procedure, from amendments increasing the mayor's authority. In 1969, the department's political role became more overt, and some participants subsequently credited the LAPD with defeating Bradley and re-electing Yorty.[5]

Chief Edward M. Davis was well-qualified to direct the police bureaucracy but seemed unwilling to confine himself to such mundane matters. Parker-like, he took it upon himself to instruct the world in its duties. District attorneys, city attorneys, judges, legislators, liberals, the mayor and even the head of a foreign state, found themselves called to account by the doughty police chief of Los Angeles. He called the U.S. Attorney General a liar. Unfortunately, Chief Davis' provocative bombast did more than delight his friends and irritate detractors. It set a dangerous example.

If, in television and newspaper interviews, the chief could safely deride the political Left; if white, middle class liberals ("swimming-pool communists") could be publicly ridiculed; if Davis' rhetoric fused the entire spectrum of social protest into a single threat to the nation's survival; then why should street-level police officers exercise restraint in dealings with militant blacks and browns, dissident students, draft evaders, war protesters, anarchic youths and "liberated" homosexuals who denied policemen respect and vilified them as willing tools of an oppressive state? Especially after those who ran amok at Century Plaza in 1967 and UCLA in 1970 heard their acts condoned by the conservative political majority? No reason, some might say, and evidence indicated that an increasing number of officers refused to accept summary departmental punishment for alleged "excessive" use of force.[6]

In the 1970's, liberals in municipal public life declined to criticize the police for fear of ruining their political careers. LAPD officers openly solicited votes for conservative political candidates.[7] The 1973 mayoralty campaign provided a good example. Five strong candidates entered the contest: Mayor Yorty, known as the LAPD's captive, who "gave the joint away" at budget time, ex-chief Thomas Reddin, city councilmen Thomas Bradley and Joel Wachs, and ex-assemblyman Jesse Unruh. Bradley, Unruh and Wachs were relative liberals but they joined Yorty and Reddin in taking strong "law and order" positions. All supported expansion of the police department. None dared affront the department or its chief. Instead, they criticized one another's statements, especially Unruh's implication that a new mayor could unseat Chief Davis. They all knew better[8]

Bradley won the election but the new mayor could effect few changes in the management of the police department. Stringent civil service rules blocked promotion, demotion and dismissal except under specified conditions. Indeed, the architects of commission government and the municipal civil service had designed it to prevent the sudden overthrow of a departmental administration. Though discrepancies existed between charter provisions and political realities, to get a police commission appointed that would exert the mayor's will against the chief's expressed opposition remained a formidable, impractical and perhaps unsolvable problem.

To depose the chief was unthinkable. Given the laws and the state of Los Angeles politics, it was probably impossible. Nor did it seem likely that an honest mayor would seek the chief's removal. Since the Bowron recall victory in 1938, Vollmer's "two generations of reform" had passed. William Parker and his successors epitomized the progressive ideal: conservative, competent and incorruptible. They guarded a thoroughly progressive city, long after the progressives and their movement had passed away. The professional policemen's opposition to vice and to "subversive" political doctrines seemed as adamant as that of the old progressives themselves. In this light the progressive triumph seemed to be complete and permanent.

The department would have been invulnerable, except for the continuing, inappropriate use of deadly force. Chief Davis had a reputation for taking the officer's part in departmental trials involving "excessive force" complaints. After his appointment, he returned the briefly independent internal affairs division to the special services bureau. Policemen who shot innocent people were seldom punished, no matter how unprofessional their conduct, unless they missed their targets. If they missed, and were found to have fired in violation of policy, then they might be fined or suspended. If they hit their targets, the department fell back on the state criminal code, which provided wide latitude for officers to shoot at suspected "fleeing felons." Shooting incidents were not entered on an officer's personal file, even though civil suits and negotiated settlements cost the city millions in damages for police malpractise.

Davis was a brave officer who, on at least one occasion, risked his life to prevent the death by police gunfire of an armed and dangerous criminal. He said afterward that it was better to save a life than to kill someone. During his administration, however, although numerous inexcusable shootings occurred, only two LAPD officers faced criminal charges, and then only because of a misunderstanding on the part of the grand jury that indicted them. They later were exonerated. A United States attorney who attempted to bring some detectives to trial for shooting two innocent men found himself subjected to extreme vilification by civic officials and lost his post soon afterward.[9]

Officers shot the owner of premises where a burglar alarm had sounded. A man waving a king-size cigaret was shot because the officer thought it was a gun. Another was shot because his identification bracelet appeared to be a "shiny object" in his hand. Unarmed suspects were killed. Officers killed a man who allegedly attacked them with a nightstick one had dropped. A man was killed over a traffic dispute. Unarmed, teenage burglary suspects were shot. Bystanders were shot. Hostages were shot. Off-duty officers were shot. On-duty officers were shot.

In April, 1977, after yet another unarmed suspect was shot by police, Councilwoman Pat Russell initiated an inquiry into the use of deadly force. Russell believed that "the department's attitude is that the public thinks (the use of deadly force) is OK." In May, a television station broadcast an interview with a masked LAPD officer who said that most officers wanted to be involved in shootings because it was exciting; that officers often beat people and then falsified reports; that a majority of the police force was prejudiced and a minority was racist; and that a civilian review board should be established.

Chief Davis accused the television news director of "yellow electronic journalism" and the "lying masked marvel" of being a communist sympathiser. Davis claimed that "everything the officer said was printed in the *People's World* 10 and 15 and 20 years ago and these are the kinds of raw allegations that are made over the years by people who hate policemen." The department undertook a long, sophisticated but ultimately unsuccessful attempt to identify the masked marvel. Technicians tried to recreate the informant's voice, which had been electronically altered to hide his identity. Photographs of his hand and forehead were distributed to the rank and file. Various means were tried to identify the number on his badge, which had been covered with tape. Employees of the television station and members of their families were interrogated, as were many police officers.[10]

The controversy over fatal shootings led to a review and revision of official LAPD policy on the use of firearms. Mayor Bradley noted that there had been thirty deaths in 1975 and thirty in 1976 but by August of 1977, twenty-seven persons had already been killed. (The final tally for 1975-1977 was 221 shot, 93 fatalities). The council committee on police, fire and civil defence held a long meeting with a citizens' group, the Committee Against Police Abuse. Afterward, the police commission announced that shooting policy would be made more restrictive.

The new policy included a preamble stating that "the value of human life" must be the guide, and that LAPD officers did not shoot to kill. Assistant Chief D.F. Gates, speaking for the LAPD, opposed a statement that the use of deadly force was not justified merely to protect property interests. Gates also argued against the new rule that an officer could use deadly deadly force against a fleeing felon only if the person had committed a violent crime and if the escape of that person presented a substantial risk of death or bodily injury to others. Given that police officers often shot at suspects they thought might be fleeing felons, the department preferred the old rule.

The commission pointed out that even the new policy was less restrictive than the shooting policies of other departments. The county coroner announced that his department henceforth would conduct independent inquiries into deaths by police action. Councilwoman Russell preferred that the county district attorney investigate police shootings and recommended that the police commission also have sufficient staff to investigate use of force by police. In her view, the commission "never acted as head of the department."

Chief Davis said that he had been "short circuited" by the process. He wanted the new policy changed. He believed that reduced hiring standards, i.e., the employment of minorities and women, led to an increase in shootings. (A preliminary study did not bear out his hypothesis.) Davis asserted that officers would be "walking into situations with their guns in their holsters and bullets through their heads." Shifts in policy could undermine morale, possibly creating "a jungle of crime" in Los Angeles. The chief argued that if the police commission rejected his proposals it should hold public hearings and allow the public to express its views. Police Commissioner Stephen Reinhardt responded that "every portion of (Davis') statement was factually incorrect."

The department and the police commission were of one mind with respect to the county coroner, however. When the coroner attempted to hold a public inquiry into the death of a nude man, who was climbing a utility pole when he was shot six times by police, LAPD officers refused to testify at the hearing and would not release relevant records. The police commission also opposed the coroner's action and did not press the chief to cooperate with him.[11]

The police did not care for citizens who filed complaints against the department for excessive use of force. One defensive tactic backfired completely, however. The department shredded its complaint files, ostensibly because "criminal defendants" obtained information from the files, thus creating "an adverse effect on police morale." The shredded files were those where the plaintiff had been charged with assault on an officer, pursuant perhaps to the police maxim that "if you hit him, charge him." Consequently, defence attorneys could not gain access to the records.

Judge George Trammell charged that the destruction of files was intended to deny evidence to plaintiffs. He described the police action as "gross professional misconduct." The city attorney was severely criticized by Judge Trammell and barred from dozens of prosecutions by outraged judges. Eventually, all the "shredding cases" were dropped. The LAPD response was that the department had "erred" in shredding active files less than a year old. Permission had been sought to destroy files that were more than one year old, and that was said to be the intent. In fact, the city council had agreed only to the destruction of files more than five years old.[12]

With respect to inane public statements, Ed Davis outdid any previous chief. As one police commissioner remarked, "usually, people say 'do what I want or I'll club you over the head.' Ed starts clubbing and then says 'do what I want and I'll stop.'" Looking ahead, "like a boy scout," Davis trained police officers to quell food riots in Los Angeles. He had an extensive spy network on the UCLA campus. Regardless of civil service regulations and the mayor's request to end discriminatory hiring, he refused to hire homosexual officers because to do so would "destroy both the morale and the efficiency of the police department."

Speaking to the National Rifle Association, Davis said that citizens needed weapons because the police could not protect them. He claimed to believe that if there were no handguns, the city would need a larger police force. Legislators who proposed to legalize marijuana were "irresponsible no-good sons of bitches." According to Davis, it was "obvious that Mickey Mouse and Goofy and all the other characters are alive and well in Disneyland North," otherwise known as the state capitol at Sacramento. Drug smugglers should be "hanged at the airport."

It also was obvious to the chief that "a fifteen percent liberal minority who believe in a licentious and libertine existence are going to force it on all of us, even if it kills us." Davis informed the Los Angeles Breakfast Club that women's liberation was partly to blame for the rise in crime, especially juvenile crime. The new woman wanted to "play around" as men were alleged to do. Children observed this behavior and reacted in criminal ways. The chief predicted that crime would go up and up, at a rate "never seen in the world before."

He denounced "the new morality which condones lying, stealing and killing,...a philosophic concept that has penetrated everyone who has gone to a university." The chief also uttered the traditional warning about eastern gangsters, announcing that "several eastern mafia families" were looking toward Los Angeles. The Los Angeles *Times*, he said, was "poisoning" its readers.

Robert Strauss, national chairman of the Democratic Party, chose New York over Los Angeles for a national convention because of the chief's tendency to "over-reaction." Davis immediately resigned from the Party. The U.S. Senate Committee on the C.I.A. wrote to the police commission, requesting information on police intelligence operations. Davis said that "it would be a cold day in hell" when he provided data.

He rebuffed a second request on the ground that the LAPD had never accepted federal grants for intelligence purposes. Records of the Law Enforcement Assistance Administration (LEAA), however, showed two such grants, amounting to $1.5 million.

Chief Davis had warm praise for State Senator Alan Robbins, who was thinking of running against Mayor Bradley. He had hot criticism for State Senator Alan Serioty, chairman of the Assembly Criminal Justice Committee. Davis asserted that while Serioty and the ACLU controlled the committee, no "good" legislation was passed. The ACLU had again made a "determined effort to destroy America." Police executives urged the ouster of Serioty and others "slanted" against law enforcement. They argued that thirty-one "beneficial" criminal justice bills had died in committee.

With a year to go until retirement, Chief Davis announced that he would seek the gubernatorial nomination of the Republican Party. He was "very frustrated" with Governor Jerry Brown, whom he blamed for increases in drug use, heroin deaths and overt homosexuality. Davis said he had been pressed to run against Mayor Bradley but he was not interested in the mayor's job because mayors did not appoint judges. He denounced Bradley because of bad appointments to the police commission and opposition to the Public Disorder Intelligence Division.

Davis accepted the chairmanship of a committee raising money to lobby (successfully) for restoration of the death penalty. A few weeks later, he announced his decision to enter the race for the governor's office. He expected the support of gun owners and the extreme right of both parties. The chief believed that he could campaign on his own time if he did not wear his uniform. From that time, he stuck mainly to politics. Sometimes he combined law enforcement with his campaign, as when he told supporters about outrageous developments in the state prisons, where "Mexican mafia gangs" were subsidized under state and federal programs for drug rehabilitation. His fear was that Governor Brown would abolish ("blow up") the prisons before he, Davis, could become governor.

Chief Davis retired in January, 1978. In June, just before the primary election, he announced that he would support the recall of any state supreme court justice who attempted to invalidate Proposition 13, the controversial tax-reform initiative. He also opposed abortion, the personal income tax, U.S. membership in the United Nations and a proposed international anti-genocide treaty. On voting day, he received twenty-eight percent of Republican votes. Davis later campaigned as a conservative Republican and won a seat in the state senate, where he proved to be more liberal and more thoughtful than he was as chief of police.[13]

The formal search for a new chief began in October, 1977. The *Times* wondered if the new executive would be "another Ed Davis, someone who shares Davis' much publicized views on sex, drugs, handguns, single mothers, gays, public morality, civilian review boards and the American Civil Liberties Union?" The police commission recommended that the competition be open to candidates outside the LAPD. The assistant chiefs, deputy chiefs and commanders opposed open competition. The Police Protective League supported the senior officers.

The rank and file denounced open competitions as a return to spoils politics. Fearing similar examinations for outside entry to junior positions, the Protective League claimed that open competitions were illegal and that the League would support a law suit. Chief Davis also opposed the proposal although a committee of the International Association of Chiefs of Police, chaired by Davis, had voted in favor of open competitions.

The police commission and the civil service commission rejected the complaints. LAPD captains and higher ranks would be eligible; outsiders holding ranks equivalent to or higher than LAPD commander also could apply. Forty percent of the mark would be based on a written examination and sixty percent on a personal interview. Some of the best-known police officials in America expressed interest but few entered the competition. Of the twenty-five who wrote the qualifying examination, only three were neither serving nor former members of the LAPD.

To be chosen as chief, an outsider had to stand first after LAPD candidates had their long-service bonus points added to their scores. Consequently, the first place finisher did not win. Chief George Tielsch, Ph.D., of the Santa Monica police department, made the highest scores on both the written and the oral examinations. When LAPD seniority points were added, however, Assistant Chief D.F.Gates stood first and Tielsch was eliminated from the competition. The police commission was left to choose among three senior LAPD officers.

The commissioners chose Gates, as most observers of the police department had predicted. Political experts asserted that if an outside chief were appointed it would be because "those in the City Hall establishment believed the department under Davis and chiefs before him had gotten too strong, too powerful and too far from the mainstream of city government." The departmental rank-and-file were overjoyed by the appointment. Gates was viewed as a virtual clone of the revered Bill Parker. Conversely, Mayor Bradley wanted change. With Gates in command, reform would be foreclosed until the day he retired. Civil service regulations denied the reformers their opportunity.[14]

Gates had long been considered "the heir apparent." He joined the department in 1950, although he had earlier declared that he would never be "a dumb cop." He had a batchelor's degree and later undertook some graduate study. He became William H. Parker's driver and spent about seven years in total as Parker's aide, adjutant and executive officer. He rose rapidly through the ranks, being appointed sergeant in 1955, lieutenant in 1958, captain in 1963, commander in 1965, deputy chief in 1968 and assistant chief in 1969. He was "Ed's right-hand man" during the Davis regime.[15]

The new chief was presented with a challenge and an opportunity to reorganize and reform the department, while retaining all that was good about the existing structure. Los Angeles had undergone a profound transformation since 1950, when Daryl Gates was a rookie patrolman and William H. Parker was chief. The white, conservative population on which Parker's political influence was based had been significantly eroded. Non-white, "visible" minority populations were increasing and the time could be foreseen when they would form a collective political majority.

There had been a great riot in 1965, that the LAPD had not handled well. Black and brown militants, civil rights advocates, war protesters, members of the the so-called "counter-culture," communists, homosexuals, women and even juveniles demanded equality and justice. Some were willing to fight for it in the streets, while others used the courts. These were Americans, moreover, demanding only the rights and liberties guaranteed by the U.S. Constitution. Given the social changes that he had observed, a thoughtful chief might have wondered whether traditional methods of hiring, training, promoting and leading police officers would suffice.

For anyone seeking new operational directions, help was at hand. In a sense, the post-World War II era was "the age of the police" in social science research. By the early 1970's, the research effort had matured. A number of seminal studies of police operations had been published.

A comparison of one-officer motorized patrol with two-officer patrols, in San Diego, demonstrated again what August Vollmer had known in Berkeley 1916 and his disciple, O.W. Wilson, had illustrated in Kansas City in 1930: one-officer cars, for obvious reasons, provided almost double the coverage of two-officer cars; they were more productive because lone officers were more alert and spent more time actually working; and they were safer because lone officers had no need to impress their partners with their bravery or toughness. Consequently, they approached difficult situations with caution, called for support when necessary and did not provoke needless confrontation with suspects or citizens.

A study of random, motorized, "preventive" patrol, conducted in Kansas City, Missouri, indicated that the presence or absence of motorized police patrols had no effect on the number of crimes committed in a patrol district. Traditional police theory held that patrol deterred criminals but the number of crimes prevented could not be estimated because they did not occur and were not reported. The Kansas City study was based on overloading some districts, leaving some unchanged and leaving some without any patrols. The study was flawed by the refusal of police officers to follow the strategy during the test period and their massive response to calls from the supposedly "unprotected" areas. Nevertheless, the study showed those who could read it without prejudice that one or two officers in an automobile, driving aimlessly about, wasted resources that could be better used solving known problems.

Detective work also received systematic scrutiny. Research established that most of the information on which detectives based their investigations was obtained from patrol officers who responded to calls for service. Very little information was obtained from dull, painstaking, door-to-door inquiries because many detectives simply did not do it. Based on this evidence, an "enhanced role for patrol officers" was proposed, such that officers responding to calls would do both preliminary and follow-up investigations of residential burglary and similar crimes. It also was suggested that detectives and patrol officers work much more closely together and that the practise whereby a detective arrived and took over the case be discontinued. Given that most officers would spend their entire careers in patrol, these measures were expected to increase both effectiveness and morale.

The study of detective work established what the police had always known but the public did not want to hear: many crimes, especially property crimes, were unsolvable because there were no witnesses, identifiable fingerprints, known time of occurrence or other evidence. The obvious conclusion was that unsolvable crimes should not be investigated. Analysis of thousands of completed cases identified the data elements necessary to a successful investigation. A weighted, thirty-point system was devised, applicable to non-violent residential burglary, break and enter, theft and similar crimes. Unless a case merited ten points, it would be "screened out" and the victim would be informed that the case was closed. The police department would, however, conduct secondary analysis of unsolved cases, in the hope that patterns might emerge that could lead to further investigation.[16]

Daryl Gates was seen by his officers as the direct descendant of William Parker. He received departmental loyalty without cavil. Reform was possible. The Parker legend was based as much on innovation as on cost-efficient administration and ruthless internal discipline. Unfortunately for the city, the department and his own career, Chief Gates did not see the opportunity, let alone seize it. His operations were not innovative, his administration was not cost-efficient and his internal discipline was anything but ruthless, except in the case of administrative infractions.

Autonomy, like other forms of power, tended to corrupt the individual. Daryl Gates proved to be the last proconsul, an inflexible, self-righteous chief who brooked no criticism from any source. To the extent that suggestions for change implied criticism of the status quo and therefore of himself, they were not welcome. Research findings from studies done in other police departments had nothing to teach him. Gates was Parker without Parker's determination to find methods that would make the department better. He was Reddin without Reddin's concern for good relations between the department and the minority communities. He was Davis without Davis' political insight and ability to get things done. He resembled his predecessors only in his abrasive, arrogant self-confidence, encouraged by secure tenure and departmental autonomy. The day that Daryl Gates became chief of police, however, the erosion of departmental autonomy began.

Chief Gates made little apparent effort to develop a rapport with the council, the mayor or the police commission. He acted as though he had always been chief, perhaps because he knew he could not be dismissed or perhaps because the only part of the job he had studied was the aggressive use of power. Whatever the reasons, Gates did not gain the political constituency that other chiefs enjoyed. The political influence of the chief and the department did not vanish overnight, but during Gates' first year in office, polls showed that public approval was down from sixty-nine percent to fifty-one percent. This finding held across all groups but was most pronounced among blacks.

After the appointment, the police commission called on the chief for "changes," "new directions" and "flexibility," but Gates marched confidently into the past. Within a year of taking office, he abolished Team Policing, one of Ed Davis' proudest accomplishments. Davis established an extensive system of sixty-five teams, integrating patrol officers and detectives into organizations responsible for crime prevention, detection and apprehension in specific geographic areas. Gates considered team policing and similar ideas to be "airy fairy" law enforcement. He separated the patrol and detective functions, to recreate the system he knew when he was a recruit. "Aggressive law enforcement" overrode community relations, to the ultimate detriment of the police and the community.[17]

Gates had the misfortune to be appointed just when Proposition 13 (the "Jarvis Amendment") reduced the residential tax rate. This brought about a reduction of forty to sixty percent in municipal tax revenues. The new law cut local property taxes, statewide, from twelve billion to about five billion dollars. The crisis was compounded by the fact that where federal grants to cities required matching funds that no longer were available, the federal government could not waive the "matching" requirement. Municipal governments were forced to impose drastic reductions in services.

In the areas of operational budgets, wages and pensions, the LAPD had maintained its traditional position at or near the top of American law enforcement. Mayors Samuel Yorty and Thomas Bradley did all they could to give the department what it needed. The inflationary 1970's, however, were increasingly difficult times in Los Angeles and the cost of municipal government was a continuing issue. Mayor Bradley argued against tax increases and the part of the budget that was under his control rose relatively slowly, although frequent vetoes were required.

In the mid-1970's, a third of the municipal budget was allocated to the police department. The annual increase in police salary and pension costs alone was about twenty million dollars, and rising year by year. Over the previous decade, the population had grown by only about three percent, the municipal workforce by forty-seven percent and the budget by 177 percent.

Bradley generally vetoed salary increases for senior police executives, who were not covered by the Jacobs formula, and was usually overridden by the council. The formula caused rank and file police wages to rise at rates that the mayor and the city administrative officer believed were too rapid. On one occasion, the mayor and council declined to pay but the Protective League successfully sued the city and forced the municipal government to meet its obligations.

Tough labor negotiations were the norm. One year, the Protective League wanted a salary increase of 17.7 percent. The city offered ten percent in wages and three percent in fringe benefits. A serious slowdown in the issuance of traffic tickets cost the city about one million dollars a month. There also was talk of "Blue Flu," a euphemism for large-scale absences for non-existent illnesses. A strike vote was taken but no strike occurred, in part because certain council members suggested that "the department could lose a lot of friends."

The League accused Chief Gates of seeking an end to binding arbitration, and the power to decide who would get a proposed uniform allowance. Mayor Bradley was accused of using the dispute to enhance his campaign for a third term, and of trying to provoke the League into a job action to gain public support for a ballot initiative intended to abolish existing "going wage" and pension rules. The council and the mayor did try to gain control over salaries through a ballot initiative in November, 1978. The proposition was lost by 41/100 of one percent of the vote, after a vigorous police and fire campaign on which municipal employees spent about $450,000, against $40,000 by proponents of the initiative.[18]

The state-wide California tax revolt was relatively limited. In 1980, a proposition to reduce the state income tax was defeated. This was hailed as a great triumph for the public sector unions. In Los Angeles, on the other hand, attempts to pass special tax levies specifically for the police failed. The financial crisis nevertheless produced a significant victory for the mayor, the council and the public over the police and fire unions. In April, 1983, voters repealed the charter provision that required the city to pay "the prevailing wage." After forty years of automatic pay and pension increases, control over municipal finances was again in the hands of elected officials, those who raised the money to operate the department.[19]

The growth of pension costs constituted a serious problem for decades before the passage of Proposition 13. The unfunded liability of the police plan rose to $3.2 billion in 1981 and continued to grow. The city administrative officer viewed the system as "a longterm threat to the financial health of the city." Mayor Bradley noted that the city paid $200 million a year into the pension plan but raised only $148.4 million from property taxes. It seemed that, due to bad decisions in the 1930's, the assets of the police and fire plan amounted to only seventeen percent of liabilities. Experts recommended that forty to fifty percent of assets should be fully funded.

To make the situation worse, officers were retiring earlier and living longer. City bureaucrats had once joked bitterly that they had "one police department coming, one working and one on pension." In the 1980's, the fear was that in the near future there would be two departments on pension. The classic hypothetical example was a thirty-year veteran who could retire at age fifty and receive seventy percent of salary, with an unlimited annual cost-of-living increase. A single pension could cost $629,000, of which eighty-eight percent was paid by the municipal taxpayer. To fund it, the city needed to invest $625,000 at 5.25 percent interest.

There was also a sudden, serious rise in the number of young officers receiving generous pensions due to "stress-related" illnesses. Disability pension costs amounted to fifty million dollars a year. Here the hypothetical example was an officer disabled on his first day of service who received a tax free, lifetime disability pension, equal to the pension he would have earned after thirty years of service, and which also included an unlimited annual cost-of-living increase.

The disability pension was a phenomenon unknown to previous generations, but it spread like a virus through North American police departments. Mayor Bradley averred that it had not been available in his day. He urged the pension commission to conduct very serious inquiries into requests for disability pensions. It even was possible for officers who had been dismissed for shooting or excessive force violations to obtain pensions after the fact, the idea being that the event for which they were terminated was so traumatic that they could not earn their livings.

By 1985, an average of thirty-five tax free disability pensions were being awarded each year. The value ranged from $823,000 to $2.7 million, assuming death at age seventy-two. Even if the recipients found other jobs, the pensions, between fifty percent and ninety percent of salary, were paid. A proposal to give officers suffering from stress less stressful, "light duty" positions in municipal government was rejected by the Protective League as "demeaning." Many proposals for reorganization, investigation, reduction of benefits and more stringent criteria were made. Publicity, however, seemed to be the most potent factor. In 1986, the number of claims underwent a significant decline, to the lowest number since 1976.[20]

The municipal government and the voters dealt with the problem as best they could. It was decided that all future police and fire officers should belong to the less generous municipal employees pension plan. Officers would not be permitted to retire unless they had reached the age of fifty and had at least twenty years of service. Ballot initiatives in 1980, 1982 and 1983 reduced the pension from "at least fifty percent of salary" to at least thirty percent, limited the annual cost of living increment to three percent and stopped employee contributions at thirty years, in an attempt to induce veteran officers to remain with the department. For the same reason, there was a move to prevent officers from "double dipping," i.e., retiring from the department and competing for civilian jobs in the municipal civil service. Double dipping allowed an officer to collect the police pension, a municipal salary and, eventually, a second municipal pension.[21]

Proposition 13, by creating a financial crisis, gave the police commission an opportunity to propose a "budgetary philosophy" to Chief Gates. The commission suggested that much could be saved through elimination of unnecessary activities, consolidation of functions, reduction of administrative costs and overhead and reorganization of the top-heavy command structure. Proposals were made to reduce the number of police lockups from thirteen to four, to "freeze" police and other employee salaries and to impose new taxes in areas other than residential property. Chief Gates opposed every attempt to economise. He described the commission proposal as a flowery attempt to deceive the public. Predictably, the Police Protective League threatened to sue if wage increases were denied.

The number of police was the most crucial issue. Mayor Bradley proposed to lay off 1080 LAPD officers and 350 civilian employees of the department, because of a shortfall of thirty-eight million dollars caused by the Jarvis amendment. Chief Gates foresaw "a catastrophe" if the "drastic" reductions were made. Later, he admitted that he had developed the number to be laid off and the proposal to freeze wages, and presented them to the mayor.

The "last-in, first out" nature of layoffs based on seniority compounded the problem because the impact would fall most heavily on the significant number of visible minority and female officers that had recently been recruited. It was suggested that a reduction in the number of police could be accomplished through attrition and a freeze on hiring. An inordinate increase in the number of officers taking their pensions, costly though it was, supported that hypothesis.

Governor Jerry Brown, whose $5 billion state surplus and refusal to cut taxes had helped to provoke the tax revolt, promised to help avert layoffs of police. The Los Angeles city council finally decided that, in voting for Proposition 13, the public had not voted against safe streets. No layoff occurred but hiring was discontinued and the police band was abolished.[22]

Two years after passage of Proposition 13, Chief Gates complained that total LAPD strength remained about 900 officers less than before. (This may have been one reason why there were fewer lethal shootings). The chief proposed a sixty million dollar property tax to hire 1400 additional police. Mayor Bradley noted that more than 560 vacancies existed. He suggested that Chief Gates concentrate on filling them before worrying about others.[23]

In mid-1979, federal aid to the LAPD was suspended, pursuant to a suit filed by the federal Department of Justice, alleging bias in hiring. The suit affected ten million dollars from the LEAA. The department at the time employed 6930 officers, of whom 82.6 percent were white, 9.9 percent were hispanic, 6.2 percent were black, 1.1 percent were Asian, 0.2 percent were American Indian and 2.3 percent were female. The Justice Department asked that, of the 450 officers to be hired in the coming six months, 25 percent be female and 30 percent black. A federal judge rejected the plea, citing the "aggressive" recruitment of women by the LAPD, but the plaintiffs eventually obtained a compromise. Women and blacks combined accounted for more than 25 percent of the next class of recruits.

The requirement to hire females and members of visible minorities created a particular difficulty for the department. The average female and the average Asian male tended to be shorter in height and lighter in weight than the average white or black male. Police tradition favored large males, although the value of those characteristics was a matter of controversy. Chief Parker claimed that men smaller than the average got into more confrontations and received more injuries than men larger than the average. Chief Davis thought that smaller officers might need to use more force, including deadly force. Court rulings, however, took precedence over practical considerations.

The department could not draft people of the height, weight and intelligence believed to be required; it had to make do with those who applied. Only thirteen percent of women were five feet, six inches or taller, whereas ninety-five percent of adult women were at least five feet tall. Chief Gates therefore requested that the minimum height requirement be lowered to five feet from five feet, six inches, so that the department could comply with the federal court interim order that twenty-five percent of new recruits be female. The final court judgement, handed down in November of 1980, bound the department to increase the number of female officers to twenty percent of the total. No physical standard was allowed that would be failed by more than fifty percent of women. The numbers of black and hispanic officers would have to be raised to the proportion of blacks and hispanics in the work-force of metropolitan Los Angeles.

Chief Gates and the department responded well. Within three years, the percentage of female officers almost tripled. One female captain and seven lieutenants were appointed. The percentage of black officers increased by more than fifty percent and the percentage of latinos by more than thirty percent. By 1986, the percentages were latinos, fifteen percent (1045), blacks, eleven percent (775) and females eight percent (556).

In 1991, the proportions were twenty-two percent latino (1798), fourteen percent black (1137), three and one-half percent Asian (259) and three tenths of one percent American Indian (24). Female officers accounted for thirteen and one-third percent (1091). The city population was approximately forty percent latino, thirteen percent black and ten percent Asian and other categories. Whites constituted thirty-seven percent of the population and held sixty percent of LAPD positions.[24]

The court order made recruitment problematic but also presented an interim opportunity. Each year, officers took more than 125,000 "days off" in lieu of payment for overtime. Unspent salaries attached to vacant positions could be used to pay serving officers cash for their overtime work. The equivalent of 200 trained personnel could be put on the street immediately, if officers were compelled to accept cash for at least half of their overtime hours. Alternatively, it was estimated that "on call" overtime would save the city almost twenty million dollars per year.

For several years, departmental strength remained below 7000 officers, while the chief, the mayor and the council searched for new revenues to pay additional personnel. A special property tax initiative, proposed by Mayor Bradley to pay for more police, failed in June, 1985. Another, specifically directed to the needs of south-central Los Angeles, was defeated in June, 1987. Then an economic recovery in the last years of the decade permitted a rapid increase in police personnel. By mid-1991, there were about 8450 officers, exceeding the 8000 for that year proposed in the Bradley plan of 1985 and approaching Chief Gates' objective of 8500 sworn staff.

The chief's longer-range objective was an increase in proportion, from about 2.3 police per thousand to a minimum of three officers per thousand residents. Three per thousand was a benchmark established by the International Association of Chiefs of Police as a minimum staffing level for American urban departments. Given a population of about 3.48 million residents, Los Angeles needed to enlarge the department by 2000 officers to reach the benchmark number of 10,440. Unfortunately, it appeared that the recruitment process would be reversed rather than reinforced. Mayor Bradley, intent on reducing 1993 municipal expenditures by $100 million below 1992, proposed a reduction of 700 police officers from a department that many experts believed was already significantly understaffed.

The economic health of the city had worsened. In addition to the general recession, thousands of jobs and millions of dollars in corporate taxes were lost, as aerospace, defence and heavy manufacturing plants were shut down or moved away. The 1992 police budget was approved at only $578 million, down from more than $600 million in 1987. The projected budget for 1993 was $533.2 million. These enormous sums amounted only to fifteen percent and fourteen percent of the respective 1992 and 1993 municipal budgets, less than half the percentage allocated to the LAPD in 1976.[25]

The most serious and most damaging controversies in the life of Chief Gates, however, arose less from budgets, wages, pensions and staffing problems than from the department's illegal surveillance of law-abiding citizens and legitimate organizations, inappropriate use of deadly force, excessive use of physical force and from his own aggressive personality.

The LAPD had spied on citizens at least since the first World War. During the Ed Davis administration, the intelligence division was a farcical and dangerously mismanaged operation, as testimony before federal committees showed. Police surveillance of citizen groups became almost as infamous as the activities of the Red Squad during the 1920's and 1930's.[26]

A law suit brought against the chief for LAPD surveillance on the Los Angeles campus of the University of California was upheld on appeal to the state supreme court. The justices ruled that in the absence of "a compelling state interest," police could not pose as students to compile dossiers on students and members of the faculty. The police commission subsequently announced that the department would purge its files of almost two million secret dossiers, going back nearly fifty years.

New guidelines for LAPD intelligence activities changed the focus from "subversive activities" to "acts disruptive of the public peace." Before, there had seemed to be no limit. Police examined even library cards, to identify users who borrowed materials that police officers thought might be communist, subversive or obscene. The state assembly eventually passed a law requiring warrants to justify the identification of library members. The police commission forbade the LAPD to open or maintain files based on race, sex, sexual orientation, position as a public official or candidate for office, drinking, sexual behavior, ecological preference "or any other dimension of an individual's style of life."

The *Times* wondered if the LAPD intelligence files actually had been destroyed. It appeared that the department had abandoned its list of allegedly dangerous black juveniles after the existence of the list became known, although large anti-drug raids on high schools indicated that some sort of surveillance was in place. The ACLU later filed a suit to bar police spies from the schools, charging that undercover officers instigated drug offences. The police implied that they had the tacit approval of the school board, although a member of the board denied the allegation.

The city council asked the police commission to review alleged LAPD cooperation with the Federal Bureau of Investigation in the suppression of groups such as the Black Panthers. It appeared that the police force also had spied on such associations as the Beverly Hills Democratic party organization, the Los Angeles Press Club and an anti-nuclear bomb group. The police could not, or would not, explain why they were operating in the city of Beverly Hills or why any of the groups had been targets.

Chief Davis said that Mayor Bradley opposed the intelligence squad "except for the year he ran for mayor." Davis maintained that Bradley's police commissioners had reduced the squad from 106 personnel in 1975 to 76 in 1976, and planned a further reduction to thirty operatives in 1977. This would ensure "an increase in terrorist activities."

Shortly after Daryl Gates became chief, the *Times* reported rumors that the department spied on about 200 activist groups. An organization called the "Coalition Against Police Abuse" (CAPA) claimed to have the list, which included many left-wing organizations, some white racist groups and zionist, homophile, feminist and black organizations. Councilman Zev Yaroslavsky proposed reform, including a local "access to information" law. Chief Gates asserted that he did not know "what police spying is." He doubted that local people would want access to their police files because of the cost of the process.

The CAPA brought a suit against the LAPD, asking for a court ban on infiltration of private associations. The coalition had just found the sixth police spy in their group. Members asserted that the police motto was, "you criticize us, we spy on you." Chief Gates suggested that if a group had done nothing wrong, its members had nothing to fear.

Although both the city council and the police commission wanted an end to pointless police surveillance of community associations, some doubted that public access to police intelligence files would prevent abuse. The council had always been seen as a "friend" of the department. Nevertheless, the LAPD refused to tell the finance and revenue committee how the budget of the intelligence division was spent. Assistant Chief Marvin Iannone claimed that to do so would put lives at risk. Whether the police commission would be told would depend upon what questions were asked.

Councilman Yaroslavsky asked Chief Gates for the data but was told by the commander of the intelligence division that even innocuous answers could be extremely interesting to persons planning a terrorist attack. The commander said that Los Angeles was relatively free of terrorist activity because of the reputation of the Public Disorder Intelligence Division (PDID). Chief Gates concurred. He thought it would be

"foolishness" to release intelligence information to satisfy a single councilman. He also believed that "if you're a terrorist it isn't difficult to make
an assessment" of intelligence operations. Whether the chief thought
Yaroslavsky was a potential terrorist was not made clear.

Councilman David Cunningham also took the chief to task. Gates'
"disdain for the councilmen's legitimate and bona fide inquiry is a direct
effrontery to the council as a whole," he wrote. Chief Gates then spent
several hours in a private meeting with some council members and satisfied their concerns. Yaroslavsky argued that other issues, especially
political spying, had not been resolved. The compromise satisfied the
Times, however, which took it as evidence that the LAPD was losing its
political clout. It appeared that the city council and the police commission, however slowly, were gaining control over the police department.

Mayor Bradley asked the police commission to establish tighter
guidelines for the PDID. Bradley said that disclosure of the intelligence
budget would not be dangerous and that political spying, which might
have violated the rights of citizens, was "absolutely unacceptable." Chief
Gates was unhappy because serious issues were being debated in the
media, but Yaroslavsky pointed out that only after a lot of publicity did
the chief and the commission seriously discuss reform. The two had a
sharp verbal dispute, during which Gates urged the public to "rise up and
support PDID and call for a stop to all this harrassment." Yaroslavsky and
John Mack, president of the Los Angeles chapter of the Urban League,
wanted a "spy law" more restrictive than the PDID guidelines. They
asked the chief and the commission to issue a statement that no surveillance of "peaceful, law abiding groups" was in progress, and were critical
of Chief Gates for failing to admit proven errors by the intelligence squad.

One police spy explained that he attended meetings of opponents
of police spying to impress members of a different group, one that the
police thought might become violent. A spy who had infiltrated native
Indian organizations "blew his cover" when members happened to see
him in uniform. Chief Gates hoped that the case would not cause trouble,
because surveillance was "absolutely essential" to the security of the
city. He stated his intention to continue along the same course "until
someone—the court or someone else—makes us stop."

One lawsuit alleged that the LAPD had, between 1972 and 1979,
infiltrated La Raza Unida, a hispanic association. The group charged
that one of the police spies was elected treasurer. As such, he had a key
to the office and access to all files. The association claimed that in
1978, Chief Gates and the police commission had sworn that no sur-

veillance was in place, yet the spying had gone on, in "flagrant violation of the U.S. Constitution." The hispanic group requested that police
be barred from spying without judicial approval, that there be access to
information about police surveillance and that the police commission
monitor intelligence operations.

It was revealed that the police had spied on private meetings
between Mayor Bradley and the United Farm Workers of America. The
spy argued that it was not possible to judge the propriety of the surveillance after the fact without re-evaluating the circumstances at the time.
Chief Gates found the situation humorous. He said he would have liked
to know whether the mayor "could make a decision on anything."

In February of 1982, the police commission issued new guidelines
for the intelligence division. Chief Gates pronounced himself "comfortable" with the regulations. The ACLU was not comfortable. A question
subsequently was raised about whether the chief had lied about the
actions of the PDID. According to the commander of the PDID, although
Gates denied it, a paid informant was used to identify organizations critical of police intelligence activities.

Councilman Yaroslavsky was convinced that Gates had mislead
the council. It became clear that information about the Coalition Against
Police Abuse (the ACLU and the American Friends Service Committee)
went directly to the chief. Gates said that information about the coalition
was "absolutely of no interest to the department." Yaroslavsky said that
Gates' remark was "a bald-faced untruth." There were then six law suits
in progress, involving twenty groups and eighty-eight individuals.

Evidence proved that police had not destroyed intelligence files as
ordered the city council. Chief Gates asked the district attorney to investigate. Gates and ex-chief Davis claimed to have no knowledge of the
matter. Gates added that he had not realized that rules governing intelligence files applied to briefing notes and similar records. Ninety boxes of
files were returned by an officer involved in the deception, who had hidden them in his home.

The police were found to have a dossier on Judge Jerry Pacht
stretching back thirty-eight years. Pacht said that the LAPD had tried to
intimidate him. Assistant Chief Marvin Iannone and the head of the internal affairs division visited him to complain that he sided "either too much
or too frequently" with police officers appealing departmental disciplinary actions. The LAPD admitted that Chief Gates sent the two officers.

Mayor Bradley averred that the conduct of the operation had
"exceeded the bounds of legal, moral and reasonable conduct." The chief

said he had been let down by officers who had erred. He also attacked critics of the PDID. Gates admitted his failure to guide the PDID, although it was known that the police chief approved the targets of intelligence activity. Councilwoman Joy Picus claimed that Gates was practicing deception in the spy case. The chief defended the PDID before the police, fire and public safety committee. He claimed to know nothing about police misconduct.

The city attorney, Ira Reiner, who had been defending LAPD officers in the "spy case" law suits, said that some officers were zealots who engaged in clandestine surveillance. Reiner expressed "no confidence whatsoever in the ability of the PDID to legitimately and properly gather intelligence." Chief Gates suggested that the department needed private defense attorneys. Reiner was removed from the case.

After considerable discussion, the police commission abolished the police intelligence unit. In May of 1983, the Anti-Terrorist Division (ATD) was created to replace the PDID. The new unit had "adequate" powers but restraints on police actions were expected to protect the public. The unit reported directly to the chief of police but the police commission and the city attorney were given more authority over its activities. The police commission was given a role in staffing and choice of activities, and authority to review PDID documents before they were released to the Anti-Terrorist Division.

Formation of the ATD did not end the "spy case" scandal. An officer was charged with providing police intelligence to the Western Goals Foundation, which was said to be affiliated with the John Birch Society. The officer worked with the Western Goals Foundation to computerize a data bank on suspected communists and left-wing organizations. In return, the LAPD attained access to the WGF database. Files in his possession showed that among the targets of the PDID were the ACLU, the National Lawyers Guild, numerous judges and the city attorney. This evidence refuted Gates' claim that the officer kept only newspaper clippings.

The captain who approved the arrangement retired; he refused to comment on the issue. A spokesman for the Foundation said that Chief Gates had not asked the WGF to confirm or deny the allegation. The grand jury and the district attorney entered the case, on the grounds that to remove, hide or steal public records was an offence. John Rees, of the WGF, lost a legal struggle and was compelled to testify. Observers found it inconceivable that no one in authority knew about the surveillance; indeed, members of the PDID testified under oath to their belief that senior LAPD officers approved their work with the Western Goals Foundation.

A police lieutenant, who also kept intelligence files at home, opened an envelope that had been sealed by the court, in order to add documents that the officer thought were relevant. The documents concerned the Revolutionary Communist Party, against which charges had been brought. The officer failed to appear in court "because he felt nervous." The judge in the case threatened to cite him for contempt of court. Chief Gates resolved the problem by withdrawing the charges against the communist group.

A detective claimed to have information about political spying, destruction of records and other offences. Lawyers for the city tried to bar his testimony but the ACLU, representing 131 people in six law suits, got a favorable court decision. The police department then filed multiple disciplinary counts against the officer.

O'Melveny and Myers, one of the most respected law firms in Los Angeles, charged that one of their supposed clients, claiming to be a Black Panther, actually was a police spy. The spy monitored discussions between the defendants and their attorneys. At the time, the law firm was in negotiations with Chief Gates. The former spy, then a defendant in a suit brought by the ACLU, said that his superiors knew what he was doing. His superiors, including Gates, denied knowledge of the spy's activities.

A black detective who served in the PDID said that the division provided material to the Yorty mayoralty campaign that was used to try to smear Thomas Bradley. The false allegation that Bradley had Black Panthers in his organization was used several times in the last days of the campaign. The officer maintained that much of the work of the PDID was worthless. A senior officer retorted that the chief of police was in a much better position than the detective to assess intelligence needs.

A member of the new Anti Terrorist Division testified that a lieutenant ordered nine PDID officers to hide intelligence documents before the management audit in 1982. Afterward, the records were brought back. Three officers testified that two of them had been told to spy on Councilman Yaroslavsky and to keep it secret. Their retired superior denied the claim, as did Chief Gates.

As the spy cases progressed, as more testimony and the content of more files revealed the extent of police intelligence activity, Yaroslavsky's criticism became more pointed. In his view, the system was out of control. He charged that the LAPD had not limited its activities to spying on alleged subversives but had collected information to increase its political influence at city hall and elsewhere. As proof,

Yaroslavsky pointed to files on individuals that recorded their sexual practises, medical conditions and business affairs.

The councilman blamed the city council and the police commission for failing to control the LAPD. Only the mayor had opposed the department but he was legally powerless to change it. Yaroslavsky proposed that the intelligence activities of the LAPD be limited to the investigation of criminal actions. If the police were found to have undertaken political surveillance, they should be punishable by fines, prison sentences or both. Oversight of the intelligence division should be independent of the council or the police commission and should be provided by a judge.

The continual revelations, the enormous amount of bad publicity, the charges and counter-charges, the rancorous relationships between the chief and the mayor, the chief and most of the council, the chief and most police commissioners, between the chief and police officers being sued for spying and between the chief and those who brought suit against the department, brought the process to an end. A consent decree was signed. The *Times* reported that the city would pay $900,000 to the ACLU and $900,000 toward the costs of attorneys.

The accord included stringent requirements for the evidence required to initiate an intelligence probe, for the recording of how and by whom the surveillance was conducted, for public disclosure of the number of authorized inquiries, for freedom of access to some criminal and intelligence records and for oversight of the agreement by a judge until 1991. The city attorney maintained that the consent decree could not be overturned, even after 1991.

The investigation showed the department, especially Chief Gates, in a very bad light. The chief attacked the credibility of everyone, in or out of municipal goverment, in or out of the police department, who criticized the LAPD or challenged his version of events. His senior subordinates followed suit. It appeared that a handful of authoritarian men at the pinnacle of the departmental bureaucracy alone understood law, justice and morality.

After the consent decree was signed, a retired police captain said that he had told the chief that PDID files were being moved to avoid a police commission audit but the chief did nothing about it. The former officer said that Gates discussed the matter privately with Assistant Chief Marvin Iannone. Afterward, "either (misconduct) was not investigated or was condoned. If Gates denies that, then he's a liar." A departmental spokesperson responded that the LAPD had "absolutely no idea what the motivation may be behind (the captain's) misunderstanding," but Gates did not deny the charge or personally respond.

Stephen Yslas, president of the police commission, said that no action would be taken against senior officers of the LAPD for their part in illegal surveillance and the subsequent cover-up. The police commission held, however, that the spy scandal was "the ultimate and direct responsibility of top sworn management, including past and present assistant chiefs and chiefs of police....It is they who must bear responsibility."

This appeared to end an unpleasant and unsavory chapter in LAPD history. Chief Gates said that his men were professionals who would abide by the agreement, but many doubters remained among the hundred and forty-four groups and individuals involved in the seven-year struggle against improper police surveillance. There was no requirement that a warrant be obtained before surveillance was authorized. Judicial oversight of the counter-terrorism division limited its scope of operations but provided no guarantee that all future surveillance would be lawful.

A study of police "internal restraints," produced by the RAND Corporation in 1981, had shown how officers circumvented rules by carrying records in their automobiles, entering them in home computers, storing them with private security firms and other irregular means. Moreover, other intelligence sections, to which judicial oversight apparently did not apply, operated within the department. In July, 1992, only weeks after Chief Gates retired, the longstanding police surveillance of political and entertainment celebrities was revealed by a former officer who worked as a spy. The book, titled *Los Angeles' Secret Police: Inside the LAPD Elite Spy Network,* was a salient factor in the decision by Chief Willie L. Williams to padlock the offices of the Organized Crime Intelligence Division. An investigation of the OCID was imminent.[27]

During the Ed Davis regime, the improper, inappropriate, unprofessional use of deadly force by a minority of police officers led the police commission to make departmental shooting policy somewhat more restrictive. After taking office, Chief Gates proposed a review of the policy, to ensure that all proper steps were taken and that the public was kept informed. Nothing significant came of this, perhaps because Gates did not view the incidence of "bad" shootings as a problem to be resolved.

Mayor Bradley was greatly concerned about conflict between the LAPD and poor black and hispanic residents. He said, with terrible prescience, that he feared "another Watts." The Southern Christian Leadership Conference and the National Association for the Advancement of Colored People supported the Coalition Against Police Abuse in a request that the U.S. Civil Rights Commission investigate the city police. They did not believe that the harrassment, the stop-and-frisk tactics and the quick resort to physical or deadly force would happen in a white community. They pointed out that most of the forty people shot by police during the first eight months of 1978 were black or brown.

The killing of Eulia Love, in January of 1979, seemed to justify every charge ever made against the LAPD. It was winter in Los Angeles. Mrs. Love, a widowed welfare mother, was in arrears with the gas company. When an employee of the gas company came to cut off the gas, Mrs. Love drove him off. The man came back with two police officers to protect him. Mrs. Love had a knife in her hand and was pacing in her yard. When she turned her back on the officers, one knocked the knife from her hand with his baton. There was a scuffle and Mrs. Love recovered the knife. She turned to confront the police, who testified that she attempted to throw it at them. The two officers then emptied their revolvers into her body. Some of the bullets were fired after she fell to the ground.

The police commission at first declined to probe into the Love case because both the department and the district attorney had investigations under way, although the mayor asked the police commission to take a vigorous role. Chief Gates assailed the news media for conducting a public lynching of the police officers. Then and thereafter, Gates defended the two officers who had killed Eulia Love against all critics, referring to them as "surrogate victims."

Police commissioner Sam Williams said that either the shooting violated policy or else the policy had to be changed. Commissioner Stephen Reinhardt argued for new policies, specifically that the police should not help to collect overdue bills. Chief Gates disagreed; he claimed that once he had been poor and had had his gas cut off. The significance of this comment was not clear.

In memory of Eulia Love, the Reverend M.M. Merriwether led a protest march from the Convention Center to City Hall. The police photographed the 400 marchers. They assured Merriwether that he was not under surveillance; they were watching other, unnamed people. Chief Gates told reporters that the marching ministers were not representative of the views of the black majority in south central Los Angeles. He did not explain how he arrived at that conclusion.

The long-promised review of the case by the police commission was presented in October, ten months to the day after the death of Euia Love. The report was a comprehensive criticism of the two officers and the LAPD. It described "serious errors" and directly contradicted the LAPD internal report. The shooting review board, the report said, did a poor job and based its conclusions on "erroneous or misconstrued facts."

Doubts were raised about the quality of departmental training. The district attorney said that he would evaluate the new facts.

The police commission report was praised by black activists, who wanted charges laid against the officers. Black associations called for Gates' resignation but Mayor Bradley demurred, asking whether it would bring the dead woman back. He argued that Chief Gates would institute a new shooting policy. Chief Gates said that the shooting was "clearly self defense and...right within the shooting policy." The chief asserted that the LAPD was threatened by the same sort of conspiracy "that practically destroyed the FBI and the CIA." "The liberal press and those people who are the enemy of the CIA and intelligence gathering" wanted to destroy "the finest municipal institution in the world."

Police Commissioner Reinhardt suggested that Gates, having already found the officers innocent, could not afterward discipline them. Over four thousand members of the LAPD signed a petition of non-confidence in the police commission. The Protective League spent $24,000 for newspaper space to eulogize slain police officers. The League won a point in court, allowing the rank and file to comment on the police commission report. Mayor Bradley finally brought the chief and the commission together and put an end to the unseemly public dispute.

Advocates of a ballot initiative to create a civilian review board began to collect signatures. Chief Gates threatened to resign if a civilian review board were instituted. The police commission also opposed the idea. The commission admitted that the existing system did not inspire public confidence but promised to take a larger role in deadly force inquiries and to make decisions as to the propriety or impropriety of police actions in particular cases. This decision was denounced, for different reasons, by the Protective League and the ballot campaigners.

The Protective League filed a class action suit in superior court on behalf of 6800 officers, asking the court to overturn the decision by the police commission to take responsibility for shooting investigations. The grounds were that officers would be denied due process of law; i.e., a hearing before the police Board of Rights, as established in the city charter. The defendants were the city, the chief and the members of the police commission.

As for the ballot campaigners, two were arrested, handcuffed and charged under a state law forbidding "circulation of a petition within 100 feet of a polling place." The two were standing outside the Vine Street School, which would have been a polling place had there been an election in progress. The city prosecutor refused to prosecute. The police commission asked for a formal report on the incident. In the end, the petitioners failed to gather enough signatures to get the proposition on the ballot, which was perhaps as much a defeat for amateurs in politics as an indication of public opinion.

The police commission established a few new rules and made some sensible proposals for change. Henceforth, officers would be required to present their business cards to anyone they stopped, identifying themselves by name and division. The police department was directed to make a formal response, providing the results of disciplinary action and relevant comments, to anyone who complained about police misconduct. Police officers were forbidden to assist in bill collecting, repossession and similar activities that could be dealt with through civil proceedings.

There also were new provisions relevant to the use of deadly force. In future, there would be more emphasis on "target discrimination," i.e., why, when and where to shoot. The LAPD "rapid fire" method would be modified. Veteran officers would be evaluated to establish whether retraining were needed. A study of the effectiveness of computerized shooting simulation would be carried out, with emphasis on when not to shoot. Monthly tests in "defence and disarm" tactics, continuing research into non-lethal weapons, a reward system for police who did not shoot, crisis intervention training for field officers and a review of the effects of stress on police officers also were approved.

Chief Gates showed no talent for timing. Two weeks later, he recommended that a new bullet be adopted by the department. The controlled expansion round (CER) was a hollow-point projectile, alleged to have three to five times the "stopping power" of conventional ammunition. The CER spent all its force in the body and did not go through or ricochet. Many police departments used it, more likely because of the policeman's love of firepower than because of its proven effectiveness.

It was not uncommon for officers who thought about shooting people to have an illegal round ("a hot load") as the first bullet in their weapons, to disable the target person with one shot. Yet L.A. county sheriff's deputies testified that, using the CER, they had been forced to empty their weapons at a range of ten to fifteen feet because suspects "just kept coming." Chief Gates made a comment to the effect that if the police who killed Eulia Love had been armed with the CER, only one bullet might have been fired and she might still have been alive. An expert who understood the relationship between force of impact and extent of trauma made the best rebuttal: "it is bunk to say that you can hit harder and hurt less."

The police commission made a strong effort to repair relationships between the police and the black and hispanic communities. Steering committees of leaders from each group were created to work with Chief Gates. The committees chose their own issues and were promised full cooperation from the department and the police commission. The initiative was viewed with suspicion by most participants. The minority leaders doubted that they would have substantive influence. Some suggested that the committees were meant to defuse the civilian review board issue. Conversely, the Police Protective League suspected that the police commission intended to become an unofficial civilian review board.

The black steering committee soon found reason to doubt the sincerity of the liason program. The committee wanted to know whether officers who had histories of conflict with members of racial minorities were still assigned to the black community. The steering committee believed that officers with as many as ten complaints for excessive use of force still worked in the black neighborhoods. The committee requested statistics rather than names but the department refused to release the information.

The request then went to the city attorney for review. The city attorney, Burt Pines, announced that the files in shooting cases would not be opened. Pines based his decision on state senate bill 1436, allowing for release of police personnel information only on defined judicial grounds. The right to privacy of individual officers and the fact that the reports would be placed in their personnel files meant that very little could be revealed.

The mayor and the district attorney were opposed to the decision by the city attorney. Councilman Robert Farrell described the new law as "a trick." The police commission insisted upon a more open process. Chief Gates argued that there was no attempt by anyone in the police department to keep anything secret, and criticized the courts because they did not "deal in truth."

The police chief and the city attorney finally agreed that there would be two reports of shootings, one for the media and one for the personnel file. When ordered to release files on two shooting incidents, however, Chief Gates said that to do so would "destroy the integrity of this department." The files eventually were released because they were helpful to the defence. Otherwise the presiding judge would have dismissed charges against the defendants for assaulting police officers.

The city council, normally the department's strongest ally, threatened to create a civilian review board. The council suggested that there should be an active review of shootings and excessive force cases; continuous monitoring of the police disciplinary process and review of citizen and staff complaints of serious misconduct; more staff to enable the police commission to review discipinary actions; crisis intervention teams to deal with non-criminal matters in south central Los Angeles; a stress management program for the LAPD; a reconsideration of shooting policy, especially to counter people wielding knives and clubs; and summaries of reviews undertaken by the commission. Chief Gates responded that there was no money for crisis intervention teams.

The federal government became involved in the long-standing controversy over police shootings when research funding was provided to the county district attorney. The district attorney received a federal grant of $255,000 to study "Operation Roll-Out." The program was initiated in February, 1979. In theory, when a shooting occurred anywhere in the county, the district attorney was immediately informed, so that the investigation could begin at the earliest possible moment. Twelve prosecutors and thirteen investigators were assigned. The district attorney said that it made possible "independent and more objective" investigations of shooting incidents.

The district attorney's special investigations division found the LAPD to be the least cooperative department in the county, to the degree that it was accused of unprofessional conduct. The head of special investigations remarked that some inquiries took a week, some, conducted by the Sheriff's department, took a month, and LAPD cases took at least four to six months. In one LAPD shooting case, an investigation initiated in June of one year was still not completed in April of the following year.

The first problem with inter-agency cooperation was alleged to lie with LAPD Lieutenant Charles Higbie, head of the officer involved shooting unit. Prosecutors suggested that, somewhere along the way, Higbie had "lost his objectivity." The second problem was that Higbie was said to wield "great influence" with Chief Gates. The frustration of the district attorney's staff was as nothing compared with that of Councilman Yaroslavsky, however. Yaroslavsky asked for a certain police report in 1975. He was still waiting in 1981.

Gerald M. Caplan, a respected legal scholar and head of the National Institute for Law Enforcement and Criminal Justice, designed the evaluation for Operation Roll-Out. Caplan expressed the opinion that "the LAPD is not willing to go to great lengths to avoid shooting a civilian when the rules permit it...Not only has Chief Gates refused the district attorney's personal request to promulgate (shooting) guidelines— Chief Gates doesn't think that they are needed—but the spirit of resistance has permeated to the bottom of the department and manifests itself in important ways."

Gates said that the report was "a wonderful monument to the bias and inefficiency and critical treatment that goes on in Washington." To Caplan's statement that there had been shootings condoned in Los Angeles that in other jurisdictions would have led to disciplinary action or even criminal charges, Gates reponded that "Caplan is a liar." The final report, eighteen months later, characterized Operation Roll-Out as "a symbolic struggle over the autonomy of the Los Angeles police agencies." Among other measures, the report recommended that a special grand jury be established to interview police officers when a shooting occurred.

The insurmountable problem with Operation Roll-Out and other attempts to reduce shooting deaths by what amounted to bureaucratic deterrence (i.e., "do not shoot anyone without very good reasons because an independent agency will investigate it") was that "senatorial courtesy" would be practised by other law enforcement agencies, including the district attorney's department. Although a criminal charge against a police officer for killing a suspect by shooting or choke hold was the rarest of rare events in the city or county of Los Angeles, if it occurred it would be publicly justified by other agencies. Regardless of private opinions, individuals would come forward to say that an act was "within policy," "necessary," "according to training," and so forth. Juries would be carefully screened. The prosecution would be defensible but not vigorous. There would be no conviction.

An example of this phenomenon occurred in 1980. A police officer killed an unarmed suspect with a shotgun blast. The suspect was lying face down on the sidewalk, with his arms handcuffed behind his back. The officer said that the handcuffed man appeared to be withdrawing his hands from inside his waistband. Therefore, the officer fired his shotgun at point blank range. After a long investigation, the district attorney's department decided that the officer fired in justifiable self defence. Since the officer apparently used good judgement, no reason existed to prosecute him. In a similar vein, no charges were laid against the officer who, using a choke hold, killed a man whose arms were cuffed behind his back and whose legs also were manacled.

Representative John Conyers, a black congressman conducting congressional hearings on police use of force, was critical of Los Angeles police officials. He observed that "the police clearly operate apart from the rest of government and above it. And apparently the rest of government here has that feeling because I noticed that the mayor's people were noticeably absent." Representative Julian Dixon of Los Angeles, speaking to the National Organization of Black Law Enforcement Executives, asserted that Gates should recognize the fact that many residents feared his officers. Dixon argued that Gates saw himself "as the defender of the LAPD (but) he should see himself as a community leader who must recognize that a large segment of the community is frightened."

At that point, the police commission issued a report on police shootings, undertaken for the commission by Marshall W. Meyer of the University of California at Riverside. The study compared Los Angeles with eight other cities, during the period 1974-1979. The findings showed that LAPD officers fired their guns less often but killed the person shot more often than officers in the other cities. The department stood first in deaths per shooting.

The number of blacks involved was disproportionate in several ways. Of persons shot by LAPD officers, 55 percent were black and of persons killed, 50 percent were black, although blacks accounted for only 18 percent of the population and 36 percent of persons arrested. Thirty-three percent of shootings occurred in black neighborhoods but only 26 percent of rapes, robberies and homicides occurred there. Of blacks shot by police, a larger proportion was shot for "failure to obey" or "furtive gestures," a larger proportion (28 percent) had no weapon, a lower proportion (22 percent) was deemed to have been shot in violation of policy and a lower proportion of officers who shot blacks (7 percent) was disciplined by the department.

The good news, so to speak, was that the number of persons killed each year showed a decline in 1978 and 1979, after LAPD shooting policy was revised to indicate that "an officer does not shoot to kill." Specifically, the number shot for failing to obey or making furtive gestures declined. The totals for the period were 26 in 1974, 30 in 1975, 30 in 1976, 33 in 1977, 20 in 1978 and 14 in 1979. The number of bullets fired per incident also declined, although the LAPD fired more shots per incident than the other departments. There was "administrative disapproval" in 18 percent of LAPD shootings and disciplinary action was taken in ten percent of cases. Law suits arising from police actions declined from 448 in 1977 to 246 in 1980.

Reformers appeared to win a small victory in mid-1981. The traditional method of "de-briefing" officers involved in shootings was for all to be interviewed in the same room, within hearing distance of the person describing the event. The critics knew that police would not interview suspected criminals under those conditions. They assumed collusion in preparing an account of the event, although they could not know whether it occurred. Successive chiefs gave weight to their suspicions by their determined opposition to separate interviews. Chief Gates decided to "go along with the nonsense" and have separate initial interviews for participants in shooting incidents.

As was so often the case, the victory was more apparent than real. The Christopher inquiry in 1991 found "serious flaws in the investigation of shooting cases. Officers are frequently interviewed as a group, and statements are often not recorded until completion of a 'pre-interview.'" In addition, officers often were interrogated under "duress," such that their accounts could not later be introduced as evidence against them in a criminal prosecution. The result was that the department treated deadly force violations more leniently than it treated other types of officer misconduct.

Critics of the department railed against the commander of the "officer involved shooting team," responsible for investigating incidents where shots had been fired. Between 1988 and 1991, LAPD officers shot and killed 112 persons. During that period, the shooting team undertook 290 inquiries but no criminal indictments arose from the investigations. Critics wrongly viewed the absence of prosecutions as evidence of incompetent work by the shooting team. Police officers thought the team was brilliant.[28]

Despite periodic public outrage provoked by the chief's defence of officers involved in "bad" shooting incidents, and the growing demand for change at the top, it was not deadly force but the use of excessive physical force by his officers that brought the long career of Daryl F. Gates to a disappointing and notorious close. Chief Gates and the LAPD had often come under fire for the use of excessive force by officers. This was especially the case with "bar arm" and "carotid" holds, used to subdue unruly individuals. One of Gates' first directives as chief was a request for a study of "the most efficient and humane" methods of restraint.

There had recently been two deaths of black men in custody. The city council therefore asked the police commission to impose a moratorium on potentially lethal suspect control techniques. The LAPD responded that the bar-arm and carotid holds were necessary to subdue users of PCP, also called "angel dust," a powerful drug that sometimes made some users uncontrollable. The council then withdrew its request for a moratorium.

Shortly afterward, the Reverend Milton M. Merriwether, a leading opponent of "choke holds," was arrested outside his church because he intervened when police were citing a woman for jaywalking. Nine police cars arrived on the scene and three persons were arrested. The clergyman took it as an attempt to intimidate those who criticized the LAPD. Black leaders reacted in anger, claiming that harrassment and use excessive force were too prevalent in south-central Los Angeles. A protest march was organized, ending at McArthur Park. The police said the marchers had violated the terms of their permit, in that they failed to use sidewalks in designated areas and had marched the entire route in the street. A police complaint against the marchers was sought.

In December of 1980, federal judge Robert M. Takasugi ordered the department to forego bar-arm and carotid holds. It was alleged that at least ten deaths since 1971 could be traced to the holds. A deputy city attorney argued that only two deaths could actually be proven to have resulted from choke holds. Judge Takasugi found that the holds constituted deadly force as applied by LAPD officers, who were not adequately trained to know when a situation became dangerous enough to justify the holds. Takasugi ruled that the lethal holds could be used only if an officer's life were in danger.

Not long afterward, police subdued a rabbi with a carotid hold because his praying was too loud. Chief Gates sent his regrets. Councilman Yaroslavsky, as chairman of the council committee on police, fire and public safety, ordered a review of the choke hold controversy but noted that the council favored the holds. His concern was that the police might become even more aggressive if Judge Takasugi's decision were not overturned. The council requested that the police commission establish guidelines for use of the holds, police training with respect to the holds and a reporting procedure to inform the council when use of a hold resulted in injury.

The city attorney petitioned the 9th U.S. circuit court of appeal to reconsider Takasugi's injunction. The department received permission to use the holds until a decision could be obtained from the U.S. Supreme Court. Several additional deaths occurred, from what was described as "blunt force trauma to the neck." The police commission changed the guideline to allow use of the holds only if the subject became "violently combatative." Chief Gates recommended that the bar arm hold be discontinued "for the sake of the officers." That would bring the LAPD in line with the Sheriff's Department, the California Highway Patrol and other major police departments across the United States.

Unfortunately, it seemed that Gates could not do something right without doing something wrong. The disputed count of persons killed during the previous seven years by LAPD officers using bar arm and carotid holds was sixteen, of whom fourteen were black. Gates mused that perhaps blacks had some physical characteristic that made them "more susceptible than normal people" to the holds. The remark caused a furor, reminding minority residents of comments about Jews and latinos that members of those groups found distasteful. The mayor, the council and the police commission expressed outrage. Various associations called for the chief to be ousted. Chief Gates apologized but the image remained of a thoughtless, unconsciously racist white chief in a multiracial community.

The police commission placed a six-month ban on the use of the controversial procedures but investigations of "illegal" use of the holds were soon in progress. Two deaths ocurred within months of the ban, including that of a man whose arms were handcuffed behind his back and whose ankles also were manacled. The financial cost of police malpractice also was an issue. A local doctor, who sued the city after an officer used a choke hold on him, was awarded $1.3 million in damages. Twelve additional cases were before the courts.

The long-awaited U.S. Supreme Court ruling on the holds overturned the Takasugi injunction. The court held, five to four, that the plaintiff had no legal standing to ask a federal judge to prohibit use of the holds. Injured persons had recourse through civil and criminal courts. Although Chief Gates was said to be "buoyed" by the decision, the police commission maintained its moratorium. The department announced that experiments were in progress on the use of alternative non-lethal methods, such as a net to subdue unruly persons, a new type of baton and the Taser Gun, which delivered a severe but non-fatal electric shock. Chemical sprays, such as Mace, also were tested.[29]

Despite the ban, some officers used the holds, and although use declined, belief endured. Years later, a Protective League spokesman argued that the fateful beating of Rodney King, on March 3, 1991, might not have occurred had police been allowed to use the forbidden procedures. Given that there were twenty-seven police officers at the scene when King was arrested, an argument might be made that the suspect could have been immobilized by sheer weight of numbers. Instead, he received two very high voltage shocks from a Taser gun and suffered more than fifty kicks and blows from police batons.

The event was filmed by a bystander who gave the film to a television station. Within a short time, the assault by white police on a lone black suspect was seen around the world. King's doctor, Edmund Chien, reported that King had suffered a fractured eye socket, a broken cheekbone, a broken leg, facial nerve damage, a severe concussion and burns from the stun-gun. Chien feared that some of the damage might be permanent. Americans from all walks of life, including President George

Bush, expressed shock, outrage and dismay. What offence could justify such a violent assault by officers sworn "to protect and to serve"? The civil rights division of the federal Justice Department, the FBI, the county grand jury, the district attorney and the LAPD internal affairs division all announced that investigations would be undertaken.

Chief Gates, so often the uncritical defender of "my guys," called in this instance for criminal indictments. Charges were preferred against the supervising sergeant and three patrolmen. Gates admitted that the force used was excessive but described it as "an aberration" in an otherwise well-disciplined department. In a videotape directed to his officers, the chief hewed to the traditional line. "We've been the model, the LAPD. Those thoughtless officers, in those couple of minutes, destroyed that image, and its going to take us a long time to rebuild that image." Gates declared that all of the officers present at the event would be disciplined. He also assured the police force that he would not step down. He would stay on to ensure "that what I say is done."

The ACLU was first to call on Gates to resign. In short order, local black and latino leaders, the Reverend Jesse Jackson, Senator Joseph Biden, a Democrat from Delaware, and Councilman Michael Woo joined the chorus. President Bush thought the chief deserved a fair hearing. Mayor Bradley said that it was up to Gates to decide when to go, disappointing the black community and, apparently, many other supporters. The ACLU claimed to have 20,000 signatures on a petition calling for the chief to leave.

On April 2, a month after the beating, Mayor Bradley finally asked Chief Gates to resign. The chief refused. On April 4, the police commission suspended him with pay for sixty days, and appointed Assistant Chief David Dotson to act in his place. Chief Gates brought suit against the police commission to overturn the suspension. The fifteen-member council, by a ten to three majority, instructed the city attorney to seek an agreement with Gates by which he would be restored to his position and would not sue the city. Chief Gates agreed, and by April 9 was back on the job. The mayor, the president of the city council and the chief of police then issued a joint statement calling for calm reflection and cooperation on everyone's part.[30]

Civil rights and other groups went to court to argue that the council violated the city charter when it usurped the commission's right to discipline the chief. The suspension of the chief by the commission was held in abeyance for several weeks, while the judge studied the case. The decision, when it came, was a startling misreading of the progressive city charter of 1925. The judge held that the progressives had designed a unitary form of government in which the city council was paramount. The ruling effectively overturned sixty-five years of commission government. The ACLU filed an appeal but the action was rendered moot in June, 1991, when voters approved Proposition 5, granting power to the council to overturn the actions of appointed commissions. It remained to be seen whether the power to override decisions implied the right to make decisions.[31]

Mayor Bradley and Chief Gates both appointed commissions of inquiry to investigate the Rodney King affair. Later the two were joined together under the chairmanship of Warren Christopher, a former deputy secretary of state and deputy attorney general of the United States, who was then chairman of the O'Melveny and Myers law firm. The group was known formally as the Independent Commission on the LAPD, and informally as the Christopher Commission. The commissioners began their work early in April, and reported to the mayor, the city council and the chief of police on July 9, 1991.[32]

The report of the Christopher Commission praised where praise was possible but in sum it constituted a damning indictment of the LAPD and Chief Daryl F. Gates. The commission noted that between 1960 and 1989, crime in Los Angeles increased at twice the national rate; i.e., it rose seven fold. The LAPD was busier than any other department among the six largest American cities. It had the fewest officers per thousand residents and per square mile but made more arrests per officer than other departments.

On the other hand, the commission found "a significant number of LAPD officers who repetitively misuse force and persistently ignore the written policies and guidelines...regarding force. The evidence...shows that this group has received inadequate supervisory and management attention." A retired assistant chief described the lack of accountability as "the essence of the excessive force problem. We know who the bad guys are. Reputations become well known (to sergeants, lieutenants and captains)....But I don't see anyone bring these people up." A serving assistant chief agreed that the LAPD had "failed miserably" to hold supervisors accountable for the use of excessive force by subordinates.

The commission pointed out that between 1986 and 1990, one officer had forty-seven complaints and reports against him, including one shooting. Another had thirty-eight complaints and reports, including three shootings. A third had fifty-two complaints and reports, including one shooting. At least forty-four officers had six or more allegations of excessive force or improper tactics during the period. Yet, "the perfor-

mance evaluation reports for these problem officers were very positive."
The evaluations "did not give an accurate picture of the officers' disciplinary history," did not "record 'sustained' complaints or...discuss their
significance," and did not "assess the officer's judgement and contacts
with the public in light of disturbing patterns of complaints."

The commission's examination of a sample of computer messages
sent from terminals in the patrol cars found "hundreds of improper messages, including scores in which officers talked about beating suspects....Officers also used the communications system to express their
eagerness to be involved in shooting incidents." The transmissions further showed that "some officers enjoy the excitement of a pursuit and
view it as an opportunity for violence against a suspect."

The commission reviewed the department's actions in the eighty-
three civil suits alleging excessive or improper force that resulted in
judgements of $15,000 or more during the period 1986-1990. The com-
missioners found that "a majority of cases involved clear and often egregious officer misconduct resulting in serious injury or death to the victim. The LAPD's investigation of these 83 cases was deficient in many
respects, and discipline against the officers was frequently light and
often nonexistent."

In addressing the problem of racism in the LAPD, the commission
found a connection between race prejudice and excessive or improper
use of force. A quarter of the officers who responded to a departmental
survey agreed that "racial bias on the part of officers toward minority citizens currently exists and contributes to a negative interaction between
police and community." A slightly higher percentage agreed that "an
officer's prejudice toward the suspect's race may lead to the use of
excessive force." [33]

Excessive force complaints doubled between 1983 and 1988. Payouts for police malpractise rose from less than a million dollars in 1980
to $14.7 million in 1991. One riotous exercise by dozens of police offi-
cers had already cost $3.8 million in payments to residents and the case
was not over. Less than one percent of 1800 officers investigated for
excessive use of force were terminated. Councilman Yaroslavsky was
concerned about the rising cost of rogue police officers. He feared that
payouts might reach $20 million in 1992, which would have put hun-
dreds of additional officers on the street. Yaroslavsky, rebutting a
remark by Gates that the Christopher Commission was "fueling" lawsuits, noted that the council had just approved $1.75 million to settle nine
cases, yet not one of the officers had been disciplined in any way.

Several other recent cases were illustrative. Joe Morgan, a black sports broadcaster and Hall of Fame baseball player, was awarded a $540,000 judgement against the city after he was detained, abused and accused of being a narcotics courier. Jamaal Wilkes, a black business-man who had been a notable basketball player at UCLA and with the Los Angeles Lakers, filed a $250,000 civil suit after he was arrested on Wilshire Boulevard early one evening and placed in handcuffs because the light over the license plate on his car was out. Wesley Snipes, star of a popular motion picture, was handcuffed and forced to lie face down on the ground because officers thought his rental car was stolen. Snipes said the officers put a gun to his head and held him for two hours before releasing him without apology. If well-known black figures were not safe from police harrassment, went the argument, what chance had ordi-nary black residents? [34]

Transmissions from LAPD mobile data terminals indicated that racist attitudes were commonplace within the LAPD, that they were often in the context of discussing pursuits or beating suspects, and that officers sending the messages had no fear of disciplinary action for mak-ing such remarks. The commission concluded that LAPD senior man-agers had not used training, counselling, rewards and incentives to reduce the incidence of improper behavior in its various forms.

The commission found much to criticize in the hiring and promo-tion of visible minorities, females and homosexuals. It was dissatisfied with the background investigations of recruits, which failed to identify many violence-prone males. It had grave doubts about the training of probationary staff by field training officers (FTO's) because too many FTO's had been disciplined for excessive use of force. Yet, the commis-sion pointed out, "the most influential training received by a probationer (is) the example set by his or her FTO."

The operational style of the LAPD was found wanting. Confronta-tion with citizens produced enormous hostility toward the department, especially among minority groups. Some officers recognized that fact. Sixty-three percent of those who responded to the LAPD survey believed that increased interaction with the community would improve their relations with residents. The commission strongly endorsed a shift to "community policing," a somewhat amorphous concept that empha-sized problem-solving and community participation with the police in deciding which local problems were most important.

The Christopher Commission noted that "no area of police opera-tions received more adverse comment than the Department's handling of complaints against LAPD officers, particularly allegations involving the use of excessive force. Statistics make the public's frustration understandable. Of the 2152 citizen allegations of excessive force from 1986 through 1990, only 42 were sustained." Examination of more than 700 complaint files revealed the fundamental weakness of departmental investigations of accused officers. Even to file a complaint was difficult, due to the reluctance of LAPD members to assist plaintiffs.

The commission recommended sensible measures to reform the LAPD system of internal discipline and make it more effective and accountable to the public. To begin, the Office of the Inspector General should be reconstituted and located within the police commission, rather than the police force. The inspector general would oversee the disciplinary process. Where serious allegations were involved, the IG would participate in the judgement and, if the officer were found guilty, the penalty phase of the case.

The commission recommended that the police commission be responsible for the complaint intake process, so that plaintiffs could be more confident that their complaints were fairly investigated. Complaints of excessive force should be investigated by the internal affairs division rather than the accused officer's divisional colleagues, the IAD investigations to be audited by the inspector general. The police commission should set disciplinary guidelines and hold the chief responsible for following them.

The Christopher Commission proposed a substantial reorganization of the police commission and new procedures for hiring and terminating the chief of police. The police commission would retain its form, mandate, method of selection and tenure, but with increased compensation. It would gain a civilian chief of staff who would manage civilian employees with skills as management auditors, computer systems data analysts and investigators. The chief of police would be required to be more responsive to the police commission. It also was recommended that the chief be more responsive to "the City's elected leadership," presumably the mayor and council. Given local politics, the attempt to serve three masters might be a recipe for disaster, or, more likely, an invitation to engage in the political machinations for which every chief since Parker had been criticized.

To protect the chief from "improper political influences," he or she would be appointed by the mayor with the advice of the police commission and the consent of the council, after an open competition. The chief would serve a single five-year term, renewable for one additional five-year term at the discretion of the police commission. The police commission, with the mayor's agreement, could terminate the chief at any time but the termination could be reversed by a two-thirds vote of the city council. Not least, the selection, tenure, discipline and termination of the chief would not be subject to existing civil service regulations.

Members of the Christopher Commission believed that, more than any other factor, the attitudes and actions of the leaders of the police department and other city agencies would determine whether the recommendations of their report would be adopted. They argued that to make genuine progress on issues relating to excessive force, racism and bias, leaders should send clear signals. Police, politicians and other civic leaders were urged to give priority to stopping the use of excessive force and curbing the practise of racism and bias, in order to bring the LAPD to a new level of excellence and esteem throughout Los Angeles.[35]

To start the reform process, and in "the interests of harmony and healing," the Christopher Commission suggested that the serving chief of police and police commissioners make way for others, people who had not been partisans in the recent controversy. The police commission subsequently underwent a gradual influx of new members. Chief Gates announced that he would retire. He was unsure about the date: first it was April 30, then June 2, and finally June 30, 1992. In any case, it would be at some point after the verdicts in the Rodney King case were handed down.

Although the police commissioners and the chief had agreed to go, "healing and harmony" were in short supply during the months that followed. Two contentious issues—the choosing of a new chief and the amendment of charter provisions governing the hiring, tenure and firing of the chief—kept partisans and antagonists of the police force in conflict. In both cases, the result was a humiliating and instructive defeat for Darryl Gates and the Police Protective League.

As in 1978, when Gates was appointed, the police commission and the civil service commission ordered an open competition for the chief's position. The police commission would choose among the three highest finishers. In order to considered, an outside candidate had to achieve the highest score after LAPD candidates had seniority bonus points added to their scores. (The value of departmental longevity was not as great as in 1978.) An assistant chief and three deputy chiefs of the LAPD were among the finalists but the victory went to an outsider. W. "Willie" Williams, a black officer who was at the time the commissioner (chief) of police in Philadelphia, scored highest on both the oral and written exams after seniority points were added to LAPD scores.

The "chief designate," a forty-eight year old native of Philadelphia, had joined his hometown park police in 1964. After the park police were integrated with the city police, Williams was promoted to detective in 1972, captain in 1984, inspector in 1986, deputy commissioner in March, 1988 and commissioner in June of 1988. He had served in the head-knocking Philadelphia police force commanded by Frank Rizzo, a department that once dropped a bomb on a houseful of black activists, killing nearly a dozen people and destroying a square city block of residences. That was not the Williams style.

Williams saw himself as "an agent for change." He was said to have an encyclopedic knowledge of the Christopher Commission report. He was a strong advocate of community-based policing and two-way police-community communication. He favored police "mini-stations" in the poorer, immigrant and minority districts, close to the people and the events that concerned them. Minority group representatives and civil rights advocates might love him for the enemies he had made: the Philadelphia local of the Fraternal Order of Police charged that Williams put too much emphasis on community relations and was too quick to punish officers for excessive use of force.

Chief Gates, although opposed to open competitions, at first said only that he knew Williams and liked him. Later, he suggested that Williams should not have been appointed because he had only a two-year, community college diploma, not a four-year degree. A hispanic city councilman was concerned because a hispanic member of the Sheriff's Department who stood third in the initial competition was eliminated by LAPD seniority points. He wanted the charter revised, ex post facto, so that the police commission could consider the officer. (The councilman's concern probably arose from the fact that latinos made up forty percent of the city population, compared with thirteen percent for blacks.) Senior LAPD officers and the Protective League criticized the choice because Williams did not know the city and would require years to understand it.

Williams declined to respond. He might have said, but did not, that he already had a better understanding of Los Angeles than Chief Gates and senior LAPD managers. He came from a city that was forty percent black but had a police force that was more than seventy percent white, to a city that was only thirty-seven percent white but had a police force that was more than sixty percent white. As a black person, he undoubtedly understood the concerns of blacks and other minorities in Los Angeles better than Gates or any previous chief.[36]

Proposition F, the other contentious issue, incorporated the recommendations of the Christopher Commission governing the hiring, tenure and termination of future chiefs of police. The initiative included a provision for a civilian to sit on police disciplinary tribunals, so that the public could have a better idea of how trial boards were conducted. The initiative also included new penalties and stronger investigative powers. Former chiefs Tom Reddin and Ed Davis supported Proposition F, which came as a surprise. Chief-designate Williams also supported the initiative.

Chief Gates, leader of the "No on F" campaign, criticized Williams for meddling in local politics. Gates charged that the initiative would "politicize the department right down to the man on the street." Councilman Michael Woo retorted that "the man who says he doesn't want politics in the police department was attending a political fundraiser in Brentwood while this city exploded around him. Let's face it. You don't get much more political than Chief Gates."[37]

The Proposition F campaign was overshadowed, in April 1992, by the trial of the four officers accused of using excessive force against Rodney King. After extensive legal manoevering, defence attorneys had obtained a change of venue. The proceedings were moved from Los Angeles to the conservative, suburban, middle-class white community of Simi Valley, about forty miles away in Ventura County. The jury, six men and six women, included eleven whites and one Asian, but no blacks.

The defence attorneys set out to persuade the jurors that the officers had acted properly and within LAPD policy. This looked like a difficult task. Chief Gates described the use of force as "excessive." The chairman of the LAPD "use of force review board" also maintained that excessive force had been used. He testified that the videotape showed that the officers had five separate chances to arrest the suspect without further force. The arresting Highway Patrol officer said that King was severely beaten about the head, although police were trained not to strike a suspect on the head. One of the participants in the beating said that the others were out of control. The supervising sergeant said that the beating was the worst he had seen in sixteen years of police work. The prosecution, moreover, had the tell-tale videotape.

As it turned out, everyone who had seen the video was appalled except the jurors. On April 29, 1992, they found the four officers innocent on all counts save one, against one officer, on which a mistrial was declared. News of the verdicts spread rapidly throughout Los Angeles. In black neighborhoods, anger led to violence against whites, latinos and Asians. Fires were set and looting began. The Second South Central Los

Angeles Riot was underway. When it was over, preliminary statistics indicated fifty to sixty dead, 2,400 injured, 13,000 arrested, about a billion dollars in damages and 25,000 jobs lost.

After the riot, everyone with a podium had an explanation. The Police Protective League blamed Mayor Thomas Bradley's "inflammatory" campaign in support of Proposition F. Apologists for Presidents Nixon, Reagan and Bush were only slightly more cynical. They argued that inner city problems stemmed from Great Society programs, rather than abolition of those programs by conservative politicians. The standard causes—poverty, unemployment and white racism—had broad liberal support. Black racism was also a possibility, given the sustained attacks by blacks on Korean-owned enterprises that left Koreatown in smoldering ruins. Greed was proposed because television showed the looters to be of all races and all ages, and generally happy in their work. The police introduced crime as a causal factor because forty percent of captured rioters had criminal records, because black street gangs were in action from the outbreak of the riot and because some of the attacks on property appeared to have been planned.

Politically, Chief Gates and the LAPD were the biggest losers. From every direction, from Washington, D.C. to the county sheriff's department, Gates was assailed for lack of leadership and lack of a plan to maintain public order in the wake of the verdicts. Gates claimed that there was a plan but subordinates had not carried it out. He blamed the lieutenant commanding the area where the first assaults on whites took place for failing to control the situation in the early stages of the riot. The lieutenant said there was no plan and that the chief had sold him out. Many confused and frustrated line officers also believed, rightly or wrongly, that the chief had let them down.

Ironically, the LAPD stood accused of being too timid. Gates said that criticism about excessive use of force had hindered the police response. The chief had been at a political meeting, raising funds to oppose Proposition F, as the riot gained momentum. When the looting and burning were over, any political influence that he might have had, or any hope of defeating the reform initiative, were gone. Post-riot opinion polls showed that eighty-one percent of respondents opposed the chief and favored Proposition F.[38]

Gates was not finished, however. His autobiography, *Chief: My Life in the LAPD*, was released late in May, 1992. In the book, Gates held forth in the usual style, accusing his senior subordinates of treachery and malice and denouncing the mayor, members of the city council, the district attorney and the ACLU. Not even William H. Parker was safe. This was entirely in keeping with previous conduct. As retired Assistant Chief Jesse Brewer remarked, "ever since I've known him he's always accused everyone of conspiring against him."

For all the talk of "my guys" and the failure to discipline street police for malpractise, there was no loyalty downward from the chief and no premium on constructive criticism. Like William Parker in his latter days, Gates was a suspicious, opinionated man who drove independent thinkers out of the department. Some remained, of course, although their careers seldom flourished after they crossed Chief Gates.

Deputy Chief Marshall Anderson alone among senior LAPD executives described the slaying of Eulia Love as "faulty judgement and poor tactics." Other deputy chiefs exonerated the officers. Gates in private described it as "a bad shooting." In public he said it was "clearly self defence and...right within shooting policy." He said the two policemen were as much victims as Mrs. Love, and attacked the media for conducting a "public lynching" of the officers.

Deputy Chief Lou Reiter left the department at only forty-two years of age. He said that the LAPD had many problems: "a seige mentality, too many brass who are paid too well, wasteful deployment of officers and stifling of innovative management practises....The department justifies some shootings on technicalities....The system doesn't require you to be innovative or creative. It will reward you if you do business as usual, be a hard charging street army to show them who is boss, and as a consequence the tactics are terrible most of the time and the shootings we get show that the tactics are terrible."

In nineteen years of service, Deputy Chief Reiter had been a patrolman, a field sergeant, a watch commander, an instructor at the police academy, the head of field services in Central Division, head of the Operations West Bureau, a financial planner and, finally, head of the personnel and training division. He said that he was leaving because the department would not force street officers to change their behavior, would not employ innovative measures to increase efficiency and would not implement sensible reductions in the bureaucracy. Chief Gates said that "poor Lou just has no idea of the overall management and why his ideas won't work."

Commander Darryl Hickman, Ph.D., undertook a survey to collect information on the attitudes of supervisors toward the department. It was alleged that during the interviews, Hickman was critical of senior departmental management. Subsequently, the department reinterviewed more than forty captains. This was taken as an indication of how far Chief

Gates would go to stamp out dissent. An officer who remained anonymous said that there was a silent constituency of veterans who believed
that some senior managers had gone stale. They remained silent because
"the department is good at ostracizing you."

Hickman was concerned about the LAPD garrison mentality and the
"we-them" attitude of officers toward citizens. He wanted to start "a ren-
naissance of thinking, reasoning and questioning." Chief Gates charged
that Hickman had acted "damn near seditiously." Hickman responded that
"loyalty is the ultimate value that is always called into question when you
speak your mind. I think blind obedience is disloyalty."

Nor was disaffection evident only in the upper echelons. The leadership of the Police Protective League was consistently critical of Chief
Gates. The rank and file and the senior managers were united only by
crises such as Proposition F. In Los Angeles, from Parker's time onward,
it was usual for the chief of police to be the biggest booster of the Police
Protective League. Most chiefs and senior officers had held executive
positions in the League at some point in their careers. Chief Gates, however, attacked the PPL leadership for overt political partisanship when it
recommended the re-election of Governor Jerry Brown over a Republican
opponent. Gates, who often campaigned for candidates or threatened to
campaign against candidates or even to run for mayor, pronounced himself "shocked, dismayed and saddened" by the PPL descent into "partisan
political machinations."

This comment was either hilarious or the most odious hypocrisy,
depending upon the point of view. The president of the PPL saw no
humor in it. He declared that Gates was "well aware that since before Ed
Davis served on this board, the Protective League has been involved in
politics. The difference is that until recently, board endorsements met the
favor of the management of our department."[39]

The Protective League suffered a great fall during the Gates
administration, and there was no likelihood of the League or the chief
ever regaining their pre-eminent places in municipal politics. Ed Davis
said that when he lobbied for the League, the political homework was
done before salary proposals were made. League officials first persuaded
L.D. Hotchiss, editor of the influential Los Angeles *Times*, that their
requests were reasonable. "Then you went to see the mayor, but it was all
set up before you got there."

When Ed Davis was chief, the same careful planning was evident.
Davis' liason officer to the city council claimed that they never let any
issue come to a vote in the fifteen-member council unless they had eight

committed votes. This produced an appearance of great power. Davis "let the police commission win sometimes," just to let them win. Under Daryl Gates, the LAPD had been "quixotic," fighting when it could not win. Council members began to see that the department was beatable. They no longer feared it nor feared being punished by the voters if they voted against the police force.[40]

The Protective League too, was corrupted by success. The remarkable wage and pension initiatives approved at the polls by the voters of Los Angeles in the 1950's and 1960's, and the defeat of initiatives designed to curtail those benefits, combined with victories in court over the mayor and council in the 1970's, apparently persuaded League officials and members that they were the dominant force in municipal politics. During the Davis administration, the League tried to obtain a formal part in personnel matters such as discipline, transfers and promotions. The union published a monthly bulletin that, according to Davis, was "two-thirds critical of the department."[41]

When the city fell upon hard times, however, the officers' unrestrained greed and refusal to bear part of the burden may have turned the public against them. Several special tax levies for police failed at the ballot box. Then, after years of support, the voters passed initiatives that terminated both the mandatory "prevailing wage" settlements and the generous pension plan. League campaigns against local politicians failed. In the immediate aftermath of the Rodney King case, the League proposed a campaign to recall Mayor Bradley but quickly aborted it because there was no public support. Instead, a half-million dollars was borrowed from the pension fund to oppose Proposition F.

Proposition F was Gates' last, crucial, desperate battle. If passed by the voters of Los Angeles, the initiative would signify the inglorious end of the Parker era. All of the victories would have been turned into defeats. This consequence would properly be traced directly to the fourteen-year administration of Daryl F. Gates. Chief Gates and the Protective League campaigned against Proposition F to the end—June 2, 1992—but lost the vote by two to one.

It is tempting, if fruitless, to speculate about whether the results would have been different if the "No on F" campaign had not been interrupted by the riot in south-central Los Angeles. Had the "No" forces prevailed, Gates would have received the retirement gift he most desired: to pass on the office of Chief of the Los Angeles Police Department in the same state and with the same inherent powers and tenure that it possessed when he received it. That was not to be; moreover, the dimension of the reform victory indicated that many other significant administrative changes would follow the removal of the chief's tenure and the opening up of the disciplinary process.

Chief Willie L. Williams was sworn in and took office on 30 June, 1992. The fact that he was a black man, combined with his quiet personal style and community policing philosophy, made him the man of the moment, a breath of fresh air in the stultifying upper echelons of the LAPD. He faced many obstacles. A substantial cadre of rogue officers remained to be reformed, curbed or dismissed, not an easy task under the disciplinary rules entrenched in the city charter. The crime rate continued to rise. Police-community relationships were unsettled. The municipal treasury was empty and the department, already understaffed, might be further reduced. Other Los Angeles chiefs, police commissions, mayors and city councils had faced similar problems, however, and they had survived.

The reformed LAPD, to its discredit, had been corrupted by success. The old progressives wanted to isolate the police from venal politicians and underworld bosses. They had not foreseen that their reforms, the initiative, civil service tenure and commission government, could be used by police professionals against the public interest. They would not have approved of the autonomous LAPD. The new progressives, however, if they could be called that, had used the initiative as their predecessors had meant it to be used, and brought the police department once more under civilian control. Given time, it might be possible again in Los Angeles to quote Sir Robert Peel: "The police are the public and the public are the police."

NOTES

[1] Reddin information is from *L.A. Times* file "Thomas Reddin" and Robert Conot, "The Superchief," *West Magazine* (June 9, 1968) 16-21. Also, *Christian Science Monitor*, 7/20/67, *Wall Street Journal*, 8/2/67, UCLA *Docket*, 5/7/68.

[2] See Reddin's comments in *L.A. Times*, 8/23/67, 3/26/68, 10/25/68, 11/24/68 and esp. 4/17/69; also his speeches in support of his candidacy for 6th Vice President of the International Association of Chiefs of Police. *The New Yorker* (Oct. 26, 1968), 157-162.

[3] *L.A. Times*, 2/13/75; *ibid.*, 4/1/76, 4/8/76.

[4] The campus incident is described in *Violence at U.C.L.A.: May 5, 1970*, A Report of the Chancellor's Commission on the Events of May 5, 1970. Student violence, in the form of broken windows, doors, and display cases, precipitated the assault. The vice chancellor of the university requested the aid of the LAPD to quell student violence.

[5] See the Protective League correspondence in council file. Re the park, see *L.A. Times*, 8-2-72, 11-8-72.

[6] Jerry Cohen, "Lore and Legend of Ed Davis," *The LAPD: How Good Is It?*, 26-32; For criticism of the Century Plaza incident see *Day of Protest, Night of Violence: The Century City Peace March* (Los Angeles: ACLU-SC, July 1967); also Andrew Kopkind, "America's Blue Fascism," *New Statesman* 74 (July 7, 1967) 3-4; compare *L.A. Times* reports on police actions, 7/2/67 and 8/2/67; the police view is set out in *Operation Century 67*, a 92-page report to the police and fire committee of the city council; Most observers and participants viewed the event as a "police riot." Daryl F. Gates prepared the police plan and was in command at the scene. He claimed that he acted because "In a minute, we believed, the crowd was going to riot." He considered the dispersal of the crowd to be a big success. D.F. Gates, *Chief: My Life in the LAPD* (New York: Bantam Books, 1992), 111-112; In 1967, a rule change resulted in all "excessive force" complaints being investigated by I.A.D. The conviction rate doubled at once, but the new rate was only 11.2%. Divisional punishment was more sure (95%) than I.A.D. (38.4%). However, when City Councilman Arthur Snyder began to hold open hearings, at which citizens aired complaints against police, the department opposed the move. The police commission promised to begin hearings if Snyder stopped. (This proved to be less than true in practice.) Linda M. Wallen, "Disciplinary Procedures: Rules and Trends," report completed for the Institute on Law and Urban Studies, 1972, *passim*.

[7] Earlier campaign organizations used retired men or luminaries such as Mrs. William Parker and ex-chief Thad Brown to solicit votes. On Nov.5, 1972, however, "Police Officers for Joe Busch," engaged in television commercials showing the incumbent district attorney in conversation with uniformed LAPD officers. Busch won. *L.A. Daily Journal,,* 11-16-72.

[8] *L.A. Times,* 1-8-73, 2-27-73, 3-3-73, 3-4-73, 3-7-73, 3-9-73.

[9] *L.A. Times, The LAPD: How Good is It?* (Los Angeles, December 18, 1977) 30; for an account of the infamous "Seventh Street Incident" see Julia B. Kessler, "Peace Keeping in the City of the Angels," prepared for the Institute on Law and Urban Studies, June, 1972.

[10] *L.A. Times,* 4/29/77, 5/12/77, 12/19/77; *The LAPD: How Good Is It?,* 53.

[11] *L.A. Times,* 10/10/75, 8/28/77, 9/2/77, 9/9/77, 9/16/77, 9/22/77, 10/25/77.

[12] *L.A. Times,* 1/24/77, 1/25/77, 4/8/77, 4/13/77, 5/9/77.

[13] *L.A. Times,* 1/23/75, 3/18/75, 3/22/75, 5/2/75, 5/8/75, 5/14/75, 7/10/75, 7/11/75, 8/7/75, 8/14/75, 8/22/75, 8/29/75, 10/3/75, 10/16/75, 12/23/75, 1/22/76, 11/4/76, 12/26/76, 2/14/77, 3/14/77, 10/15/77, 10/28/77, 1/16/78, 3/22/78.

[14] *L.A. Times,* 10/22/77, 10/29/77, 11/4/77, 11/16/77, 11/19/77, 12/5/77, 12/16/77, 12/29/77, 1/11/78, 1/15/78, 1/19/78, 2/11/78, 2/20/78, 2/23/78, 2/24/78, 3/4/78, 3/24/78, 3/25/78, 3/29/78.

[15] *L.A. Times,* 3/25/78.

[16] A quick understanding of the scope of police research in the United States, the United Kingdom and Canada may be gained from the bibliographies of two recent books by Robert Reiner, *The Politics of the Police* (Sussex: Wheatsheaf Books, 1985) and *Chief Constables* (Oxford University Press, 1991); George Kelling, et al., *The Kansas City Preventive Patrol Experiment* (Washington, D.C.: The Police Foundation, 1974); Peter Greenwood, et al., *The Criminal Investigation Process* (Lexington, Mass.: D.C. Heath, 1977); J. Boydstun, M. Sherry and N.P. Moelter, *Patrol Staffing in San Diego: One or Two Officer Units?* (Washington, D.C.: The Police Foundation, 1977).

[17] Chief Gates believed that he had highly developed political skills and claimed he had "conned the City Council out of the biggest pay raise in department history." Gates, 129-130; When the mayor and council managed to rescind the Jacobs formula after Proposition 13 became law, Gates described their action as "a tremendous amount of short-sightedness." Gates, 129-130; *L.A. Times,* 9/3/80; *L.A. Times,* 3/25/28, 2/1/79.

[18] Negotiations tended to be drawn out as the parties moved from one strategy to another, giving the effect of a continuous process not limited by given years. *L.A. Times*, 5/23/78, 6/7/78, 6/22/78, 6/28/78, 11/5/78, 3/7/80, 6/26/80, 8/8/80, 8/14/80, 8/14/80, 8/23/80, 9/3/80, 9/11/80, 9/12/80, 9/27/80, 10/8/80, 10/13/80, 4/29/82, 10/15/82.

[19] The flat refusal of the Protective League to reduce its requests during the recession, combined with demands for police tax initiatives and threats of lawsuits against civic officials, seem to have tried the public patience to the point where voters turned against the police. *L.A. Times*, 6/27/79, 8/17/79, 9/5/79, 9/6/79, 9/13/79, 11/7/79, 5/30/80, 6/4/80, 7/1/80, 9/8/80, 9/12/80, 9/13/80, 9/21/80, 9/23/80, 9/27/80, 11/26/80, 2/27/81, 4/16/81, 6/3/81, 3/13/82, 9/22/82, 4/13/83, 4/26/83, 5/10/83, 5/25/83, 11/7/84.

[20] *L.A. Times*, 5/28/75, 11/27/75, 10/23/77, 11/3/77, 1/22/78, 1/3/80, 1/5/80, 4/8/80, 1/6/82, 2/3/85; In less than two decades, the unfunded liability almost tripled in size, and the amount per dollar of wages to support the pension plan increased from fifty cents to more than seventy-six cents. The changes made in the early 1980's interrupted the increases. In 1992, the unfunded liability was $3.671 billion and the amount per dollar of wages had declined to 44.6 cents. Staff officer, Los Angeles Police and Fire Pension Commission, 6/22/92.

[21] There were serious problems with the overgenerous pension plan; e.g., a deputy chief retired at forty-two years of age. He could be expected to draw a pension for thirty years, with annual increases to maintain his income at the percentage of a deputy chief's salary that he was entitled to at retirement. *L.A. Times*, 6/17/78, 6/28/78, 6/30/78, 7/1/78, 9/13/78, 12/22/78, 4/6/79, 12/27/79, 12/28/79, 1/3/80, 1/11/80, 4/8/80, 4/17/80, 4/23/80, 10/13/80, 10/23/80, 10/31/80, 11/4/80, 2/13/81, 2/20/81, 3/29/81, 4/16/81, 7/14/81, 12/24/81, 1/6/82, 3.23.82, 4/8/83, 4/13/83, 5/7/83, 9/30/84, 2/3/85, 2/4/85, 2/6/85, 2/8/85, 1/19/86.

[22] Gates said that the conflict over layoffs arose from a misunderstanding. Gates, 181-185; Chief Gates was as intransigent as the Protective League when the subject was trimming the departmental bureaucracy. An attempt to move desk officers into street patrol was overturned. Gates could ignore and insult the police commission, the mayor and the city administrative officer but his quarrels with council members hurt him and the department. *L.A. Times*, 5/23/78, 6/7/78, 6/7/78, 6/9/78, 6/10/78, 6/14/78, 6/17/78, 6/20/78, 6/22/78, 6/23/78, 6/28/78, 6/30/78, 7/1/78, 7/31/78, 8/1/78, 9/20/78, 12/22/78, 2/16/79, 6/6/79, 7/21/81, 7/22/81, 7/24/81, 7/28/81, 7/29/81, 9/10/81, 3/13/82, 4/20/82.

[23] *L.A. Times*, 9/11/80, 11/26/80, 12/3/80, 2/25/81, 3/9/81.

[24] Chief Davis was strongly in favor of larger people: "the turkeys in my profession who caved in to liberal pressures have filled their departments with undersized people, with people who just can't do the job, have burdened the taxpayers for twenty or thirty years with people who cannot do the job." *L.A. Times*, 5/15/79, 5/18/79, 12/19/79, 12/20/79, 2/27/80, 7/23/80, 9/24/80, 11/21/80, 3/11/81, 3/12/81, 4/6/81, 4/10/81, 7/10/81, 7/20/81, 7/21/81, 8/17/81, 9/11/81, 6/15/82, 11/6/82, 11/7/82, 12/19/83, 7/24/85, 6/20/86, 9/28/86, 10/6/91; Warren Christopher, chairman, Independent Commission on the Los Angeles Police Department, *Summary Report* (Los Angeles: The Commission, July 9, 1991), 6,7; staff member, office of Councilman Zev Yaroslavsky, 6/18/92.

[25] *L.A. Times*, 9/24/80, 11/17/83, 1/7/85, 1/24/85, 1/31/85, 2/6/85, 2/18/85, 3/2/85, 6/5/85, 6/23/87; U.S. Attorney William Barr asserted that the LAPD was too small to do a proper job and was limited to "response policing," *ibid.*, 5/19/92; Christopher, 2; David Shaw, *L.A. Times* reporter, 6/16/92.

[26] One of the more revealing LAPD espionage blunders became known as "the Thoms case." Officer Thoms, in testimony before a U.S. Senate committee, accused many innocent citizens of membership in subversive organizations. After a great deal of criticism, Chief Davis requested that Thoms' testimony be withdrawn but apparently it was not possible to expunge the record of a Senate committee hearing. Later, one of the falsely accused persons was barred from an art show on a military base, presumably as a threat to national security; *L.A. Times*, 3/25/70, 3/28/70; *Santa Monica Evening Outlook* editorial, 3/28/70; "Extent of Subversion on the 'New Left.'" Testimony of Robert J. Thoms: U.S. Senate, Committee on the Judiciary, 91st Cong., 2nd Sess., *Hearings,* 1/20/1970. See also "The Symcox Incident," Chancellor's Commission on the Events of May 5, 1970, *Report,* 46-49; Citizens' Research and Investigating Committee, *The Glass House Tapes* (New York: Avon Press, 1973; insight into police thinking can be gained from Donald O. Schultz and Loren Norton, *Police Operational Intelligence* (Springfield, Ill.: Charles C. Thomas, 1968), esp. 90-102 and appendix, "Guide to Subversive Organizations." The book is dedicated to "the giants of the police intelligence community," including Chief William Parker; *L.A. Times* editorial, 10/2/69; *L.A. Times*, 3/14/73.

[27] The spy scandal dragged through the legal and political processes for six and a half years. It is a tribute to the ACLU and other organiza-

tions that they stayed the course. *L.A. Times*, 7/19/78, 8/11/78, 9/5/79,
10/10/79, 3/26/80, 4/7/80, 5/7/80, 5/9/80, 5/12/80, 5/13/80, 5/14/80,
5/15/80, 5/16/80, 6/5/80, 6/21/80, 7/1/80, 7/21/80, 7/26/80, 11/21/80,
11/22/80, 9/9/81, 2/25/82. 9/22/82, 10/11/82, 10/12/82, 10/13/82,
11/8/82, 11/10/82, 1/5/83, 1/19/83, 1/25/83, 2/8/83, 3/4/83, 3/16/83,
3/24/83, 5/10/83, 5/25/83, 6/5/83, 6/28/83, 7/7/83, 7/21/83, 7/27/83,
8/12/83, 8/13/83, 8/17/83, 8/20/83, 9/2/83, 9/9/83, 9/13/83, 9/15/83,
9/16/83, 9/24/83, 9/28/83, 9/30/83, 10/12/83, 10/18/83, 10/19/83,
10/27/83, 10/28/83, 11/16/83, 11/17/83, 11/28/83, 11/29/83, 12/12/83,
12/13/83, 12/14/83, 12/15/83, 12/16/83, 12/23/83, 12/28/83, 12/31/83,
1/4/84, 1/19/84, 1/25/84, 1/28/84, 2/1/84, 2/4/84, 2/6/84, 2/23/84,
3/9/84, 3/14/84, 3/20/84, 3/29/84, 4/5/84, 4/26/84, 5/1/84, 5/4/84,
7/22/84, 8/27/84; the culpable officers identified by Yslas were Marvin
Iannone, Robert Vernon, Ed Davis and Daryl Gates; *ibid.*, 1/11/85. For
the chief's version, see Gates, 220-230. Gates said that the amount ot be
paid was $640,000, "to parties we agreed were legitimately injured by
our surveillance. It also crammed down our throats the most restrictive
guidelines of any police department." He seemed to think the LAPD had
won a victory. See Ivan T. Goldman, *Los Angeles Secret Police,* (New
York: Simon and Shuster, 1992).

[28] *The LAPD: How Good Is It?,* 33-35, 53-56; *L.A. Times*, 4/1/78,
8/10/78, 9/21/78, 11/30/78, 1/4/79, 2/7/79, 2/9/79, 3/1/79, 3/2/79,
3/7/79, 4/26/79, 4/27/79, 5/2/79, 5/17/79, 6/2/79, 6/30/79, 7/7/79,
7/25/79, 8/11/79, 9/4/79, 9/5/79, 9/11/79, 10/4/79, 10/7/79, 10/9/79-
10/17/79, 11/24/79, 12/19/79, 1/21/80, 3/21/80, 3/23/80-3/26/80, 4/5/80,
5/13/80, 6/2/80 6/24/80-6/28/80, 8/13/80, 8/16/80, 8/26/80, 9/17/80,
10/12/80, 11/12/80, 11/18/80, 11/22/80, 2/13/81, 4/1/81, 6/29/81,
7/15/81, 10/3/81, 10/30/81, 1/14/82, 1/17/82, 2/9/82, 7/29/82, 1/5/84,
10/14/86, 9/14/87, 4/7/92.

[29] *L.A. Times*, 5/11/78, 5/20/78, 7/13/78, 8/10/78, 8/27/78, 9/21/78,
12/19/80, 2/25/81, 8/22/81, 8/27/81, 9/30/81, 4/20/82, 5/7/82, 5/8/82; for
Gates' "racist" remarks see *ibid.*, 5/4/78, 5/11/82, 5/12/82, 5/13/82, 6/2/82;
Brennan, Blackman, Stevens and Marshall dissented; *ibid.*, 4/21/83,
4/26/83, 11/19/83. For the chief's version, see Gates, 214-221. Gates made
the point relevant to the "big versus small officers" argument, that a female
sergeant told him that due to her short stature, the bar arm hold was the only
one that worked for her when subduing a suspect. *Ibid,* 215.

[30] *New York Times*, 3/7/91, 3/8/91, 3/10/91, 3/11/91, 3/12/91,
3/15/91, 3/18/91, 3/20/91, 3/22/91, 3/25/91, 3/28/91, 4/3/91, 4/5/91,
4/6/91; Chief Gates said that, according to Dr. David Gianetto of the

L.A. County-USC Medical Center, King suffered a broken fibula, a broken cheekbone, bruising and contusions. Gates, 316-317.

[31] See Los Angeles Superior Court No. BS 006789, Hon. Ronald S. Sohegian, Judge; Christopher, *op. cit.*, 15; This appears to have been a colossal blunder my Mayor Bradley, who approved the porposition instead of vetoing it. His attempt to correct the mistake was rejected by the court. Gates, 340.

[32] *L.A. Times*, 4/1/91; the other members were: John A. Arguellas, a retired justice of the supreme court of California; R.A. Anderson, chairman emeritus of the Lockheed corporation; W.R. Barnes, a former state commissioner of corporations; L.F. Estrada, an associate professor of architecture at UCLA; M. Kantor, chairman of the board of the Los Angeles conservation corps; Andrea Ordin, a former U.S. attorney; J.B. Slaughter, the president of Occidental College; and R.E. Tranquada, a professor of medicine at USC.

[33] Christopher, 2-7.

[34] *New York Times*, 3/12/91, 4/12/91; *L.A. Times*, 5/26/92.

[35] Christopher, *Summary, passim.*

[36] *L.A. Times*, 3/8/92, 4/16/92, 4/17/92; Victor Valle and Rudy D. Torres, "The Wrong Way to Pick a Latino as L.A. Police Chief," took issue with the councilman. *ibid.*, 3/22/92.

[37] Michael Woo, "What Could Be More Political Than Gates?", *L.A. Times*, 5/27/92. Woo also asserted that Gates "plays politics inside the department, inciting rivalries, playing favorites and putting officers against one another. He refused to speak to many of the officers in his top command even when they were pleading with him to develop a plan for protecting the public against an outbreak of violence. He campaigns for candidates in close political races; he smirks and drops hints about having secrets on politicians." For example, see Gates, 230-232.

[38] *L.A. Times*, 5/6/92, 5/15/92, 5/19/92, 5/24/92. The supervising sergeant, after the trial wrote an essay that bore out the charges made by the Christopher Commission. He sought publication but had not succeeded as of July, 1992.

[39] *L.A. Times*, 10/7/78, 11/10/78.

[40] Davis said that when he was the legislative advocate for the LAPD and the Protective League, "I learned where the power bases were. I try to figure out everthing I go into and learn how it works. The legislative process in the city council, in Sacramento and, to some extent, in Congress. I learned what made the difference between successful legislative advocacy and unsuccessful legislative advocacy. When I made a speech, I learned what the loves and the phobias were. I did my work in

advance and I had the votes counted." *The LAPD: How Good Is It?*, 32; L.A. *Times*, 11/11/84, 11/12/84, 11/13/84.

[41] *Ibid.*, 11/12/84.

EPILOGUE

THE PROGRESSIVES AND THE POLICE: DEFEAT AND VICTORY

During William Parker's administration, it appeared that the reformers had achieved their fondest goals. After years of struggle, cooperation between progressives and professionals produced a nationally famous law enforcement agency, much praised for its businesslike management. The new model policeman— honest, intelligent, disciplined— embodied the progressive faith in personal merit. The "efficient" new model department—well trained, well equipped, well housed—justified the vast expenditures that police professionalism required.

True, crime persisted; indeed it increased at double the national rate, but critics blamed society, not the police force. Organized crime troubled only distant eastern cities, and protected crime (specifically vice) did not exist. The past had almost been forgotten. The colorful days of police corruption and reform crusades lived in the memories of a dwindling number of participants, and came to light only in occasional newspaper obituaries.

The great transformation owed much to personnel management and technological sophistication but neither ranked as the first cause of successful reform. Conventional wisdom awarded that place to operational autonomy, i.e., the elimination of "political meddling" in departmental administration. The police continually emphasized this point rather than its complement: the people's elected representatives had no legal power over the police force.[1]

At best, bureaucratic independence violated democratic principles. At worst, an appointed, civil service police chief commanded a body of armed men, loyal to himself and the department rather than to the public which ostensibly they served. The legal bases of LAPD autonomy seemed unshakable. The significance of police autonomy might have remained forever a theoretical question, had not the department vigorously and deliberately attempted to enforce its own solutions to social and political problems.

While Parker commanded the LAPD, critics of the police became increasingly concerned with civil rights violations, including verbal and physical abuse, harassment and surveillance. Police misconduct usually involved racial minorities and adherents of unpopular political philosophies. Organizations such as the ACLU and NAACP could not attract enough public support to accomplish municipal police reform. In the end, Parker proved himself as unconcerned with constitutional rights as his predecessors in the days when Merchants and Manufacturers Association policies guided the department.[2]

In the post-Parker era, the LAPD easily defeated the so-called "counterculture," black and brown militants, middle-class civil rights and antiwar protesters (in the streets and on the campus)and municipal government reformers. The reformed, "de-politicized," police force took an overt role in municipal politics, occasionally becoming the major point of contention in city elections devoid of practical issues.

The LAPD suffered from corporate schizophrenia. Perhaps twenty percent of the certified personnel held college degrees; possibly half of the remainder had attended college part time. The department included idealistic young officers who embodied the highest professional concepts, including acceptance of court decisions which, though "handcuffing" the police, protected the citizen's constitutional rights. Whether these officers and their counterparts elsewhere represented the vanguard of academic police professionalism could not be ascertained. Professionalism, the conventional wisdom, appeared to have strong momentum. At the same time, a disturbing antiprofessionalism within the department threatened to halt professional progress.[3]

Violent acts, generated by the beliefs of the officers, negated the ideal of efficient, impersonal, non-partisan "professional" police service. Police officers appeared to view public demonstrations not as professional problems to be dealt with as a routine matter, but as enemy battalions to be defeated. Police anti-professionalism seemed to be part of an inchoate but nationwide conservative reaction that glorified the simplistic use of force. The frontier returned to urban America. Producers of motion pictures found that neo-fascist roles need no longer be restricted to private detectives and criminals. Badge-wearing civil servants, sworn to uphold the Constitution, could settle all arguments in a hail of gunfire.[4]

Novels, too, presented the policeman as avenger. Joseph Wambaugh, an LAPD officer, wrote a number of successful books. The first two bore interesting and perhaps revealing titles: The *New Centurions*, and *The Blue Knight*. Wambaugh portrayed the Los Angeles police milieu with such fidelity that Chief Davis tried to censor The *New Centurions* before publication. The author's refusal to accept the chief's editorial advice resulted in disciplinary action.[5]

The success of fictional neo-fascist policemen perhaps reflected public acceptance of the actual police violence that underlay the LAPD's political strength. Policemen who killed innocent people accidentally were seldom punished, no matter how egregious their conduct. Stringent civil service rules blocked demotion and dismissal except under specified conditions because the architects of commission government had designed it to prevent the sudden overthrow of a departmental administration.

As events proved, the most important progressive reforms, though of enormous future significance, had little beneficial effect on the conditions they were designed to correct. The progressives established the civil service in 1903 and extended it to the chief in 1923; the regulations were strengthened in 1931, 1932 and 1937. Yet political considerations effected the removal of many individual policemen and every chief thereafter until Parker, including the first two reform chiefs of the Bowron administration. The rule that pension rights could not be lost for any reason, meant to reassure depression-era men and keep them working past 20 years, and the amendments to section 202, designed to protect policemen from machine politicians, in practise insulated the department from public accountability; not, to be sure, during the machine era, but after the reformers took office. William Parker wove the statutory but previously undependable legal provisions into *de facto* autonomy. When he died, the old ways had been forgotten and the new independence prevailed.

What irony! The progressives betrayed their most cherished ideal. They attempted to return government to the people but unwittingly placed the most important municipal bureaucracy outside public control. The police used such progressive apparatus as the initiative to benefit the department at public expense. Furthermore, though the police credited the reputed efficiency of the LAPD to its political independence, reform was solely a function of politics. Perhaps none of the constitutional safeguards that insulated the police from political and underworld bosses had any actual beneficial effect at the time they were established.

Finally, the will to power affected honest civil service policemen as well as ordinary mortals and power corrupted them as it corrupted others. The progressives designed the professional department as an agency of social control, to the end that gambling, prostitution and liquor operations would be eliminated. In the 60's, 70's and 80's, however, it appeared that the progressives had created a Frankenstein. The department, freed of political trammels, chose its own targets. Social protest, in a broad sense, took the place of vice as the prime objective, to be suppressed by vigorous police action in the streets and by political work on behalf of conservative candidates.

Events in Los Angeles fitted a national pattern. Voters in several cities elected policemen to municipal leadership. Police discussed the formation of an activist national organization for political purposes. The rise of police officers to positions of political strength reflected a nationwide conservative resurgence, evident from the grass roots to the U.S. presidency. This had grave potential consequences. In the past, the conservative majority often excused the unbridled use of force against the minority, and denial of its constitutional rights, as Pullman strikers, copper miners, Wobblies, anarchists, communists, racial militants, hippies, homosexuals and liberals could testify.

The results of a union between reactionary politicians and professional police diplomats remained to be observed, but the Los Angeles experience gave slight reason for hope. This "most professional" force had no history of regard for democratic or constitutional principles. With one major difference, it remained the anti-democratic force it had been in the past. The difference was that, after 1950, it chose its own targets rather than taking direction from the financial interests.

This presented a challenge. The LAPD could choose the role of political bully, suppressing progress and intimidating local government. Or it could, in the hands of dedicated professionals, become the ultimate nonpartisan peacekeeping agency, an honorable calling that could attract society's most talented people to its ranks. In either event, for about four decades the choice lay not with the sovereign public but with the police force. The progressives would not have approved this result of their labors.

Hubris, on high and in the ranks, toppled the seemingly impregnable police department. The leaders and a good part of the rank and file lost sight of the purpose spelled out in their motto: "To Protect and to Serve." The people were generous but their servants were greedy, intransigent and lawless. The department fell from grace with the public, allowing a new generation of reformers to gain control of the police force.

There were lessons enough for everyone, especially municipal politicians. The first might be that there is no place in a democratic America for an armed, autonomous bureaucracy such as the LAPD became between 1950 and 1992. The second might be that the big lie— "the LAPD (or any other police force) is the best in the world" — endlessly repeated by Chief Gates without a hint of supporting evidence, should be shouted down whenever it is uttered. There is no proof, even of the fabled absence of corruption. During the Gates regime, LAPD ranks harbored every sort of criminal from rapists to contract murderers, including some who protected vice. As one clear-sighted LAPD officer said, long before the Rodney King debacle, "if we are the best, the others are really in trouble."

A third lesson might be that police work, although it could be and should be a vocation such as education or law, does *not* meet the standards of recognized professions. Police officers, therefore, should not be called professionals, treated like professionals and paid like professionals if they refuse to act like professionals. Nor does six months or less in a police academy, with half the time spent in physical combat and on the pistol range, amount to professional training. That is not to say that there are no professional police officers, only that they are rare and are seldom found in patrol cars.

A fourth might be that the quality of personnel is more important to success than any other factor. The objectives of the organization should therefore be established and published for all to know. Personnel should be recruited who agree with the objectives, and should be rewarded and promoted in direct relationship to achievement of those objectives.

August Vollmer held that police work ought to be recognized as "the highest form of social work." Most police officers reject that view. Indeed, they are quick to say emphatically that they are not social workers. If they are not, they should not have been employed. They should have chosen another line of work. It will always be necessary to direct adequate resources to the apprehension and conviction of violent criminals, but that is a difficult and uncertain activity that does not meet the needs of most people. It should not be the first order of police business. But the police cannot do it alone. In the 1990's, the spirit of the age is problem-oriented and community based. The central objectives are to maintain the civil peace, to enhance the feeling of safety in urban neighborhoods and to involve individuals in the protection and improvement of their own communities.

Community policing is a difficult concept because it can be traced back to the precepts expressed in 1829 by Sir Robert Peel, yet it is as contemporary as the next good idea for bringing the police and the public closer together. The Christopher Commission expressed a strong preference for community policing as they understood it. In effect, they charged Chief Gates with nourishing, if not creating, "an organizational culture that emphasizes crime control over crime prevention and that isolates the police from the communities and the people they serve."

Gates (as would any veteran officer of the NYPD, the London Metropolitan Police or other forces) argued that the LAPD had pioneered in community policing. In the late 1960's, he had put the Basic Car Plan and Team Policing into effect for Chief Ed Davis. Mayor Bradley, who had a line-item veto over the police budget, was responsible for the cutbacks in community policing. As chief, Gates said, he had kept the programs alive in spite of reductions in financial and personnel resources.

Gates might have been more generous, given that it was chiefs Parker and Reddin who, after the Watts Riot, initiated and extended the program of community relations officers (CRO's), commanded by James Fisk. Ed Davis added the basic car, assigned permanently to a specified area, and the senior lead officer (SLO), who was responsible for coordinating the three shifts of officers assigned to the basic car. Directed patrol also was initiated. Unlike "random preventive patrol" by officers aimlessly waiting for calls to action, directed patrol required that the officer deal with specific problems in the patrol area while waiting for calls. Later, community crime prevention programs such as Neighborhood Watch were introduced.

These measures had beneficial effects that LAPD officers recognized, even though some began with the idea that police were "not coffee pourers and nice talkers to people. We joined up to put people in jail." Unfortunately for the communities of Los Angeles, Chief Davis used the CRO's as community organizers, to get people out to city hall when the chief wanted them there to support his proposals. After Tom Bradley was elected mayor, funds for CRO's were cut from the police budget to derail the Davis political machine. The public thus was victimized by two powerful and egotistical public officials.

In 1979, Chief Gates abolished team policing and returned the department to the conditions that team policing was meant to ameliorate. He maintained to the end that, "refusing to give up on community-based policing, (he) continued to use it in a viable and effective way." These comments were contradicted by a study of the issue, prepared in 1987 by a researcher from outside the LAPD, based on the recollections, observations and judgements of LAPD officers who had served through the period. The study indicated that community relations had been generally neglected, to the dismay of many committed officers.

In 1986, the department made another effort to establish systematic relationships with residents of the basic car areas. It appears that the program was not carefully organized or monitored. Most officers perceived that the program was not a high priority. They avoided the requisite meetings and communication with the community. A few dedicated officers, from captains to street cops, made the effort and achieved considerable success. They learned what the chief knew but seemed not to care about — in general, people worried most about small things that made their immediate safety and "quality of life" problematic, but that the police could resolve. Major crimes were secondary, although local contracts sometimes led to the arrest of serious criminals.

In the Wilshire district, a local Community Mobilization Project produced gratifying examples of what police and community could accomplish together. They developed an effective program but response times for calls for service declined to the lowest in the city. Although research had shown that response time meant very little to victims or witnesses unless a crime was actually in progress when the call was made, departmental pressure forced the officers responsible for community liaison to spend forty percent of their time back on routine patrol. The officers resented this, for good reason: "The department is striving for the wrong thing. They want fast response time. What fast response time means is nothing but two policemen in a radio car, driving around making no contact with the community." Again, the community was the victim.

The chief made his fundamental attitude clear. He attended Harvard seminars on community policing with the chiefs of the largest American police forces, the U.S. Attorney General and selected academics, but thought they should switch focus "to something, maybe, like crime." It seemed unimportant to him that community policing was developed by serious, career police officers, not politicians or professors. For all the defensive comments about protecting community-based policing, Gates was explicit with respect to his innermost views: "At some point, as crime continues to stalk this city, people are going to cry, 'We don't want lollipops! We want arrests!'" "Did they honestly think that a bunch of cops grinning at people and patting kids on the head was going to prevent crime?"

Yet LAPD programs with the most potential to prevent crime, one to help young people avoid joining youth gangs (Jeopardy) and one to guide them away from drugs (DARE), were prime examples of effective community policing. In January, 1992, Chief Gates responded to the recommendations of the Christopher Committee by "initiating" community policing in seven of the eighteen LAPD divisions. He claimed that his officers were amused and the city council by the fact that the proposed "new" programs were already in place. In any event, Gates thought that community policing was ineffective.

"Always," said Chief Gates, "I…emphasized crime fighting." He was immensely proud of his anti-crime programs, the names of which pointedly established his view of police work: SWAT, CRASH, OPER-ATION HAMMER, the high-powered weapons, the battering ram, the noisy "flashbangs" and so on. In this regard, a former LAPD chief made a succinct point: "the attitudes and the statements and the actions of the individual on top have a tendency to trickle down to the man working in the street." This was the case in Los Angeles, where the killing of Eulia Love and the beating of Rodney King constituted powerful symbolic "proof" of the way the police viewed the public. The continuing depredations of a relative few "hard-nosed" officers infuriated the neighborhoods and finally brought down the hard-nosed chief who set the style.

The new chief of the LAPD appeared to understand that aggressive, confrontational policing had not solved social problems and that more of the same would not help. Whether community policing would succeed in Los Angeles remained to be seen, but one thing seemed sure: it would not provoke a riot.[6]

NOTES

[1] See the *Annual Reports,,* 1950-1991, *passim.*

[2] Deputy Chief Thad Brown accepted an interim appointment from 7-18-66 to 2-17-67; Thomas H. Reddin commanded from 2-18-67 to 5-5-69; Roger Murdock served as interim chief until 8-28-69, when Edward M. Davis assumed control. Daryl Gates took command on March 25, 1978 and retired on 30 June 1992.

[3] The author, taking Parker-like positions, has discussed court decisions with young LAPD officers, some of whom asserted that police powers must be limited. They do not wish to be identified.

[4] Films such as *Dirty Harry, The French Connection, Robocop, Murphy's Law* and a hundred others extol the jury-judge-executioner role of fictional detectives.

[5] Joseph Wambaugh, *The New Centurions* (N.Y.:Dell Publishing Co.,1972); *The Blue Knight* (Boston: Little, Brown & Co.1972). Wambaugh also wrote successful television and motion picture scripts portraying police officers.

[6] *The LAPD: How Good It It?*, 12: Christopher, 8-9: David M. Kennedy, *Neighborhood Policing in Los Angeles* (The President and Fellows of Harvard College, 1987), *passim;* Gates, 1, 280, 306-311, 344, 354-355; *L.A. Times,* 5/26/92. For community policing, see Francis X. Hartman, Lee P. Brown and Darrel Stephens, *Community Policing: Would You Know It If You Saw It?* (Lansing, Mich.: National Neighborhood Foot Patrol Center, 1988); Christopher Murphy and Graham Muir, *Community-Based Policing: A Review of the Critical Issues* (Ottawa: Solicitor General Canada, 1985).

BIBLIOGRAPHY

MANUSCRIPT COLLECTIONS

American Civil Liberties Union Archives.
Ainsworth, Edward M. *Papers*.
Biscailuz, Eugene Warren. *Papers*
Blake, Harry E. *Papers*.
Chamberlain, Ernest. Collection.
Clinton, Clifford E. *Papers*..
Cole Family *Papers*
Cory Family *Papers*
Davis, Joseph Le Compte. *Papers*.
Dickson, Edward Augustus. *Papers*.
Field, Robert, Jr. *Papers*
Gerson, Theodore Perceval. *Correspondence and Papers*.
Haynes, John R. *Papers* and *Correspondence*
Hichborn, J. Franklin. *Papers*.
Johnson, Hiram W. *Papers*. Bancroft Library, University of California
    at Berkeley.
Kelley, John R. Collection.
Leeds, Charles Tilesten. *Correspondence and Papers*.
Lybeck, Ruth. *Papers*.
Moreland, Walt Loren. *Papers*.
Nadeau, Remi A. *Papers*.
Neylan, John F. *Papers*.
Redpath, Kenneth. *Papers*.
Riseley, Jerry B. *Papers*
Shaw, Joseph Edward. *Papers*.
Shuler, Robert P. "Sermons and Broadcasts." Doheny Library,
    University of Southern California
Stimson, Marshall. *Papers*.
Vollmer, August. *Papers*. Bancroft Library, University of California at
    Berkeley.
Woolwine, Thomas Lee. *Correspondence*. Henry E. Huntington
    Library, San Marino, California.

315

PUBLIC DOCUMENTS

Boston, Massachusetts. *18th Annual Report of the Police
    Commissioners for the City of Boston for the Year Ending
    November 30, 1923.*

California. Bureau of Criminal Statistics. *Crime in California.* 1952.

California. Bureau of Industrial Education. *Report of Teacher Training
    for Police Services.* 1935.

California. *Crime Commission. Report.* 1931.

California. Crime Problem Advisory Committee. *Report.* Sacramento:
    California State Printing Office. 1933.

California. Department of Public Health. *Alcoholism and California
    Related Statistics, 1900-1956.* Sacramento, 1958.

California. Governor's Commission on the Los Angeles Riots. *Violence
    in the City—An End or a Beginning?* 1965.

California. Governor's Special Crime Study Commission. *Reports,*
    1948-1953.

———. Board of Civil Service Commissioners *Annual Reports.*1904-1925.

———. City Council *Minutes.* 1919-1941.

———. *Charter Provisions and Rules and Regulations,* 1928.

———. Board of Pension Commissioners. *Minutes.* 1919-1971.

———. Board of Police Commissioners. *Minutes.* 1919-1971.

———. City Administrative Officer. *Fire and Police Salary
    Recommendations for the Fiscal Year 1956-57.*

———. *City Charter,* 1926-1972.

———. *City Council Files.* 1890-1972.

———. *Minutes.* 1875-1971.

———. Mayor. *Annual Message.* 1940.

———. Police Department. *Administration of Discipline Within the
    Los Angeles Police Department.* n.d.

———. *Annual Reports,* 1891-1971.

———. *Board of Rights Manual.*

———. *The Beat,* 1947-1960.

———. Crime Prevention Division *Report,* 1934-1935.

———. *Daily Bulletin,* 1910-1955.

———. Helicopter Section *Annual Report,* 1970.

———. *New Development in Crime Prevention,* 1936.

———. Public Relations Division *Bulletins,* 1928-1929.

———. *Scope of Responsibilities and Duties Performed by Each
    Position or Detail.* 1951.

———. *Territorial Imperative.* 1971.

———. *Tomorrow's Policeman Today.* 1970.

———. *Transiency in Southern California.* 1937.

Los Angeles County. Bureau of Efficiency. *Survey of Radio Equipped Patrol Cars.* 1933.

———. *Survey of the Sheriff's Department of Los Angeles, California.* 1929.

Los Angeles County. Grand Jury. *The Pattern of Vice Protection.* Los Angeles, 1965.

New York. *Annual Report* of the Police Department for the Year 1923.

U.S. Bureau of the Census. *Reports of the Decennial Census., 1860-1970.*

———. *Fifteenth Census of the United States: 1930-Population.*

———. Mortality Statistics *Annual Report.* 1914-1936.

———. *The Prisoner's Antecedents Washington:* U.S. Government Printing Office,1929.

———. *Vital Statistics.* 1900-1940.

U.S. Bureau of Labor Statistics. *Monthly Labor Review.* 1924-1972.

U.S. Commission on Civil Rights. California Advisory Committee. *Police-Minority Relations in Los Angeles and San Francisco Bay Area.* Washington, 1963.

U.S. Congress. *Report on the Enforcement of the Prohibition Laws, 1931.* 71st. Congress, 3rd Session. House Document 722. Washington, 1931.

U.S. Department of Justice. Federal Bureau of Investigation. *Uniform Crime Reports for the U.S. and its Possessions.* Washington: U.S. Government Printing Office, 1930.

U.S. Senate. Committee on Education and Labor. *Violations of Free Speech and the Rights of Labor.* 76th Congress, 3rd Session. Senate Resolution 266. Washington: Government Printing Office, 1940.

———. Special Commission to Investigate Organized Crime in Interstate Commerce. *Part 10-Nevada-California.* Washington: U.S. Government Printing Office, 1950-1951.

U.S. National Commission on Law Observance and Enforcement Report No. 10. *Crime and the Foreign Born.* Washington: U.S. Government Printing Office, 1931.

———. Report No. 11. *Lawlessness in Law Enforcement.* Washington: U.S. Government Printing Office, 1931.

U.S. President's Commission on Law Enforcement and Administration of Justice. *The Challenge of Crime in a Free Society.* New York, 1963.

————. *Task Force Report: The Police.* Washington: U.S. Government Printing Office, 1967.

BOOKS

Adamic, Louis. *Dynamite: The Story of Class Violence in America* .London: Jonathan Cape, 1931.

————. *Laughing in the Jungle: The Autobiography of an Immigrant in America.* New York: Harper & Bros., 1932.

Ahern, James F. *Police in Trouble.* New York: Hawthorn Books, Inc., 1972.

Allen, Frederick Lewis. *Only Yesterday.* New York: Harper and Row 1964.

————. *The Big Change 1900-1950.* New York: Bantam Books, 1965.

Allen, Robert S., ed. *Our Fair City.* New York: Vanguard Press, Inc., 1947.

Allsop, Kenneth. *The Bootleggers and Their Era.* Garden City: Doubleday and Company, 1961.

American Bar Association. *Standards Relating to the Urban Police Function.* March 1972.

American Civil Liberties Union, Southern California Branch. *Police Malpractice and the Watts Riots.* Los Angeles, 1965.

Anderson, Clinton H. *Beverly Hills is My Beat.* New York: Popular Library, 1962.

Astor, Gerald, *The New York Cops: An Informal History.* New York: Charles Scribner's Sons, 1971.

Banfield, Edward C. *Political Influence.* Glencoe: The Free Press, 1962.

————. *Big City Politics.* New York: Random House,1965.

————. ed., *Urban Government.* New York: The Free Press,1969.

————. and James Q. Wilson. *City Politics.* Cambridge, Mass.: The Harvard University Press, 1965

Banton, Michael. *The Policeman in the Community.* New York: Basic Books, 1964.

Bartlett, Dana W. *The Better City.* Los Angeles: Neuner Company Press, 1907.

Beattie, Ronald H. *A System of Criminal Judicial Statistics for California.* Berkley: University of California Press, 1936.

Becker, Harold, K. *Issues in Police Administration.* Metuchen,N.J.: The Scarecrow Press, 1970.

Bell, Daniel. *The End of Ideology.* Glencoe: The Free Press,1960.
Bell, Horace. *Reminiscences of a Ranger.* Los Angeles: Yarnell, Caystile and Mathes, 1881.
————. *On The Old West Coast: Being Further Reminiscences of a Ranger.* New York: William Morrow & Co., 1902.
Berkley, George E. *The Democratic Policeman.* Boston: Beacon Press, 1969.
Bigger, Richard and James D. Kitchen. *How the Cities Grew: A Century of Municipal Expansion in Metropolitan Los Angeles.* Los Angeles: Haynes Foundation, 1952.
Bittner, Egon. *The Functions of the Police in Modern Society.* Public Health Service Publication No. 2059.
Blau, Peter M. and Scott, Richard W. *Formal Organizations.* London: Routledge and Kegan Paul, 1966.
Bollens, John C., and Henry J. Schmandt. *The Metropolis.* New York: Harper & Row, 1965.
Bonelli, William G. *Billion Dollar Blackjack.* Beverly Hills: Civic Research Press, 1954.
Bontemps, Arna and Conroy, Jack. *They Seek a City.* New York: Harcourt, Brace & Co., 1931.
————. *God Sends Sunday.* Garden City, N.Y.: Doubleday, Doran & Co., 1945.
Bopp, William J. *The Police Rebellion: A Quest for Blue Power.* Springfield, Ill.: Charles C. Thomas, 1971.
Bordua, David J., ed. *The Police: Six Sociological Essays.* New York: John Wiley and Sons, 1967.
Boydstun, J. et al. *Patrol Staffing in San Diego: One of Two Officer Units?* Washington, D.C.: The Police Foundation, 1977.
Brandstatter, A.F. and Radelet, Louis A., eds. *The Police and Community Relations.* Beverly Hills: The Glencoe Press,1968.
Bynum, Lyndley and Jones, Idwal. *Biscailuz: Sheriff of the New West.* New York: William Morrow & Co., 1950.
Burpo, John H. *The Police Labor Movement: Problems and Perspectives.* Springfield, Ill: Charles C. Thomas, 1972.
Carse, Robert. *Rum Row.* Rinehart & Co., 1959.
Chalfant, Harry M. *These Agitators and Their Ideas.* Nashville: Cokesbury Press, 1931.
Chalmers, David M. *Hooded Americanism: The History of the KKK.* Chicago: Quadrangle Paperbacks, 1968.
Chandler, Raymond. *Farewell My Lovely.* New York: A.A. Knopf, 1940.

————. *Killer in the Rain.* New York: Houghton Mifflin Co., 1964.
————. *The Simple Art of Murder.* New York: William Norton & Co., 1968.
Clark, Donald. *A Forward Footstep: Educational Backgrounds for Police.* Springfield, Ill., 1968.
Clark, Norman H. *The Dry Years.* Seattle: University of Washington Press.
Clark, Ramsey. *Crime in America.* New York, 1970.
Cleland, Robert G. *California in Our Time.* New York: A.A. Knopf, 1947.
Clover, Samuel T., ed. *Constructive Californians.* Los Angeles: Saturday Night Publishing Co., 1926.
Cochran, Thomas C. *The Pabst Brewing Company.* New York: New York University Press, 1948.
Cottrell, Edwin A. and Helen L. Jones. *Characteristics of the Metropolis.* Los Angeles: The Haynes Foundation, 1952.
Conot, Robert. *Rivers of Blood, Years of Darkness.* New York: W.H. Morrow & Co., 1967.
Cooper, Courtney R. *Here's to Crime.* Boston: Little, Brown & Co., 1937.
Coppock, Robert W. *How to Recruit and Select Police and Firemen.* Chicago, 1958.
Crawford, Fred G. *Organization and Administrative Development of The Government of the City of Los Angeles During the Thirty Year Period July 1, 1925 to September 30, 1955.* Los Angeles: University of Southern California School of Public Administration, 1955.
Critchley, T.A. *A History of Police in England and Wales, 900- 1966.* London: Constable & Co. Ltd., 1967.
Crockett, Thompson S. *Guidelines for Law Enforcement Education Programs in Community and Junior Colleges.* Washington, D.C.: American Association of Junior Colleges, 1968.
Crouch, Winston and Beatrice Dinerman. *Southern California Metropolis.* Berkeley: University of California Press, 1963.
Dahl, Robert A. *Who Governs? Democracy and Power in an American City.* New Haven: Yale University Press, 1961.
Danforth, Harold R. and James D. Horan. *The D.A.'s Man.* New York, 1951.
Dorsett, Lyle W. *The Pendergast Machine.* New York: Oxford University Press, 1968.

Durant, William C., ed. *Law Observance.* New York, 1929.
Edwards, George. *The Police on the Urban Frontier: A Guide to Community Understanding.* New York: Institute of Human Relations, 1968.
Erikson, Erik H. *Childhood and Society.* New York: Norton and Co., 1963.
Erskine, John. *Prohibition and Christianity.* Indianapolis: Bobbs-Merrill Co., 1927.
Feldman, Herman. *Prohibition: Its Economic and Industrial Aspects.* New York: David Appleton & Co., 1927.
Finney, Guy W. *Angel City in Turmoil.* Los Angeles: Amer Press, 1945.
———. *The Great Los Angeles Bubble.* 1929.
Fogelson, Robert M. *The Fragmented Metropolis: Los Angeles 1850-1930.* Cambridge: Harvard University Press,1967.
———. *Violence as Protest: A Study of Riots and Ghettos.* Garden City: Doubleday & Co., 1971.
———. *Mass Violence in America: The Los Angeles Riots.* New York: The Arno Press, 1969.
Ford, John Anson. *Thirty Explosive Years in Los Angeles County.* 1961.
Fosdick, Raymond B. *American Police Systems.* New York: Century Press, 1920.
Francis, Lee. *Ladies on Call.* Los Angeles: Holloway House, 1965.
Fricke, Charles W. *Criminal Investigation.* Los Angeles: D.W. Smith, 1930.
Gates, Daryl F. *Chief: My Life in the LAPD.* New York: Bantam Books, 1992.
Garrigues, Charles H. *You're Paying for It! A Guide to Graft.* New York: Funk and Wagnalls, 1936.
Germann, A.C. *Police Personnel Management.* Springfield: Charles C. Thomas, 1958.
———. et al. *Introduction to Law Enforcement and Criminal Justice.* Springfield: Charles C. Thomas, 1971.
Ginger, Ray. *Eugene Debs: The Making of an American Radical.* New York: Collier Books, 1966.
Glaab, Charles N. and Theodore A. Brown. *A History of Urban America.* New York: The MacMillan Co., 1967.
Gock. Blye W. *Police Sergeants' Manual.*
Gordon, Ernest B. *The Wrecking of the Eighteenth Amendment.* Francetown, N.H.: Alcohol Information Press, 1943.
———. *When the Brewer Had the Stranglehold.* New York: Alcohol Information Committee, 1930.

Gouldner, Alvin W. *Patterns of Industrial Bureaucracy..* Glencoe Free
    Press, 1954.
Gourley, G.D. *Public Relations and the Police.* Springfield: Charles S.
    Thomas, 1953.
Governor of the Commonwealth Club. *The Population of California.*
    San Francisco, 1946.
Greenstone, J. David. *Labor in American Politics.* New York: Alfred
    A. Knopf, 1969.
Greenwood, Peter et al. *The Criminal Investigation Process.* Lexington,
    Mass.: D.C. Heath, 1977.
Guinn, J.M. *Historical and Biographical Record of Southern Calfornia.*
    Chicago, 1902.
Gusfield, Joseph R. *Symbolic Crusade.* University of Illinois Press, 1966.
Handlin, Oscar. *Boston's Immigrants.* New York: Atheneum, 1968.
Hamilton, John J. *The Dethronement of the City Boss.* New York: Funk
    & Wagnall Co., 1910.
Hamilton, Charles, ed. *Men of the Underworld.* New York: Macmillan
    & Co., 1952.
Hanson, Carl and Paul Beckett. *Los Angeles: Its People and Its Homes.*
    Los Angeles: The Haynes Foundation, 1944.
Hartman, Francis X., Lee P. Brown and Darrel Stephens. *Community
    Policing: Would You Know It If You Saw It?* Lansing, Mich.:
    National Neighborhood Foot Patrol Center, 1988.
Heidenheimer, Arnold J., ed. *Political Corruption: Readings in
    Comparative Analysis.* New York: Holt, Rinehart & Winston,
    1970.
Higham, John. *Strangers in the Land: Patterns of American Nativism,
    1860-1925.* New York: Atheneum, 1968.
Hofstadter, Richard. *The Age of Reform.* New York: Vintage Books, 1955.
Hopkins, Ernest J. *Our Lawless Police: A Study of the Unlawful
    Enforcement of the Law.* New York: Viking Press, 1931.
Hopper, Hedda. *From Under My Hat.* Garden City, N.Y.: Doubleday &
    Co., 1952.
———. *The Whole Truth and Nothing But.* Garden City,
    N.Y.:Doubleday & Co., 1963.
Howe, Frederick C. *The City: The Hope of Democracy.* New York:
    Charles Scribner's Sons, 1905.
Houghton, Robert A. *Special Unit Senator: The Investigation of the
    Assasination of Senator Robert F. Kennedy.* New York: Random
    House, 1970.

Jackson, Kenneth T. *The Ku Klux Klan in the City*. New York: Oxford University Press, 1967.

Jacobs, Paul. *Prelude to Riot: A View of Urban America from the Bottom*. New York: Random House, 1966.

Jenkins, Hubert. *Keeping the Peace*. New York: Harper & Row, 1970.

Jennings, Dean. *We Only Kill Each Other*. Greenwich, Conn.: Fawcett Publications, Inc., 1967.

Kavanaugh, Marcus. *The Criminal and His Allies*. Inianapolis: Bobbs Merrill, 1928.

Kelling, George, et al. *The Kansas City Preventive Patrol Experiment*. Washington, D.C.: The Police Foundation, 1974.

Kendall, Sydney C. *The Soundings of Hell*. Los Angeles, 1903.

———. *Queen of the Red Lights*. Los Angeles, 1906.

Kephart, W.A. *Radical Factors and Urban Law Enforcement*. Philadelphia: University of Pennsylvania Press, 1957.

Kimbrough, Jesse L. *Defender of the Angels: A Black Policeman in Old Los Angeles*. The Macmillan Company, 1969.

Lahue, Kalton C. *Mack Sennett's Keystone: The Man, The Myth, and the Comedies*. New York: A.S. Barnes & Co., 1971.

Lamott, Kenneth. *Chronicles of San Quentin*. New York: David McKay Co., Inc., 1961.

Lane, Roger. *Policing the City: Boston 1822-1885*. Cambridge: Harvard University Press, 1967.

Lee, Henry. *How Dry We Were*. Englewood Cliffs: Prentice Hall, 1963.

Los Angeles: A Guide to the City and Its Environs. Compiled by the Workers of the Writers Program of the W.P.A. in Southern California. New York: Hastings House, 1941.

Lundberg, Ferdinand. *Imperial Hearst: A Social Biography*. New York: Random House, 1937.

Lynch, Dennis Tilden. *Criminals and Politicians*. New York: The Macmillan Co., 1932.

McWilliams, Carey. *Southern California Country*. New York: Duell, Sloan, and Pierce, 1946.

Maas, Peter. *The Valachi Papers*. New York: Bantam Books, 1969.

May, Henry F. *Protestant Churches and Industrial America*. New York: Harper Torchbooks, 1967.

Mayo, Morrow. *Los Angeles*. New York, 1933.

Merz, Charles, *The Dry Decade*. New York, 1931.

Millen, Gilmore. *Sweet Man*. New York: The Viking Press, 1930.

Miller, Zane L. *Boss Cox's Cincinnati: Urban Politics in the Progressive Era*. New York: Oxford University Press, 1968.

Moeller, Beverly Bowen. *Phil Swing and Boulder Dam*. University of California Press, 1971.

Mowry, George E. *The California Progressives*. Chicago: Quadrangle Books, 1963.

Muir, Florabel. *Headline Happy*. New York: Henry Holt & Co., 1950.

Murphy, Christopher and Graham Muir. *Community-Based Policing: A Review of the Critical Issues*. Ottawa: Solicitor General Canada, 1985.

Nadeau, Remi A. *City Makers*. Garden City, N.Y.: Doubleday & Co., 1950.

————. *Los Angeles: From Mission to Modern City*. New York: Longman's Green & Co.,1960.

Nicholas, Alex. *Black in Blue: A Study of the Negro Policeman*. New York: Appleton Century Crofts, 1969.

Neiderhoffer, Arthur. *Behind the Shield: The Police in Urban Society*. Garden City, N.Y., 1967.

Neiderhoffer, Arthur and Abraham S. Blumberg, eds. *The Ambivalent Force: Perspectives on the Police*. Waltham, Mass.: Ginn & Co., 1972.

Newmark, Harris. *Sixty Years in Southern California*. New York: The Knickerbocker Press, 1916.

Noble, John Wesley and Bernard Averbuck. *Never Plead Guilty: The Story of Jake Erlich*. New York: Farrar, Strauss and Cudahy, 1955.

Odegard, Peter H. *Pressure Politics: The Story of the Anti-Saloon League*. New York: Octagon Books, 1966.

Olender, Terrys T. *For the Prosecution: Miss Deputy D.A.* New York: Chilton Co., 1961.

Ostrander, Gilman H. *The Prohibition Movement in California, 1848-1933*. Berkeley: University of California Press, 1957.

Ostrom, Vincent. *Water and Politics: A Study of Water Policies and Administration in the Development of Los Angeles*. Los Angeles: The Haynes Foundation, 1953.

Parker, Alfred E. *Crime Fighter: August Vollmer*. New York: Macmillan Co., 1961.

Parker, William H. *Parker on Police*. Edited by O.W. Wilson. Springfield, Ill.: Charles C. Thomas Co.,1957.

Patrick, Clarence H. *Alcohol, Culture and Society*. Durham: Duke University Press, 1952.

Perry, Louis B. and Richard S. Perry. *A History of the Los Angeles Labor Movement, 1911-1940.* University of California Press, 1963.

Peterson, Lorin. *The Day of the Mugwump.* New York: Random House, 1961.

Pittman, David J. *Conference on Crime and Corrections.* St. Louis: Washington University, 1960.

Preiss, J.J. and H.J. Erlich. *An Examination of Role Theory: The Case of the State Police.* Lincoln: University of Nebraska Press, 1966.

Puzo, Mario. *The Godfather.* New York: G.P. Putnam's Sons, 1969.

Reid, Ed. *The Grim Reapers.* New York: Bantam Books, 1970.

Reiner, Robert. *Chief Constables: Bobbies, Bosses or Bureaucrats?* Oxford University Press, 1991.

———. *The Politics of the Police.* Brighton: Wheatsheaf Books, 1985.

Reiser, Martin. *The Police Department Psychologist.* Springfield, Ill.: Charles C. Thomas, 1972.

Reiss, Albert J., Jr. *The Police and the Public.* New Haven: Yale University Press, 1971.

Reith, Charles, *The Police Idea: Its History and Evolution in England in the Eighteenth Century and After.* London: Oxford University Press, 1938.

———. *A Short History of the British Police.* London: Oxford University Press, 1948.

Richardson, James F. *The New York Police: Colonial Times to 1901.* New York: Oxford University Press, 1970.

———. *Spring Street: A Story of Los Angeles.* Los Angeles: Times-Mirror Press, 1922.

Richardson, James H. *For the Life of Me: Memoirs of a City Editor.* New York: G.P. Putnam's Sons, 1954.

Robinson, Louis Newton. *History and Organization of Crime Statistics in the United States.* Boston: Houghton Mifflin Co., 1911.

Robinson, W.W. *Tarnished Angels: Paradisiacal Turpitude in Los Angeles.* Los Angeles, 1969.

———. *Los Angeles From the Days of the Pueblo.* California Historical Society, 1959.

Rogin, Michael P. and John L. Shover. *Political Change in California: Critical Elections and Social Movements, 1890-1966.* Westport, Conn.: Greenwood Publishing Corp.,1970.

Royko, Mike. *Boss: Richard J. Daley of Chicago.* New York: Signet Books, 1971.

Samish, Arthur H. *The Secret Boss of California: The Life and High Times of Art Samish*. New York: Thomas Crown Publishers, Inc., 1971.

Schlesinger, Joseph A. *Ambition and Politics*. Chicago: Rand, McNally & Co., 1966.

Scott, William R. *Revolt on Mount Sinai*. Pasadena: Login Printing Co., 1944.

Shannon, Dell. *Chance to Kill*. New York: William Morrow & Co., Inc., 1967.

Shevsky, Eshref and Marilyn Williams. *The Social Areas of Los Angeles*. University of California Press, 1949.

Sinclair, Andrew S. *Prohibition: The Era of Excess*. New York: Little, Brown, and Co., 1963.

Skolnick, Jerome H. *Justice Without Trial*. New York: John Wiley and Sons, Inc., 1966.

Smith, Bruce, et al. *Chicago Police Problems*. Chicago: University of Chicago Press, 1931.

Spenser, James. *Limey: An Englishman Joins the Gangs*. London: N. Spearman, 1957.

Stave, Bruce M. *Urban Bosses, Machines and Progressive Reformers*. Lexington, Ky.: D.C. Heath & Co., 1972.

St. John, Adela Rogers. *Final Verdict*. Garden City, N.Y.: Doubleday & Co., 1962.

Steffens, Lincoln. *The Autobiography of Lincoln Steffens*. New York: Literary Guild, 1931.

———. *The Shame of the Cities*. New York: Peter Smith, 1948.

Steinbeck, John. *Cannery Row*. New York: Viking Press,1945.

Stewart, Justin, Wayne Wheeler, *Dry Boss*. New York: Fleming H. Revell Co., 1928.

Stimson, Grace H. *Rise of the Labor Movement in Los Angeles*. Los Angeles: University of California Press, 1955.

Stoker, Charles F. *Thicker'n Thieves*. Santa Monica: Sidereal Press, 1951.

Terman, Lewis and Catherine C. Miles. *Sex and Personality: Studies in Masculinity and Femininity*. New York: McGraw Hill Book Co., 1936.

Tillitt, Malvern H. *The Price of Prohibition*. New York: Harcourt, Brace, and Co., 1932.

Turner, William W. *The Police Establishment*. New York: G.P. Putnam's Sons, 1968.

University of California at Los Angeles, Bureau of Governmental
Research. *Intergovernmental Cooperation in the Los Angeles
Area.* Los Angeles, 1940.
University of California School of Criminology. *The Police and the
Community.* Washington, D.C., 1966.
Vollmer, August. *The Police and Modern Society.* University of
California Press, 1936.
Vorspan, Max and Lloyd P. Gartner. *History of the Jews of Los
Angeles.* San Marino, Cal., 1970.
Walker, T. Mike. *Voices From the Bottom of the World: A Policeman's
Journal.* New York: Grove Press, Inc., 1969.
Wambaugh, Joseph. *The New Centurions.* New York: Dell Publishing
Co., 1972.
————. *The Blue Knight.* Boston: Little, Brown & Co., 1972.
Ward, David. *Cities and Immigrants: A Geography of Change in
Nineteenth Century America.* New York: Oxford University
Press, 1971.
Weaver, John D. *Warren: The Man, The Court, The Era.* Boston: Little,
Brown and Co., 1967.
Webb, Jack. *The Badge.* Englewood Cliffs, N.J.: Prentice-Hall, Inc.,
1958.
Weber, Adna Ferrin. *The Growth of Cities in the Nineteenth Century: A
Study in Statistics.* New York: Cornell University Press, 1967.
Weinstock, Matt. *My Los Angeles.* New York, 1947.
Whittemore, L.H. *Cop.* Greenwich: Fawcett Publications, Inc.1969.
Wiebe, Robert H. *The Search for Order, 1877-1920.* New York: Hill &
Wang, 1967.
Wilcox, Robert F. *Law Enforcement.* Los Angeles: The Haynes
Foundation, 1952.
Willard, Dwight. *The History of Los Angeles* City. Los Angeles, 1901.
Willoughby, Malcolm F. *Rum War at Sea.* Washington, D.C.: U.S.
Government Printing Office, 1964.
Wilson, Clarence T. *The Case for Prohibition.* New York: Funk &
Wagnalls Co., 1923.
Wilson, Edmund. *The American Earthquake: A Documentary of the
Twenties and Thirties.* Garden City, N.Y.: Doubleday Anchor
Books, 1958.
Wilson, Herbert Emerson. *I Stole $16,000,000.* New York: New
American Library, 1956.
Wilson, J. Albert. *History of Los Angeles.* Oakland: Thompson Co., 1880.

Wilson, James Q. *Varieties of Police Behavior*. Cambridge: Harvard
    University Press, 1968.
Wolsey, Serge G. *Call House Madam: The Story of the Career of
    Beverly Davis*. New York: Martindale Corp., 1942.
Zink, Harold. *Government of Cities in the United States*. New York:
    The Macmillan Co., 1939.

ARTICLES

"A Basic Reading List." *Atlantic*, 233 (March, 1969), 135.
"A Tale of Two Cities and the Open Shop." *Current Opinion*, 69
    (August, 1920), 248-250.
Adamic, Louis. "L.A.: There She Blows." *Outlook*, 155 (August 13,
    1930), 562-565.
Adams, L.G. "Police Officer Difficulties in Enforcing the Liquor
    Laws." *Annals of the American Academy of Political and Social
    Sciences*, 109 (September, 1923), 196-200.
Addams, Jane. "Democracy and Social Ethics." *Urban Government*.
    Edited by Edward C. Banfield. New York: The Free Press, 1969.
"AFL Police Unions in Disfavor." *Literary Digest*, 63 (November,
    1919), 16.
Aggeler, William T. "Defense of the Helpless and Unfortunate." L.A.
    Bar Association *Bulletin*, 2:12 (1928), 19.
Alper, Benedict. "Comparative Costs of the Administration of Criminal
    Justice in American Cities." *The Journal of Criminal Law,
    Criminology and Police Science*, 26:3 (1935), 366.
Anderson, W.H. "Ignorance as a Factor in Criminal Law Enforcement."
    L.A. Bar Association *Bulletin*, 5:4 (December 19, 1929), 110-113.
"Astounding Story of L.A. Reformer." *San Francisco News Letter and
    Wasp*, September 15, 1939.
"August Vollmer Retired." *The Journal of Criminal Law, Criminology
    and Police Science*, 23:3 (1932), 496-497.
Barger, Bob. "Raymond L. Haight and the Commonwealth Progressive
    Campaign of 1934." *California Historical Society Quarterly*, 43
    (September, 1964), 1115-1125.
"B-Girl Crackdown." *Newsweek*, 41 (june 15, 1953), 26.
Beatty, J. "Justice Cracks the Whip." *The American Magazine*, 117
    (June, 1934), 72-73, 129-130.
————. "Justice Moves Like a Fire Brigade." *North American Review*,
    239 (February,1935), 126-130.

Bell, Daniel."Crime As An American Way of Life." *Antioch Review,* 13 (Summer, 1953), 131-154.

"Best Police Force Versus Worst Crime Wave." *Newsweek,* 43. (February 8, 1954), 50-53.

Black, Don J. "Production of Crime Rates." *American Sociological Review,* 35:4 (August, 1970), 733-748.

"Black Legion." *Newsweek,* 20 (August 24, 1942), 34-35.

Blauner, Robert. "Whitewash Over Watts." *TransAction,* 3:3 (March-April, 1966), 3-9, 54.

Bliven, Bruce. "Los Angeles, The City That's Bachanalian in a Nice Way." 51(July 13, 1927), 197-200.

Bloom, Hannah. "The Passing of Red Hynes." *The Nation,* 175 (August 2, 1952), 91-92.

Bopp, William J. "The Boston Police Strike of 1919." *Police,* 16:11 (July, 1972), 54-58.

Bordua, David J. and Edward W. Haurek. "The Police Budget's Lot." *American Behavioral Scientist,* 13:5 & 6 (May-August, 1970), 667-680.

Borough, Reuben W. "Law and Order in Los Angeles." *The Nation,* 125 (July 16, 1927), 12.

Bostwick, A.L. "Relative Size of Municipal Police Departments." *American City,* 12 (February, 1915), 154.

"Boy Meets Girl at Cliftons." *Focus,* July, 1938, 5.

"Brenda's Revenge." *Time,* 54 (July 11,1949), 20.

Bunn, E.M. "Salaries of Policemen and Firemen: A Quarter Century Review." *Monthly Labor Review,* 70 (June, 1950), 633-634.

Caldwell, Bernard R. "Police Motors of Los Angeles." *American City.* 57 (January, 1942), 13.

"California Police Training." *The Journal of Criminal Law, Criminology and Police Science,* 24:3 (1933), 591-597.

"California Report." *The Journal of Criminal Law, Criminology and Police Science,* 24:2 (1933), 458-459

"California Study." *The Journal of Criminal Law, Criminology and Police Science,* 25:2 (1934), 291.

"Calfornia Supreme Court Adopts Exclusionary Rule." *The Journal of Criminal Law, Criminology and Police Science,* 46:3 (1955), 430-433.

Campbell, Dorothy. "Bibliography on Training of Police." *The Journal of Criminal Law, Criminology and Police Science,* 24:3 (1933), 591-597.

Canan, James W. "Crime and the Supreme Court." *Garrett Newspapers.* Rochester, N.Y., 1965.

Cannon, L.J. "Survey of the Salaries of Police and Fire Departments." *American City*, 25(December, 1921),459-462.

Cardarelli, Albert P. "An Analysis of Police Killed by Criminal Action: 1961-1963." *The Journal of Criminal Law, Criminology and Police Science*, 59:3 (1968), 447-453.

Carney, Francis M. "The Decentralized Politics of Los Angeles." *The Annals of the American Academy of Political and Social Science*, 353 (May, 1964), 107-121.

"Centralized Law Enforcement—How." *Tax Digest*, 14 (July, 1936), 228-229.

Chwast, Jacob. "Value-Conflicts in Law Enforcement." *Crime and Delinquency,*, 11:2 (April, 1965), 151-161.

"City Mothers Bureau." *Outlook*, 138 (December 3, 1924), 528.

"City of Sin: Los Angeles." *Real Detective*, April, 1939.

"Clay Pigeon." *Time*, 54 (August 1, 1949), 14.

Clinton, Clifford. "Has Los Angeles a New Boss?" *American Mercury*, May, 1941, 633-635.

"Clinton's Big Job." *Time*, 40 (September 14, 1942), 23.

"Column Campaign." *Time*, 29 (May 27, 1939), 18-19.

"Constitution and the Police." *Survey*, 29 (October 26, 1912), 93-94.

Corliss, Carroll P. "The Public's Right to Know." *Police*, 16:7 (March, 1972), 26-31.

Counts, G.S. "Social Status of Occupations." *School Review*, 33 (1925), 16-27.

Cray, Ed. "The Police and Civil Rights." *Frontier*, 13 (May, 1962), 5-11.

"Crime Prevention Work in Los Angeles." *The Journal of Criminal Law, Criminology and Police Science*, 23:1 (1932), 121.

Crump, Guy R. "The President's Page." L.A. Bar Association *Bulletin*, 5:1 (September 19, 1929), 14.

Cumming, Elaine, Ian Cumming and Laura Edell. "Policeman as Philosopher, Guide and Friend." *Social Problems*, Winter, 1965, 276-286.

Davis, Leon T. "The City Attorneys of Los Angeles." L.A. Bar Association *Bulletin*, 25:8 (April, 1950), 226-246.

Detler, K. "Why Hoodlums Hate Bill Parker." *Readers Digest*, 76 (March, 1960), 239-240.

Dillon, J.J. "How a Cop Sizes Folks Up." *American Mercury*, 88 (August, 1919), 40-41.

Dorsey, Susan M. "How Citizenship is Taught in Schools of Los Angeles." *National Education Association*, 9 (1920), 66-68.

Farrar, Larston Dawn. "In Defense of the Third Degree." *American Mercury,* 179 (November, 1938), 330-333.

"Filmland Fleecing." *Newsweek,* 35 (May 8, 1950), 27.

Fitts, Buron. "Buron Fitts Defends L.A." *Liberty,* March 16, 1940.

Gabard, E. Caroline and Charles Gabard. "The Present Status of Police Literature." *The Journal of Criminal Law, Criminology and Police Science,* 48:6 (1958), 664-665.

Glover, K. "Stopping Crime at its Source: Neighborhood Councils of Los Angeles." *Women's Home Companion,* 63 (September, 1936), 28.

Griswold, Tom. "A Bum's Guide to Los Angeles." *American Mercury,* 51 (December, 1940), 408-413.

Guzman, Ralph. "The Function of Anglo-American Racism in the Political Development of Chicanos." *California Historical Quarterly,* 50:3 (September, 1971), 321-337.

Haight, Raymond. "Indicted! How a City Political Gang Got Its Man." *Scribner's* 44:3 (March, 1934), 195-198.

Haller, Mark H. "Police Reform in Chicago, 1905-1935." *American Behavioral Scientist,* 13:5&6 (May-August, 1970), 649-666.

———. "Organized Crime in Urban Society." *Journal of Social History,* Winter, 1971-72, 210-234.

Halliburton, Richard. "Half a Mile of HIstory: Main Street in the City of Los Angeles." *Readers Digest,* 31 (October, 1937), 70-73.

Harper, Harry L. "Where Summer Spends the Winter." *Who's Who in L.A. County,* 1932-1933.

Hodge, Robert W., Paul M. Siegel and Peter H. Rossi. "Occupational Prestige in the United States, 1925-1963." *American Journal of Sociology,* 70:3 (November, 1964), 286-302.

"Holding Prisoners Incommunicado." L.A. Bar Association *Bulletin,* 3:8 (December 15, 1927), 20.

"How To: Books on Race Attitudes of Police." *Report,* 32 (May 20, 1965), 14-15.

Hunger, A.A. "Attack on Crime Gains Ground." *Christian Century,* 15 (December 8, 1937), 1534.

Hutmacher, J. Joseph. "Urban Liberalism and the Age of Reform." *Mississippi Valley Historical Review,* 49 (September, 1962), 231-241.

"Intermarriage in Los Angeles, 1924-1933." *American Journal of Sociology,* 47 (March, 1942), 690-701.

"In the World of Graft." *McClure's Magazine*, 16 (April, 1901), 327-334: 17(June, 1901), 115-121.

Jacobs, Paul. "Los Angeles Police." *Atantic*, 218 (December, 1966), 95-101.

Jameson, Samuel H. "Controversial Areas in Twentieth Century Policing." Interdisciplinary Problems in Criminology. *Papers of the American Sociology of Criminology*, edited by Walter C. Kechless and Charles L. Newman. Columbus: Ohio State University, 1965.

Jennings, Dean. "Portrait of a Police Chief." *Saturday Evening Post*, 232 (May 7, 1960), 44-45.

Juris, Hervey A. "The Implications of Police Unionism." *Law and Society Review*, 6:2 (November, 1971), 231-245.

Klein, Herbert and Cary McWilliams. "Cold Terror in California." *The Nation*, 141:3655 (July 24, 1935), 97-98.

Kooken, D.L. "Police Unions and the Public Safety." *Annals of the American Academy of Political and Social Science*, 281 (1954), 152-158.

Kopkind, Andrew. "America's `Blue Facism'." *New Statesman*, 74 (July, 1967), 3-4.

Kullick, H.D. "Abuse of the Police Power." *Forum*, 24 (December, 1897), 487-501.

"The Lady is a Cop: Mrs. J. Summer of Los Angeles." *Look*, 20 (March 6, 1956), 48-53.

Layton, Edward. "The Better America Federation." *Pacific Historical Review*, 30 (May, 1961), 137-147.

Lawrence, C. "Police Removals and the Courts." *Political Science Quarterly*, 20 (March, 1909), 68-90.

"Les Mickey Rables." *Newsweek*, 35 (February 20, 1950), 21-22.

Levinson, Lew. "The Case of Thomas Sharpe." *Nation,*, 139 (September 5, 1934), 272.

Lineberry, Robert L. and Edmund P. Fowler. "Reformism and Public Policies in American Cities." *Urban Government*. Edited by Edward C. Banfield. New York: The Free Press, 1969.

Lipsett, Seymour M. "Why Cops Hate Liberals and Vice Versa." *Atlantic*, 233 (March, 1969), 76-83.

"Los Angeles Doubles Motorcycle Force." *American City*, 56 (September, 1941), 15.

"Los Angeles Labor Court." *Business Week*, April 26, 1941, 55

"Los Angeles Police Headquarters." *The American City*, 71 (June, 1956), 143.

"Los Angeles Record Victory in Contempt of Court Case." *Nation*, 134 (June 29, 1932), 711.

"Los Angeles Registers Her Ex-Convicts." *Literary Digest*, 116 (September, 30, 1933), 39.

"Los Angeles Stays Open Shop." *Business Week*, March 6, 1936, 15-16.

"Los Angeles, America's Wickedest City." *Look*, 3 (September 26, 1939), 28-31.

Lowi, Theodore J. "Machine Politics, Old and New." *The Public Interest*, 9 (Fall, 1967), 83-92.

McDonald, Donald. "An Interview with William Parker." *The Police*. Santa Barbara: Center for the Study of Democratic Institutions. April, 1962.

McWilliams, Carey. "Big Fix in Los Angeles." *The Nation*, 169 (August 20, 1949), 170-172.

————. "Los Angeles' Pachuco Gangs." *New Republic*, 108 (January 18, 1943), 76-77.

Martin, R.E. "Straight Shooting Cops Train on Novel Pistol Range." *Popular Science*, 132 (February, 1938), 62-63.

Marx, Wesley. "Parker: The Cop as Crusader." *Los Angeles*, August, 1962, 19-20.

Mason, Walt. "Policemen." (Poem.) *American City*, 19 (October, 1918), 278.

Matthews, F. "Character of American Police." *World's Work*, 2 (October, 1901), 1314-1319.

Maverick, Maury, and R.E.G. Harris. "Los Angeles: Rainbow's End." *Our Fair City*. Edited by Robert S. Allen. New York: Vanguard Press. 1947.

Menken, H.L. "Cops and Their Art." *American Mercury*, 22 (February, 1931), 161-163.

Moley, Raymond. "Revolt in Los Angeles." *Newsweek*, 41 (June 8, 1953), 108.

Moss, Frank. "Police Corruption and the Nation." *North American*, 173 (October, 1901), 470-480.

"Negro Police Officers in Los Angeles." *The Crisis*, 41:8 (August, 1934), 242.

Nietz, J.A. "The Depression and the Social Status of Occupations." *Elementary School Journal*, 35 (1935), 454-461.

Obatala, J.K. "The Sons of Watts: Off the Streets and Into the System." *West*, August 13, 1972, 6-9.

"Odor in Los Angeles." *Newsweek*, 34 (July 18, 1949), 19.

Olson, Bruce. "The City Policeman: Inner or Other Directed?" *Public Personnel Review,*, 31 (April, 1970), 102-107.

O'Rourke, L.J. "Use of Scientific Tests in the Selection and Promotion of Police." *Annals of the American Academy of Political and Social Science,* 147-159.

"Oscars for St. Louis and Los Angeles." *American City,* 71 (June, 1956), 143.

Packard, Rose Marie. "The Los Angeles Border Patrol." *The Journal of Criminal Law, Criminology and Police Science,* 47:6 (1957), 721-729.

Pease, Otis A. "Urban Reformers in the Progressive Era: A Reassessment." *Pacific North West Quarterly,* 62:2 (April, 1971), 49-58.

"Per Capita Costs of Police Service in 27 Cities." *American City,* 31 (September, 1924), 273.

Perham, H. "Boy Sheriffs Help Fight Crime." *Popular Science,* 137 (July, 1940), 96-98.

"Police Matrons." *Harpers Weekly,* 34 (August 30, 1890), 675.

"Police Problems in Cities." National Conference of City Governments, 1909. *Outlook,* 98 (July, 1910), 53-63.

"Police Statistics of 204 Cities." *American City,* 14 (January, 1916), 85.

"Policemen's Salaries, Hours, in 49 Cities." *American City,* 42 (April, 1930), 108-109.

Putnam, Jackson K. "The Persistence of Progressivism in the 1920's: The Case of California." *Pacific Historical Review,* 35:4 (November, 1966), 395-411.

Quinney, Richard. "Crime in Political Perspective." *The American Behavioral Scientist.* 8 (December, 1964), 19-22.

"Raising Educational Standards for Police." *American City,* 37 (September, 1927), 370.

Rankin, James H. "Psychiatric Screening of Police Recruits." *Public Personnel Review,* 20 (July, 1959), 191-196.

"Reform Election in Los Angeles." *Christian Century,* 53 (September 30, 1936), 1293.

"Reform Over Los Angeles." *Time,* 32 (December 5, 1938), 14.

Reiser, Martin and J. Leonard Steinberg. "A Human Relations Handbook for Police Officers." *Police,* 16:12 (August, 1972).

Reiss, Albert J., Jr. "Assessing the Current Crime Wave." *Crime in Urban Society.* Edited by Barbara N. McClenna. Cambridge University Press, 1970.

"Relations of the Police and the Courts to the Crime Problem." *American City,* 38 (April, 1928), 84-87.

"Results of Investigations of the California Crime Commission." *The Journal of Criminal Law and Criminology,* 22. (1931), 272-278.

"Retirement Systems for Policemen and Firemen." *Monthly Labor Review*, 27 (October, 1928), 680-695.

Riznick, Joseph. "California Racket Buster." *American Magazine*, 125 (June, 1938), 14-15, 106-109.

Rogers, Stanley. "The Attempted Recall of the Mayor of Los Angeles." *National Municipal Review*, 21 (July, 1932), 416-419.

Sagalyn, Arnold. "The Danger of Police Overreaction." *The Journal of Criminal Law, Criminology and Police Science*, 60:4 (1969), 517-519.

"Salaries in the Police Departments of Principal Cities." *Monthly Labor Review*, 30 (January, 1930), 118-138.

Schwartz, Murray L. "A Hard Lesson for the Law." *Saturday Review*, 48 (November 13, 1965), 33.

Seiler, Conrad. "Los Angeles Must be Kept Pure." *The Nation*, 122 (May 19, 1926), 548-549.

"The Ship Murder Case." *Friday Magazine*, June 13, 1941, 11-15.

Simon, Richard, "The Role Call Training Program of the Los Angeles Police Department." *The Journal of Criminal Law, Criminology and Police Science*, 40:2 (1949), 507-518.

————. "The Planning and Research Division of the Los Angeles Police Department." *The Journal of Criminal Law, Criminology and Police Science*, 44:3 (1953), 365-373.

Smith, Bruce. "Urgent Need for More and Better Police Schools." *American City*, 38 (January, 1928), 102.

Stinchcombe, A.L. "Institutions of Privacy in the Determination of Police Administration Practices." *American Journal*, 69:2 (September, 1963), 150-160.

Stoddard, Elwyn R. "The Informal `Code' of Police Deviancy: A Group Approach to `Blue-Coat' Crime." *The Journal of Criminal Law, Criminology and Police Science*, 59:2 (1968), 201-213.

"Stupid and Inefficient, Police or Critics?" Report of a Sub- committee of the National Crime Commission. *Literary Digest*, 96 (March, 1927), 14-15.

"Sun and Shade." *Time*, 32 (September 26, 1938), 12.

Sutherland, Edwin H. and C.C. Van Vechten, Jr. "The Reliability of Criminal Statistics." *The Journal of Criminal Law, Criminology and Police Science*, 25:2 (1934), 10-20.

"Tale of Violence with a Happy Ending." *Life*, 27 (August 1, 1940), 34.

Taylor, F.J. "Man with a Borrowed Shoe String." *Saturday Evening Post*, 217 (December 2, 1944), 24-25.

Terman, Lewis and Arthur Otis. "A Trial of Mental and Psychological
     Tests in a Civil Service Examination for Policemen and
     Firemen." *Journal of Applied Psychology,* I (1917).
"Third Perch." *Time,* 26 (July 15, 1935), 32.
Thompson, Pearl. "Los Angeles Sporting Girl." *Ken,* May 5, 1938, p. 33.
"Triumphant Campaign of the First Congregational Church." *Time,* 40
     (August 3, 1942), 38.
Turney, Hon. Raymond I. "The Night Court." L.A. Bar Association
     Bulletin, 4:10 (June 20, 1929), 302.
"Union Climax in Los Angeles." *Business Week,* January 29, 1938, 34-35.
"Upton Sinclair Defends the Law." *The Nation,* 116 (June 6, 1923), 116.
Vale, Rena M. "A New Boss Takes Los Angeles." *American Mercury,*
     207 (March, 1941), 299-307.
———. "Stalin Over California." *American Mercury,* April, 1940, 412-
     420.
Velie, Lester. "The Secret Boss of California." *Colliers,* August 13,
     1949, 11-13, 71-73; August 20, 1949, 12-13, 60-63.
"Vice Scandal Involves a Leading Woman." *Life,* 27 (July 18, 1949),
     30-31.
"Voice of the Prowl Car." *Popular Mechanic,* 91 (June, 1949), 81- 85.
Vollmer, August and Albert Schneider. "The School for Police as
     Planned at Berkeley." *The Journal of Criminal Law and
     Criminology,* 7:6 (1916), 877-898.
———. "Revision of the Atcherley Modus Operandi System." *The
     Journal of Criminal Law and Criminology,* 10:2 (1919), 229-242.
———. "The Bureau of Criminal Records." *The Journal of Criminal
     Law and Criminology,* 11:2 (1920), 171-180.
———. "Aims and Ideals of the Police Service." *The Journal of
     Criminal Law and Criminology,* 13:2 (1922), 251-257.
———. "Predelinquency." *The Journal of Criminal Law and
     Criminology,* 14:2 (1923), 279-283.
———. "The Scientific Patrolman" *The American Journal of Police
     Science,* 21:1 (1930), 8-12.
Waskow, Arthur. "Community Control of the Police." *TransAction,*
     (December, 1969), 4-7.
"Weird Hospital: Los Angeles County General." *Time,* 35 (March 4,
     1940), 66.
Westley, W.A. "Secrecy and the Police." *Social Forces,* 34(1956) 254-257.
———. "Violence and the Police." *American Journal of Sociology,* 59
     (May-July, 1954), 34-41.

"What the Police Read." *Literary Digest,* 48 (June 13, 1914), 1436.

White, F.M. "Said the Old Cop to the New." *Harpers Weekly,* 52 (July 11, 1908), 13.

Whitman, H. "Don't Go Out Alone At Night in L.A." *Colliers,* 126 (October, 1950), 30-31.

Whitten, Woodrow. "Criminal Syndicalism and the Law in California, 1919-1927." *The American Philosophical Society,* 49: Pt 2 (1969), 1-103.

Wickersham, George W. "Police Court Graft." *Overland Monthly,* 85 (April 1920), 331.

Wilensky, Harold L. "The Professionalization of Everyone." *American Journal of Sociology,* 70 (September, 1964), 137-158.

Wilson, James Q. "A Guide to Reagan Country: The Political Culture of Southern California." *Commentary,* 43:5 (May,1967) 37-45.

Wilson, O.W. "August Vollmer." *The Journal of Criminal Law, Criminology and Police Science,* 44:1 (1953), 91-103.

Wolfinger, E.W. "Salaries of Policemen and Firemen." *American City,* 29 (October, 1923), 410.

Wright, Willard H. "Los Angeles, the Chemically Pure." *The Smart Set,* March, 1913.

Young, Erle Fiske. "The Coordinating Council Plan in Los Angeles County." *The Journal of Criminal Law, Criminology and Police Science,* 26:1 (1935), 34-40.

PAMPHLETS AND MISCELLANEOUS PUBLISHED DOCUMENTS

American Civil Liberties Union. *The Police and the Radicals: What 88 Police Chiefs Think and Do About Radical Meetings.* 1921.

California State Peace Officers' Association. "Report of the Sub-Committee on Subversive Activities." 1936.

Carter, Royle A. *Memorandum Re Certain Major Factors of Police Administration.* July 30, 1940.

Christopher, Warren, Chairman. Independent Commission on the Los Angeles Police Department. *Report.* Los Angeles, 1991.

Citizens Budget Commission, Inc. 1938 *Compensation and Conditions of Employment and Retirement of Policemen and Fireman in the City of New York and in 292 Other Cities in the U.S.*

Citizens' Committee for the Defense of Mexican American Youth. *The Sleepy Lagoon Case.* Los Angeles, 1942.

Cohen, Bernard and Jan M. Chaiken. "Police Background Character-
      istics and Performance: Summary." New York City Rand
      Institute, 1972.
Congressional Quarterly Service. *Crime and Justice in America.* 2nd
      ed. Washington, D.C., 1968.
Epstein, Melech. *The Jew and Communism: The Story of Early
      Communist Victories and Ultimate Defeats in the Jewish
      Community, U.S.A.* New York: Trade Union Sponsoring
      Committee, n.d.
Fraternal Order of Police. *Survey of 1962 Salaries.* Philadelphia, 1962.
Greer, Sarah. *A Bibliography of Police Administration and Police
      Science.* New York, 1936.
Griffenhagen and Associates. *A Method of Determining Annual
      Adjustments in Fire and Police Salaries.* Los Angeles,1956.
Kennedy, David M. *Neighbourhood Policing in Los Angeles.* The
      President and Fellows of Harvard College, 1987.
Kuhlman, Augustus E. *A Guide to Materials on Crime and Criminal
      Justice.* New York: Social Science Research Council, 1929.
Los Angeles Crime Commission. *Reports, 1923-1924.*
Los Angeles Fire and Police Protective League. "History of the
      Department of Pensions of the City of Los Angeles." 1939.
National Safety Council. Accident Facts. n.d. The National Science
      Foundation. *Nonlethal Weapons: Research Needs and Priorities.*
      1972.
Norris, Harold. "Arrests Without Warrant." Detroit Branch, NAACP, 1958.
"Report on an Actuarial Investigation of the Fire and Police Pension
      Fund of the City of Los Angeles." 1931.
Rhyne, Charles S. "Labor Unions and Municipal Employee Law."
      National Institute of Municipal Law Officers. Washington, D.C.
      1948.
Shuler, Robert P. *The Strange Death of Charlie Crawford.* 1931.
————. *Eunice Pringle.* n.d.
————. *The Criminal Lawyer.* n.d.
————. *Contempt and the Judge.* n.d.
————. *Campaign Testbook.* n.d.
————. *Millionaires and Hired Girls.* n.d.
————. *Free Speech.* n.d.
————. *Jailed.* n.d.
————. *Julian Thieves in Politics.* n.d.
————. *$.* n.d.

Taft, Clinton J. *Fifteen Years on Freedom's Front*. Los Angeles: American Civil Liberties Union, 1939.

Tenney, Charles W. Jr. "Higher Education Programs in Law Enforcement and Criminal Justice." U.S. Department of Justice, 1971.

DISSERTATIONS AND THESES

Abrahams, Marvin. "Functioning of Boards and Commissions in the Los Angeles City Government." Ph.D. dissertation, University of California, Los Angeles, 1967.

Bond, J. Max. "The Negro in Southern California." Doctoral dissertation, University of Southern California, 1936.

Caplan, Jerry Saul. "The Role of CIVIC in the Recall of Mayor Shaw." Master's thesis, University of California, Los Angeles, 1947.

Clodius, Albert H. "The Quest for Good Government in Los Angeles, 1900-1910." Doctoral dissertation, Claremont Graduate School,1953.

DeGraaf, Lawrence B. "Negro Migration to Los Angeles, 1930-1950." Doctoral dissertation, University of California at Los Angeles, 1962.

Devine, Eugene J. "Manpower Shortages in Local Government Employment." Ph.D. dissertation, University of California, Los Angeles, 1970.

Featherhoff, Grace. "An Authentic Detailed Record of the First Supervisorial Campaign of John Anson Ford, July—December, 1934." Incomplete Master's thesis, University of California at Los Angeles.

Findley, James Clifford. "The Economic Boom of the Twenties in Los Angeles." Ph.D. dissertation, Claremont Graduate School, 1958.

Gabard, Charles E. "A Study of the History, Organization and Function of the Crime Laboratory, Scientific Investigation Division, Los Angeles Police Department." Master's thesis, University of Southern California, 1957.

Gabard, E. Caroline. "The Development of Law Enforcement in Early California." Master's thesis, University of Southern California, 1960.

Hallberg, June E. "The Fitts-Palmer Campaign for District Attorney in Los Angeles County, 1936." Master's thesis, University of California at Los Angeles, 1940.

Harmon, Wendell E. "A History of the Prohibition Movement in California." Ph.D. dissertation, University of California, Los Angeles, 1955.

Jaques, Janice. "The Political Reform Movement in Los Angeles 1900-1910." Master's thesis, Claremont Graduate School, 1948.

Kebeck, Arthur B. "Electronic Data Processing Systems in the Field of Law Enforcement." Master's thesis, San Diego State College, 1967.

Keim, T. Beverly. "The Recall of the Judges in Los Angeles, 1932." Master's thesis, University of California, Los Angeles, 1936.

Lane, Robert G. "The Administration of Fletcher Bowron as Mayor of the City of Los Angeles. Master's thesis, University of Southern California, 1954.

Leader, Leonard. "Los Angeles in the Great Depression." Doctoral dissertation, University of California at Los Angeles, 1972.

McNamara, John Harold. "Role learning for Police Recruits: Some Problems in the Process of Preparation for the Uncertainties of Police Work." Ph.D. dissertation, University of California, Los Angeles, 1967.

O'Rourke, Lawrence W. "The Office of Mayor in Los Angeles: An Administrative Analysis." Master's thesis, University of California, Los Angeles, 1954.

Ostrom, Vincent A. School Board Politics: An Analysis of Non-Partisanship in the Los Angeles Board of Education. Master's thesis, University of California at Los Angeles, 1945.

Rusco, Elmer R. "Machine Politics, California Model: Arthur Samish and the Alcoholic Beverage Industry." Doctoral dissertation, University of California at Berkeley, 1960.

Singleton, Gregory H. "Religion in the City of the Angels." Doctoral dissertation, University of California at Los Angeles, 1975.

Sjoquist, Arthur W. "From Posses to Professionals: A History of the Los Angeles Police Department." Master's thesis, California State University at Los Angeles, 1972.

Urquhart, Alexander D. "Adjudication and Rulemaking in Los Angeles Municipal Administration." Ph.D. dissertation, University of California, Los Angeles, 1957.

Van Maanen, John. "Pledging the Police: A Study of Selected Aspects of Recruit Socialization in a Large, Urban Police Department." Doctoral dissertation, University of California at Irvine, 1972.

Weintraub, Hyman. "The I.W.W. in California, 1905-1931," Master's thesis, University of California at Los Angeles, 1947.

Weintraut, Richard S. "An Inquiry into the prestige of the Public Service." Master's thesis, San Diego State College, 1966.

MISCELLANEOUS UNPUBLISHED MATERIALS

Bard, Morton. "Alternatives to Traditional Law Enforcement." Paper presented to a meeting of the American Psychological Association, Washington, D.C., September 2, 1969.

Bollinger, Bruce. "Police Unions in Los Angeles." Report prepared for the Institute on Law and Urban Studies, Loyola University Law School, 1973.

Borough, Reuben W. "Reuben W. Borough and California Reform Movements." Oral History typescript, University of California, Los Angeles, 1968.

Clark, John. "Reminiscences." Oral History typescript, University of California, Los Angeles.

Davis, Edward M. "Move Over, Chief." An Address to the League of California Cities, October 23, 1962.

"Day of Protest, Night of Violence: The Century City Peace March." A Report to the American Civil Liberties Union, Southern California Branch , July, 1967.

Erie, Steven P. "Politics, Power and the Public Interest: The Los Angeles Police Department Budgetary Process." The Institute on Law and Urban Studies, Beverly Hills, 1972.

————. "The Cognitive Structure of Los Angeles Policemen," The Institute on Law and Urban Studies, Beverly Hills, California, 1972.

————. "Who Benefited? Machine Politics in Los Angeles, 1890-1909." University of California at Los Angeles, 1970.

Fogelson, Robert M. "Institutional Change in Urban America." Paper presented at a meeting of the Organization of American Historians, Los Angeles, April 16, 1972.

Ford, John Anson. "Reminiscences." Oral History typescript, University of California at Los Angeles.

Johnson, David R. "The Origins of Police Corruption." Paper presented at a meeting of the Organization of American Historians, April, 1972.

Kenney, Robert W. "Reminiscences." Oral history typescript, University of California at Los Angeles.

Lawler, Oscar. "Reminiscences." Oral history typescript, University of California at Los Angeles.

Manes, Hugh R. "A Report on Law Enforcement and the Negro Citizen." Los Angeles, 1961.

Mitchell, Jim. "Police Shootings." Typescript, Radio Station K.F.W.B., Los Angeles, 1972.

Newman, Lawrence E. and J. Leonard Steinberg. "Consulting With Police on Human Relations Training." Paper presented to a meeting of the American Psychiatric Association, Bal Harbour Florida, 1969.

Ostrom, Elinor. "On the Meaning and Measurement of Output and Efficiency in the Production of Police Services." N.d.

Poos, Patricia A. "The Era of Do-It-Yourself Justice: The First Twenty-One Years of the Los Angeles County Sheriff's Department." Senior Project, California, State Polytechnic College at Pomona, 1972.

Quinn, John R. "Reminiscences." Oral History typescript, University of California at Los Angeles.

"Violence at U.C.L.A." A Report by the Chancellor's Commission on the Events of May 5, 1970.

Wallen, Linda M. "Policing the Police: Internal and External Alternatives." Report prepared for the Institute on Law and Urban Studies, Loyola University Law School, Beverly Hills, California, 1972.

Wilson, James Q. "Dilemmas of Police Administration." N.d.

NEWSPAPERS AND PERIODICALS

Anti-Saloon League Year Book. 1929-1933.

California Eagle. 1921-1941.

Hollywood Citizen News. 1932-1954.

International Association of Police Chiefs. *Yearbook.* 1910-1972.

Los Angeles Equalizer. 1934-1942.

Los Angeles Examiner. 1905-1971.

Los Angeles Illustrated Daily News. 1926-1954.

Los Angeles Record. 1906-1932.

Los Angeles Times. 1890-1992.

Police: The Journal Covering the Porfessional Interests of All Law Enforcement Personnel. 1969-1972.

INTERVIEWS

Brown, Thaddeus

Fisk, James

Ford, John A.

Foster, Lyndon
Franscell, George
Halstead, L.E. "Jack"
Heath, Lee
Hohmann, Arthur H.
Kenney, John P.
Kimbrough, Jesse L.
Leavy, J. Miller
Lester, Ervis
Porter, Everette
Sansing, E.B.
Weinstock, Matthew
Williams, George
Yorty, Samuel

INDEX